Mansions of the Sun

UMA ANAND

WITH PHOTOGRAPHS
BY VIVEK ANAND

Al-Falak/Scorpion

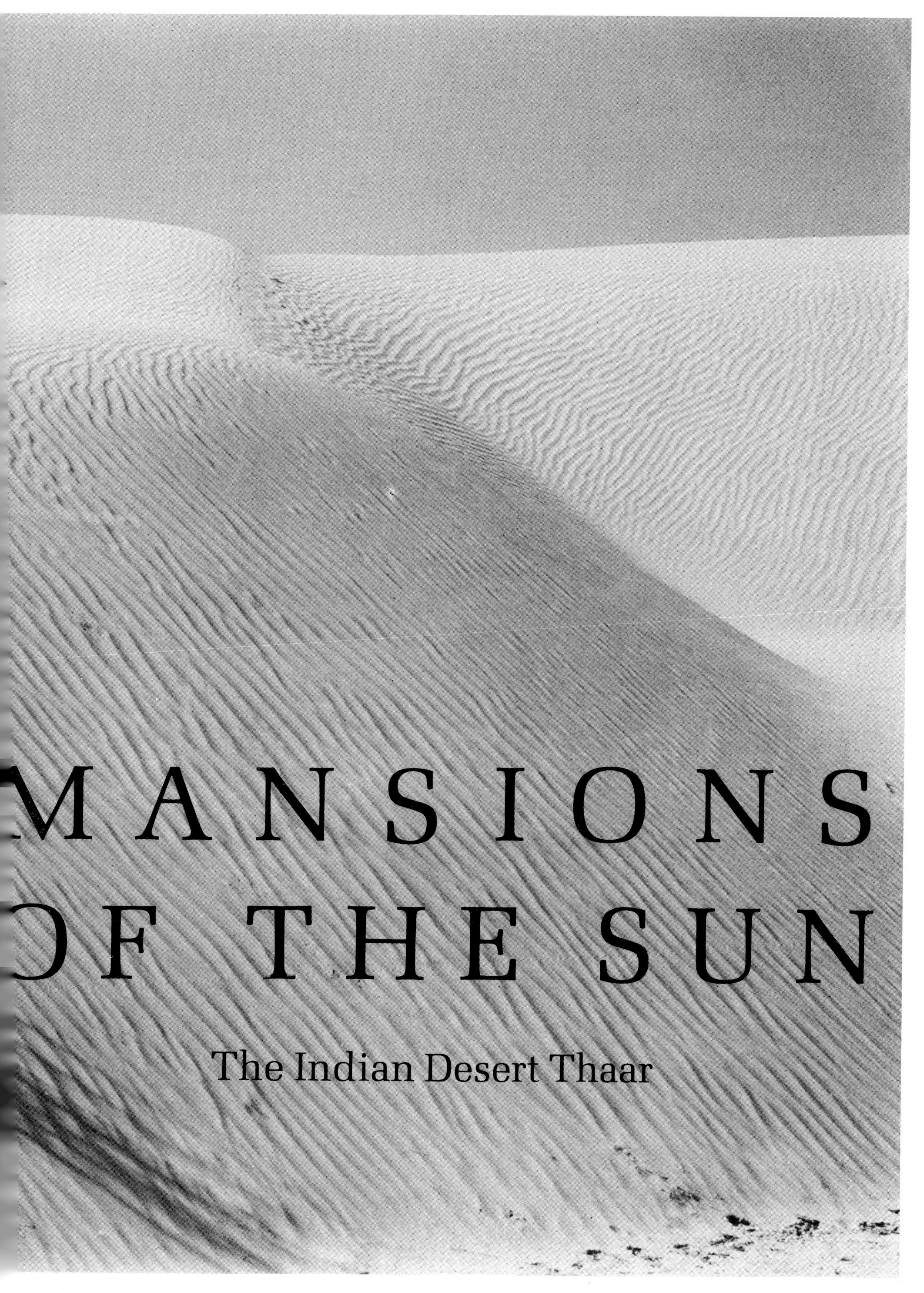

MANSIONS
OF THE SUN
The Indian Desert Thaar

First published in 1982 by
Al-Falak and
Scorpion Communications and Publications Ltd

ISBN 0 905906 29 2

Editors: E. Alkazi and L W Harrow
Design and art direction: Colin Larkin
Design assistant: Dale Dawson

Set in Linoterm Rockwell by
STS, Hervey Park Road, London E17 6LJ

Produced by
Scorpion Communications and Publications Ltd
377 High Street, London E15 4QZ

Printed in England by Penshurst Press,
Tunbridge Wells, Kent

Contents

Acknowledgements

One of the few wholly pleasurable tasks that falls to any author in writing a book is to record the help and guidance given by all those who made it possible for him to do so. It is with deep gratitude that I recall the generous hospitality of Rupayan Sansthan, Borunda, and its Directors, Komal Kothari and Vijaydan Dehta, in permitting me the free use of the Institute's archival materials and their expertise and scholarship. I am also indebted to the Director of the Census Department, New Delhi, for his permission to quote from the excellent Census Reports on the villages of the desert region. I owe my thanks to the Librarians of the Sangeet Natak Akademi, New Delhi; the Institute of Historical Studies, New Delhi; the Library of Science and Culture, New Delhi and the Archaeological Survey of India, New Delhi, for their help in tracing and obtaining references and obscure publications.
Among the many personal friends who came to my aid were Akhila Ghose who translated the poems in Chapter I and 'Kesaria' and 'Moria' in Chapter 6; Fatima Al Talib who prepared the manuscript and greatly helped by her supportive encouragement; P.L. Dhingra who typed the many drafts of the ms with uncomplaining fortitude and N. Iqbal Singh who read the near final draft and gave much helpful advice. I owe more than thanks to E. Alkazi, who not only edited the ms with perceptive and meticulous care, but whose faith and confidence in me made the completion of the book possible. Finally, I must thank my publishers, Scorpion Publications, London: Leonard Harrow for the patience and unfailing courtesy extended to me throughout our association, and Colin Larkin for the infinite pains he has taken in designing this book.

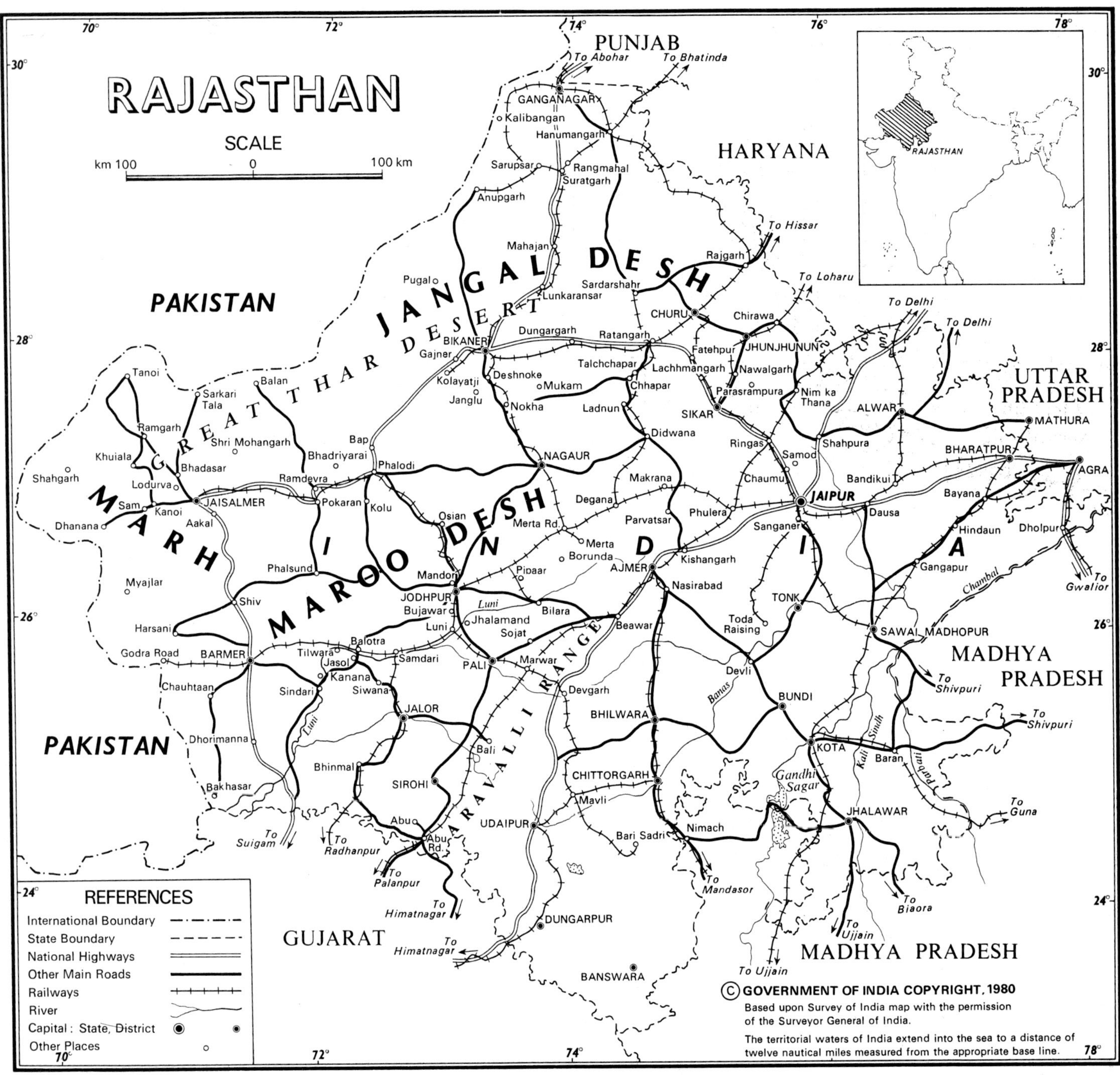

RAJASTHAN
SCALE
km 100   0   100 km

PUNJAB
To Abohar   To Bhatinda
HARYANA
GANGANAGAR
Kalibangan
Hanumangarh
Sarupsar   Rangmahal
Suratgarh
Anupgarh
Mahajan
Rajgarh
To Hissar
To Loharu
Pugal   Sardarshahr
Lunkaransar
CHURU   Chirawa
To Delhi
To Delhi
Dungargarh   Ratangarh
Fatehpur   JHUNJHUNUN
UTTAR
PRADESH
BIKANER
Gajner
Deshnoke   Talchchapar   Lachhmangarh   Nawalgarh
Parasrampura
MATHURA
Kolayatji   Mukam   Chhapar
Nim ka
Thana   ALWAR
Janglu   Nokha   Ladnun   SIKAR   Shahpura
BHARATPUR
Ringas   Samod
PAKISTAN
Tanoi
Didwana   Chaumu   Bandikui   AGRA
Balan   NAGAUR   Phulera   JAIPUR
Sarkari
Tala   Makrana   Bayana
Ramgarh   Degana   Sanganer   Dausa   Hindaun
Shri Mohangarh   Bap   Parvatsar   Dholpur
Khuiala   Bhadriyarai   Merta Rd.   Gangapur
Shahgarh   Bhadasar   Phalodi   Merta
To
Gwalior
Lodurva   Ramdevra   Osian   Borunda   Kishangarh
Sam   JAISALMER   Pokaran   Kolu   AJMER
Kanoi   Pidaar   Nasirabad   TONK
Aakal   SAWAI MADHOPUR
Dhanana   Phalsund   Mandor
Myajlar   JODHPUR   Luni   MADHYA
Shiv   Bujawar   Jhalamand   Bilara   Beawar   PRADESH
Luni   Sojat   Toda
Raising   To
Shivpuri
Harsani   Balotra   Marwar   Banas   BUNDI
Godra Road   BARMER   Tilwara   Samdari   PALI   Devli   To
Shivpuri
Jasol   Devgarh   KOTA
Chauhtaan   Kanana   Siwana   BHILWARA   Baran
Sindari   JALOR   Devgarh
Dhorimanna   Bali   To
Guna
Bhinmal   CHITTORGARH   Gandhi
Sagar   JHALAWAR
Bakhasar   SIROHI   Mavli
Abu   UDAIPUR   Bari Sadri   Nimach   To
Guna
To
Suigam   To
Radhanpur   Abu
Rd.   To
Mandasor   To
Biaora
To
Palanpur   To
Ujjain
To
Himatnagar   GUJARAT   DUNGARPUR   MADHYA PRADESH
To
Himatnagar   BANSWARA   To Ujjain

PAKISTAN
GREAT THAR DESERT
JANGAL DESH
MARH
MAROO DESH
ARAVALLI RANGE
I N D I A
Luni
Chambal
Banas
Kali Sindh

REFERENCES
International Boundary
State Boundary
National Highways
Other Main Roads
Railways
River
Capital : State, District
Other Places

(C) GOVERNMENT OF INDIA COPYRIGHT, 1980
Based upon Survey of India map with the permission
of the Surveyor General of India.
The territorial waters of India extend into the sea to a distance of
twelve nautical miles measured from the appropriate base line.
RAJASTHAN

1 Encounters in the Thaar

Even if
the nine sheep,
my home,
and all the camels were
to be drowned;

even if
I were left without children;

even so
it is good
that the rain must fall.

In the summer of 1979 I received a letter from a friend in Jodhpur dated July 10: 'Rajasthan is very, very hot. No rains up to now. We may face again a severe famine if it doesn't rain for another week.'

On the night of July 15 the clouds burst, and floods ravaged the entire Jodhpur, Pali and Barmer regions. Water poured in a constant stream from the sundered heavens with the deafening roar of a cataract. The swollen river Luni and its tributaries overflowed their shallow silt-quilted beds, obliterated the roads and cart-tracks, and inundated the fields. The flood swelled up against the railway embankments that cut across the natural gradient of the land, sucked away the earth underneath and, rising with increasing volume and force, breached the rail-track at several places. Torrents gushed down narrow village lanes, uprooting trees and sweeping off camels, goats and cattle, whose frenzied screams went unheard in the tumultuous cacophony of the skies. Huts of mud and rubble crumbled under the unceasing deluge and settled into mounds of sticky clay, becoming the graves of those they sheltered.

Next day the clouds, empty and weightless, dispersed in a light breeze, like shredded wisps of waste cotton. The meteorological office at Jodhpur had recorded 88.8cm of rain during the dark hours of that one interminable night.

Nature seems never less than dramatic in the Thaar. Yet there is no irony in the prayer of a nameless woman of the desert:

Even so
it is good
that the rain must fall.

At what precise moment experience crystallied in rhyming couplets of such terse and pithy brevity is not known. There is a desert cactus whose fibrous roots trace a nervous descent through rock and sand to some secret spring of life. The plant finally bursts into bloom just once in a cycle of years, in opaque, waxy buds that open their milky petals to the light of the moon. Perhaps the briny sap of sorrow, filtered through numberless human lives, flowered in the poem, like a wild cactus blossom with its ruff of thorny barbs.

Or it may have been a wandering mendicant-saint, one of those who often have walked among our people, eyes glazed with the burn of the maddening sun, who chanted the couplets in a sweet monotone to wash the pain of personal loss into a flood of compassion for the parched and arid earth:

Even so
it is good
that the rain must fall

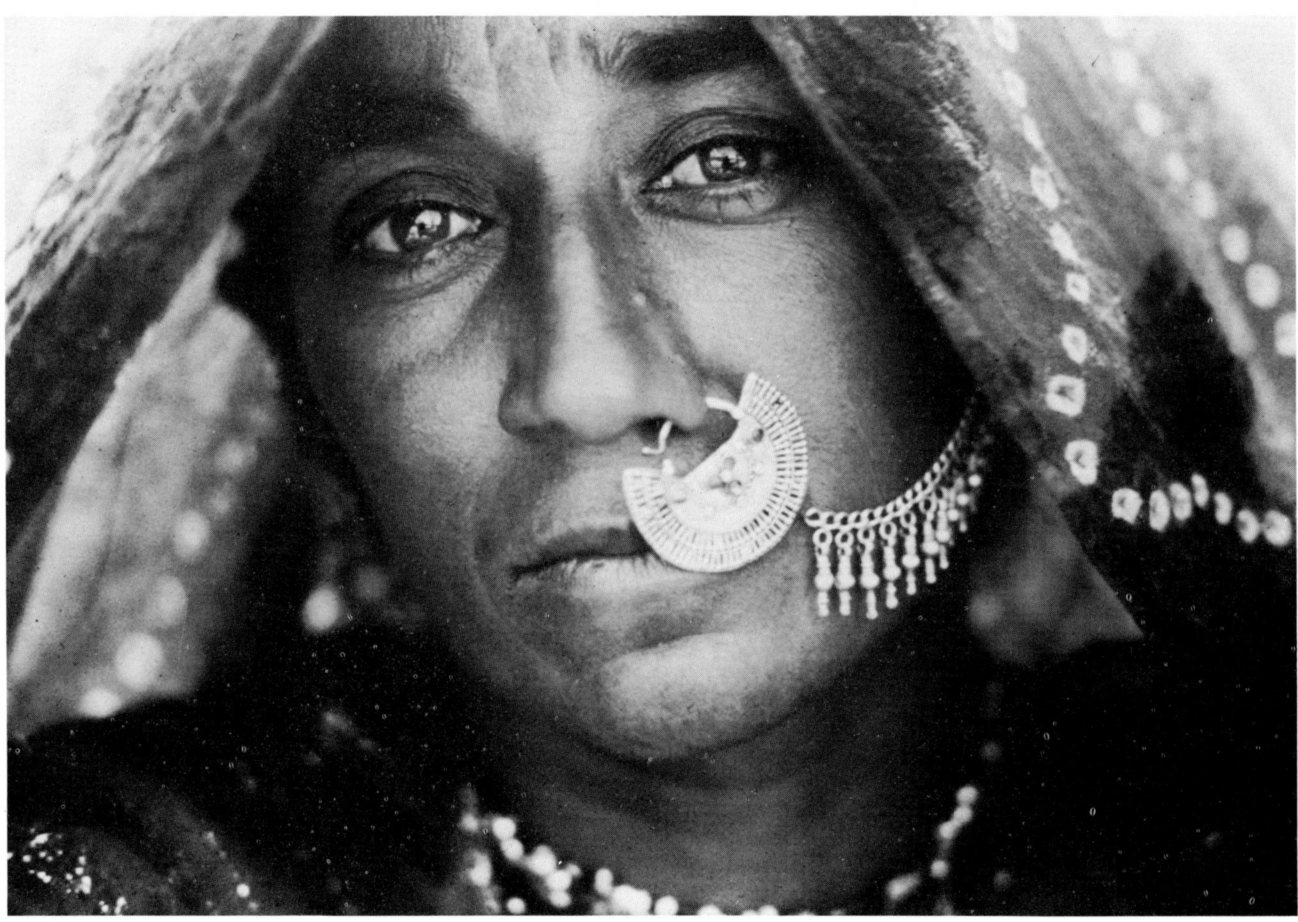

Desert woman

Alone, man cannot survive in the desert. He belongs to the body corporate like a bee to the hive, as an extension or vital cell of a sentient unit. Individual identity is defined through association with the family: *Rana ra baap,* father of Rana; *Luna ri ma,* mother of Luna. Or through the caste: *Bishnoi ra gayan,* the priest of the Bishnois. Or the professional group: *Pabuji ra bhopa,* the minstrel of the ballad of Pabu. Or the tribe: *Kalbelion ra neta,* the leader of the nomadic Kalbelias. Or through the clan: *Bhatiani rani,* the queen of the Bhatis. To be cut off from the unit is to perish. If the group survives, the individual lives on in vicarious immortality, and if the earth, the mother, is replenished, the people will endure.

Life is geared to this corporate end. There is a well-known saying on which all desert children are nurtured:

> One year in three, drought;
> one year in eight, famine.

From infancy they are brought up to frugality, to survive despite deprivation. Yet the resignation implied in an acceptance of forces they cannot control, fails to disguise the soft sift of fear that permeates the psyche of the desert people: the ever present dread of being without water.

Through
snake-bite, accident,
lightning, or the stroke
of a sharp sword,
death may approach us.
But do not kill us
by denying rain.

And so when the clouds burst over Jodhpur, the personal tragedy is submitted to as an ordeal by water.

The Terrain

Thaar, the Great Indian Desert, lies in the north-west of Rajasthan in the Indian sub-continent. Its northern reaches extend across the national boundary into Sindh, Pakistan, where the wind-whipped sands are subdued and contained by the fertile Indus valley, and the perennial waters of its major tributary, the Sutlej. To the south, the desert deflects further west, to end in the vast salt marshes of the Great Rann of Kutch, in Gujarat. North-east and south-west from Gujarat strike out the weathered Aravallis, the oldest geophysical feature of the subcontinent which, according to the Imperial Gazetteer of India (1909) 'are but the depressed and degraded relics of a far

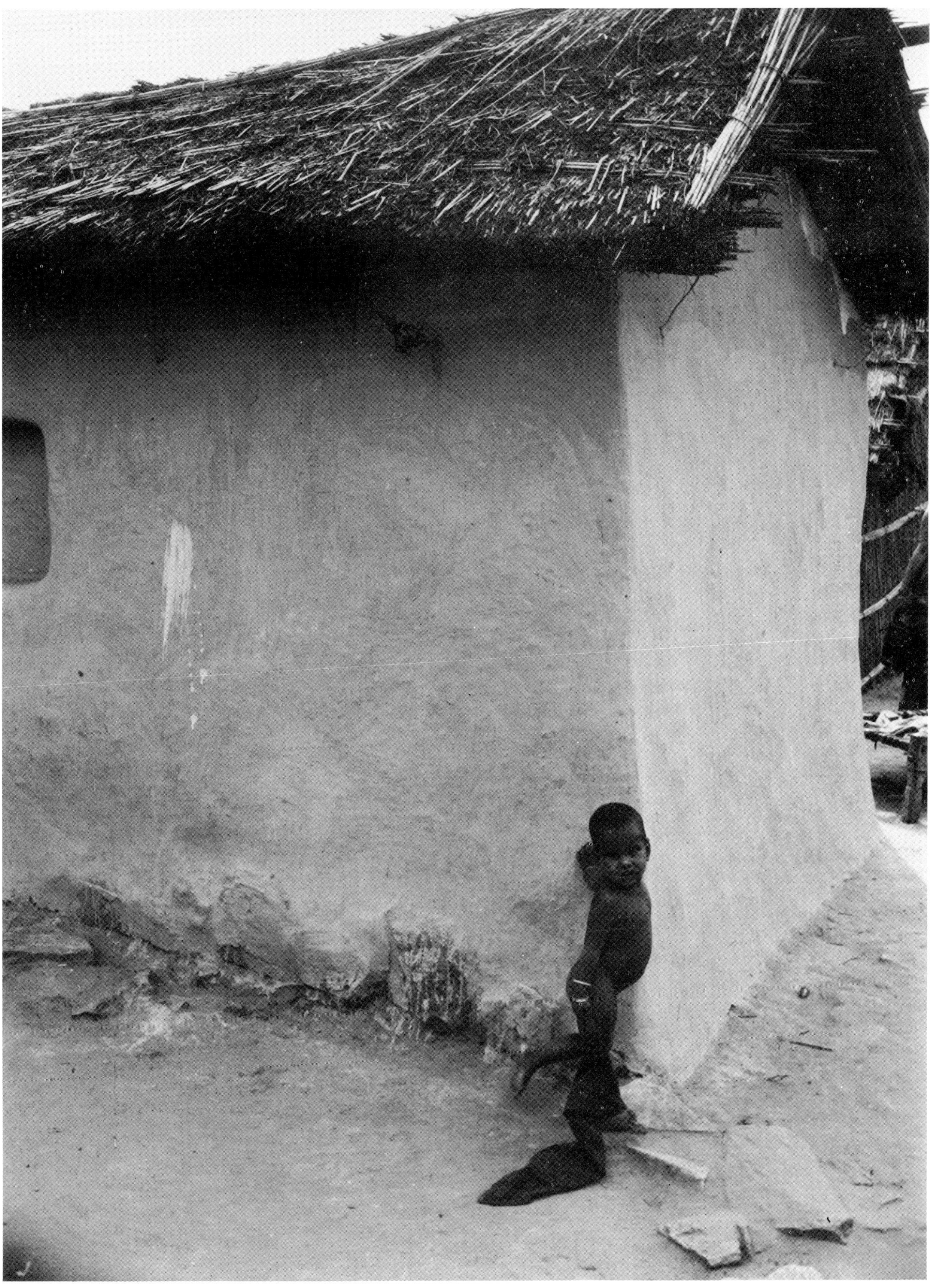

Child of the desert

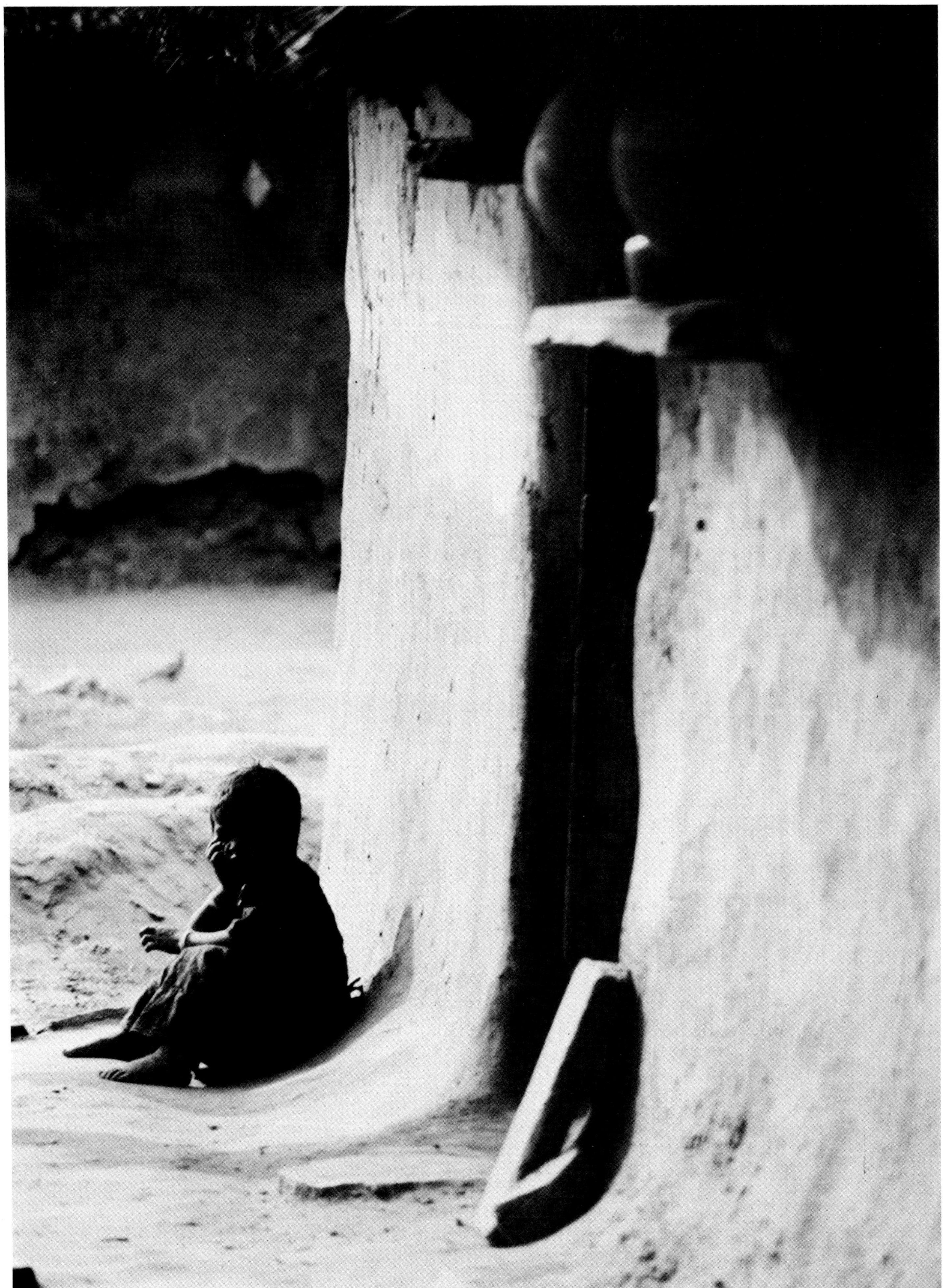

Little girl

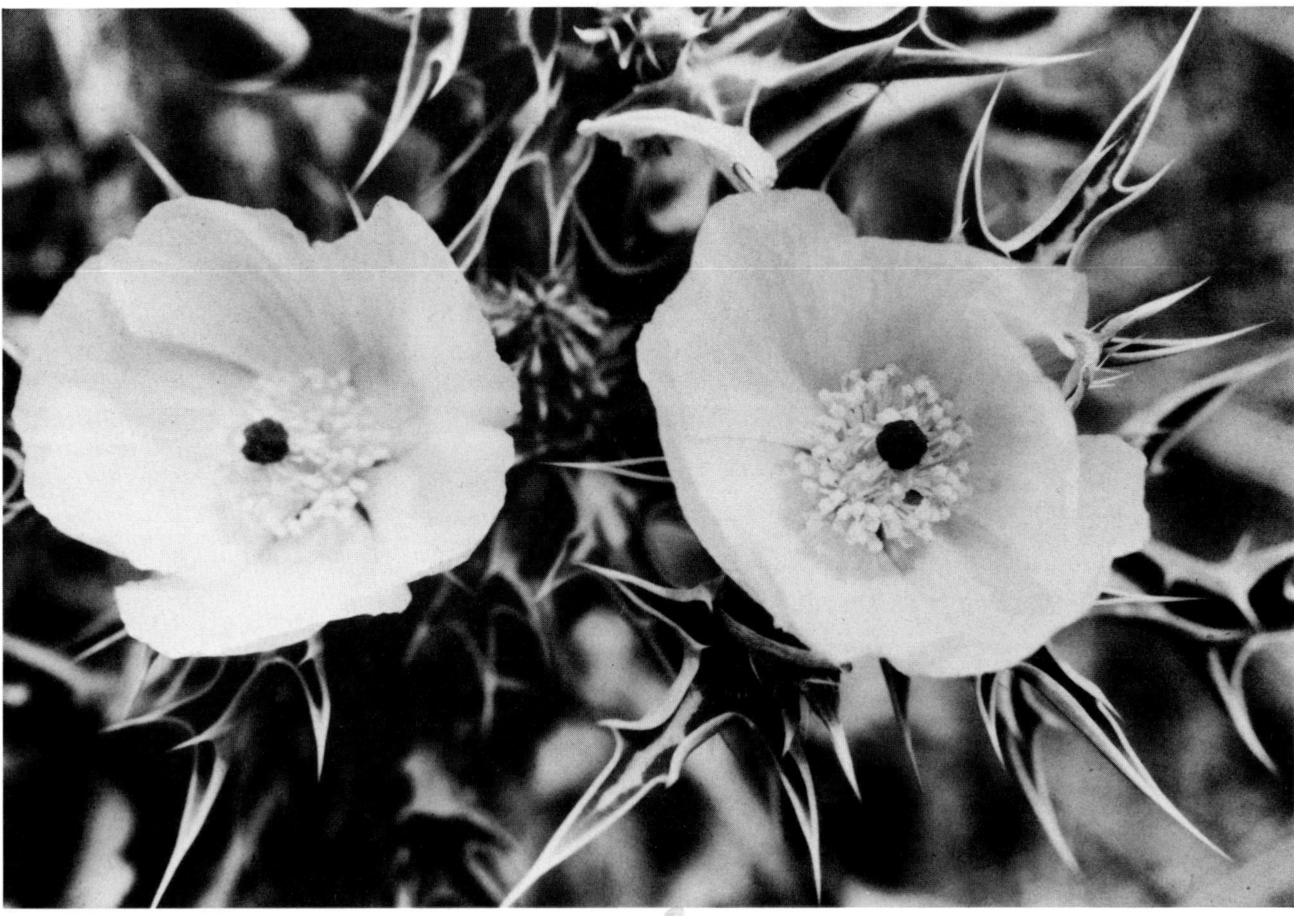

Cactus in bloom

more prominent mountain system, which stood, in Palaeozoic times, on the edge of the Rajputana sea.' The range attains its highest point (1722 metres) in the granite peak of Guru Shikar, Mt. Abu, in the south, an offshoot cut off from the central axis. The tightly packed quartz, metamorphic and igneous rocks of the main outbreak curve into an imposing spur almost 80 km wide at Udaipur, after which they straggle in attenuated form.

The Aravallis provide the natural divide in Rajasthan, separating the 'land where the aola blooms' in the east from Maroodesh, the 'dead land' of the west – the desert Thaar.

Desert territory within the borders of Rajasthan covers an area of 196,150sq.km and comprises Maroodesh in the south, with Jodhpur as its centre and including Barmer, Jangaldesh, the wilderness in the north, around Bikaner; and Marh, the petrified region of the west, surrounding the wind-sculpted jurassic limestone of Jaisalmer.

West and north of Jodhpur lies the true desert, hard compact earth covered by shifting sands, the horizon broken by dunes and sparsely dotted with scrub, cactus and the thorny *babul*. In early summer rise the fierce sandstorms that darken the sun, turning day into night.

In Marh and Jangaldesh water is often found at a depth of a hundred to two hundred and fifty metres below the surface. The Mughal conqueror, Babar (1526-30),

in his keenly critical and finely observed memoirs, the *Babarnama*, writes of wells:

> At the well edge they set up a fork of wood, having a roller adjusted between the forks, tie a rope to a large bucket, put the rope over the roller and tie its other end to the bullock. One person must drive the bullock, another empty the bucket. Every time the bullock turns after having drawn the bucket out of the well, that rope lies on the bullock track, in pollution of urine and dung, before it descends again into the well.

In the *Storia do Mogor* the Italian traveller Manucci (1653-1708) explains that

> Wells are so deep that when water is drawn out of them with the help of oxen, those who set these animals to work beat a drum as a warning that the pot is at the mouth of the well, and they are about to draw water.

Such wells are still worked in the interior of Barmer, Jaisalmer and Bikaner districts.

Temperatures in summer touch 50° C in the shade, with wide extremes in diurnal range, up to 30°C. Winters can be cold, night temperatures falling to −2° C in the dew-drenched wasteland. Rainfall on an average is 16cm annually. Many areas receive as little as 5-6cm and occasionally none at all.

Since the land cannot support a large settled population, two thirds of the people have evolved patterns of a nomadic or semi-nomadic life-cycle. Like the driven sands they are constantly on the move. The itinerant players, the wandering tinkers and blacksmiths, the snake-charmers and wayside performers, the seasonal circuit of camel-drovers and herdsmen, the regular migrations of shepherds, and the large-scale influx of landless labourers into urban centres, far from their desert homeland, are part of a general way of life imposed by environment.

Even the peasant communities and their service castes, that should normally be settled, may find their villages made uninhabitable after a sandstorm, the wells choked and unusable, the ponds dry, the fields destroyed. Such an event may mean the exodus of the entire population, usually no more than a score of households. Or the gradual drying up of water sources due to consecutive years of drought might slowly deplete a village of its inhabitants, till isolation compels the remaining families to migrate.

The wanderer, homeless and unencumbered by much domestic clutter has the need to strike roots. So he carries with him his history and culture in well-rembered ballads and songs, in rituals scrupulously observed, and customs sustained with a loving care for detail, and often at an expense he can ill afford. He clings with tenacity to the legends and lore that define his identity, the tenets of his caste, and the fabulous tales of its origin. In the treasured tablets that commemorate the spirit of his ancestors or the hero-deities of his clan, in crafts and art, dress and ornaments, he preserves the wealth of his spiritual and material well-being. He hands down to his progeny the precious skills of his ancestral profession and guards the secrets of his trade with blinkered zeal. Any concession to alien ideas and untried methods might erode the entire structure of this tenuous inner life.

Paradoxically, his wanderings bring him into contact with distant places, new people, strange customs. His ways, methods, habits, imperceptibility, are modified. Sometimes the change is abrupt, far-reaching, even devastating. A recently constructed road runs past villages on his circuit, and this might well mean that the inhabitants no longer require his humble services, since they can travel by bus to the nearest town to buy what they require. Or the influx of manufactured goods into rural areas may find him suddenly without a trade. A law passed may prohibit him from following his age-old profession. Such radical erosions are rapidly multiplying, and while this may be true of conditions faced by rural communities everywhere, the effects are clearly visible, and more devastating, seen against the stark backdrop of the desert and the singular life-style of its people.

My personal involvement with the desert began after an initial recoil from the stagnant social ethos of life in an erstwhile princely state. I was unused to the obsequious humility of domestics, the servility in the hunched-shoulder greeting of the lower orders in a strictly hierarchical society. The circumscribed living imposed by the tyranny of caste rules was a rude shock. I preferred an academic retreat into history and the romantic approach generated by an absorbed study of Colonel James Tod's *Annals and Antiquities of Rajasthan*, (1832) which, despite the personal bias and prejudices of its author, remains a classic and major work on the region.

I learnt soon enough that antiquities are no substitute for life, however fascinating or picturesque their appeal. The cloistered mind is disturbed by the throb of a distant drum, its confined conjectures swept away by the gusty vigour of events outside a window. It was the music that led me to try and discover the people; a music that invades the spaces of the wasteland, reverberates against the upturned cauldron of a brazen sky, to invest each barren hamlet with the bounty of living.

Rupayan Sansthan: Abode of Beauty

In this venture the work of a unique institute guided me through the intricate maze that forms the complicated life-patterns of the desert.

Rupayan Sansthan, an institute of folklore studies in Borunda village, about 106 km east of Jodhpur, is the creation of two men, Komal Kothari and Vijaydan Detha. It grew out of a friendship that began in student days, in a common nationalist ardour tinged with vague left-wing leanings that were endemic in youth movements in pre-Independence years, in undirected longings to rediscover roots in the culture of their native soil.

Kothari attempted poetry. For inspiration he turned to the folks songs and ballads of the people, and found such riches there that he tossed aside his own slender talent to explore these long-neglected treasures.

Vijaydan, given to a solitary pursuit of ideas, began a patient compiling of proverbs and sayings, riddles, children's rhymes and games. In his search for the core of a people's beliefs, he sought the company of wrinkled grandmothers and village elders, who related to him half-forgotten tales and local legends which he carefully noted down.

What had begun as a means to sustain and nurture themselves gradually became an end in itself. Driven by a need to discover and document, and later help promote, the folk arts, both men, much to the anxiety of their families, took a decision to shun the normal course of securing jobs, so that they could devote themselves entirely to their common obsession.

They based themselves in Borunda village, the home of Vijaydan. Here in 1960 an acquaintance gave them the use of a tumble-down *haveli* in return for its upkeep. Rupayan Sansthan came into being. They bought an antiquated second-hand printing press and housed it in one of the dilapidated cowsheds.

I first visited Borunda with my son Vivek about a

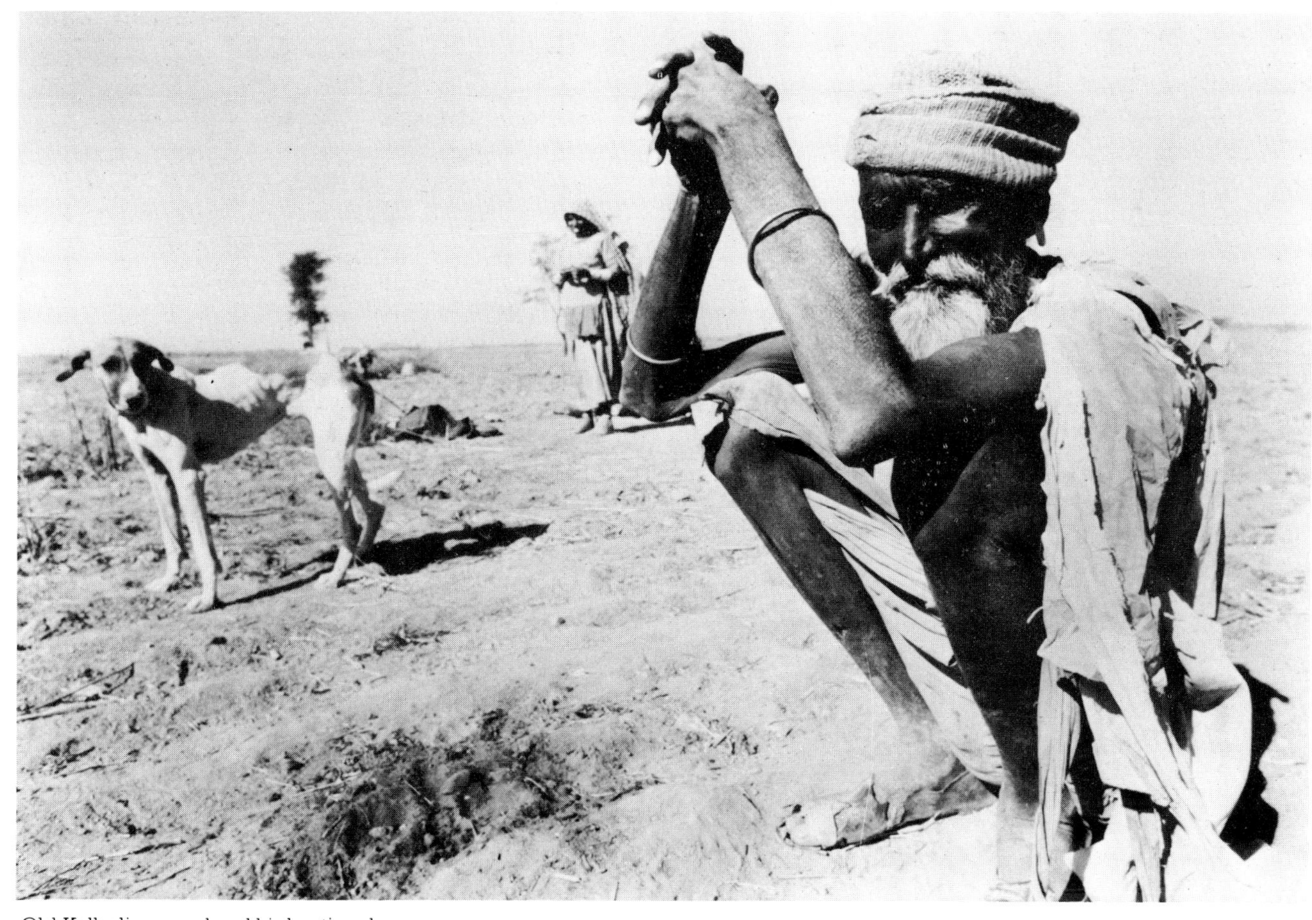

Old Kalbelia nomad and his hunting dog

On the move

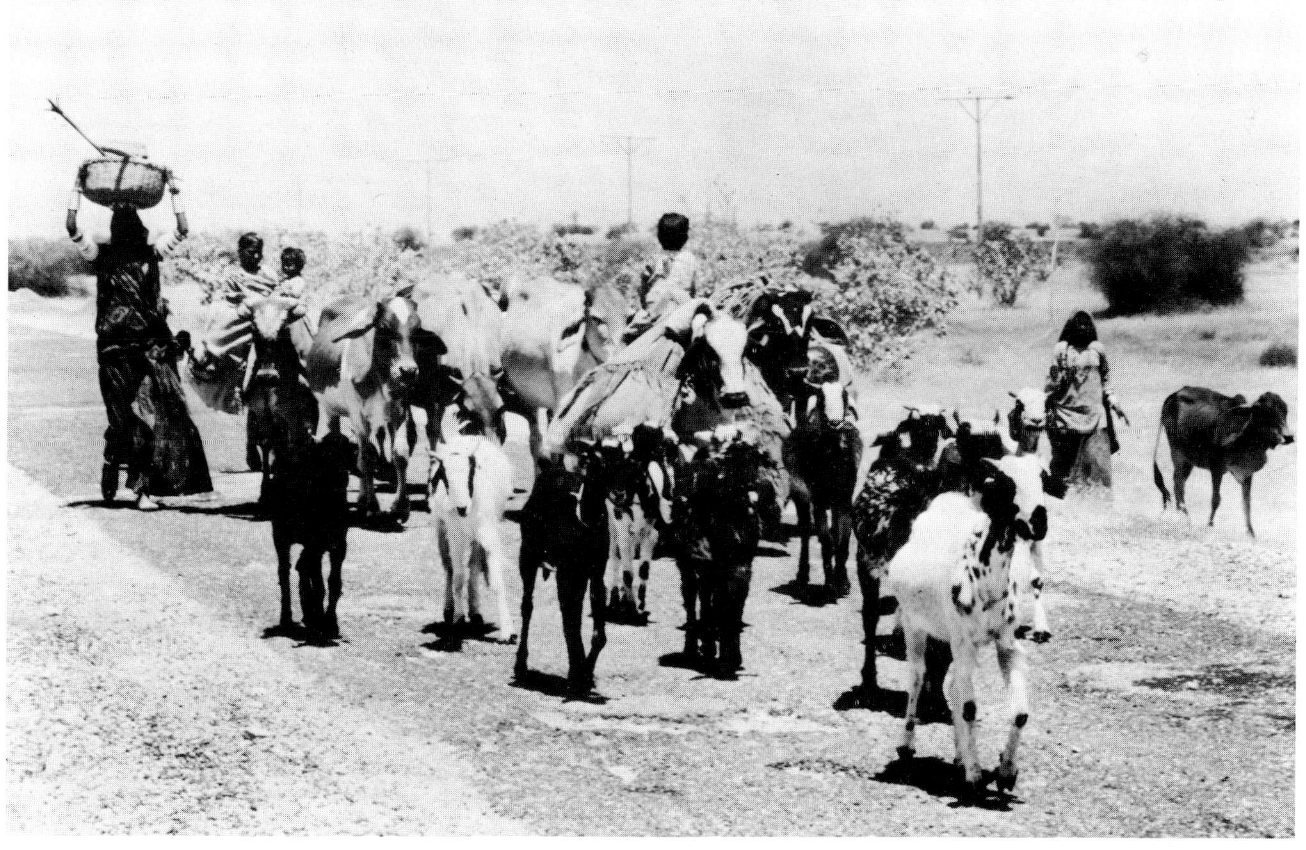

decade ago. We found Vijaydan up to the elbows in printer's ink, diligently hand-setting the formes for the latest volume of folk-tales, while Komal, surrounded by a group of Langa folk-singers, was transcribing the text of songs. In this he was helped considerably by Noor Mohammed, the senior Langa musician and singer, a highly intelligent man whose tragic death has been a grievous loss to the community and the Sansthan, as he was a reliable source of information and one of the few folk artistes who appreciated the significance of the work being done.

In 1965 the Rajasthan government recognised the importance of the Sansthan's role and since then has provided a small annual grant towards its running. The central government has also aided certain projects from time to time.

Through the years the Sansthan has brought out fourteen volumes of folk-tales in the local language. These have been translated into Hindi and a first collection has been published recently. A volume of proverbs with 3000 entries has been produced and four similar volumes are under preparation. Kothari and Vijaydan edited a monthly journal called *Lok Sanskriti* (Folklore) which appeared regularly for 18 years, from 1960 to 1978. Unfortunately they no longer have the press which had to be sold a couple of years ago.

A monograph by Kothari on the Langas was released along with a set of records. Up to now they have been able to market three sets of discs on the music of the Langas and Manganiyars. The tape archives of the institute comprise the largest available collection of Rajasthani folk music.

A subsequent visit to Rupayan Sansthan found the institute luxuriously housed in its own premises, a spacious, well-designed building on top of a hill overlooking the village. Its completion in 1972 was a dream fulfilled for the directors. They now have a permanent home and the possibility of expanding their work to include the systematic study of specific subjects. A collection of specimens has been initiated, which they hope will grow into a representative museum of rural arts and crafts.

I asked Vijaydan whether their work in Borunda in the past twenty years has had any effect on the life of the villagers. 'Not a jot!' he replied emphatically. 'Village folk are eminently pragmatic by nature. If our work had brought them direct material gain, they might have been interested. Since it does not, they merely ignore us.'

I persisted, 'The Sansthan is now well-known throughout the country; its work has been recognised abroad. Do they feel no sense of pride in what has brought Borunda recognition?'

'They are not in the least concerned, since the recognition, such as it is, brings them no tangible rewards.'

He went on to explain that new ideas, methods or projects are resisted by rural communities until the benefits accruing from them are demonstrated in concrete terms. The sinking of tube-wells, the use of fertilisers, or new types of seed grain were only accepted when the peasants were convinced that the results were profitable, and actually seen to be so.

To me the influence of the folklore institute is apparent in the simple fact of Vijaydan's nephew, Inderdan, who farms his own land in the village, devoting all his spare time to a laborious piecing together of the history of the village. When completed, this survey of Borunda with its detailed account of each community, will be a valuable sociological document, perhaps the first of its kind in Rajasthan, more thorough than the surveys undertaken by the Census Department, which are the most reliable studies available at present.

A visit we paid to the village with Inderdan as our guide was an illuminating experience. He knew every individual in each household and was a favourite with young children.

In the weaver's colony we saw the primitive mud hut in which an old weaver had lived, worked and brought up his family. Opposite this was his new home, built of bricks. The grandmother gave us a winning, toothless smile as she confided, 'The old home was better. When the wind and the rain came (referring to the cloud-burst), I ran into the shed. Even if this had fallen on my head or blown away I still would have been alive. In a *pucca* house the roof can fall on your head and kill you!'

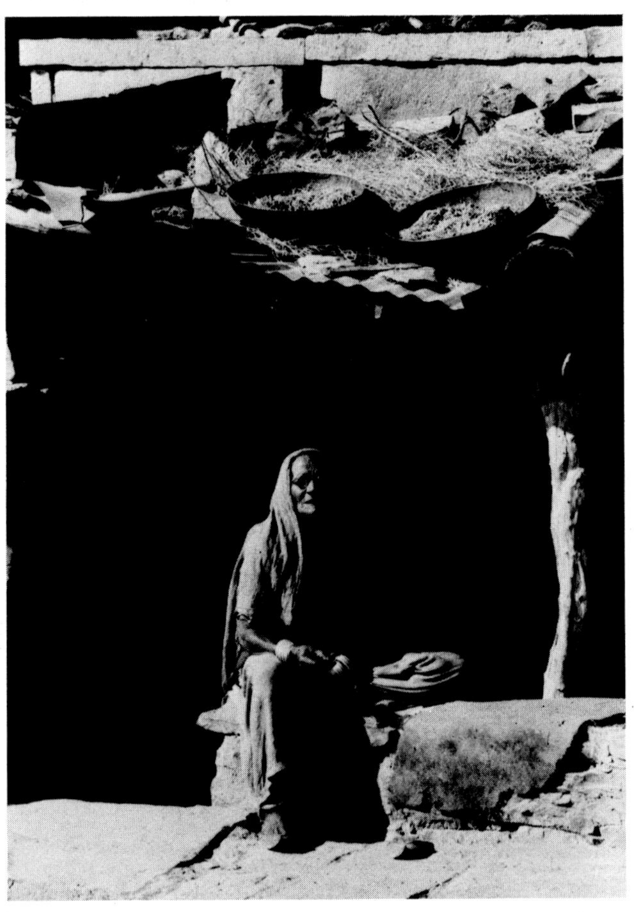
Grandmother outside the old hut

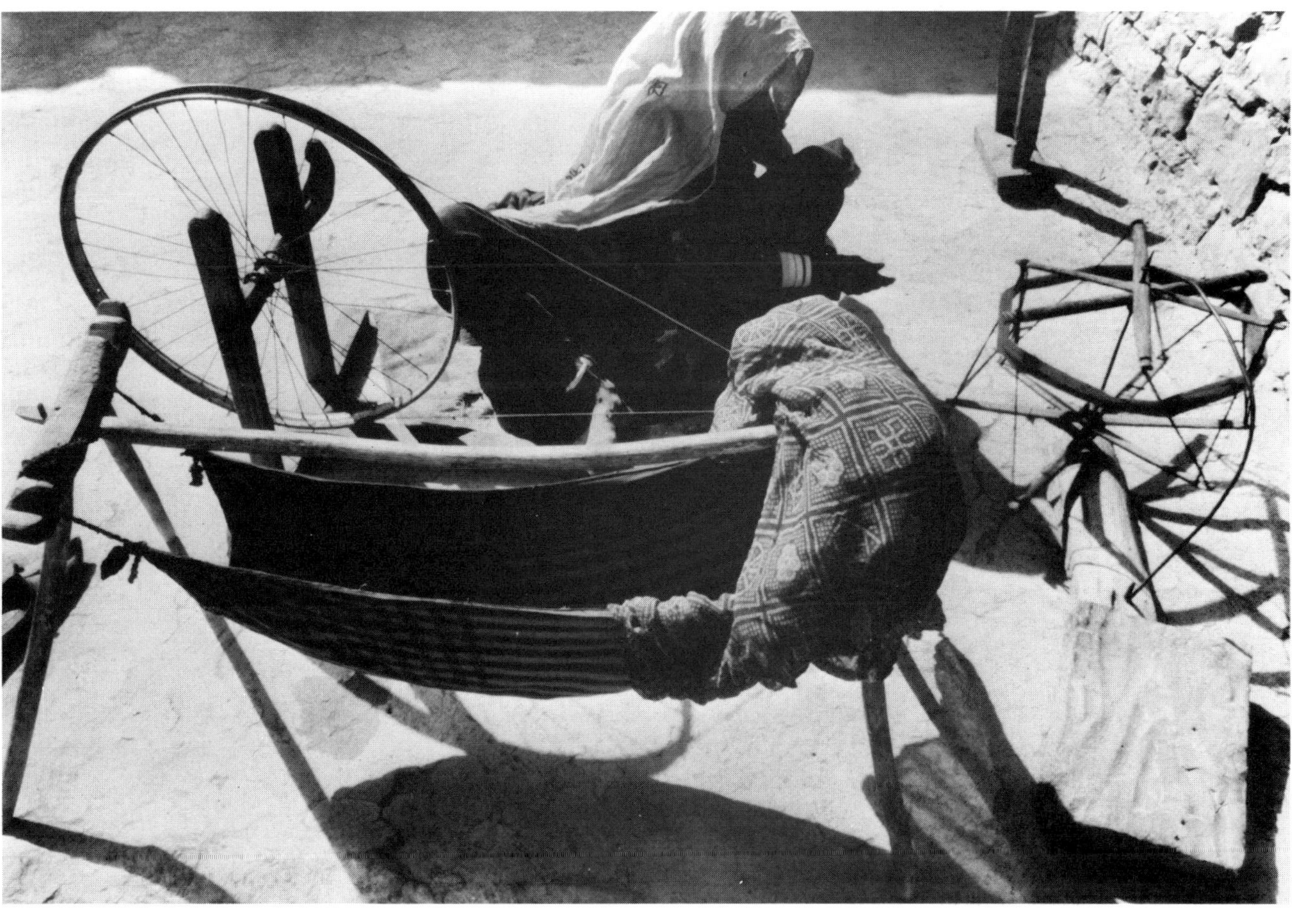

Ingenious use of bicycle wheel as spinning wheel

In another home Inderdan picked out some brightly coloured patchwork quilts, which we admired. He told us, 'Not a single scrap of cloth is ever thrown away. Rags are washed and pulled into shreds, and the shreds are used as padding for quilts and quilted jackets. The stronger and more colourful bits of cloth are pieced together in patchwork or appliqué designs.'

Time and again the ingenuity and unceasing industry of the members in village households struck us forcibly. In one home a bicycle wheel had been converted into a spinning wheel; in another a packing case transformed into an attractive child's cot. The love of colour and an acute, unerring sense of design related to function was discernible in the weaver's hut, in a display of coloured cotton spools hung on a wall. The courtyard and interior of each home we visited were spotlessly clean and neatly arranged. Dirt or untidiness, garbage and squalor are confined to the lanes of the village, or to the outskirts of the settled area.

The Ballad of Pabuji Rathor

As we returned to the institute through the pomegranate orchard, we could hear the familiar sound of a balladeer, *Pabuji ra bhopa*, recounting the heroic ballad of Pabuji Rathor, a fourteenth century pastoral hero. Among the Sansthan's guests was an ethno-musicologist who was engaged in a comparative study of Greek and Rajasthani folk music, and an eminent Indologist, whom we knew well.

Kothari has recorded eleven different versions of the Pabuji ballad so far, and he is not certain if he has exhausted all the variations.

History, myth and legend come together to form the Ballad of Pabuji. The protagonist is the illegitimate son of a Rathor prince, this much history concedes. His birth takes us to the realm of myth. The ballad related that the Rathor fell in love with a fairy who agreed to live with him at night but made him vow that he would not intrude on her during the day. She bore him a son. The prince broke his promise, and on entering her apartment came upon a lioness feeding the babe. The fairy-lioness disappeared on his entry. Her sister was Devali, a powerful Charan woman who brought up the young lad. His pranks as a child and exploits as a young man form the legendary aspects of the ballad. His birthplace was at Kolu near Pokharan. The well dug there by the boy, Pabu, and his companions still exists. As a pastoral hero he is credited with introducing a new breed of camel into the region. He is the patron deity of the Raika community who are camel drovers and herdsmen. They claim descent from the union of a Rajput with an *apsara*, a celestial nymph. Charan women who developed mystic powers were considered superhuman beings, either saints or *apsaras*. It is said that the Raikas formed part

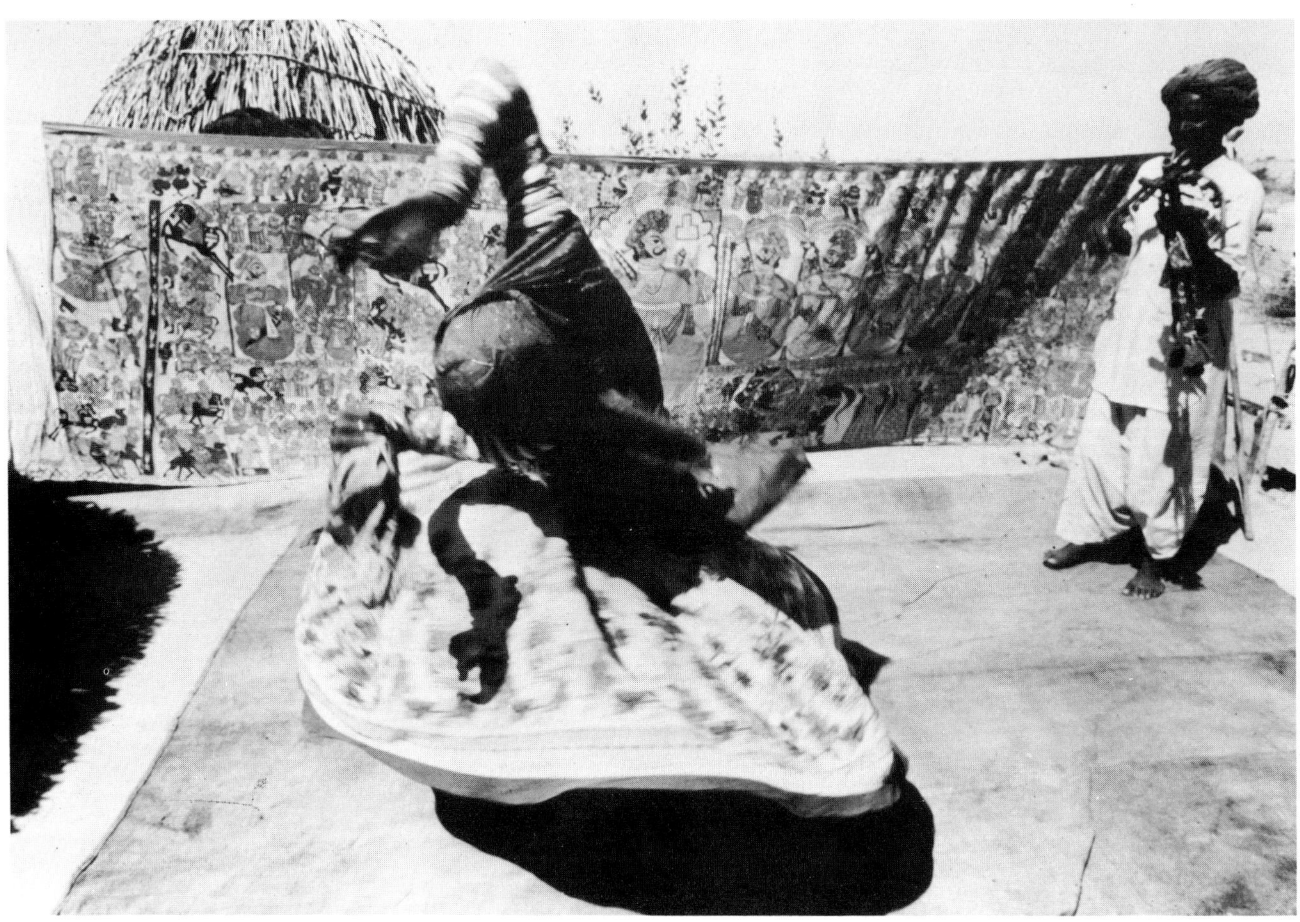

The female impersonator executes an intricate movement as the Pabuji ballad is sung

of the armed bands that fought under Pabuji.

The ballad is sung by a community of itinerant performers, usually a husband and wife team, in front of the *parh*, a painted curtain on which are depicted various episodes from the life of Pabu. The man plays a string instrument of ancient origin, called *ravanhatha*, 'the hand of Ravana', with a short bow to which jingle-bells are attached. He dances while he sings and plays, jerking the bow as he draws it across the strings, producing a marked rhythm on the bells. The woman, her face heavily veiled, carries an oil lamp in her hand with which she lights the painted pictures, one by one, as the story unfolds. Occasionally she utters a piercing note, like the cry of a wild bird, to underline a high point in the romantic tale, or to emphasise an emotional passage.

The curtain is a piece of coarse handwoven textile – 6 metres long and 1½ metres wide. A bold portrait of Pabuji in profile dominates the centre space, drawn in folk style akin to the manner of the early Jain manuscripts, but lacking the exaggerated fish-eye. Four figures, slightly smaller in size, of Pabu's companions, face their leader. His famous mare, Kali Kesari, a gift from his Charan patroness, Devali, occupies a prominent position just below the seated warriors. The major incidents of the narrative are drawn around these important panels. They are not placed in any discernible sequence. Often an episode that follows another will be found at the farthest end from it, in an obscure corner. This separation of events gives the balladeer and his partner scope for complicated action. The dancing back and forth of the singer, and the swooping and darting figure of the veiled woman with the light, as she illuminates a painted detail, now here, now there, shrilling her wild-bird calls, indicate a masterly command of choreographic movement in a confined space. The colours formerly used were the muted shades derived from herbs and minerals such as turmeric, indigo, lime-chalk, charcoal, but these have been replaced by the clear tones of poster paints. A Parh painter whom we watched at work, in Bassi near Chitorgarh, told us that he preferred the new paints which were strong and bright and could be easily seen from a distance. The firm black outline he executed with artists' brushes of varied thickness were, in his opinion, superior to the uneven, blurred effect of the earlier paintings made with brushes of local thorn. Old curtains were of value only to urban collectors with their peculiar notions of what constituted the aesthetics of folk art. These professional painters are known as *chitrakars*.

We once witnessed a performance of Pabuji out in the Barmer desert at Haathitala village near Dhorimana, in which a third performer also participated. He was a female impersonator who danced before the curtain and executed some skilled acrobatics while doing so. This is unusual and only particular families in remote villages include such a participant in their traditional performance.

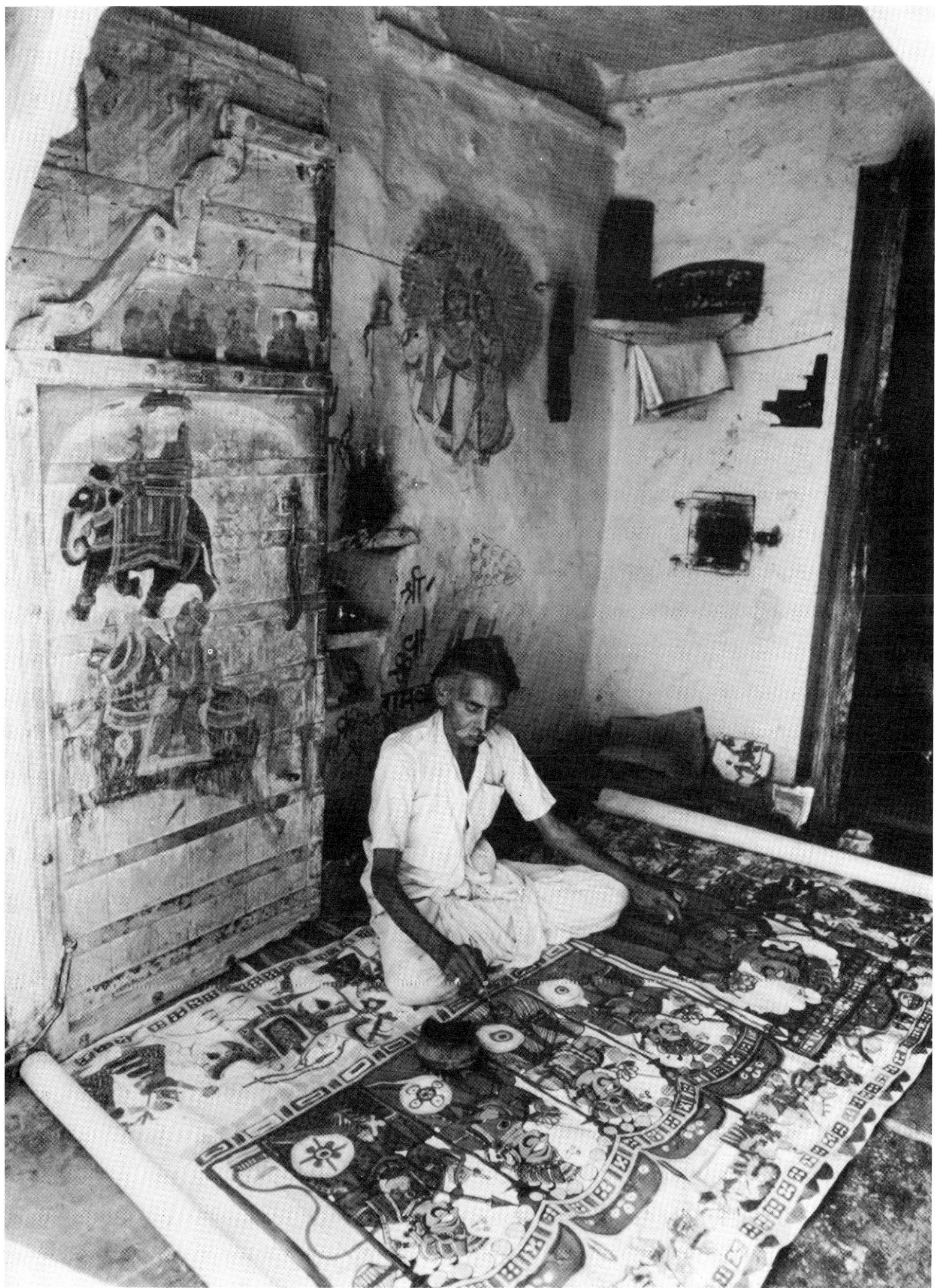

Traditional *Parh* painter at work

Although the *bhopin*, the balladeers' wife, acts as his assistant during the performance of the ballad, women do not dance in front of the *parh*. In the seclusion of their homes, however, the women of these Nayak families participate in elaborate enactments during wedding celebrations. Within the courtyard, the drummers, who are the *bhaats*, genealogists, of the Nayaks, start their strong beats. The girls and women, begin by dancing one after the other. Occasionally a second or third dancer will enter the arena. An exceptionally skilled dancer may challenge the drummers, by executing complicated figures and calling for a faster tempo. They then form groups and perform short plays, known as *vesha*. Some of the girls dress up as boys or men, and act as male impersonators.

The spectators at such gatherings include male relations of the families, but no outsiders are admitted. These enactments last throughout the night accompanied by much convivial drinking and feasting. We had the privilege of seeing some of these acts while we were with Kothari. A *bhopa*, Khiyan Ram, agreed to let the women of his family perform for documentation purposes. His dark and comely wife, Parvati, and her sister Virji, piquant of face and of a sparkling vivacity, were the principal performers. There were two other women of the families and inevitably, two tiny infants.

The girls began by challenging each other in single dance items. Then, with much off stage giggling, Khiyah Ram doffed his jacket and turban which Virji donned, tucking her pleated skirt up between her legs, to form a baggy pantaloon. They acted out the *vesha* of the marriage ceremonies. Wearing her turban at a rakish angle, Virgi led in Parvati as his bride. The other women sang the appropriate songs as the bride and groom went in for the seven perambulations round the fire-altar, then the bride left for her new home, where on arrival the couple broke into an ecstatic courtship display, like mating birds, to express their happiness. One realised how, in the intimate seclusion of the courtyard, the young people could let themselves go and express themselves with freedom. Virji, who made a dashing groom, wooed his bride with a flaunting abandon and the dance became symbolic of conjugal love. The songs were profuse in the use of *double entendre*. In the middle of the dance Virji's little babe set up a wail and refused such comfort as Khiyan Ram could offer. Quite undisturbed, Virji danced up to the baby, picked it up and continued her act as the naughty bridegroom without missing the beat and not a whit disconcerted by the now contented babe clutched to her hip and nuzzling like a little monkey.

That evening we sat over maps with Kothari and marked out the itinerary of our forthcoming tour. He was to join us some days later at Bikaner, so Vivek and I decided to visit Shekhawati, the region between Jaipur and Bikaner, before meeting him. In the past ten years we made several such tours, Manohar Lalas,

the sound recordist, documenting material for the Sansthan's archives, while Vivek covered the same subject with his camera. Often the pictorial record achieves a clarity and precision which captures the essence of a moment, an event or a place that words cannot match, and can only inadequately describe. Words explain, narrate or explore, while the visual is able to evoke an immediate response: it has a life, a validity of its own. An analogy, near enough, could be with Indian music, where melody and rhythm follow their separate norms but combine in a synthesis more meaningful than either could achieve by itself.

Scholarly works on Rajasthan have concentrated mainly on its history, architecture, art, its archaeology or anthropology. Popular accounts have tended to emphasise the seemingly romantic and exotic aspects of its past – the Rajput clans with their genealogical fantasies or their much-vaunted code of chivalry and martial valour. Few have given thought to the people. In a general survey it has not been possible to do more than provide, in words and visuals, a glimpse of the textures of everyday life through these encounters with the inhabitants of the mansions of the sun, the desert Thaar.

2 Shekhawati: On the Edge of the Desert

North of Jaipur the landscape changes. The grey land begins and gradually gives way to the desert. On the increasingly waterless expanse the sun bleaches green to ash, and brown to a sandy beige. Shade trees are replaced by scrub and brush, fields of wheat and mustard by a broad wasteland where the ubiquitous goat voraciously devours the dry grasses, pulling up roots and stripping the bark off the *khejra* trees that break the monotony of the low skyline. Shekhawati is on the fringes of the Thaar and we were on the trail of the Shekhawati murals.

In this landscape wells take on significance. Their very form proclaims their importance. A high platform surrounds the well-mouth, and four turretted pillars mark its corners. The deeper one travels into the desert the higher stand these turrets, like sentinels guarding the precious sustenance of life: water. Some of these are very ancient, and many have been gifted to villages by pious, wealthy merchants or by landlords, the Thakurs.

At Jhalar we stopped at the *Baniani ri Baori*, the Well of the Merchant's Wife. She must have been a highly esteemed person with much at stake, for the legend relates that she lost her gold bracelet at a fair in Lohargarh. It may have been at a clandestine rendezvous because she was frightened at its loss, and went to the Brahmin priest to seek his help in recovering it. He told her to dig at a certain spot and here she fortunately found the ornament. He then ordained that in expiation for her fault and as an act of piety she should dig a well at that very place for the people of Jhalar. Thus her temporary loss was a permanent gain for the villages in the vicinity.

Next to the well is a temple to Raghunathji (Lord Rama) and here we had our first glimpse of the fascinating murals that are found in many buildings throughout this area.

Although there is the usual *kirti stambh*, about one metre high with a conical top and square sides, standing outside the temple, it records no date, nor the name or emblem of the man who built it. The temple priest told us that the murals were about 100 years old, which may be a slight exaggeration. The gateway is profusely covered with many varied scenes and the colours are still fairly bright. Prominence is given to the Dhola Maru episode which is understandable. Shekhawati Rajputs are from branches of the Kachchwaha clan of Amer-Jaipur and Prince Dhola Rai is their most famous hero and the founder of the Kachchwaha kingdom. He wrested it from the former rulers, the Mina tribals, but later in a skirmish with them, accompanied on a camel by his wife, the bewitching Princess Maroni, Dhola was killed. The other paintings on this outer facade show scenes of everyday life, wrestling, hunting, falconry, and a horse and carriage with seated figures.

The doorway to the inner court has a frieze of celestial musicians playing on instruments that are still in use locally: the *satara*, double flute; *sarangi*, stringed lute; *khartal*, wooden castanets; *duff*, one-sided shallow drum like a tambourine without the jingles; *dhol*, two-faced drum; and *poongi*, snake-charmer's pipe. Though not distinguished as works of art, the murals have a spontaneous liveliness. The shrine is guarded by Balarupa Hanuman, the monkey-god devotee of Lord Rama, in his diminutive form.

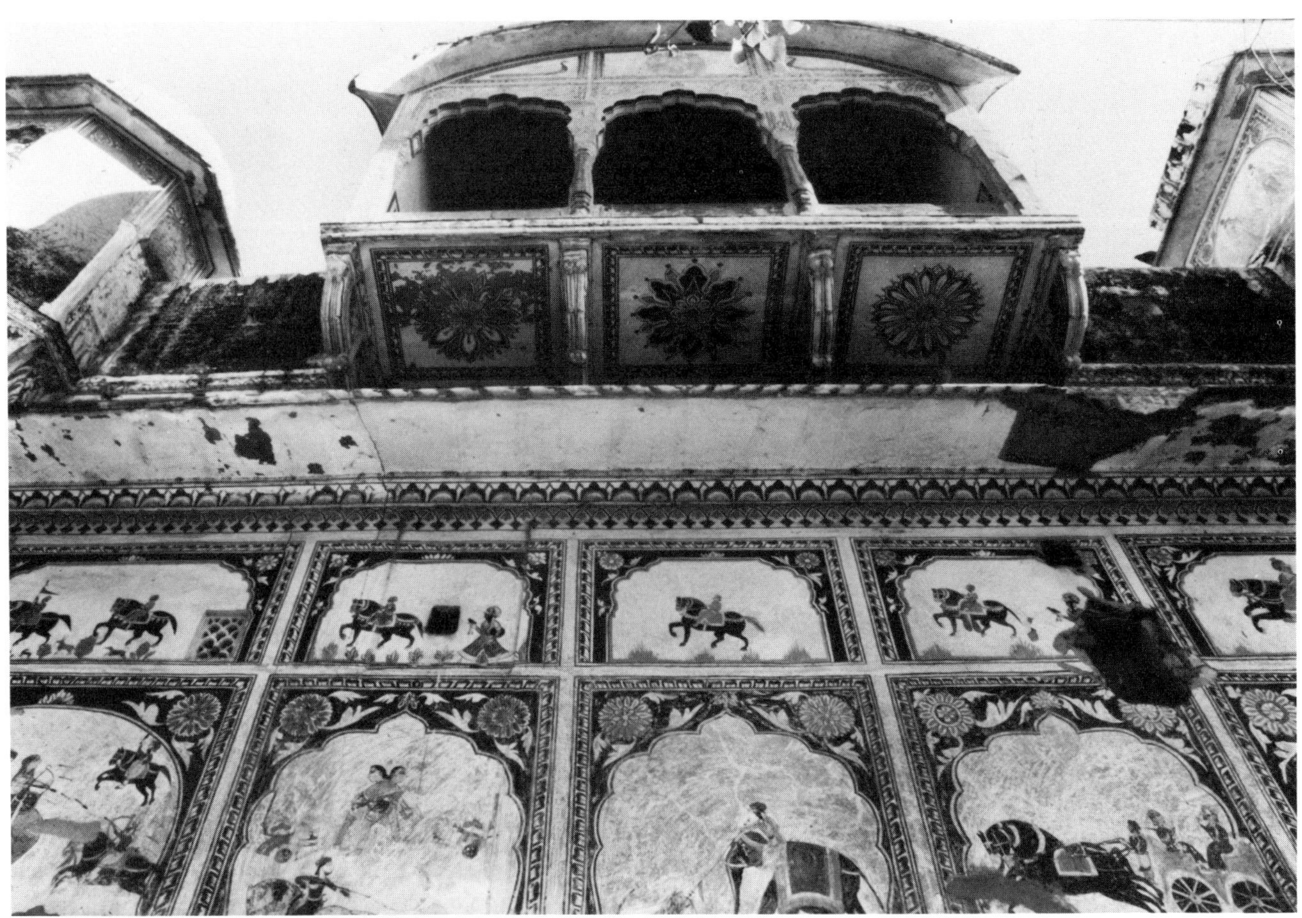

The facade of the Raghunathji temple, Jhalar

Through Shekhawati passed one of the major ancient caravan trade-routes, giving this region its strategic importance. From Bhatinda in the Punjab, through Sirsa via Churu, across Shekhawati, ran the route on to the salt lake of Sambhar, and so to Ajmer. Salt was one of the chief items of commerce, and whoever controlled its movement from the salt-beds at Sambhar – at times the Rathors of Jodhpur, at others the Kachchwahas of Amer-Jaipur – had an enviable source of revenue. This trade was curtailed later by the British who imposed an embargo on its movement outside Rajasthan, as the Raj had a government monopoly on salt throughout India. Sambhar Lake no longer yields as much salt as before because rainfall in recent years has reduced its salinity. Before the embargo, salt and grain were carried far beyond the Thaar by the Banjaras, a tribe known as the most audacious of nomads. Their route took them across the jungles of central India south up to the Deccan plateau. They are still to be found in Andhra Pradesh, where they are known as Lambadis. Their women are gorgeous creatures of a wild-eyed beauty and vigorous grace.

Bishop Heber came across these people near Ajmer during his long travels through India between 1824 and 1826. As is usual with the good Bishop, he spells their name in a curious manner, but what he has to say of them in his *Narrative* is enthralling:

> We passed a large encampment of "Brinjarrees" or carriers of grain, a singular wandering race, who pass their whole time in transporting this article from one part of the country to another, seldom on their own account, but as agents for more wealthy dealers. They move about in large bodies with their wives, children, dogs and loaded bullocks. The men are all armed as a protection against petty thieves. From the sovereigns and armies of Hindostan they have no apprehensions. Even contending armies allow them to pass and repass safely, never taking their goods without purchase, or even preventing them, if they choose, from victualling their enemies' camp. Both sides wisely agree to respect and encourage a branch of industry, the interruption of which might be attended with fatal consequences to both. How well would it be if a similar liberal feeling prevailed between the belligerents of Europe; and how much is our piratical system of warfare put to shame in this respect by the practice of those whom we call barbarians. *

As we drove through Jhalar village we noticed a group of Banjaras squatting in a semi-circle at the bus-stop. They were smoking a *chillum*, a large clay

* Heber, Rev. Reginald, *Narrative of a Journey through the Upper Provinces of India*, John Murray, London, 1828, II, 444.

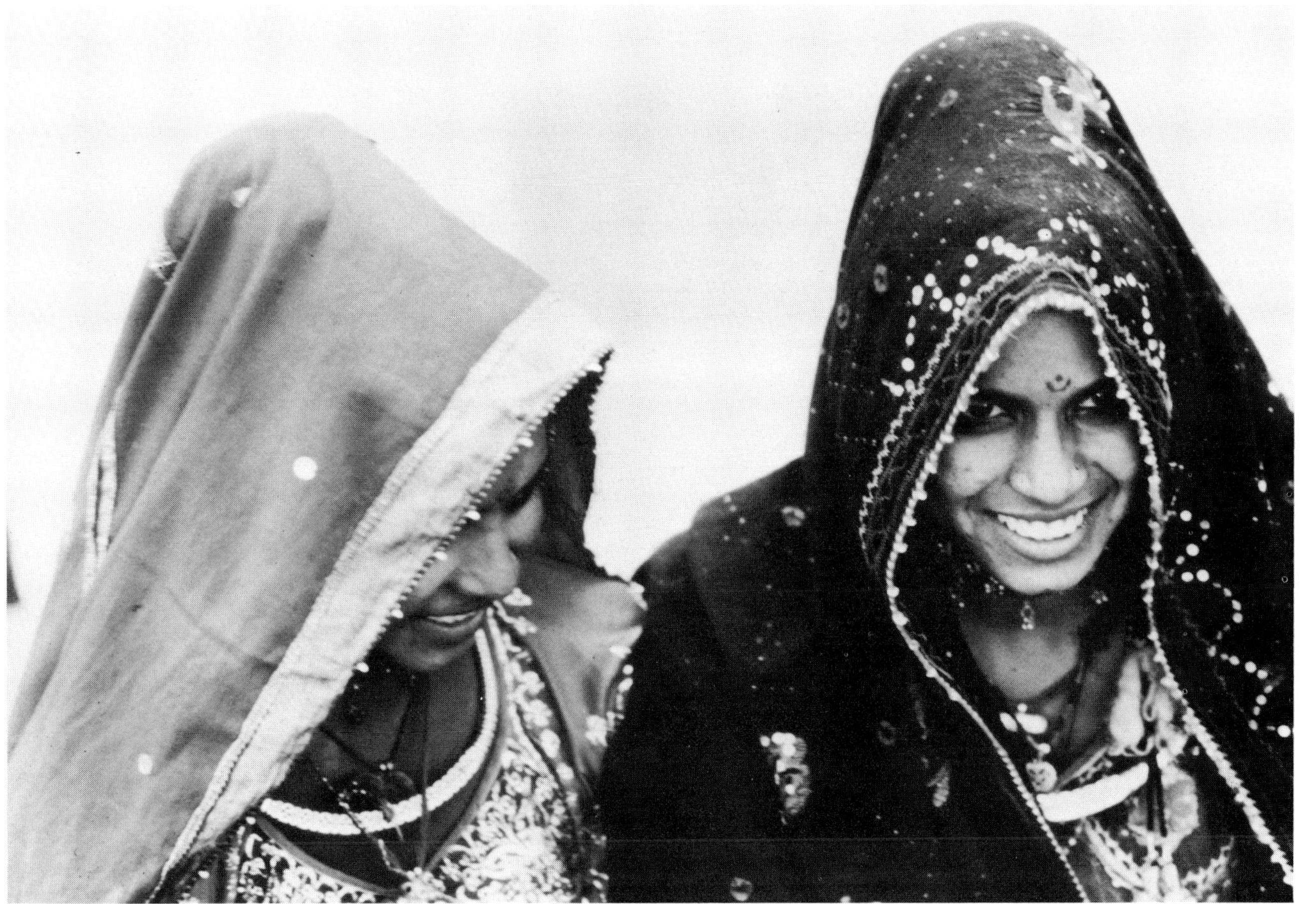

Girls dressed for a fair

pipe, each man inhaling deeply, his face assuming a look of soporific beatitude, before he passed it to his neighbour. They are now merely herdsmen, having lost out to the goods train and the noisome polluting trucks that ply between towns and villages. Desert economy can make no use today of the qualities of the Banjaras as hardy, venturesome and fearless transporters of salt and grain.

At Chaumu we branched off to Samod. The flat plain here is broken up by rocky little hills and shallow ravines. The road turned and twisted its way up the incline. A babble of voices and the light twittering of laughter, like bird-calls, filtered down from the higher reaches, echoing in the narrow gorge, tantalising us as it now seemed loud and close, but around the next bend was suddenly lost, or grew faint and distant as though borne away on an erratic breeze to some distant valley. A brief gust tossed at us, like a shower of blossoms, the opening phrase of a folk song, only to scatter the refrain that followed which whispered into nothingness, like autumn leaves rustling in a neighbour's garden.

We laboured through the gorge beyond which the road opened out into a glade of deciduous trees. Here we ran into the rear-guard of an assorted caravan of bullock and camel carts, and riders mounted on horses and camels. The laggards were the singers, two youths walking with the long swinging stride of those accustomed to open spaces. The first sang a stanza, his companion joining in the refrain. A high teasing voice from somewhere out front called out to them, and a cascade of laughter swept down the line of travellers. The carts, we noticed, were freshly painted, the bullocks hung with beads and bells, the camels caparisoned in the *gorbandh*, with its bright woven strands decorated with cowrie shells. The carts were packed with families. The women wore the traditional hand-printed skirts. These, pleated and gathered up at the waist, are made of coarse hand-woven cotton, block-printed in designs predominantly black on a red ground or red on black. Their veils were also of thick cotton in sun-yellow or red with tie-dye borders, and central motifs in a contrasting shade. The men sported the *angarkha*, short tops with flared backs, tied with tassels on the right. Were these people going to a village fair? There was an air of make-believe that puzzled us.

We ran the gauntlet of their mocking remarks as we drove slowly past them, though they made way for our dust-raising mechanised brute with good-humoured tolerance. When we turned towards the gates of the small fortified palace which was our destination, the mystery was solved. These were 'locals' who had been engaged as 'extras' for shooting on an outdoor location. A Hindi film unit had beaten us to Samod! In order to supplement his dwindled income the ex-ruler of Samod had rented out his palace as the locale for a romantic period film, a practice increasingly

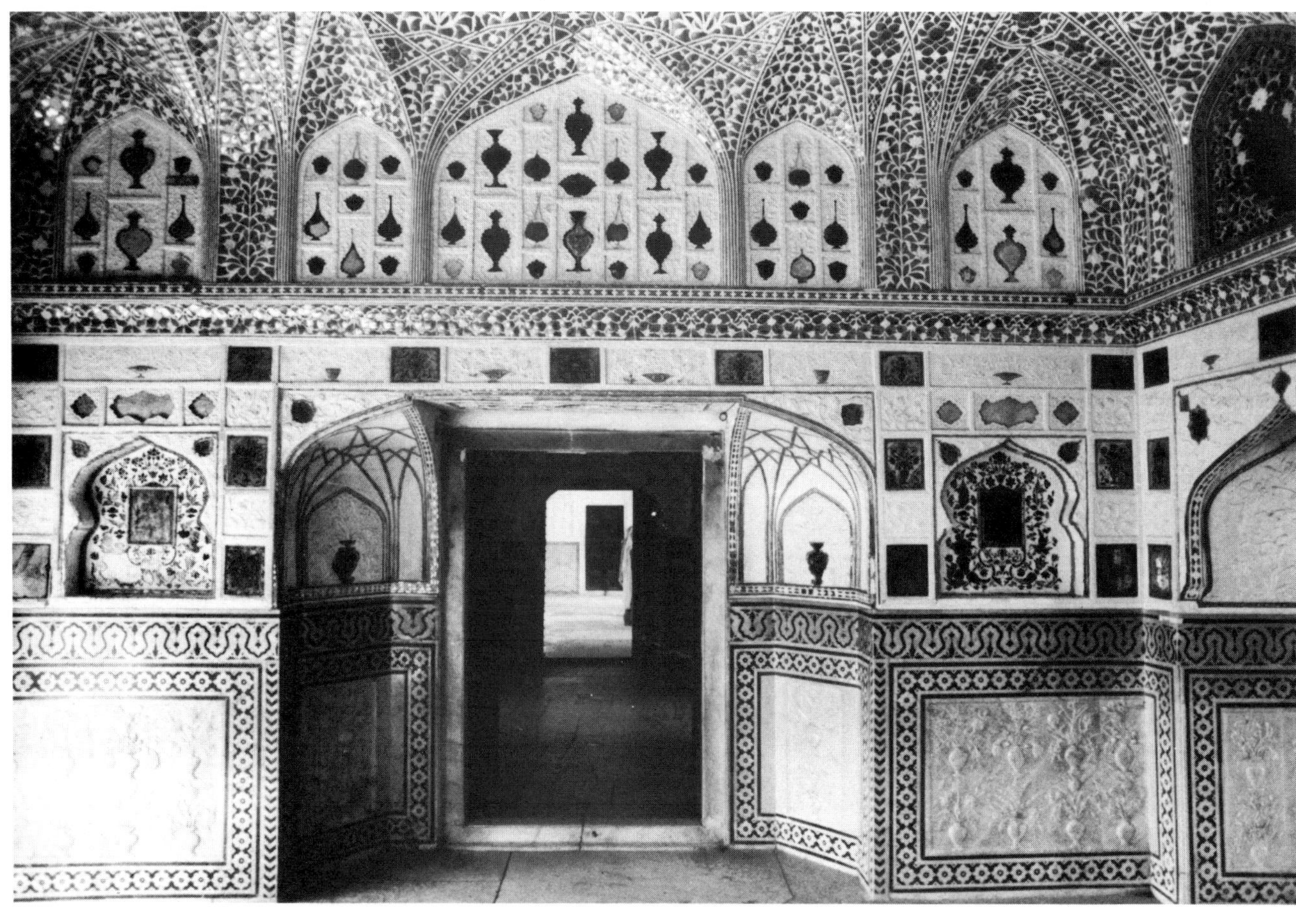

The Shish Mahal at Amer became the inspiration for mirror work as wall decoration

resorted to by the owners of royal homes they can no longer afford to live in.

Walking though the gateway of the palace, we came upon a chaotic scene. The open courtyard was crowded with people dodging between the technical crew who were setting up cameras and huge reflectors. The upper ramparts were packed with exuberant villagers perched on top who had come to see this novel type of *tamasha*, fun-fair. The facade of the palace had been slicked up with a fresh coat of paint and decked with coloured pennants emblazoned with mythical heraldic beasts flying from the battlements.

Samod's Painted Palaces

Leaving this scene of high expectation we followed a wispy, garrulous old retainer into the inner court. Here all was quiet desolation and gentle decay. The court was small and full of weeds, plaster peeling off the walls, stagnant pools of water in the corners. Odd bits of dismembered furniture littered the surrounding verandahs. Pigeons and doves cooed their refrain from little niches which once held oil-lamps at night. We turned into a corridor, mounted a staircase, and through a low entrance stepped into a miniature *Rang Mahal*, painted palace, of astonishing beauty.

It was the scale that made the difference. The celebrated Rang Mahals in the palaces of Amer, Jodhpur and Bikaner are splendid chambers for the opulent durbars of extravagant princes. But their very size and grandeur overwhelm the eye and satiate the imagination. Here all was jewelled perfection, on the diminutive scale of fairy land, an opal setting for those tender meetings of royal lovers made familiar in Rajput miniature paintings, that express with ineffable grace the most fragile sentiments.

The chamber is divided into two parts. In the outer pavilion the walls are entirely covered in red and blue floral designs, on a gold ground, with panels on top showing birds of many recognisable species, fighting, flying, mating, or singing from branches. The floors are white marble, a pristine touch of impeccable taste, and so are the fluted pillars that divide the chamber. The ceiling here sparkles with tiny bits of mirror set in coloured geometric designs. The inner room, a little *Sheesh Mahal*, palace of mirrors, has painted panels with *minakari* giving the effect of enamel inset, studded with mirrors. The lower panels depict scenes of courtly life, and one that catches the attention is a hunting scene of a princess riding a horse at full gallop, lassooing a black buck with her bow, no doubt to capture it alive, as the buck was a favourite pet. The prince at her side is taking aim at another animal.

A door at one end of the outer pavilion leads into a bed-chamber, painted entirely in pastel shades of water-greens and spring-sky blues, creating an underwater effect, very cool and soothing. The painted panels here are, appropriately, of ladies at their toilet, or dancing and playing on instruments.

To get the best effect of these elaborately painted rooms, one should look at them as they were meant to be seen: seated at ground level. When in use, such chambers are furnished with mattresses laid on a very low platform, to make a divan. The mattress is covered by a carpet of lustrous colours and formal designs. Large bolsters are placed along the back and sides, and several small cushions of varied shapes are scattered around, to be adjusted for comfort. These are covered with exquisitely worked embroidery, appliqué, or the local *abla*, mirror work, set in geometric or floral patterns in close fine stitchery.

Stools and small tables placed near the divans serve to hold cups of sherbet, a silver betel-leaf container, or a carved book-rest against which the folios of miniature paintings can be viewed in comfort.

Seated thus, the wall decorations take on a certain order. At the bottom, just below eye-level, are the incidents from everyday life, of princes hunting deer, of girls on a swing or lovers in a bower. Above these, at the level of the eyes as one sits, are the panels of formal design, floral or geometric. Leaning back against the bolsters and looking up, one watches scenes of court life, royal durbars, ceremonial processions, and triumphant victory parades. Uppermost, next to the ceiling, are the episodes from myths and epics interspersed with medallions of the deities. Finally, while reclining, the gaze is directed to the ceiling, to the stars in the *Sheesh Mahal* that twinkle in the canopied sky.

The use of mirror as a feature of wall or ceiling decoration is an art of Iranian origin, but it found its finest expression in the *sheesh mahals* of the Rajput princes. Every major palace in Rajasthan boasts a hall of mirrors, the most lavish being the renowned one at Amer, built (1639) by the brilliant and arrogant Mirza Raja Jai Singh I. There, when the doors are closed, in the light of a single candle, one loses all sense of confinement, and floats like a satellite in infinite space among the glittering galaxies.

The reason for mirror-work among the Rajputs is understandable. Essentially fighting men, used to living under the open sky, most of their time was spent in camp on warlike expeditions or raids. They were seldom in residence, and even when they were, they lived simple almost spartan lives. These public chambers were in use only on momentous occasion such as celebrations for the birth of a son, the marriage of a daughter, a visit by a royal ally, a religious ritual, or after victory in battle. At least one of the palace chambers had to sparkle with slivers of mirror to remind them of the star-clustered night sky under which they felt most at home.

Our gentle guide informed us that the artists who had executed the paintings were Muslims from nearby Rohri. They were also the masons who, according to him, had built the palace some two hundred and fifty years ago, about the time that Raja Jai Singh II set up his new capital at Jaipur (1728). No doubt the then Rawal of Samod had been inspired by Jai Singh who was the titular head of his clan.

From a terrace behind the *Rang Mahal* we could see the remains of the fort above. There, the guide told us, had once been a splendid *Sultan Mahal*, palace of the prince, but all was in ruins now. We noted the ingenious method by which water was trapped in tunnels leading down from the fort to fill huge underground water-tanks below the terrace on which we stood. This was an essential precaution against frequent years of drought, and possible siege during the petty wars with neighbouring states that were endemic and apparently the favourite pastime of the Rajput princes.

The Shuttered Mansions of Nawalgarh

Nawalgarh keeps its secret well. No one passing through this dusty, slumberous town would suspect it of being the home of twenty-two multi-millionaire families, not until he stumbles across the *Aathon Haveli*, the Street of the Eight Mansions.

The street lies beyond the main bazaar on the outskirts of the old city. It is full of ruts, no trees line it, nor are there any gardens to give a suggestion of affluence. In fact, this part of the town seems uninhabited. Except for a solitary cyclist or a horse-drawn cart chasing its shadow in the dust, the road is empty. On a slight rise one is abruptly confronted by a double-storeyed *haveli* on the left of the road, opposite which is a decline, neither tarred nor paved, a mere sandy stretch, and on both sides of this unprepossessing drive drowse large, somnolent buildings. Their architecture is undistinguished, but they nevertheless rivet one's attention. For the entire facade of each of these *havelis* is covered with wall-paintings.

These stately mansions are tightly shuttered, lifeless and uncared for, forgotten. The absent owners must indeed be very wealthy, because they have not put them out on rent, nor have they sold them. They are rich enough to let them stand untenanted, except perhaps for a few days once a year when some member of the family might return to Nawalgarh on a brief visit. Some of the dwellings have not been opened for several years, and even the caretaker could not be found.

A ghost street. And appropriately enough the first *haveli* on the main road, called *Uttariyan ri haveli* is said to be haunted. It is a guest-house where marriage parties used to be housed, but one night a murder took place here and all the guests fled, never to return. They say the murdered man calls into the empty, echoing street, and lights mysteriously flicker

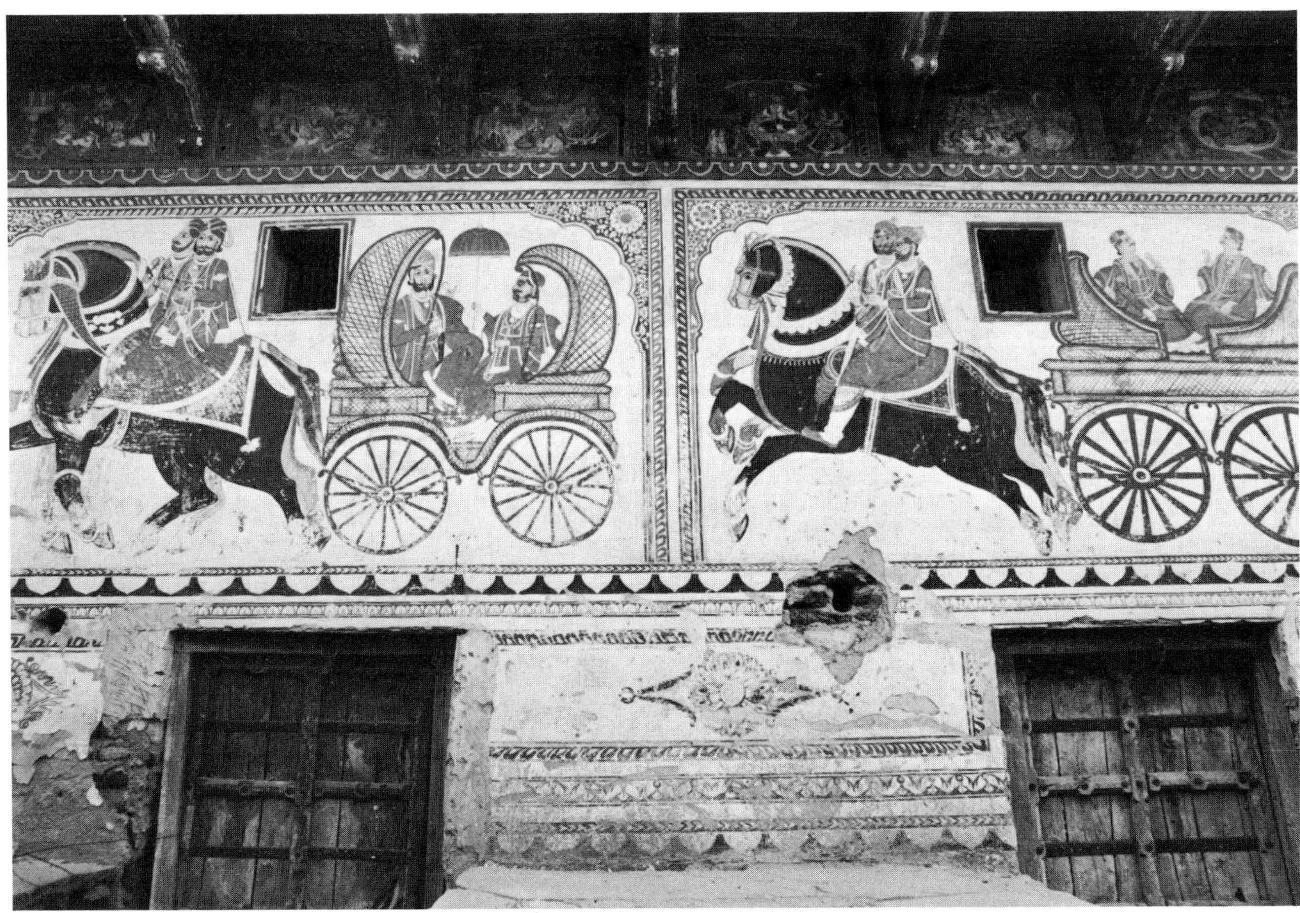

Horse carriages on a *haveli* facade at Nawalgarh

at the small windows.

The names of some of the owners of these desolate mansions, Podar, Morarkar, Sanganeria, Chhauseria, are names to conjure with in the share-bazaars, the stock exchanges and the business circles of Bombay, Calcutta, Madras and other industrial centres, for they all belong to the class of merchant-traders of the desert region known as Marwaris.

The *havelis* are three or four storeys high. Their roofs lack the usual *chhatris*, the Rajasthani version of the dome and cupola, that give the buildings of the state their distinctive character. The upper storeys jut out in overhanging balconies supported by decorative stone brackets which are their chief architectural attraction, and one of their few typically regional features. The wood panels above the central doorways are carved, but the work is not particularly fine, and the windows of some have slatted venetian blinds which replace the stone screens of traditional buildings. The overhanging balconies provide shade on the lower walls, so that the paintings immediately below are better preserved, being protected from sun and rain. The houses here are not very old as their architecture indicates. The earliest possibly may have been constructed at the turn of the century. The murals date from the early 1900s to the twenties and thirties. Their workmanship is not as refined as we had seen at Samod, nor even at the insignificant Raghunathji Temple at Jhalar. Those also differed in

character, for, however inferior in quality, they aspired to the style of the regional school of miniature paintings, whereas the murals in these *havelis* are more akin to bazaar paintings. They have a bold, almost brash, flamboyance we had not come across before, and the unorthodox mixture of subject-matter makes them a vivid record of the changing social mores of the period.

The wall surface is broken up into sections. Under the balconies and between the brackets the work is finer, and the subjects are usually religious or traditional themes. The area between these upper panels and the doorways has often been treated as one long continuous space for a frieze of horsemen and camel-riders engaged in battle, a ceremonial procession, or, with more originality, a small steam-engine puffing its way across the landscape, hauling a trail of wagons, with the engine-driver and fireman wearing European clothes complete with bowler hats! Ladies in long skirts ride side-saddle on proud chargers in one panel, while in another an English family sits in a coach to take the evening air at the esplanade. The motor-car had made its appearance and honks its way into these murals, in amusing versions of vintage models of such curious make that one suspects the artists had never seen a car, except perhaps in magazine illustrations or photographs provided by their much-travelled patrons.

At times a lower wall is split into several panels, each

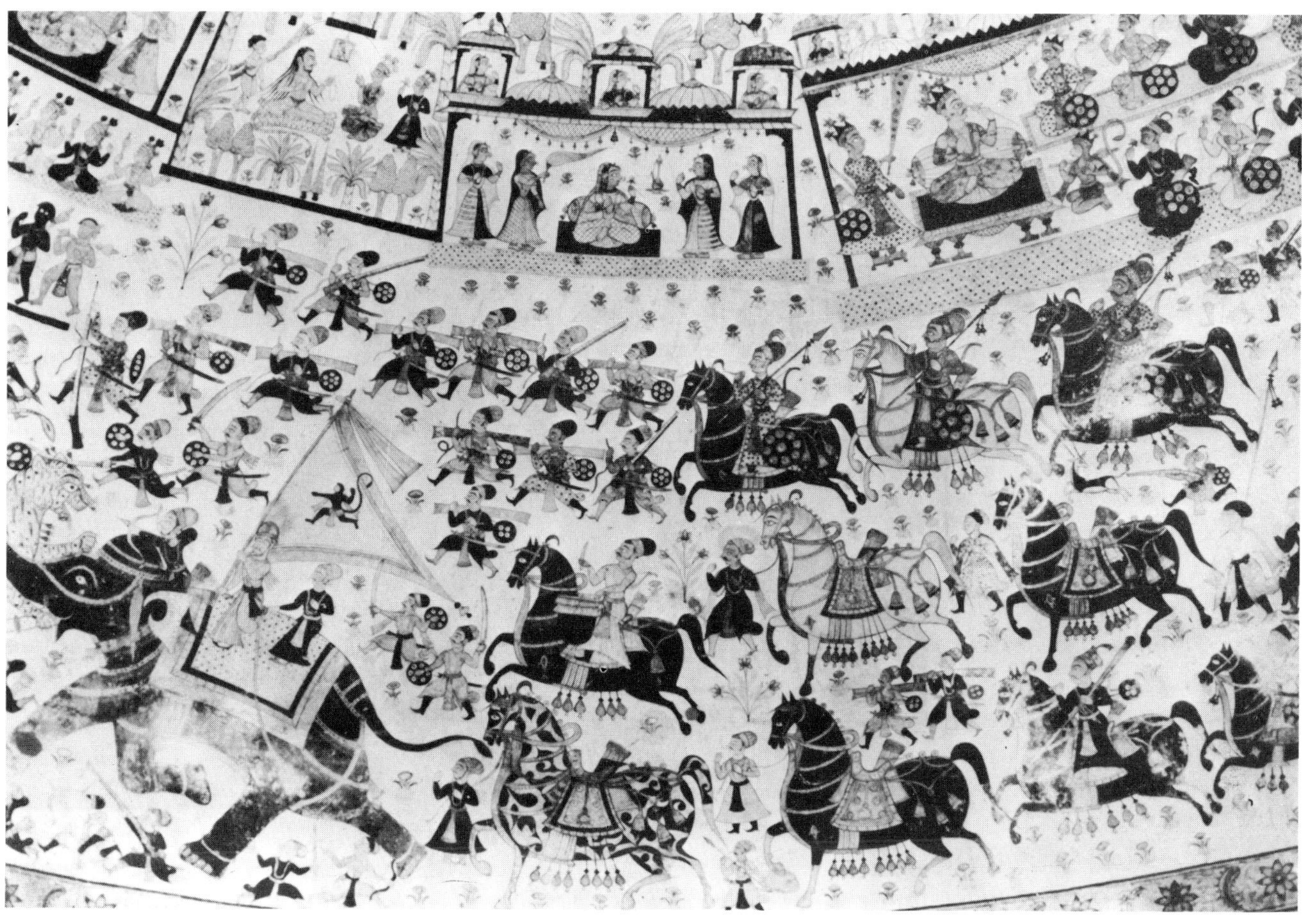

The ceiling of the Parasrampur *chhatri* showing details of battle scenes

presenting a different scene. In one a bold Rajput cavalier cradles his beloved in his lap, in another a maid pours water over English children in a bath-tub. Two winsome *chauri*-bearers wave their fans; a dashing soldier primes his old-fashioned gun. The subjects range over a wide variety of modes and manners that captured the fancy of the householder or the painter.

As at Samod, the masons who built the *havelis* were also the artists who put the 'finishing touches' to them. The buildings are in brick, with sandstone brackets and columns. The brick surface is covered with layers of plaster. The third layer, laid on smooth and fine, provided the base for the painting.

Ceilings of verandahs and the inner walls are completely covered with floral or geometric designs, and even the narrow surfaces of the stone brackets are often painted over with flowers or bird motifs.

These mason-artists belonged to traditional occupational castes and whole families worked on the buildings. The young apprentices would learn the craft by starting on unimportant trellis or geometric edgings, gradually progressing to more intricate flower and animal motifs as they grew more competent. The delicate brushwork of the small panels of mythological scenes or the grand friezes of horses and soldiers or railway trains were undoubtedly the work of the master-craftsman, who could have been either a *guru* or an *ustad* as both

Hindu and Muslim mason castes worked in these areas. Since these *havelis* were built within a decade of so of one another, a healthy rivalry seems to have existed between the owners, each vying with his neighbour in the lavishness of the decoration and the daring modernity of the designs. The artist-masons obviously were caught up in this game of one-upmanship, as the cars and carriages on one facade shout for attention over the puffing engine and galloping horses of the next.

These pre-World War II merchant patrons of Shekhawati seem to have been the last of their kind. Buildings that have been erected since, whether private dwellings or public edifices, are not such as to lend themselves to the naive and exuberant art of these craftsmen. One wonders how long the present owners of the *havelis* will permit them to stand in their neglected condition. Although the sturdy thick-walled structures show many years of life, they are slowly disintegrating, the paintings are fading and the plaster is gradually peeling off. And the brash, assertive murals slowly languish into decay in the echoing silence.

Pavilions in a Sunken Garden

Nawalgarh was built in 1746 on the site of the ancient city of Rolani. Although we could not discover any remains of this earlier city, we did find the ruins of

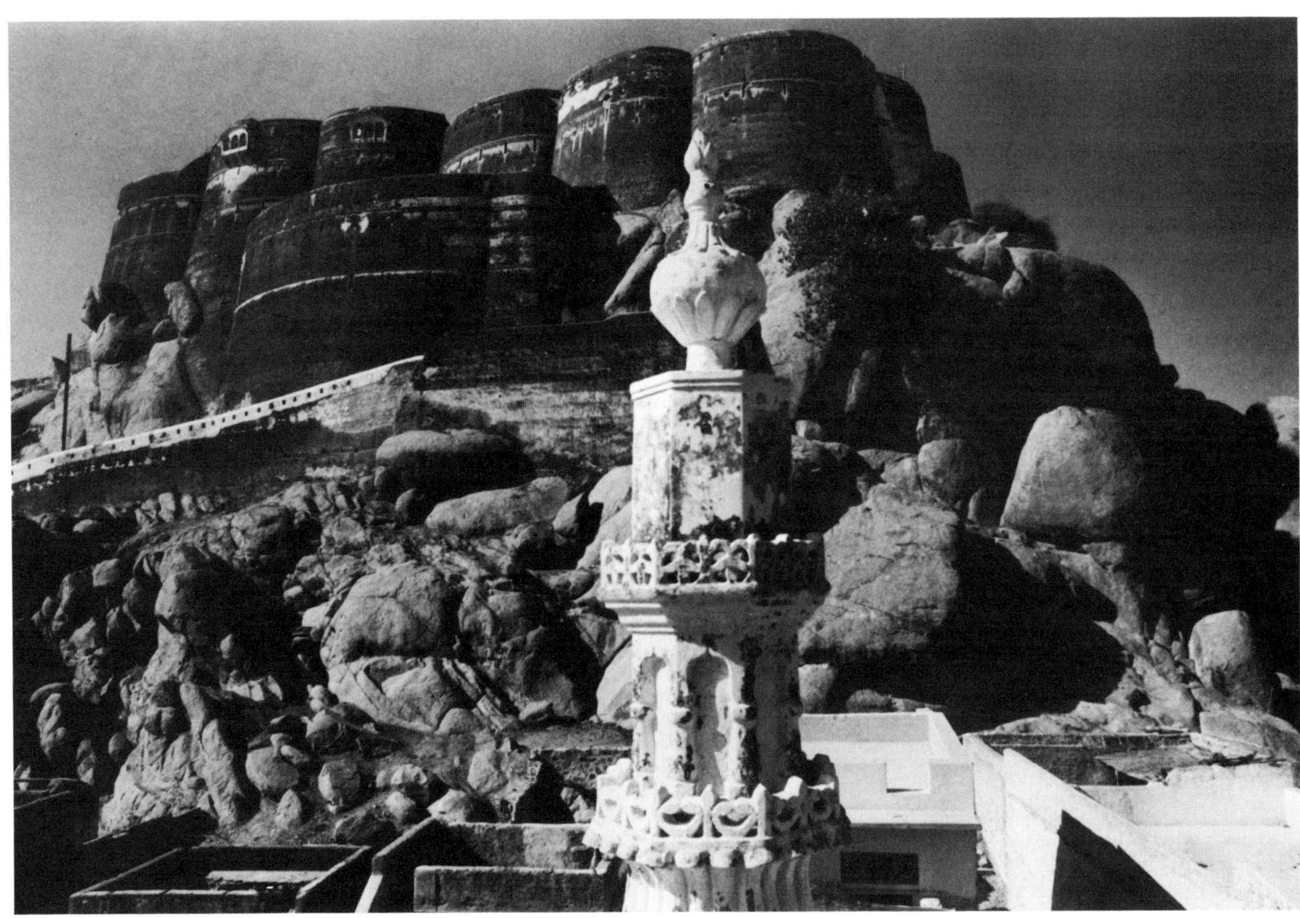

The Lachhmangarh fort

The decaying interior of the Lachhmangarh *haveli*

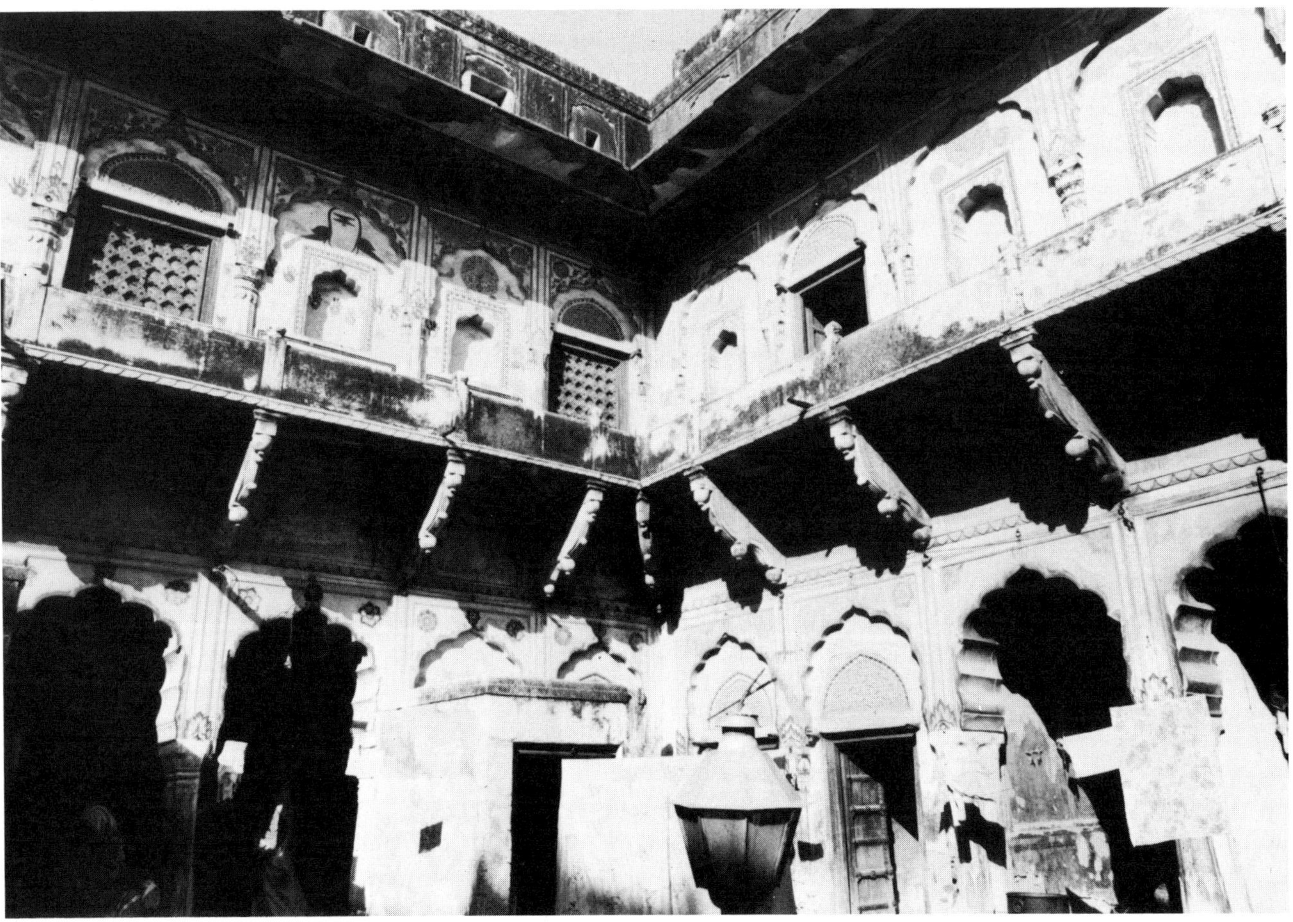

Parasrampura which predates Nawalgarh by a couple of centuries.

Here we stumbled across a group of pavilions in what must have been a sunken garden. The traces of a wall were the only vestiges of a nearby palace. The pavilions may have been royal *chhatris*, as the cenotaphs of the Rajputs are called, although they showed no trace of any commemorative tablets. We removed our shoes as a sign of respect to the dead.

The central pavilion has a dome the ceiling of which is entirely covered with extraordinarily detailed and intricate paintings. Some scenes are from the *Ramayana*, others of royal durbars, religious processions, royal hunts and battles. The work is of a high standard and shows a masterly use of the curved surface to convey a sense of rhythm and movement. Each figure is minutely executed, the features finely drawn, clothes and battle gear faithfully reproduced. The horses are shown caparisoned, painted over with patterns, as they still are at fairs and festivals, and the tigers, panthers, deer and monkeys meticulously observed, with an occasional flourish of fantasy. Since the colours have been protected from the elements they are still vivid, though in this respect the browns and reds have fared better than the blues and greens.

We had attracted quite a crowd of youngsters who regaled us with the usual horror story of how, when the artist of these paintings had begun a still finer series at the local shrine, the Raja had cut off his hands. Undeterred, he had tried to complete the work by painting with his tongue, whereupon the enraged ruler had him killed. The abominable story had followed us not only throughout Rajasthan, but also in the Himalayan hill-states. The same crime was hinted at against the Moghal Emperor, Shah Jehan, with regard to the craftsmen engaged to work on the Taj Mahal. It could not be possibly true in all, if any, of the cited cases, but its very repetition over such widely dispersed areas, and of so many rulers, is a sign of the deep-seated sense of insecurity among the common people in times of arbitrary rule. The young men of Parasrampura firmly believed in this sensational legend if for no other reason than that it added a note of tragic glamour and mystery to their otherwise dreary, inconspicuous village.

A Desert Sentinel

> The castle of Lachhman situated upon a lofty mountain (about 75 miles N.W. of Jaipur city) was erected in 1806, though probably on the ruins of some more ancient fortress. It commands a most extensive prospect and is quite a beacon in that country, studded with hill-castles. The town is built on the model of Jaipur, with regular streets intersecting each other at right angles in which there are many wealthy merchants who enjoy perfect security. (Vol. III, p.1442)

Thus Tod describes Lachhmangarh in 1814, when it was very new. The castle is still the most imposing and picturesque of all the Shekhawati forts. It actually looks much older than its mere 175 years. The walls rise sheer from the rocks of the hill it is built upon, quite an engineering feat, and their weathered, pitted surface gives it a worn and rugged look. It creates the same general effect as the magnificent fort at Jodhpur, but on a miniature scale, and it would make the perfect illustration for an ogre's stronghold in a children's fairy-tale.

The town, which Tod found to be a replica of the well laid out city of Jaipur, built on the grid plan, has not retained its intended orderliness. The basic pattern cannot now be discerned in the bursting bazaars and obtruding structures that have sprung up at every corner. But the houses of the wealthy merchants he mentions still exist, though in an unkempt condition. Unlike the *havelis* of Nawalgarh, the ones here, going back to a century earlier, are built in the traditional style. Imposing gateways lead into courtyards with fluted pillars and scalloped arches. Besides, they are occupied and in constant use. Suprisingly, two of the several *havelis* we visited belonged to Brahmin families and not to merchants, indicating the wealth and social position of some members of the priestly caste.

We were invited into one of the Marwari houses, the home of a girl we had met through a friend. She was on vacation from her college in Jaipur. The family, apart from her mother and younger brother, seemed to consist of several wispy old ladies and gentle old men, who wandered from one courtyard to the other like barely tangible ghosts. The *haveli* was large and rambling, with four courtyards, one leading to the other through pillared archways. Each court had an upper storey on the four sides, with small rooms where once the many units of the joint family lived. These rooms opened on to a narrow balcony that ran all round the upper storey. Many of these upper rooms were now closed. The lower storey consisted of deep, shady verandahs divided by the fluted pillars, and the old people seemed to favour these as living-rooms. The kitchen and store-rooms were in a corner of the courtyard.

All the earning male members of the family were away, carrying on the family-business in large cities. A young woman suddenly made her appearance from a room upstairs and looked down from the balcony. She had two small children clinging to her, who promptly began to cry on seeing strangers in the courtyard below. The young woman was related to the girl who was our hostess. Her husband, too, did not live in Lachhmangarh.

It seems a convenient system to leave all one's family responsibilities in a safe, commodious house, where the little ones romp in the courtyard under some watchful elder's care, the older children return from school or college for the holidays and the old people

are looked after by various daughters-in-law, grand-
daughters and even grand-daughters-in-law! For a
wedding in the family the whole clan makes an effort
to gather here, and when they all muster, they add up
to almost a hundred persons. Such occasions are
increasingly rare, though, when our young friend
finishes her studies and is to be married, perhaps the
old house will come alive, the courtyards resound to
the sound of the *shehnai*, and all the beautiful, old
wall-paintings glow in the light of bright lamps, as four
or five generations gather together, to celebrate the
occasion in the family *haveli*.

Patterns in the sand

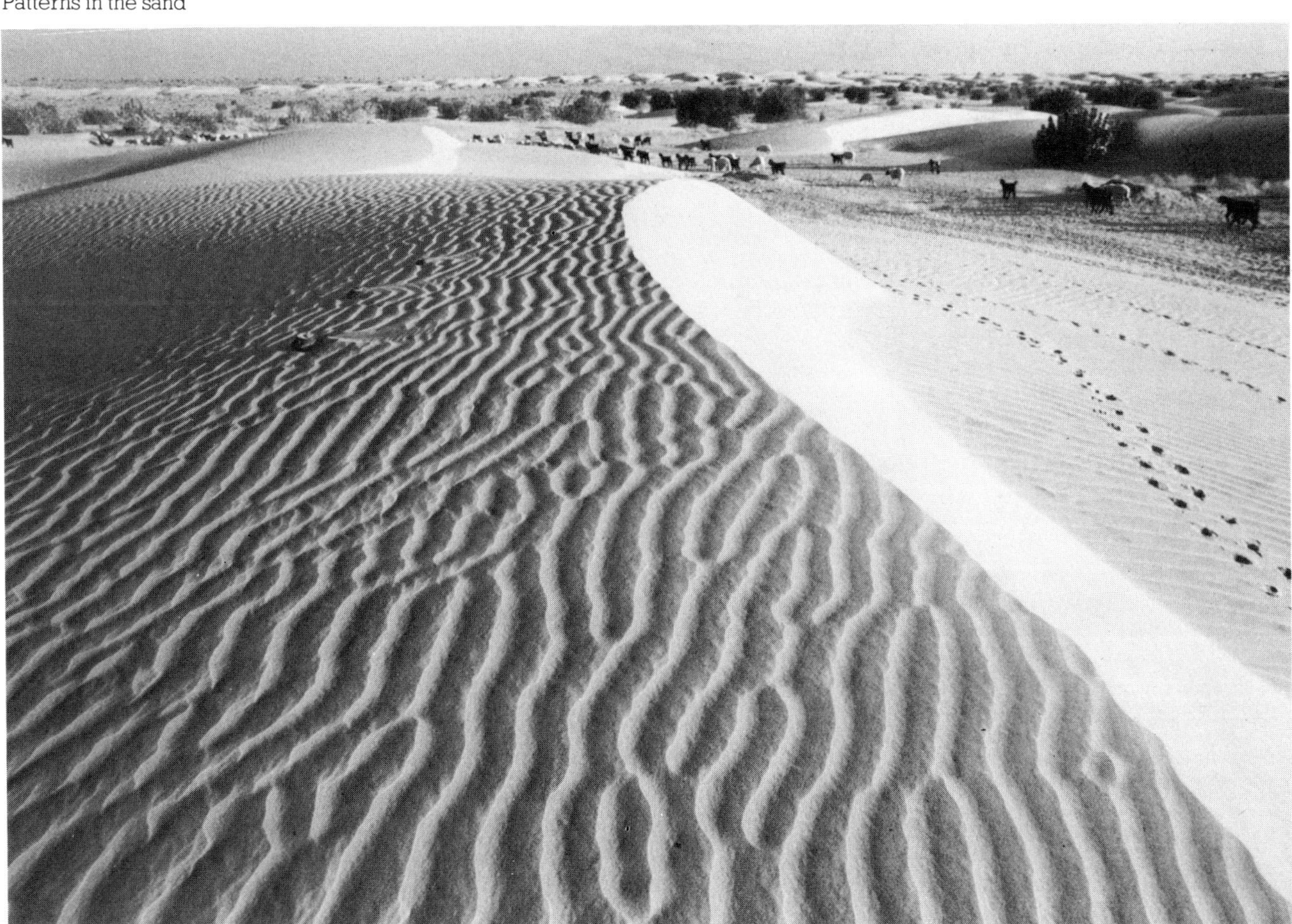

3 Jangaldesh: The Wilderness I

There are certain first impressions about a place, a person or a journey which never fade. Even when subsequent and closer acquaintance proves one's hastily formed ideas exaggerated, the effects of that early reaction linger, and one has to make a mental correction each time to achieve a sense of balance. Such was my impression of Jangaldesh, the wilderness, when many years ago I had my initial experience of the true Thaar on a journey from Jaipur to Bikaner.

The very name of the vast northern tract of the desert, Jangaldesh, was enough to provoke the imagination. 'Jungle' in my north Indian context meant an area of scrub, brush and trees caught up in a wild tangle of liana creepers, spiked with the tenacious wait-a-bit thorn; of forest floors thick with fallen leaves and dried twigs that crackled and snapped underfoot; of creatures that slouched and crawled below and flew and sang above; of elusive, four-footed denizens that disappeared from sight into the dense undergrowth before they could be identified. These were the tantalising and much loved jungles of my experience in the countryside of the Punjab and Haryana; the lower reaches of the Sivalik range in the outer Himalayas; the diminishing green belt around the ridge at Dehli, or the more fertile areas of east and south Rajasthan at Bharatpur and Abu. A desert 'jungle' would necessarily be different. I had a pre-conceived picture of an endless sea of undulating sand dunes, with formations of giant cacti, their sinister, knobbled arms silhouetted against a harsh, blue sky from which a relentless sun directed its rays through the prism of still air to shrivel up every living thing, like scraps of paper under a magnifying glass. Or swirling wind-tossed sands through which one might glimpse the haven of an oasis of swaying palm-trees, dimly perceived, like half-smudged images in a rubbing.

The reality of Jangaldesh was so unlike my romantic imaginings that it came to me as a shock. But now another image, equally extreme and unreal, involuntarily arises whenever I read, think of, or travel in the wilderness, and which I constantly have to correct.

I see a road that flies like a giant arrow, absolutely straight, to the ever-receding horizon through a bleak landscape. I recall silence.

It is obvious that no road can run straight for any considerable distance, and equally obvious that while travelling in a car, there cannot have been a moment's silence. Yet that ineradicable impression of limitless space and unbroken silence captures the essence of my experience of Jangaldesh in a way that no factual description can hope to convey.

Jangaldesh is bounded in the east by Jaipur-Shekhawati, north east by Punjab-Haryana, north and north west by Pakistan, and west by Jaisalmer. It covers an enormous area of over 36,500 square kms most of which is arid and sparsely populated. Bikaner which 'like a Fata Morgana rises in the very midst of the desert' was once the capital of a leading princely state and a centre of Rathor power. It is now the headquarters of an important division in the province of Rajasthan.

On that first journey we started out from Jaipur at the early hour of four in the morning. We had about 450 km

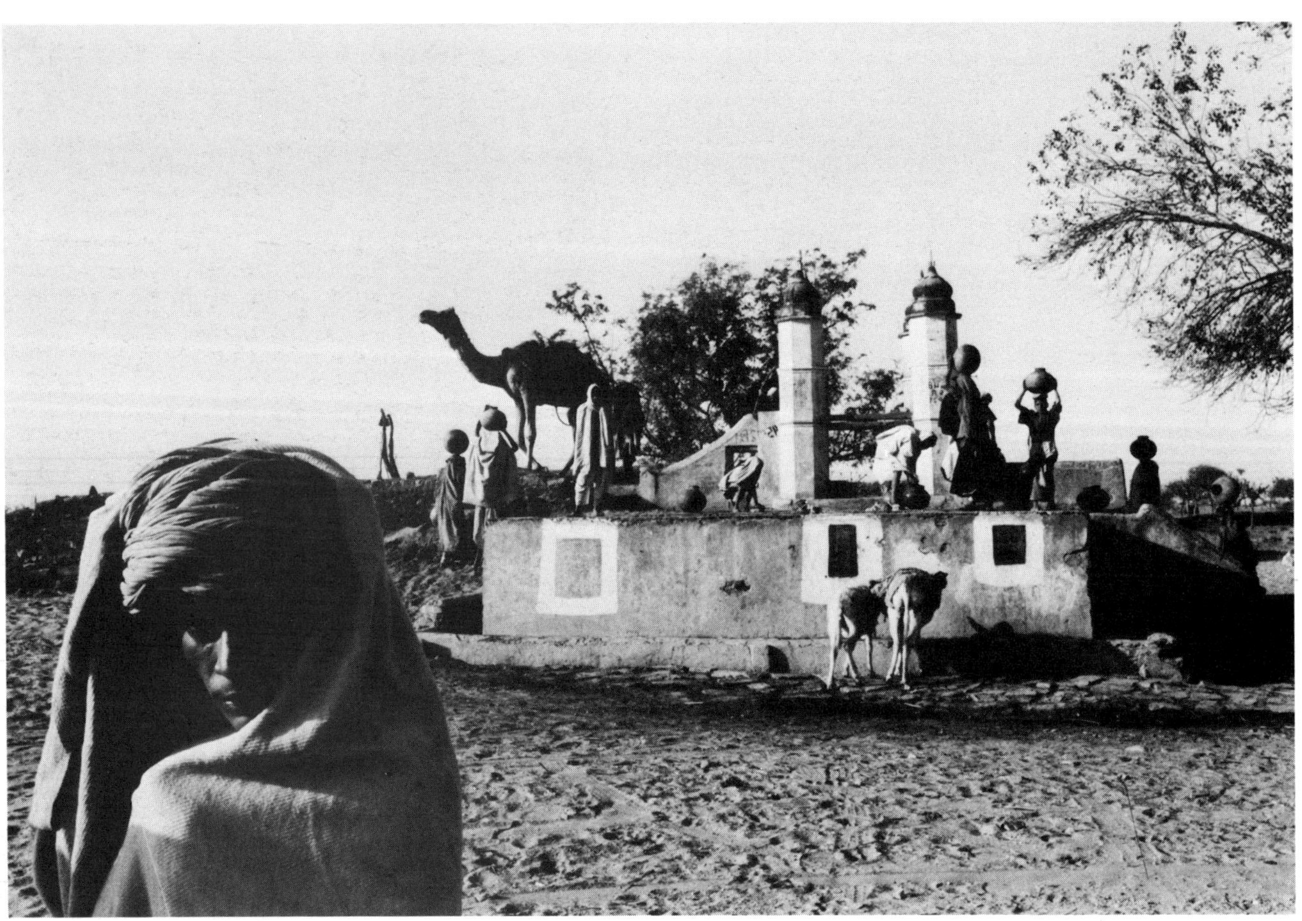

The well at Akhepura

to cover in territory that was unknown to us, and on a military road that had only recently been opened to civilian traffic. It is a superb highway, well maintained and at that time, sparingly used, since it bypasses most towns and villages on the route. As such it was not of much service to the desert people, who preferred to keep to the familiar, well-beaten dirt tracks that connected the villages of the interior. Their journeys were usually short, from one hamlet to another, and the tracks were better suited to their modest modes of transport: by camel, bullock cart or on foot.

In the pre-dawn half-light beyond Shekhawati we entered a grey world. I slowly came to realise how infinite the variations of that natural shade are. There was first the metallic charcoal of the tarred road, a dark streak cutting our space in half. Above us, the night sky melted through veils of slate-blue to the opaque luminosity of pearl till the first touch of dawn, rose-tinted in the east behind us, washed the low skyline with that lemon-grey tinge that imparts such tenderness to the throat of the yellow wagtail. On the horizon, a sharp band of silver separated heaven and earth, while a few untidy clouds, dirty white as new-plucked pods of cotton, were slowly flicked into shiny floss by some celestial carder's whipcord.

Through the hard-packed dun-coloured earth, bushes of grey-green gorse pushed against the metalled road; the clumps of *sewan* grass were palely striped above their roots; and the *khejra* trees, shorn of their leaves, lifted ugly sable stumps against the sky.

The sun came up and bleached the landscape of these subtle variations. The black ribbon of road reflected its blinding light in the dancing dazzle of water which seemed to evaporate at our approach.

The hum of the speeding car was a constant sound around which silence eddied in expanding waves. A chatter of babblers broke through briefly as the car slowed to give way to a herd of *chinkara*, which catapulted across, their tiny hooves clicking just once against the tarmac as each antelope cleared the road in a single leap.

We stopped at the old well at Akhepura, its four tall pillars intact, and watched the camels shuffle down the long ramp to work it. At Fatehpur we paused a while by the abandoned tank and water-pavilions, dry and deserted, which echoed to the shriek of parrots as they darted across in erratic flight. A tiny kingfisher fluttered its jewelled wings, paused in mid-air and then alighted on the dome of a pavilion. In distant days when water had lapped against the steps of the now parched tank, musicians and singing girls paddled across in boats on festive occasions to take their place on this central 'stage'. Their dulcet voices and yearning strains of music wafted across the water to the listeners who thronged the tiers and balconies, and soothed the ears of weary princes and their

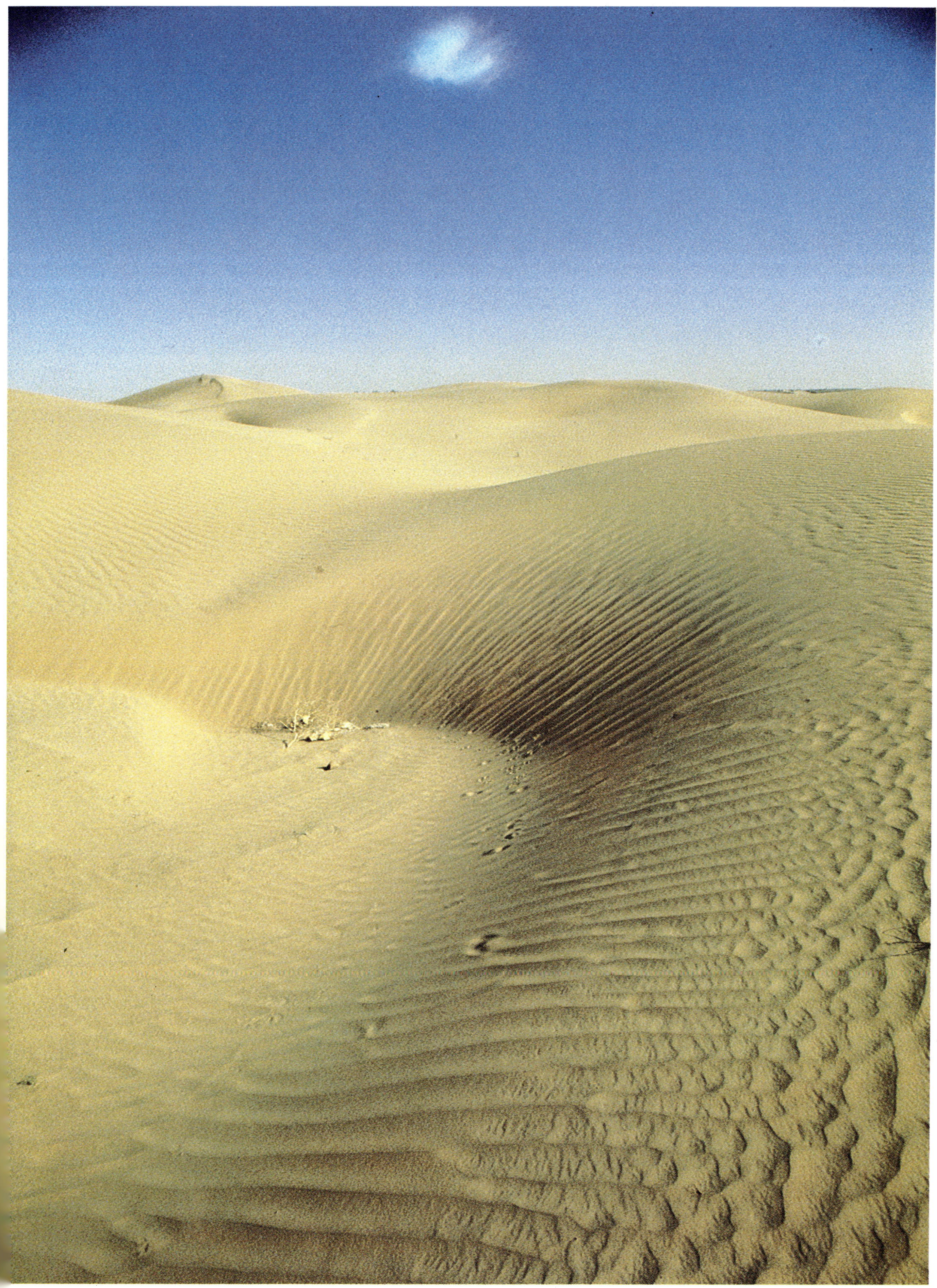

Sand dunes at Sam near Jaisalmer

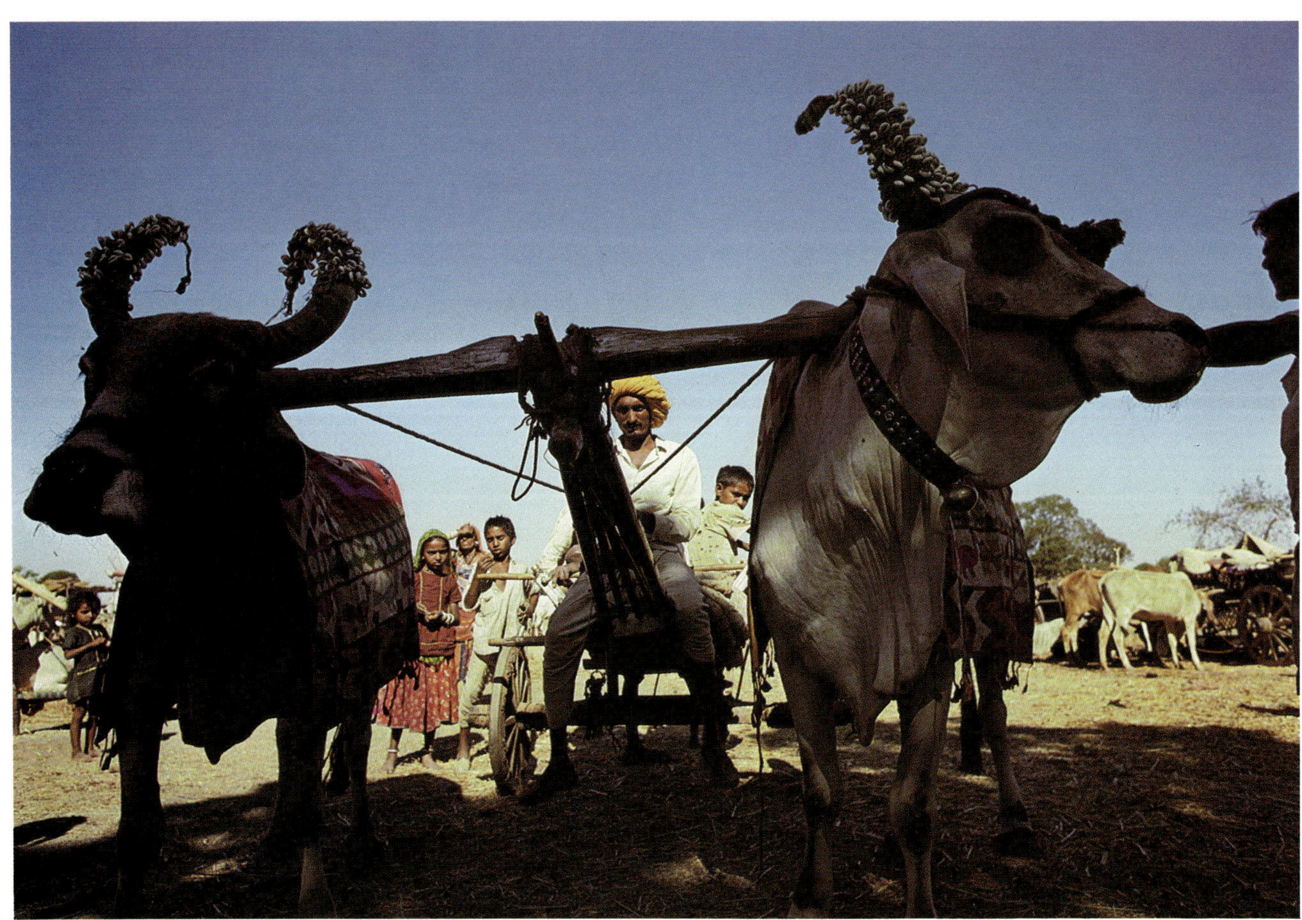

Gadia Lohars, nomadic blacksmiths and tinkers, on the road.

A Kalbelia woman. They carry their wealth, in jewellery, on their person.

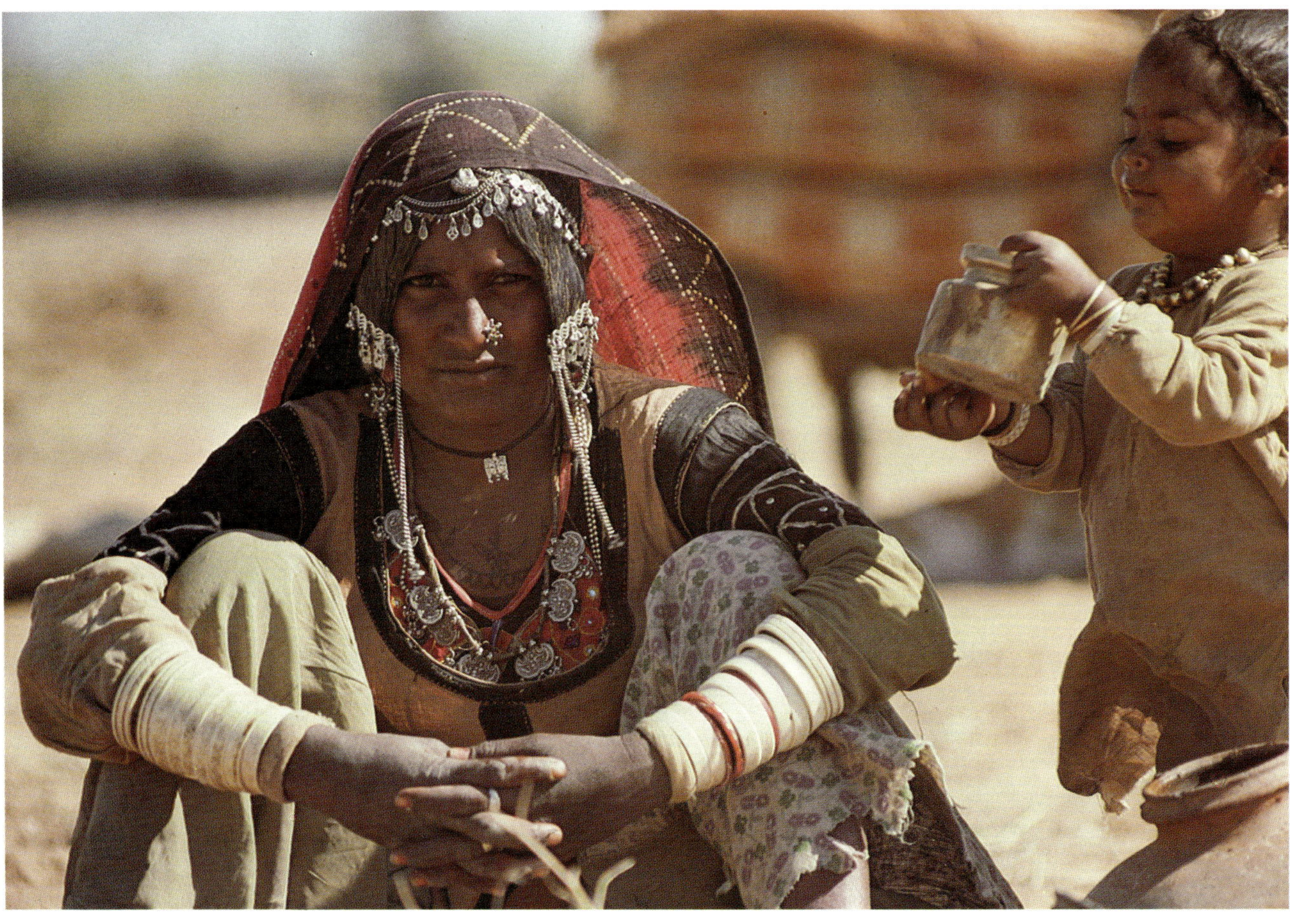

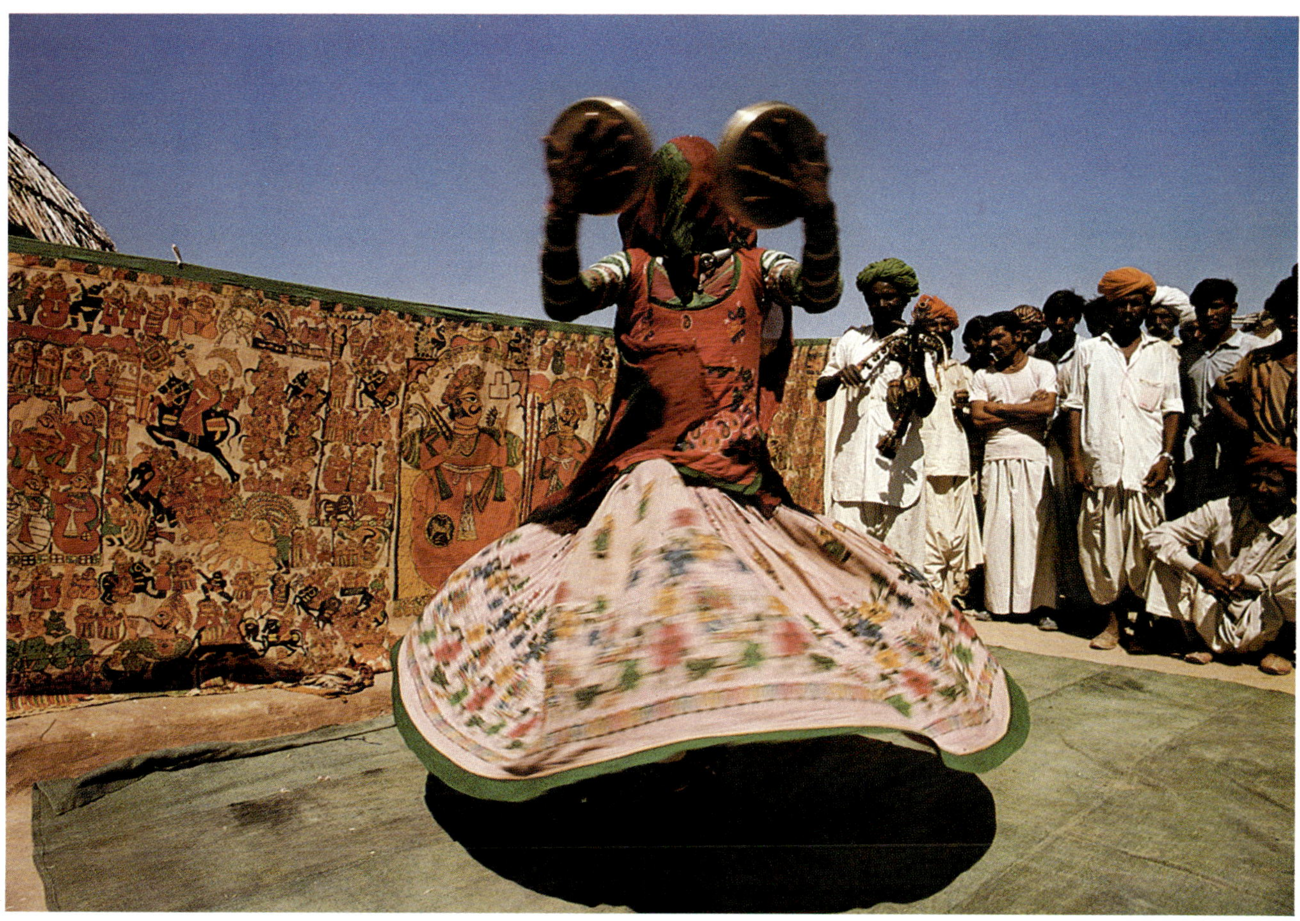

Pabuji Parh, a painted scroll-curtain. The female impersonator dancing.

A wayside Mamaji shrine. Votive horses and elephants offered to an ancestor.

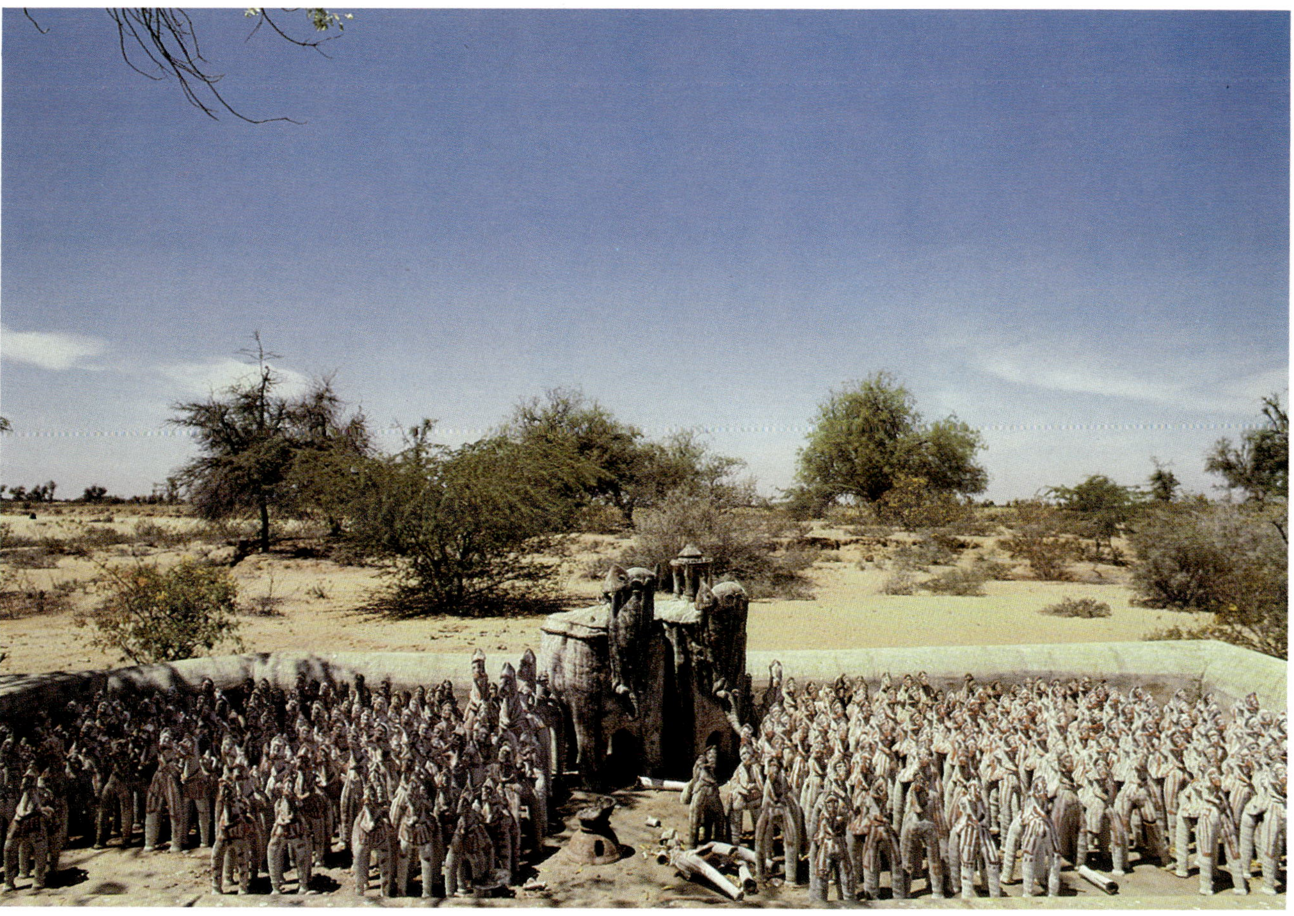

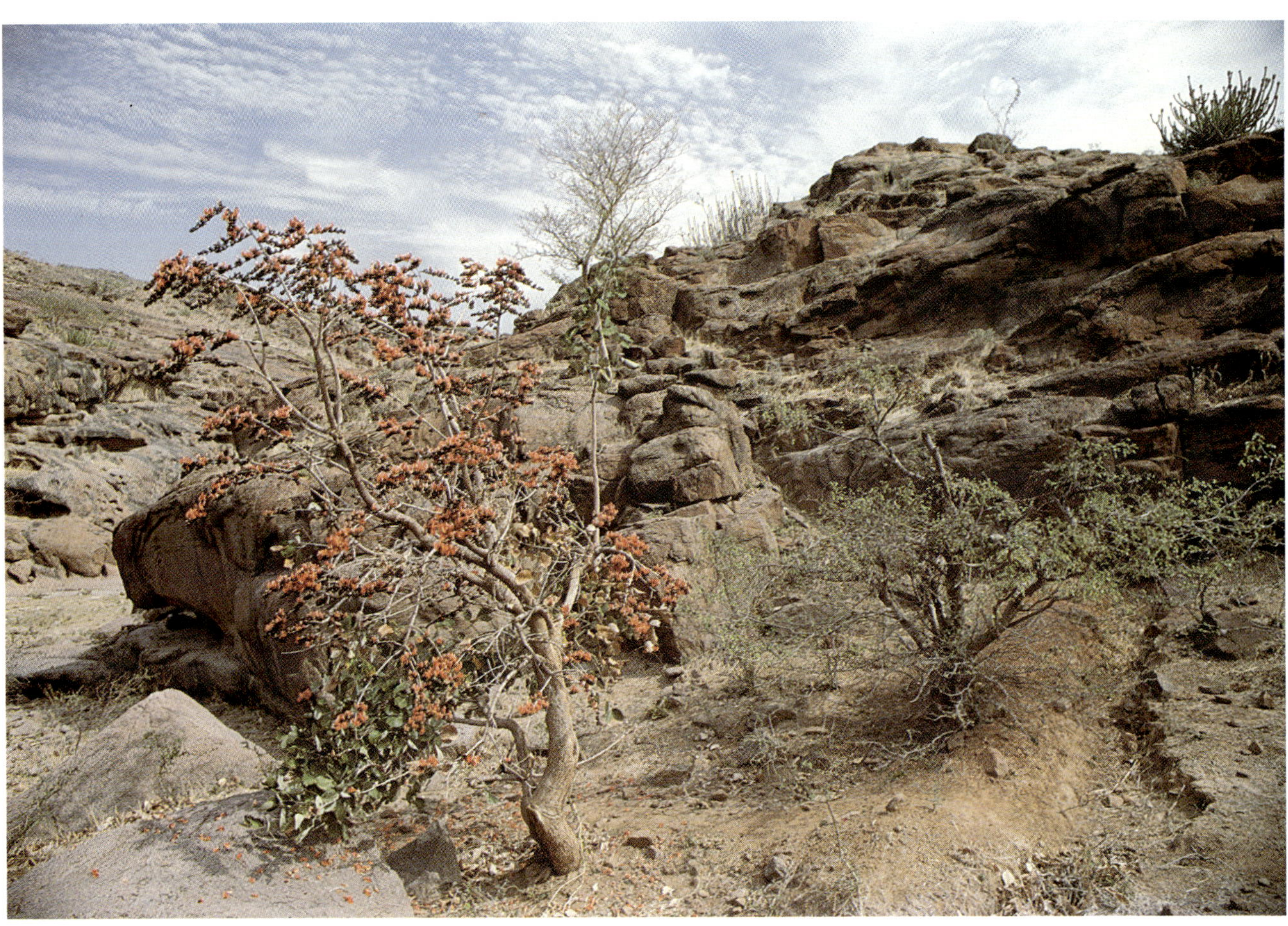

Flowers in the wilderness

Samod, in Shekhawati; built in imitation of Amer Palace, Jaipur.

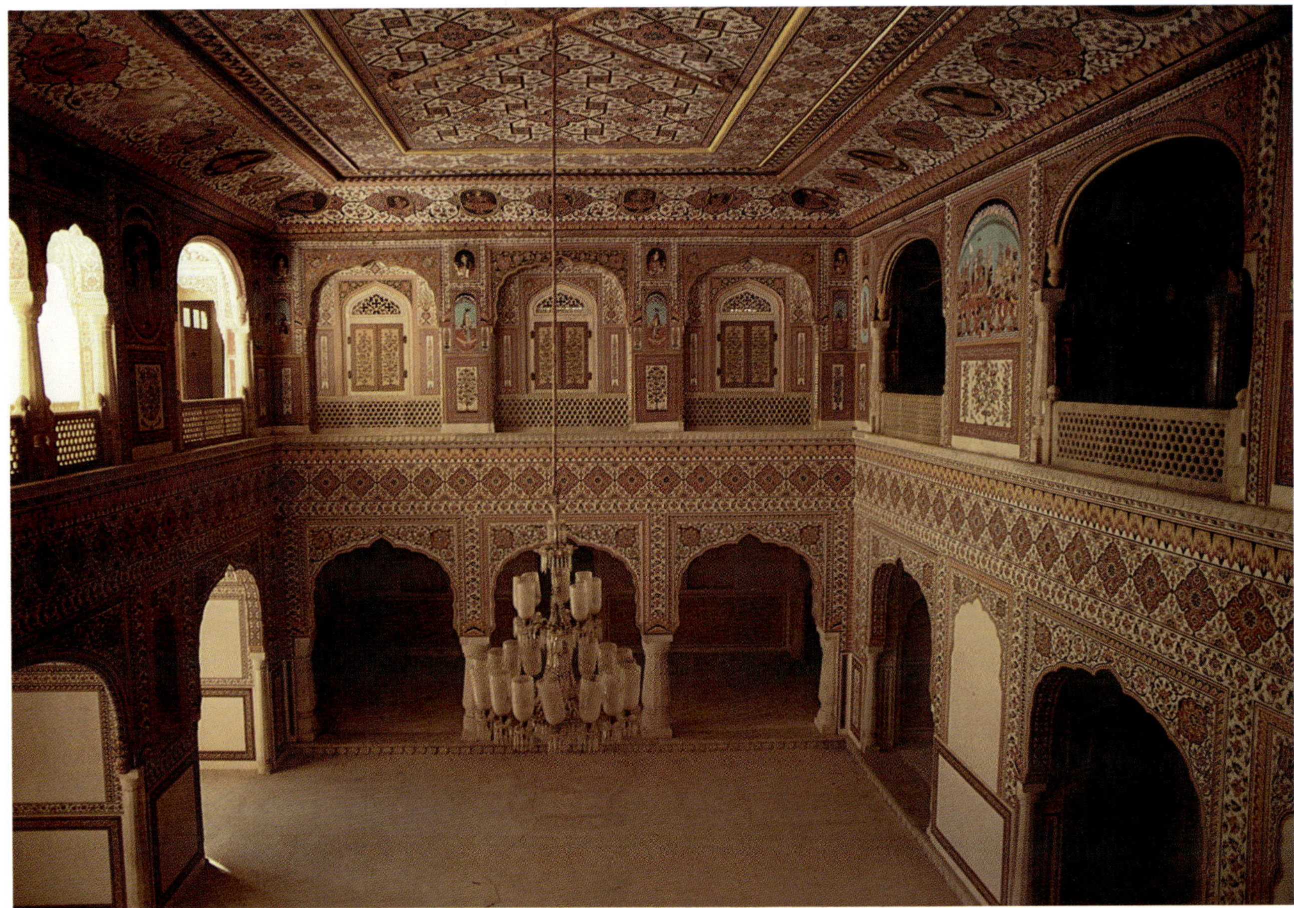

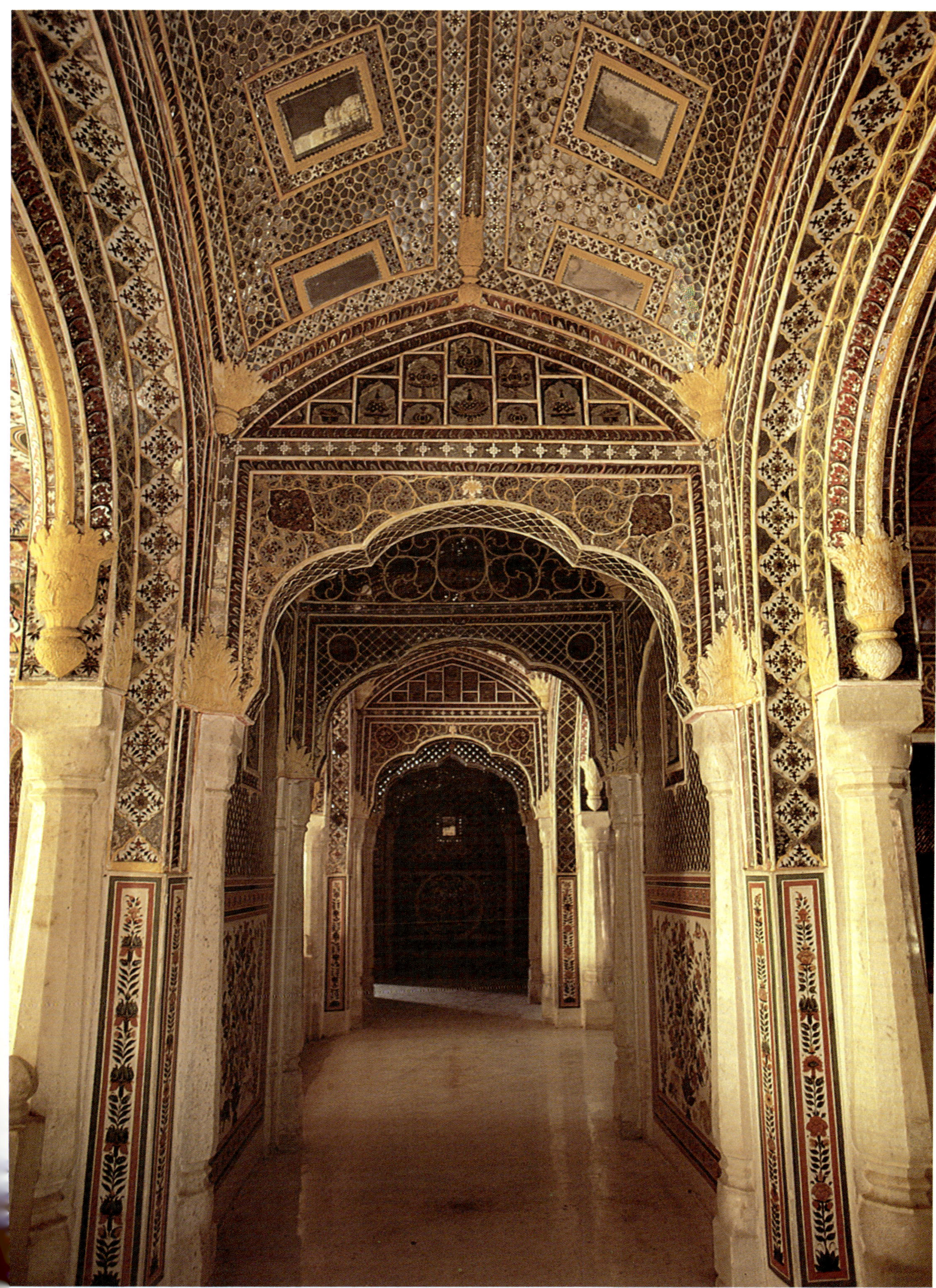

Corridor at Samod, showing the use of mirror in the ceiling.

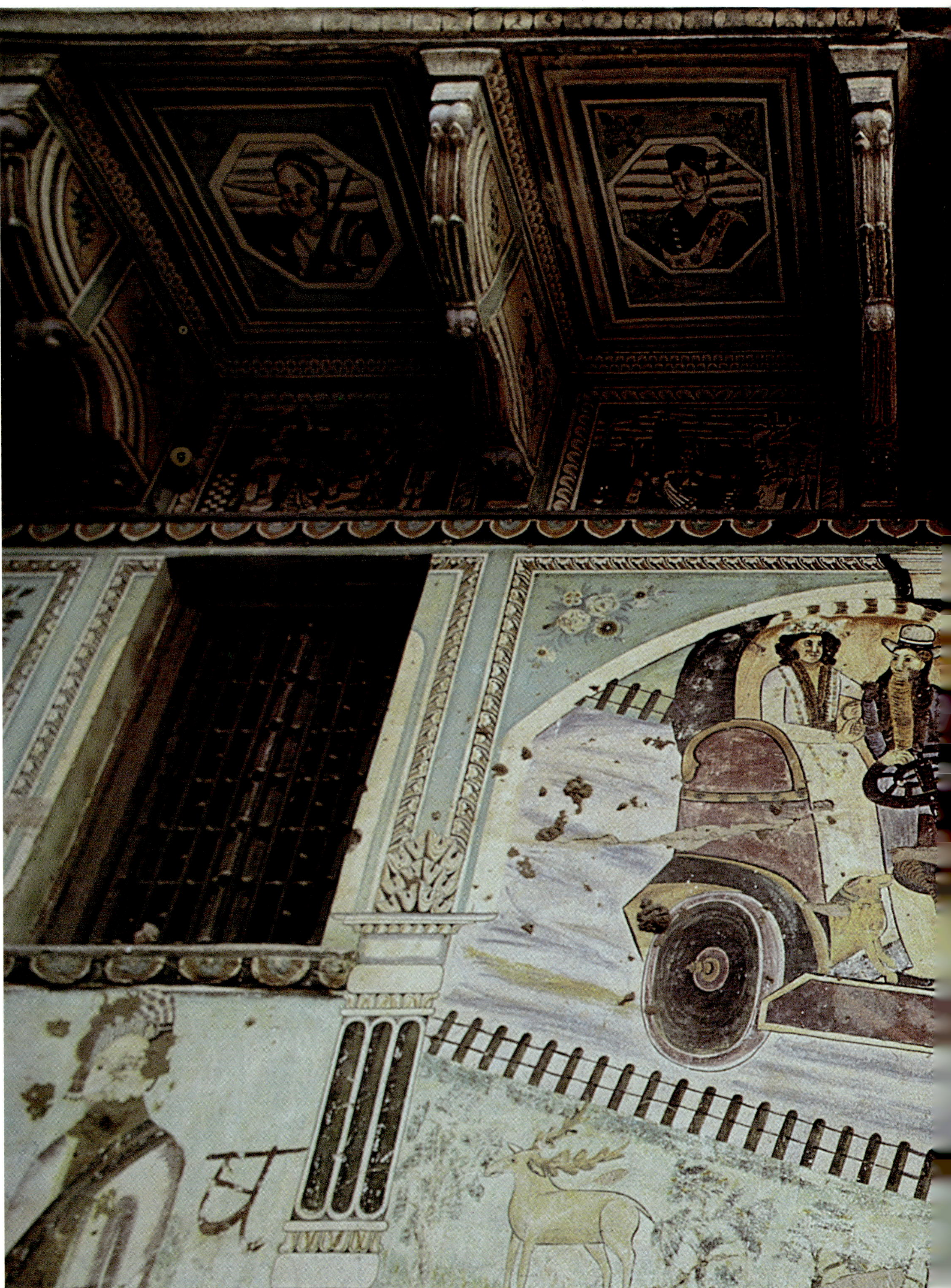

Nawalgarh wall-painting. Horse and car.

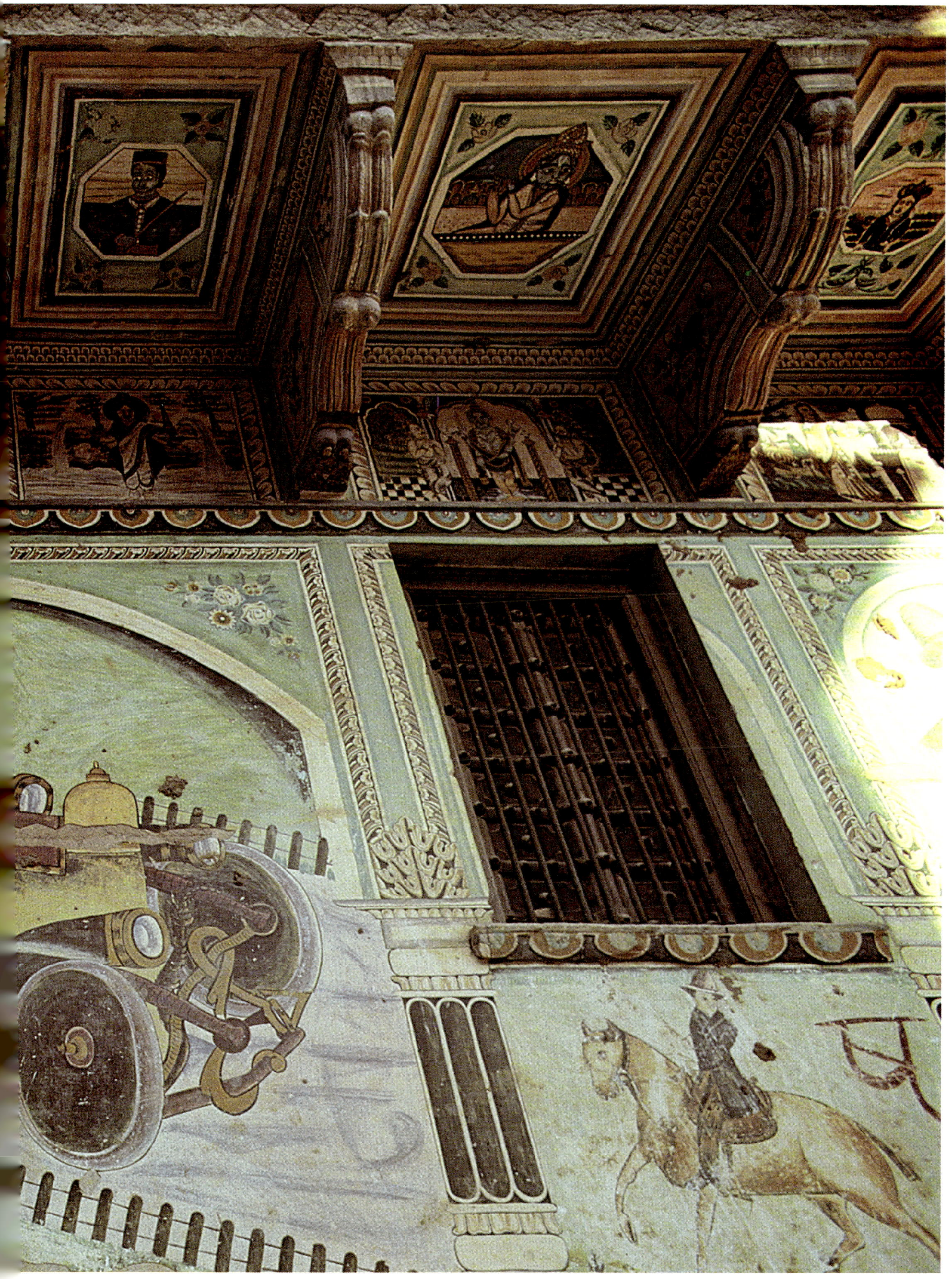

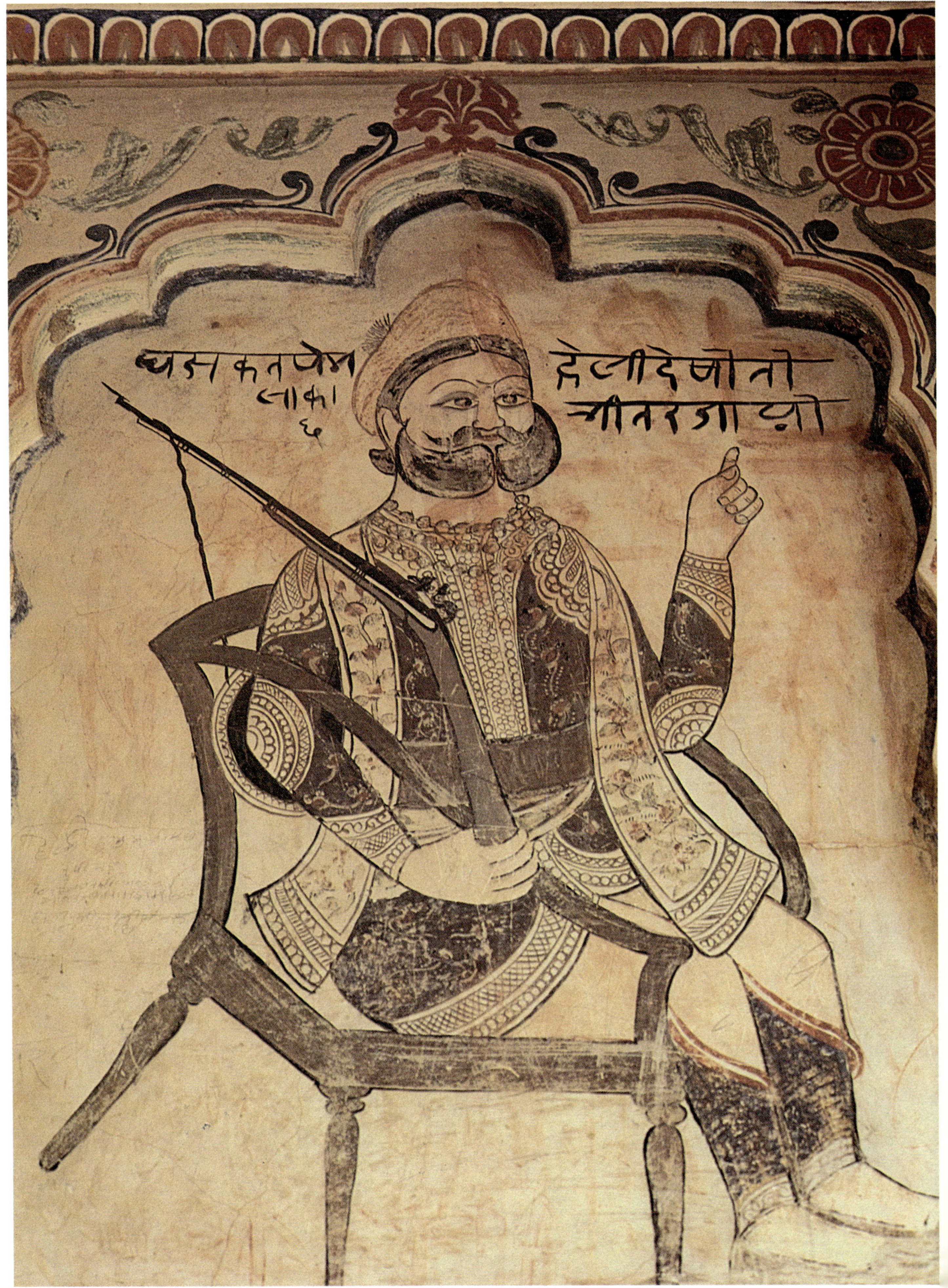

Man seated with rifle. Nawalgarh *haveli*.

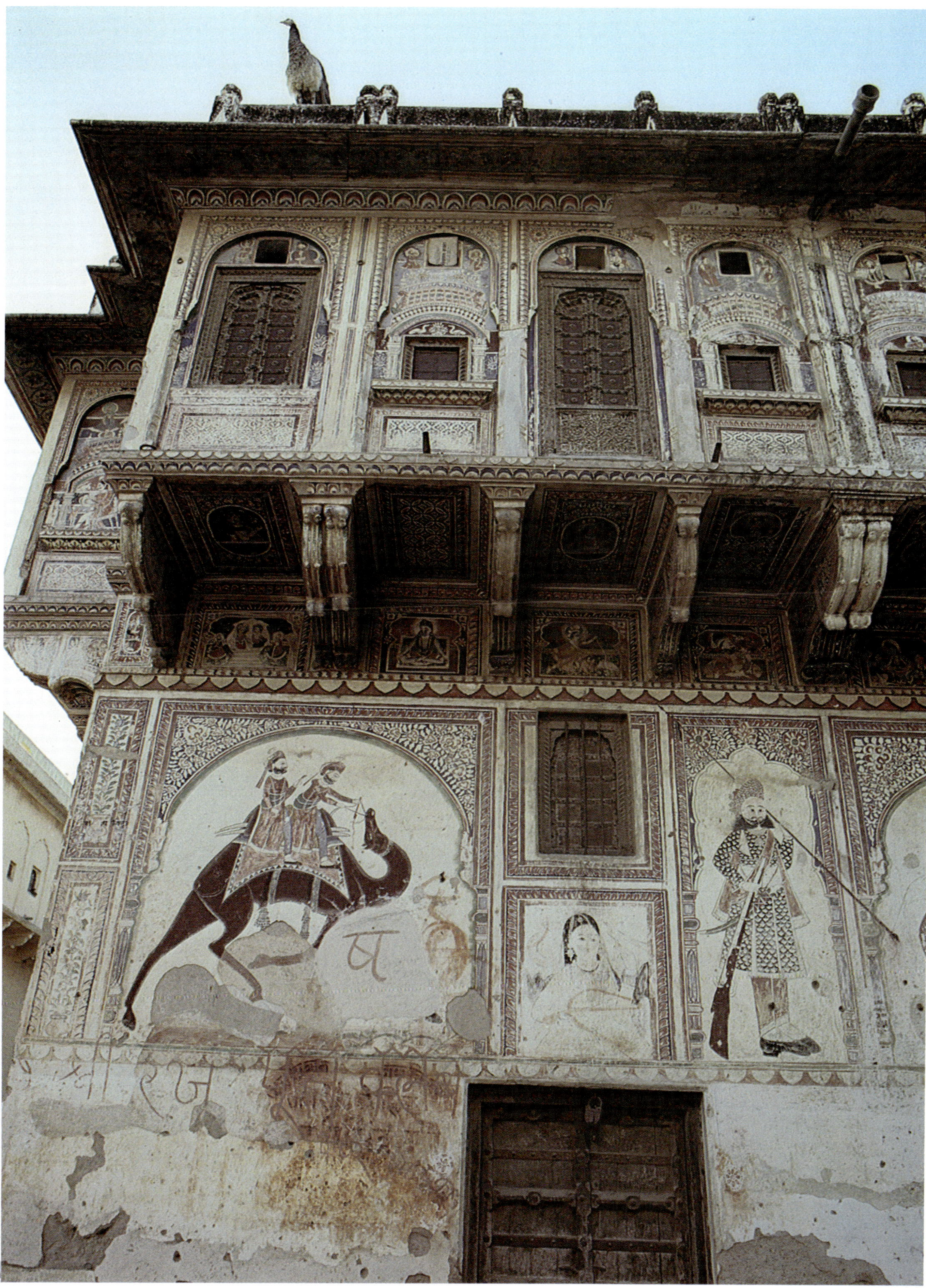

Lachhmangarh painted facade.

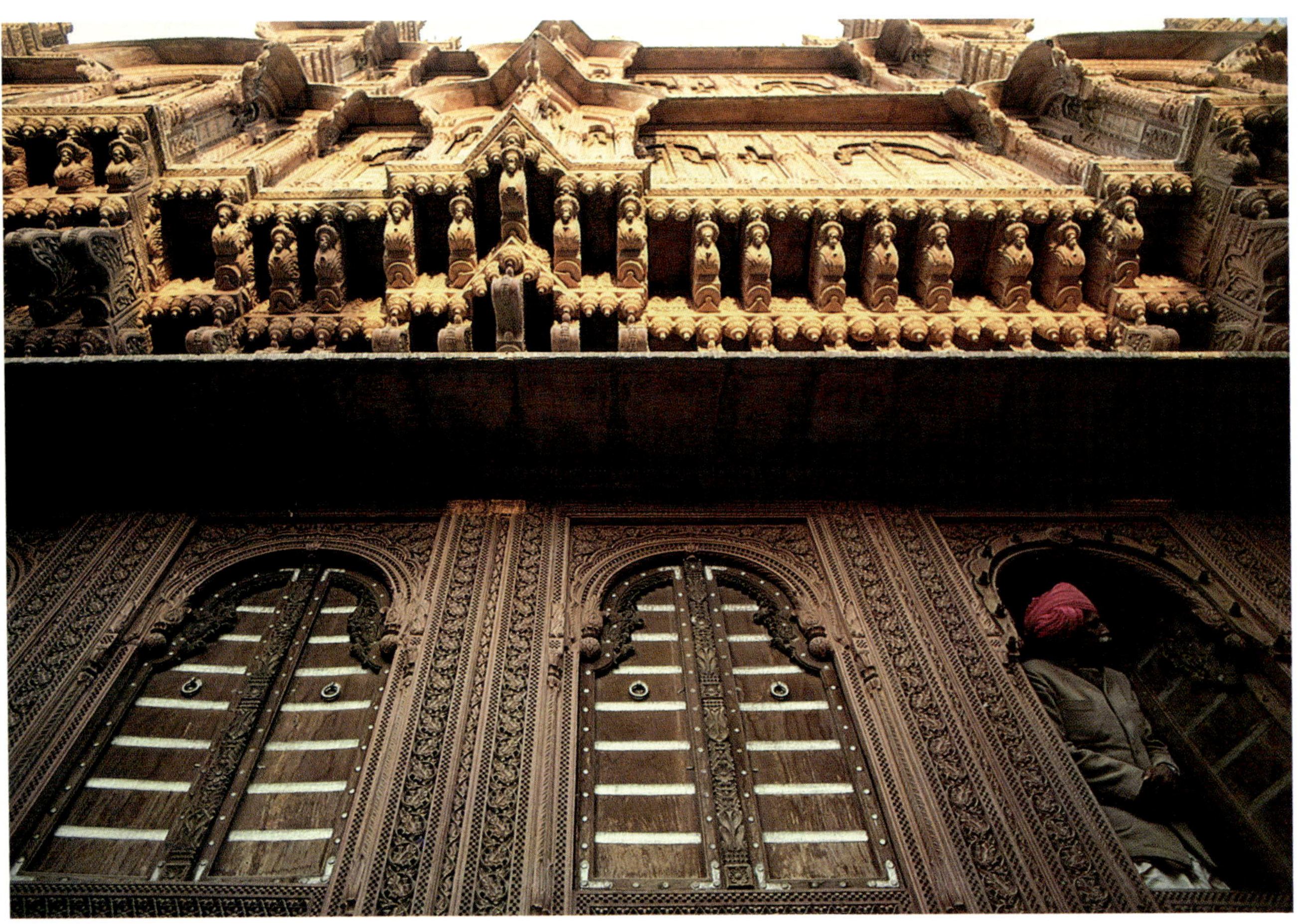

A Bikaner *havcli*, in red sandstone.

Darbar Hall, in contrast, added later, is sumptuous.

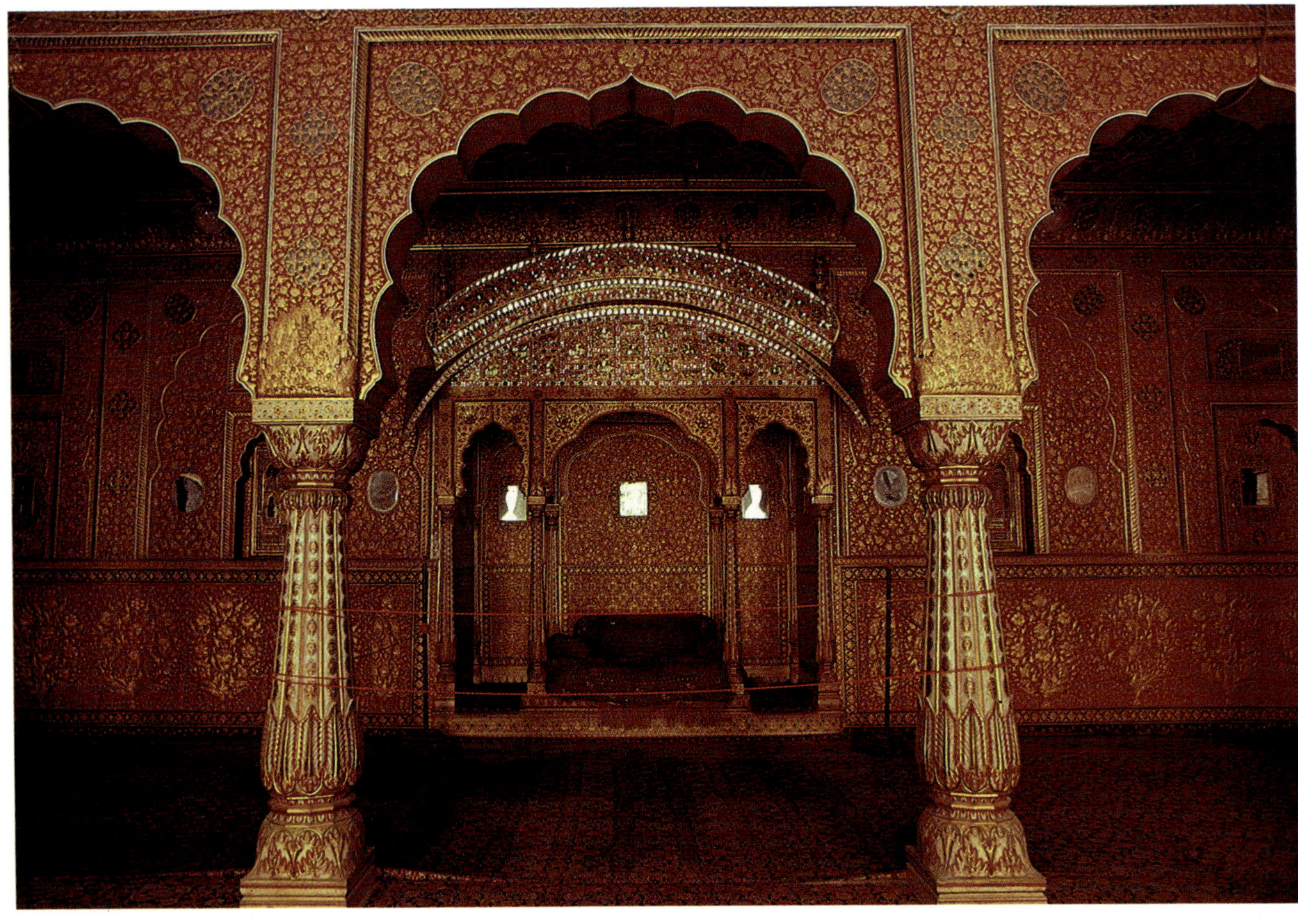

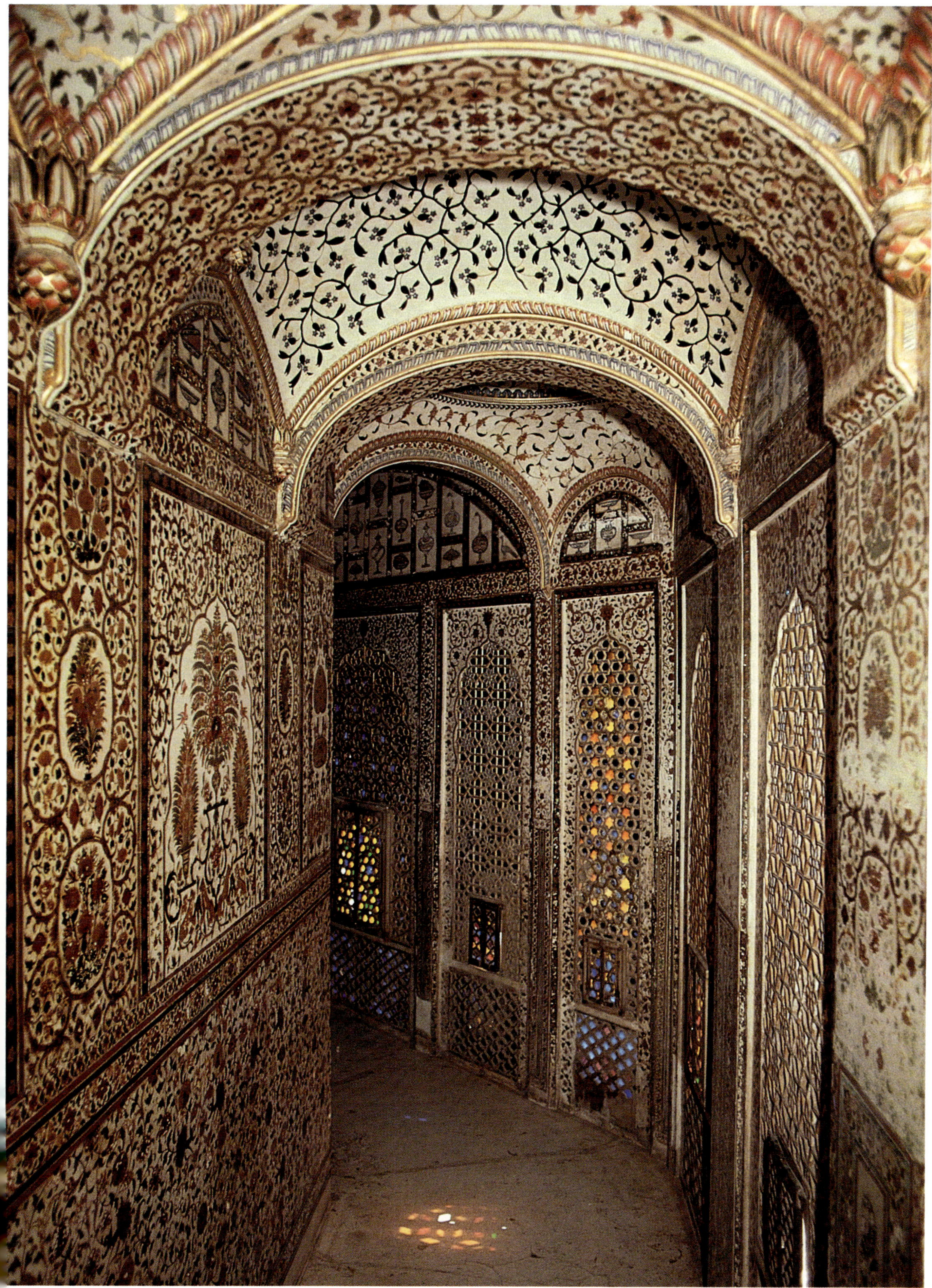

Junagarh Fort. Corridor in Phool Mahal.

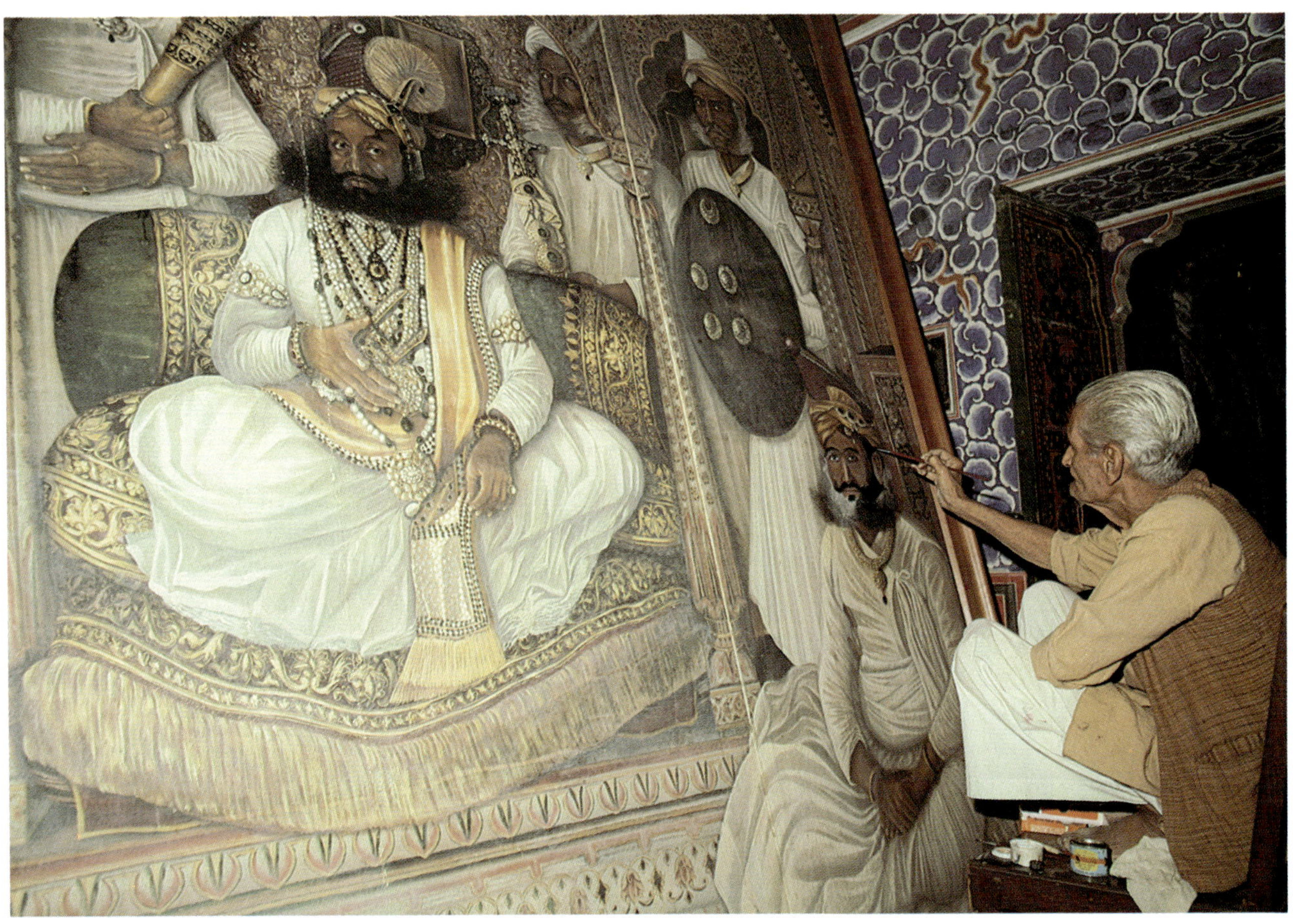

An artist retouching a royal family portrait painted by an Italian

Sun motif in wood and lacquer

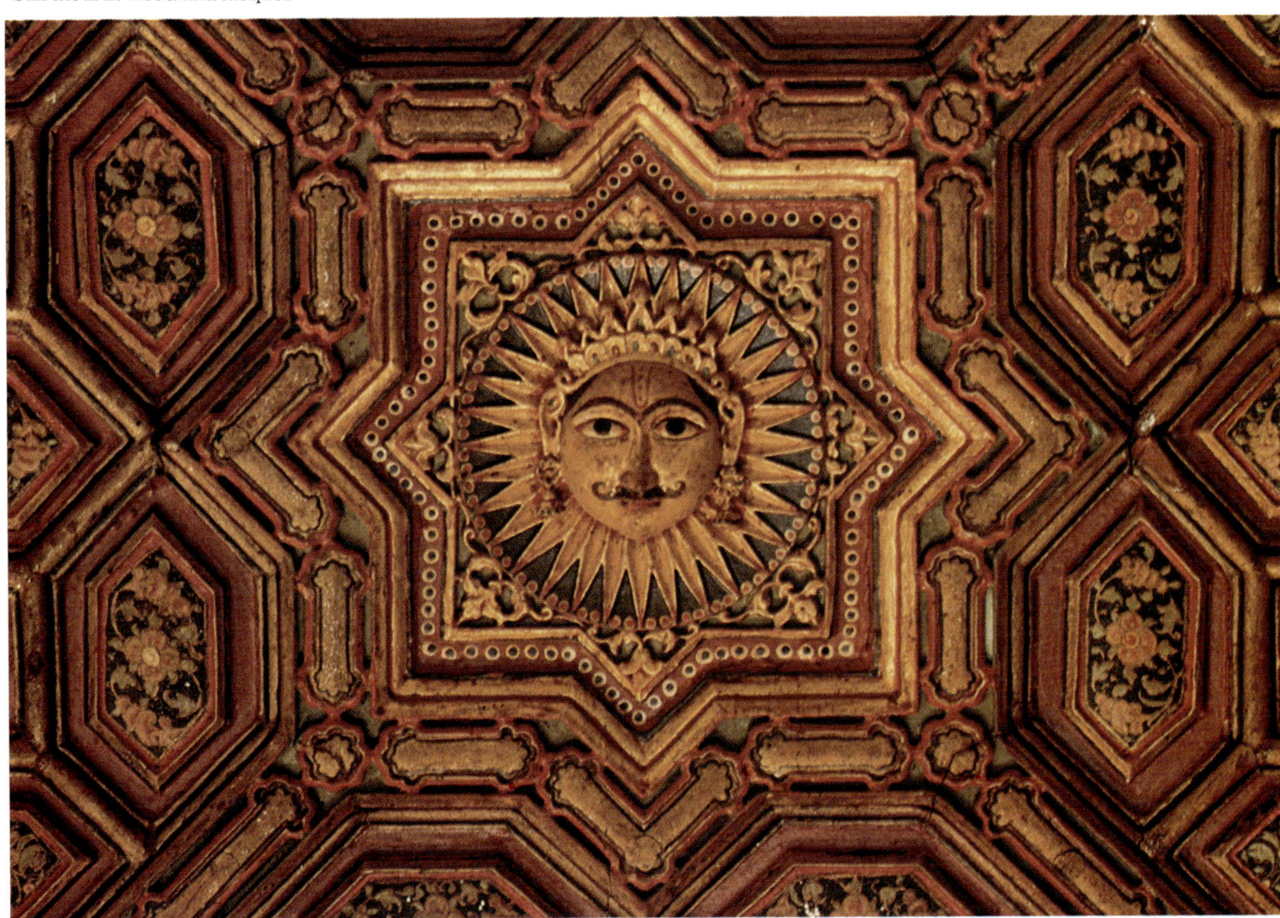

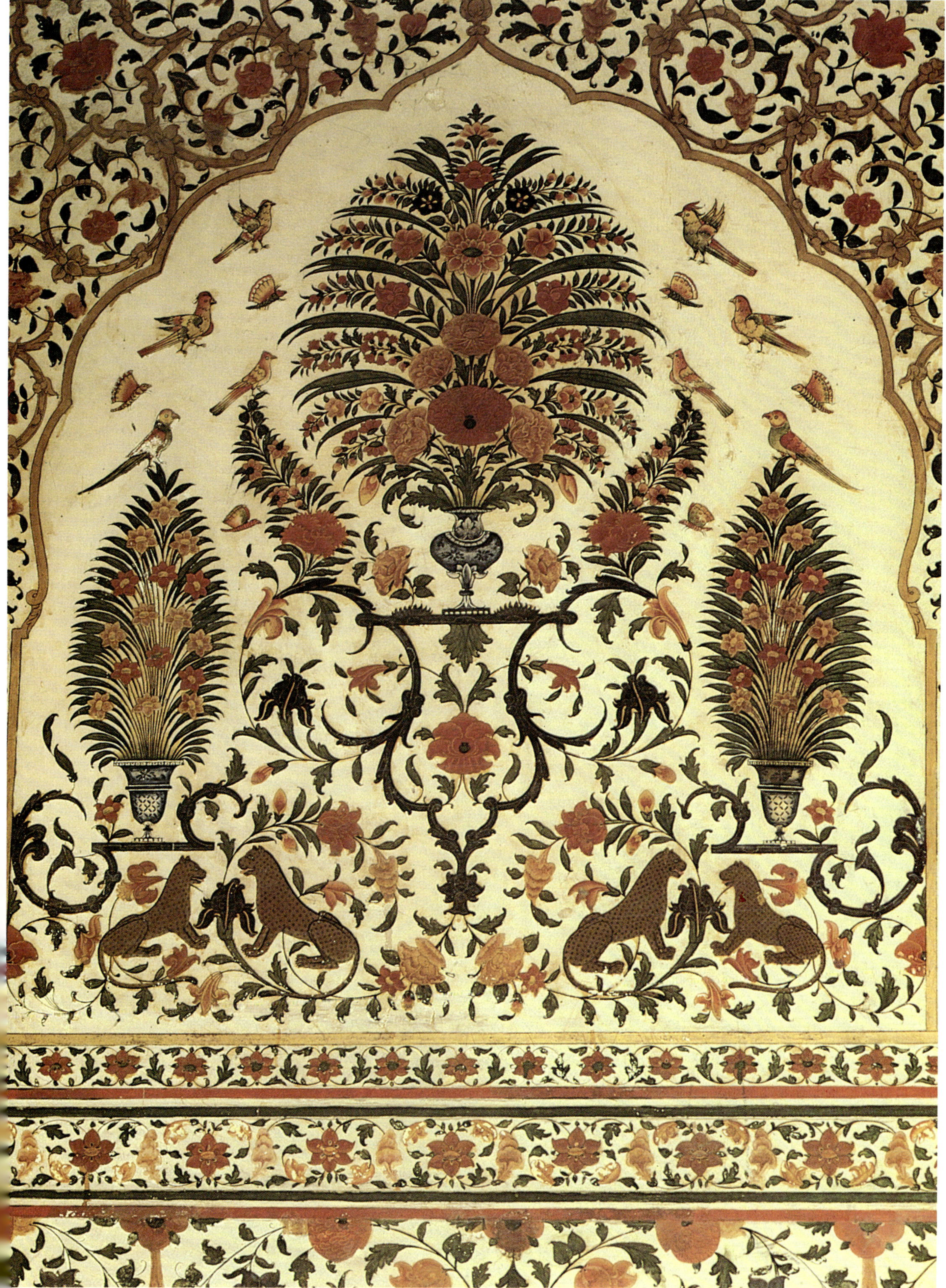

Floral decoration. Painting replaces pietra dura in Junagarh, Bikaner.

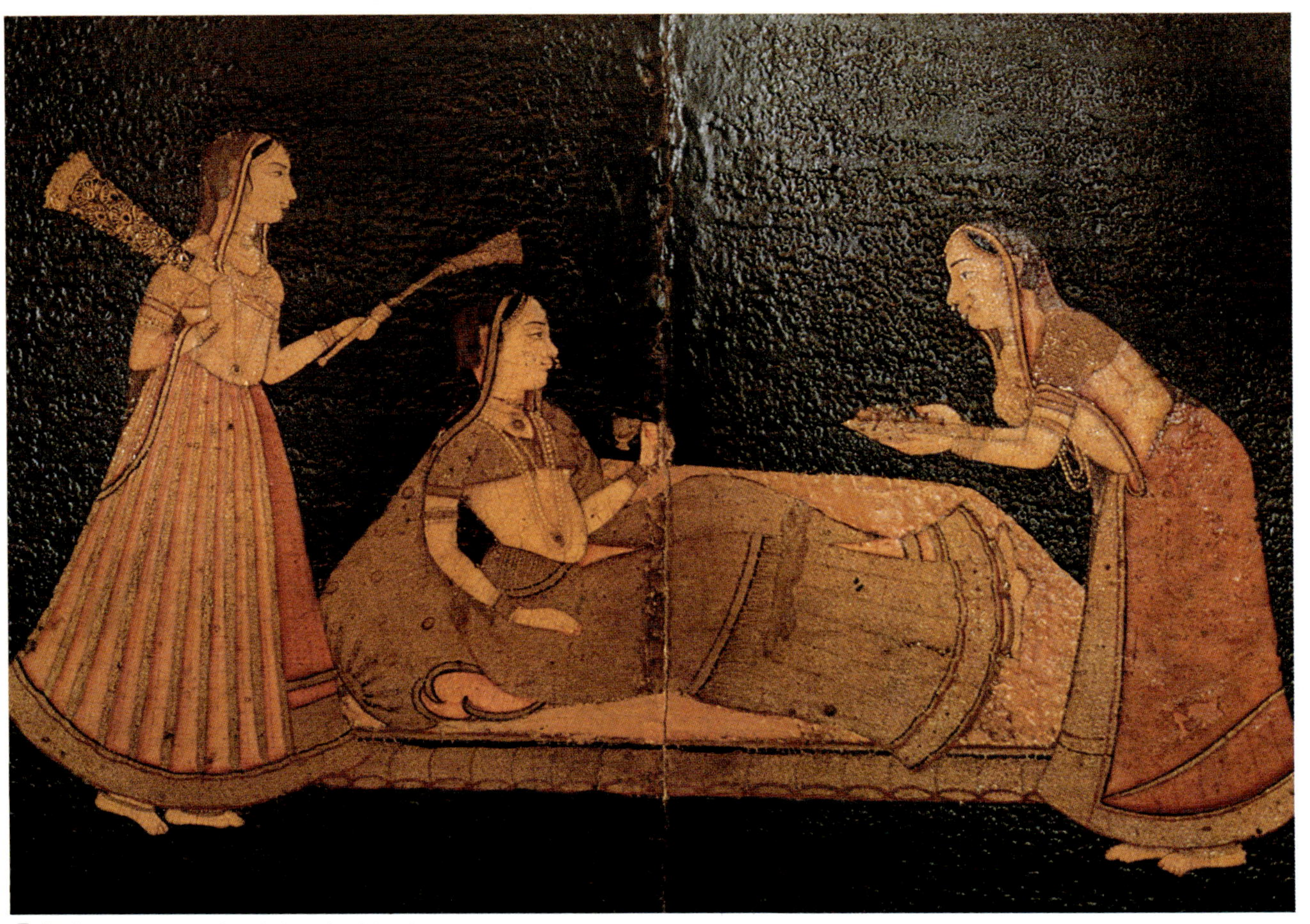

Folk elements on a painted door. Sur Mahal, Junagarh, Bikaner.

Chhattar Mahal, Junagarh. An old photograph and painted tiles.

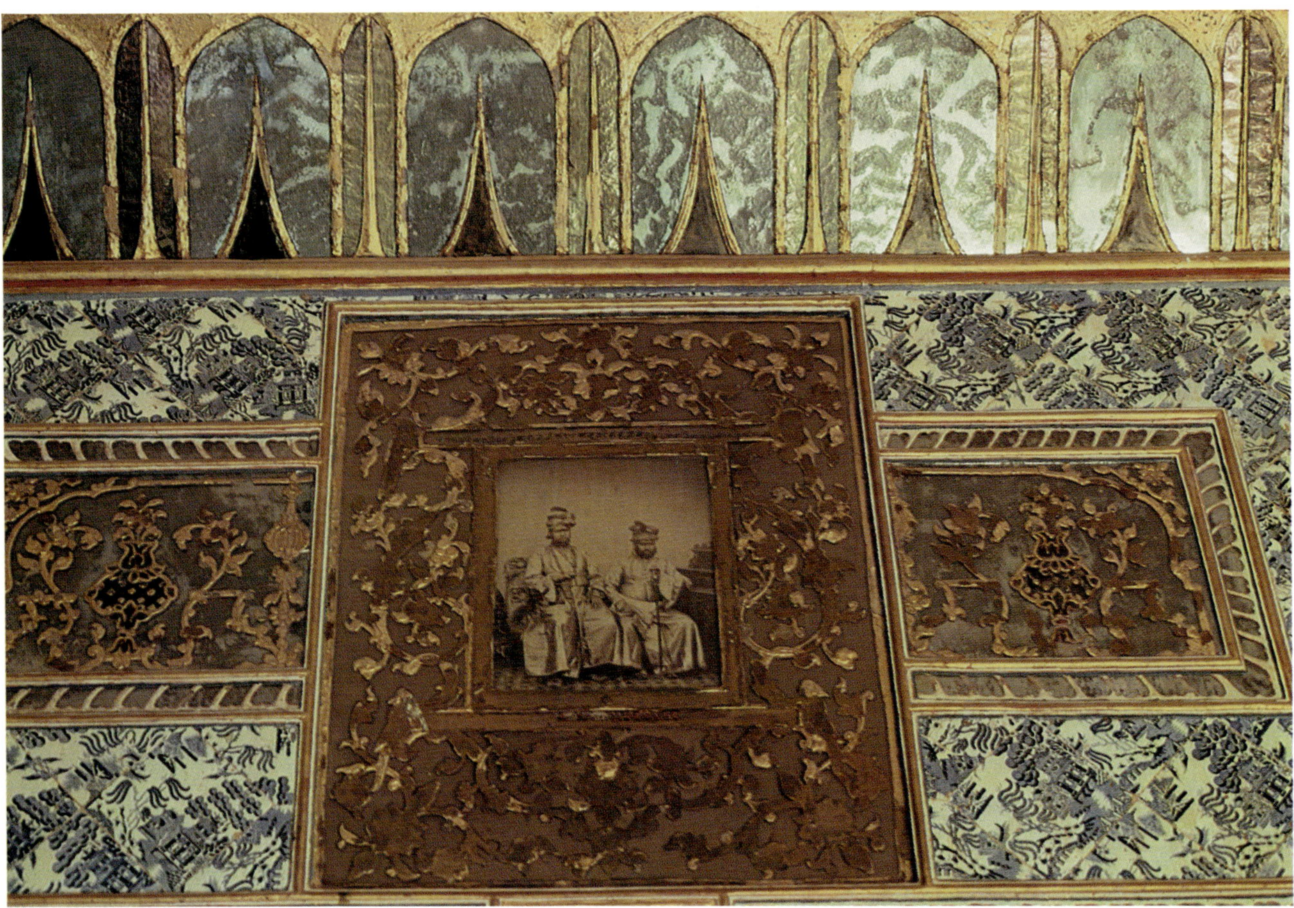

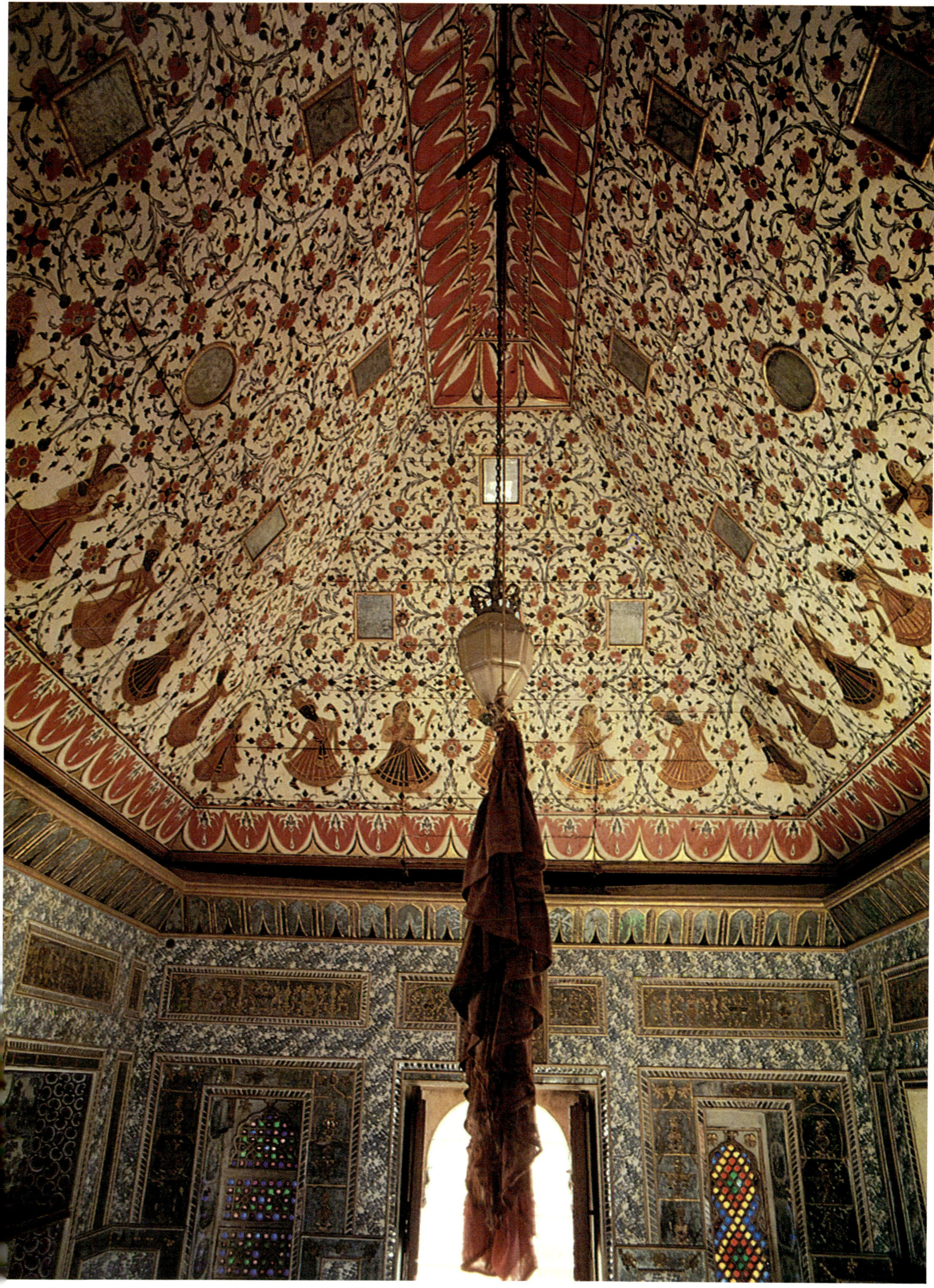

Canopy roof with scenes from the Krishna theme. Chhattar Mahal.

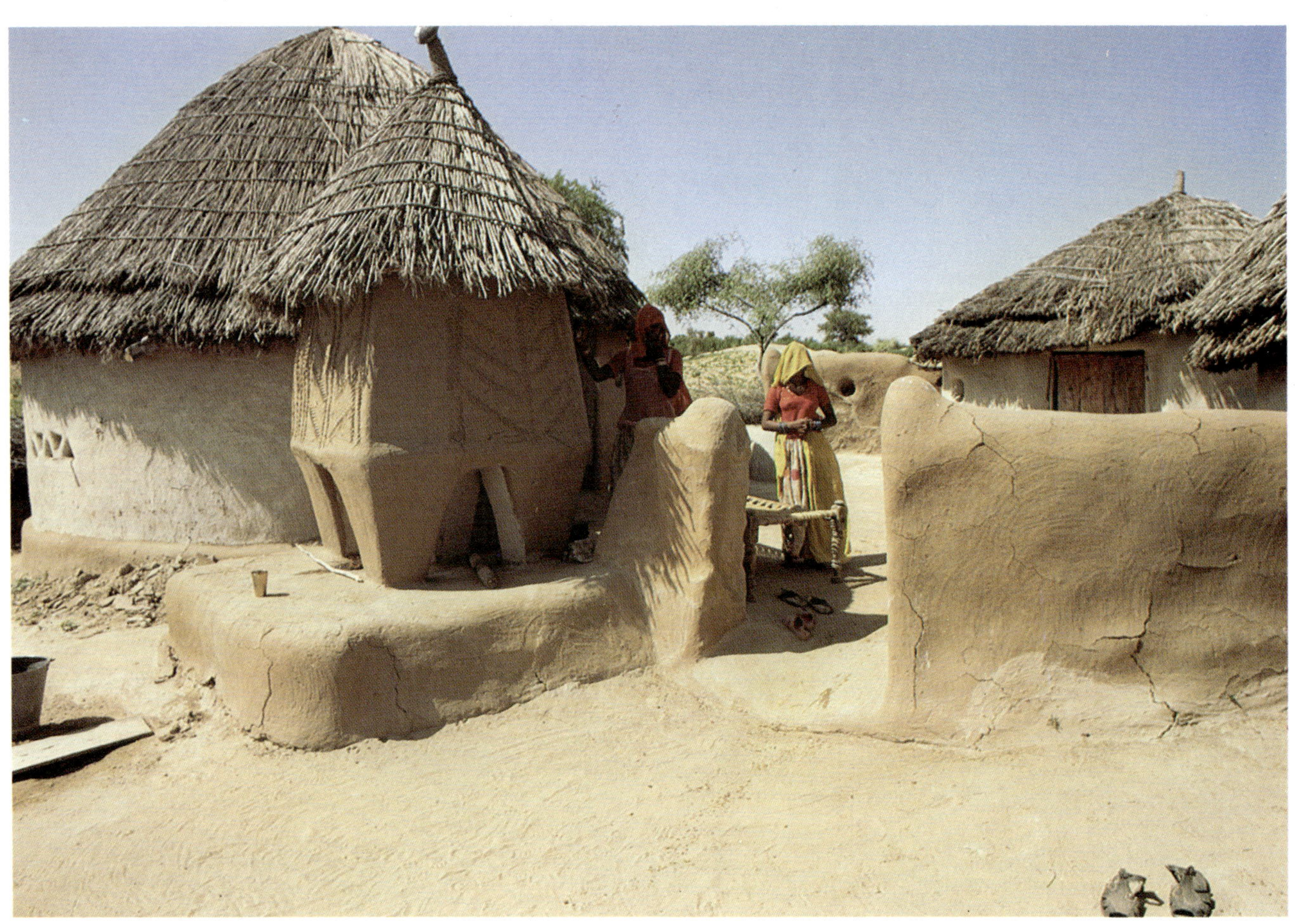

Desert village. *Kothis*, grain bins, of plastered mud and huts show use of local materials.

Interior of a village home

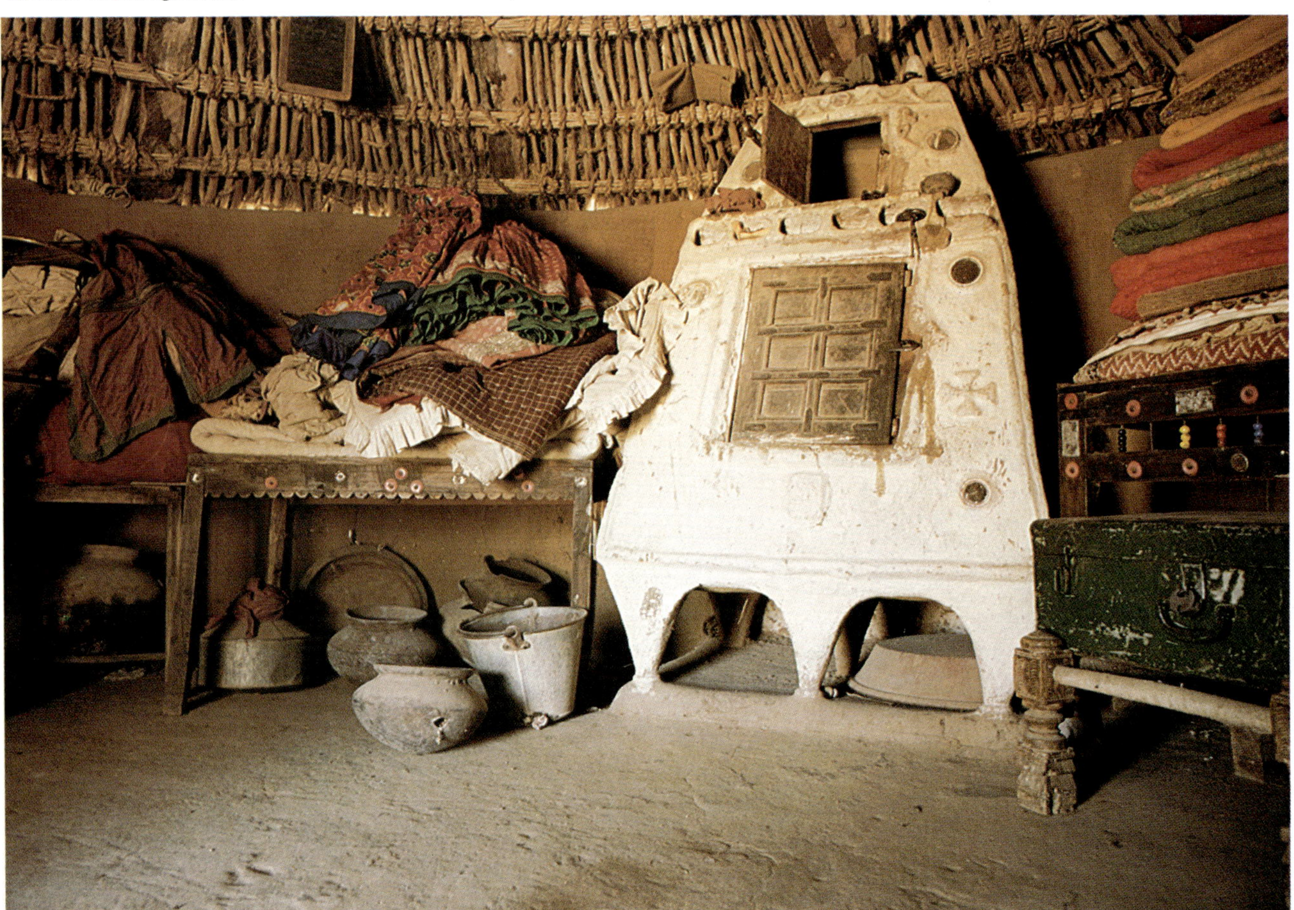

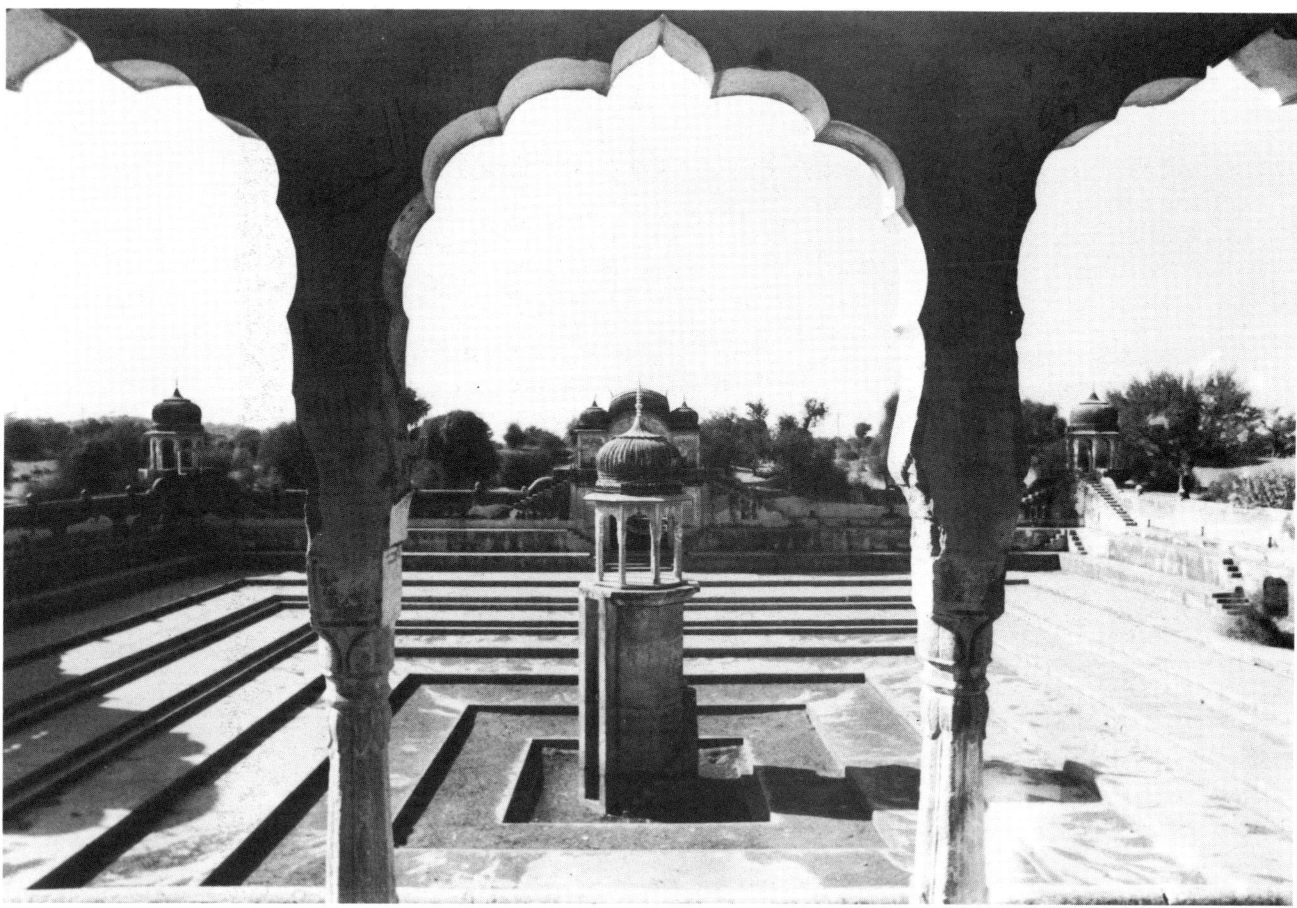

Abandoned *baori* at Fatehpur

guests as they sat in the carpeted pavilions. The kingfisher cocked its head and gazed gravely at the dry bottom of the tank before it flew off, disappointed. The sun was hot; without the cool limpid sound of water the place was like a forsaken shell. We wandered back to the car, and surprised a miniature prehistoric monster, a metre in length from its pointed snout down its scaly back to the blunt-end tail, as it waddled into a ditch. It was a monitor lizard which can grow to a length of over two metres in the desert. I was glad we had met only a juvenile member of the species, though I am told they are quite harmless.

Raptorial predators, hawks, falcons, eagles used the strung-out electric poles as watch towers from where they surveyed the scrub for rodents and other prey. Mere silhouettes against the blistering sky, they were difficult to tell apart. We sped by a pyramid of animal carcasses, the bleached bones grotesquely piled. A white-beared vulture dutifully picked the last scraps off the skull of a goat. These macabre remains are collected by *chamars* and piled by the roadside, to be transported in trucks, to be sold by traders for commercial use.

Arriving in Bikaner by three in the afternoon, I found I was shivering in the heat and running a temperature, having got what is euphemistically called 'a touch of the sun'.

No subsequent trip to Bikaner gave me quite the same insight into the desert as that first one. The very nature of the journey has altered radically. The ribbon of road is now a national highway, a broad bustling artery, with regular bus services and heavy truck transport. Several roads branch off from it into the interior, linking villages to the nearest towns. The public vehicles are filled to capacity with country folk, a sizeable overflow finding thrills and merriment on the roof. Even in the desert, the problem is of numbers. *Chinkara* and black buck formerly seen grazing in the open countryside have disappeared, and are now mainly to be found in the sanctuaries at Gajner or Tal Chhapar. Within a decade the very feel of the terrain has altered.

Caravan Routes and Mirages

The journey from Shekhawati to Bikaner which we had covered by car within eight hours, took a highly organised caravan fifteen days in 1808. I often wondered what it must have been like in the era of caravan travel to venture into that wilderness. Monstuart Elphinstone in his book, *An Account of the Kingdom of Caboul*, gives a revealing description. A British Political Agent, he was sent on a mission to the Afghan ruler, Amir Sher Shuja, by the Governor-General, Lord Minto, who feared an invasion of India by Napoleon as part of his grand design. Minto hoped to forestall the French in Kabul by a pact of friendship with the Afghans. Starting from Delhi on October 13, 1808, Elphinstone arrived on the borders of Shekhawati on October 21 where

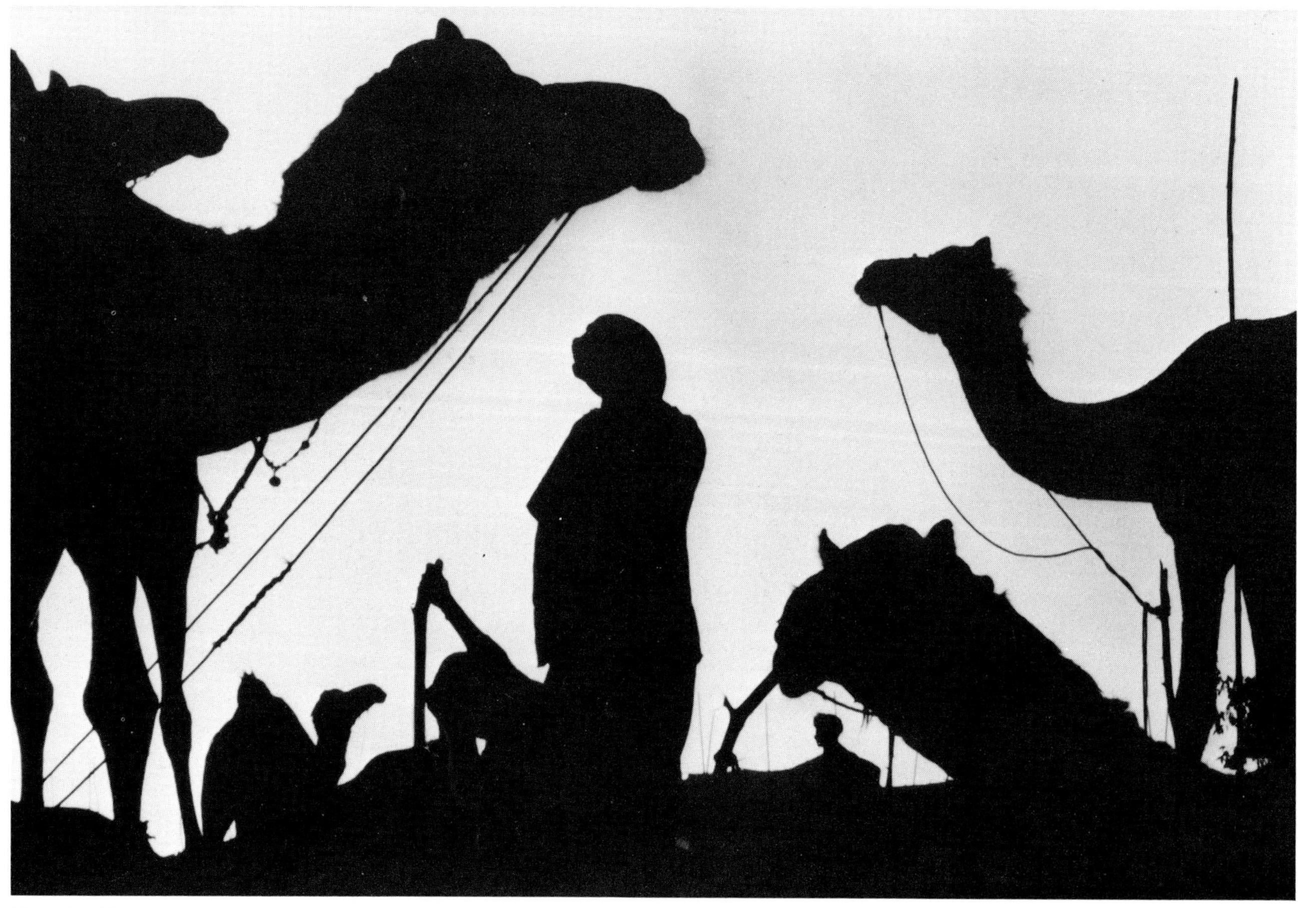

Camels silhouetted against the sky.

We had the first specimen of the desert, to which we were looking forward with anxious curiosity. Three miles before reaching that place, we came to sand-hills, which at first were covered with bushes, but afterwards were naked piles of loose sand, rising one after another, like the waves of the sea, and marked on the surface by the wind like drifted snow. There were roads through them, made solid by the treading of animals, but off the road our horses sunk into the sand above the knee.

The caravan entered Bikaner State at Churu, and from here Elphinstone took on his full complement of men, equipment, supplies and animals for the journey through Jangaldesh. Having sent back all the women camp-followers and any faint-hearted men, his caravan comprised fourteen British officers, an escort of one hundred mounted cavalry, two hundred and fifty infantry, and one hundred irregular horse, apart from the men who looked after the six hundred camels and thirteen elephants that carried provisions and water. On the march, strung out in single file, the caravan extended over two miles. It left Churu on October 30.

Water was their chief problem:

> The wells are often three hundred feet deep and one was three hunded and forty-five deep. With this enormous depth, some were only three feet in diameter, the water is always brackish, unwholesome, and so scanty, that two bullocks working for a night, easily emptied a well.

Beyond Nokha there is a well, still in use, which is almost three hundred metres in depth. The digging of such deep wells is a feat in itself, as the sandy sides are apt to crumble in and bury the diggers. The walls are reinforced with dry branches of the *phog* bush which grows wild in the desert. It is very hardy and water-resistant. It is also used in the construction of the village huts. *Phog* is known as camel-thorn and is a favourite fodder for these animals.

> In the midst of so arid a country, the water melon the most juicy of fruits, is found in abundance. It is really a subject of wonder to see melons three of four feet in circumference, growing from a stalk as slender as that of the common melon, in the dry sand of the desert. They are sown and perhaps require some cultivation, but they are scattered about to all appearances as though they grew wild.

Recourse to these melons as means of slaking their thirst was not a very wise practice as Elphinstone soon discovered:

> Such were the combined effects of fatigue, bad water and the excessive use of water-melons, that a great proportion of the natives who accompanied us became afflicted with a low fever accompanied by a dysentry – and forty persons of all description expired during the first week of our halt at Bikaner ... At last on the

5th November, in the midst of a tract of more than ordinary desolation we discovered the walls and towers of Bikaner, which presented the appearance of a great and magnificent city in the midst of a wilderness.

Conditions there were disturbed, as usual:

Bikaner was at this time invaded by five different armies.

– a somewhat excessive achievement even for those rather violent and unpredictable times.

I envied Elphinstone the sight of large herds of the wild ass in this part of the Thaar. They are now found only in the Rann of Kutch, and even there I could not get a glimpse of this fugitive creature which

resembles a mule rather than an ass, but is of the colour of the latter. It is remarkable for its shyness, and still more for its speed: at a kind of shuffling trot peculiar to itself, it will leave the fleetest horse behind.

A mere decade after Elphinstone, Colonel Tod mentioned the wild ass as found in Barmer and in the Rann of Kutch, but he did not come across it in Jangaldesh. Tod's editor, William Crooke, in a footnote adds,

Herodotus (vii, 86) noted that the Indian chariots in the armies of Xerxes were drawn by horses or wild asses.

No efforts to tame the wild ass have succeeded in the present day, although E.P. Gee, mentions, in his work on the wild life of India, that it has been attempted by army men stationed near the Rann. We seem to have lost control over, and connection with, wild creatures and can now only eliminate them, or at best, preserve them in zoos and sanctuaries.

We did manage to share the experience of a phenomenon peculiar to the Thaar that both Elphinstone and Tod had known. This was the mirage. Elphinstone's route took him northwest from Bikaner to Pugal. On leaving that town for Manjgar he records:

Towards evening many persons were astonished with the appearance of a long lake, enclosing several little islands; notwithstanding the well-known nature of the country, many were positive that it was a lake, and one of the surveyors took bearings of it. It was, however, only one of those illusions which the French call *mirage* and the Persians *sirraub*.

Tod's experience of the mirage was not in Jangaldesh but in Maroo, the desert around the Jodhpur area, north of Merta, at Jharau, travelling towards Ajmer. It was vivid, and Tod's graphic, dramatic style contrasts with the cryptic statements of the Scot:

The eye was attracted by a lofty opaque wall of lurid smoke, which seemed to be bounded by, or to rise from, the very verge of the horizon. By slow degrees the dense mass became more apparent, and assumed a reflecting or refracting power: shrubs were magnified into trees; the dwarf *kair* appeared ten times larger than the gigantic *amli* of the forest. A ray of light suddenly broke the line of continuity of this yet smoky barrier, and, as if touched by the enchanter's wand, castles, towers, and trees were seen in an aggregate cluster, partly obscured by magnificent foliage. Every accession of light produced a change in the *chitram*, which from the dense wall that it first exhibited had now faded into a thin transparent film, broken into a thousand masses, each mass being a huge lens, until at length the too vivid power of the sun dissolved the vision: castles, towers, and foliage melted, like the enchantment of Prospero, into "thin air".

After this evocative description I can only add that we witnessed a similar illusion on a morning in early February on our way south-east, to Pokharan. Both Elphinstone and Tod had experienced the mirage in November.

Because the mirage is an illusory phenomenon that hints at the tenuous frailty of our sensory link with the external world, it is defined in poetic metaphor in many languages. *Siyah kot*, castle in the air; *chitram*, picture; *sirraub*, in Persian. In Arabic *sirabh* means 'water of the desert'. In Sanskrit it is called *gandharva pura*, the 'city of celestial singers' or *mrigatrish*, the 'thirst of the deer'. Elphinstone found that the Afghans considered a mirage the work of evil spirits, as their name for it in Pashto, which he writes as *ghoolee beeabaun*, means 'ghoul of the wilderness'. According to them the ghoul creates the illusion in order to bewitch travellers in the desert and when they approach it, the phantom seizes and devours them.

From this popular superstition, they often illustrate an account of the wildness of any sequestered tribe, by saying that they are *ghoole beeabaun* (wild as the demons of the waste).

This of course is poetry of another sort, the more compelling in its imagery because of its power to project one into the chilling spaces of an unknown, malignant spirit world.

Before he left the borders of the Thaar beyond Pugal, Elphinstone seems to have been overwhelmed by the desolation of the desert which made him feel

a sort of wonder at the people who could reside in so dismal a wilderness and of horror at the life to which they seemed to be condemned.

A couple of centuries later we heard similar sentiments being expressed from a different viewpoint by two young men of Parasrampura in Shekhawati. For them the wonder was that we, who lived in the capital of the country should deliberately seek out their miserable, depressing village, in pursuit of some strange outlandish custom, or to record the snatch of an archaic song. They on their part made no attempt to disguise the feeling of being trapped by destiny in a meaningless existence that was as harsh as a life-sentence for an unknown, inexplicable crime, which they, the innocent-condemned, expiated in a Kafkaesque penal settlement.

Buried Cities and Early Peoples

Yet the Thaar has provided a homeland throughout the history of man in the sub-continent. Strangely, it was not the rich, fertile Ganga-Yamuna valley that cradled the most ancient cultures here, but the sterner clime of the Indus and its tributaries. The densely forested plains in the Indian heartland were an effective barrier to settled communities who did not know the use of iron (before c.800 B.C.). Only primitive tribes inhabited these forest belts. Fire was a quick and practical means of clearing woodland for pasture and cultivation, but it was a dangerous method and a destructive one.

We read of Arjuna, the Pandava hero, and Krishna burning the Khandava forest around Indraprastha (modern Delhi) in the *Mahabharata* (c. 1000-800 B.C.), and of their slaughtering wild animals, and rejoicing in their victory over the Yakshas of the forest, meaning the aboriginees. To a modern Indian the episode is unedifying, even when one realises that conditions in those early times called for desperate measures. But warfare in any age is ugly and 'flushing out the enemy' a familiar phrase in contemporary military parlance, is no less horrifying and reprehensible.

Although desert conditions prevailed in the Thaar in the pre-historic age, they were not as pronounced as those recorded in historic times. A vast network of rivers, known collectively as the Indus system, brought down the bounty of the melted Himalayan snows in several deep, perennial tributaries to the mighty Indus which debouched into the sea. The mythic Saraswati, worshipped as a life-sustaining river goddess by the early Rigvedic Aryans, the Drisdavati, the Ghaggar and Hakra were streams that joined the parent river south of the well-watered Punjab through which the five rivers, Jhelum, Chenab, Ravi, Beas and Sutlej, still flow.

Rivers are of course the natural site for the growth of settled communities. They provide the necessary water for agriculture, bring down enriching silt to replenish the soil, and wherever navigable, are excellent highways for transport and communication. If in addition they are not overgrown by impenetrable tropical forest, like the Gangetic plain of the early ages, they provide ideal conditions for the growth and progress of civilisations. It was on the banks of the Ravi and the Indus that the cities of the Indus valley civilisations were excavated at the sites of Harappa and Mohenjodaro, now in Pakistan. I suspect that, when after Independence, the diggings at Kalibangan, 250 km north of Bikaner in Ganganagar district, and situated on the dried terraced beds of the lost Saraswati, just within Indian territory, revealed a small, unmistakable Harappan city, this country was stirred to a sense of deep national pride. Indeed, subsequent excavations at the same site unearthed an even more ancient culture, dubbed 'pre-Harappan' for want of a more exact nomenclature.

Archaeologists are not certain who these pre-Harappans were. They may have been an earlier wave of Harappans who came in from Iran via Baluchistan, since similar sites have been found in the latter region. Also, their wheel-turned pottery has designs that show an affinity with Iranian models. These specimens are not as developed or beautiful as the later Harappan, but they show fine incised designs in white and black. Certain purely local characteristics seem to have been absorbed from indigenous sources, seen in the miniature terracotta figurines of serpent goddesses with raised arms, holding trays. Were these taken from tribal sources? Were these tribals aborigines? Were they Bhils? Dravidians? There is no definite answer. The pre-Harappan settlement was surrounded by a protective wall similar in form to the later Harappan citadels, and the houses were made of brick. What links this early culture most directly to the present is the method of ploughing and the cultivation of fields. The pattern of furrows is exactly that followed by peasants in the desert today.

For the Harappan people, whoever they were, one has nothing but admiration. It is with a certain awe that one reviews their achievements. Kalibangan fortunately provides a fairly complete picture of their model cities. The main citadel or acropolis, surrounded by a high wall, occupied a prominent position on a mound on the banks of the river. The classic features of a ritual bathing tank and public granary were present, but smaller and less elaborate than those at Mohenjodaro. The lower city at the base of the acropolis, inland from the river bank, had its own walled ramparts. The town plan followed the parallelogram pattern, divided into squares, with roads running straight down and across, north to south, east to west, intersecting at right angles. The main throughfares had covered drains, which were brick-lined with soak-pits made of ceramic pots at regular intervals. This would be considered an achievement in a modern Indian town even today, and it is unknown in any village at the present time.

The houses at Kalibangan provided amenities still dreamt of as unattainable luxuries by most contemporary desert dwellers. They were made of kiln-fired bricks and had individual wells, or one well serving a colony of houses. Each dwelling had a bathroom with proper drains and sanitary system. These drains had water-proof lining with *pucca* bricks set with gypsum. The water pipes were of terracotta and the water supply was controlled by faucets! Gypsum is still one of the major resources of this area and is mined in the Bikaner district.

The Harappan people were literate but so far their pictograph script has not been deciphered. The script appears on copper seals along with the finely engraved images of animals, god-like figures and plants. It is also incised on the pottery. The quality and workmanship of these seals, and the terracotta jars and pots that have a metallic resonance when struck, indicate great technological expertise. The carefully graded system of weights, made of cubes of agate, and measures employing unshrinkable lengths of shell, all point to a highly organised and well-regulated society. Maritime trade with West Asia is

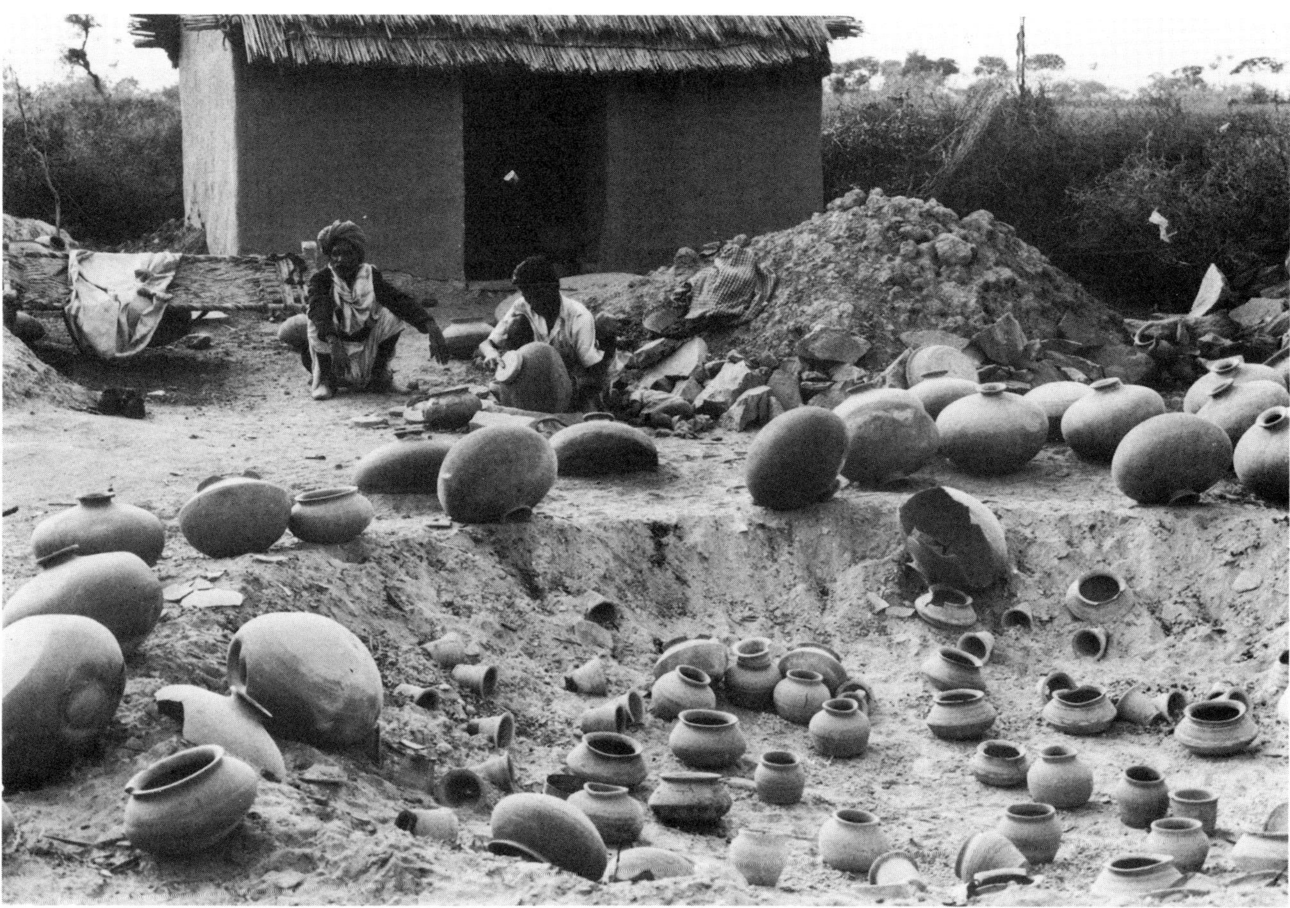

Potter at work

indicated by the excavations of the ports at Lothal in Gujarat and Sarkotada in Kutch, both belonging to this period. The presence of Harappan seals and beads in Bahrain and Mesopotamia, and spouted jugs and dishes typical of West Asian pottery in Harappan cities, confirms a close link between these cultures.

Yet the scientific town-planning of Harappan cities was unknown to the more sophisticated cultures of the same period at Ur of the Chaldees in south Iraq. Where had the Harappans developed this skill? The findings on their sites across Afghanistan, Punjab, Sindh, Rajasthan and Gujarat are all of the completely developed town. That they came into India through the Hindu Kush passes is reasonably well established, but who they were and where their original home was is not certain.

And then, just as mysteriously as it has bloomed, the Harappan culture disappeared. Possible dates of its existence, variously hazarded by scholars, are from 2500 BC to 1500 BC or more conservatively 2350 BC to 1700 BC. This means a period of at least six hundred years. Cities like Mohenjodaro seem to have been destroyed overnight, either by a natural disaster like a flash flood, or by the violence of invading hordes from the north, or both. But Kalibangan suffered no sudden death. It simply faded away. The desert sands were to keep their secret for more than three thousand five hundred years.

Pastoral Invaders

The newcomers are known to us as the Aryans, although what this name implies is the subject of debate. They were nomadic, pastoral people, who came through in successive waves, moving swiftly on horses or in chariots, driving their cattle in search of fresh pastures. The early Aryans (c. 1500 BC) still found the Saraswati a mighty river, worthy of worship:

Pure in her course
from the mountain to the ocean,
alone of streams,
Saraswati hath listened.

These offerings have we made with adoration.
O, Saraswati, accept our praises.
And placing us under thy dear protection,
May we approach thee as a tree for shelter.
(Rig Veda)

In a later period it is referred to as a seasonal stream, on whose bank the Pandava heroes of the *Mahabharata* sported in delight. Desert conditions were rapidly overtaking the Thaar region. This may have been due to the rivers changing course, as they continue to do. The damming of rivers above this area and the diverting of water in channels for irrigation purposes perhaps also contributed to this process. At present only the dried beds of the Saraswati and Drisdavati indicate their former courses, while the Hakra and Ghaggar are meagre seasonal streams.

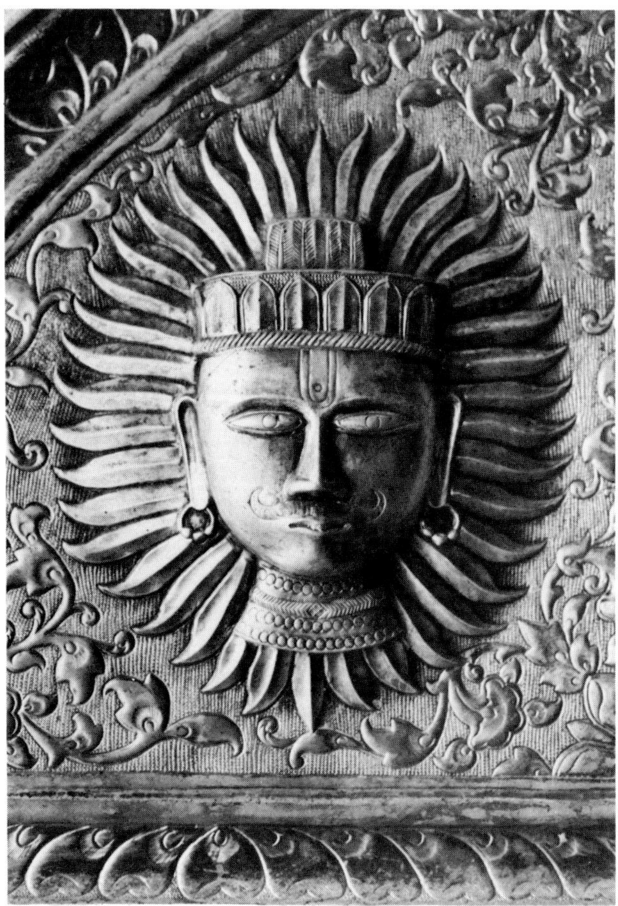
Sun motif in silver

The Aryans were a vigorous, aggressive people, determined in purpose and violent in action. Pastoral wealth is counted in herds, and the requirements of the animals are the supreme motivation of nomadic herdsmen. Vast territory is essential, as the wanderers search for fresh pastures in varying seasons, and the protection of the livestock calls for utmost vigilance.

These factors have shaped life and character in the desert all through history, and right from the epic age to medieval times, battles have been fought over cattle stolen in raids by a rival clan, or over territorial grazing rights. Gods and heroes, from Krishna and the Pandava princes down to Pabuji Rathor and Gugga Chauhan, both medieval heroes worshipped as gods, were those who successfully protected the herds of the tribe.

In many aspects the Aryan invasions marked a setback in cultural terms. Urban civilisation disappeared along with the scientifically planned cities and the ideal plumbing and sanitary systems. These were not to develop again for a thousand years, and even then not to the same degree of excellence. The written script vanished into oblivion, despite the highly developed, complex and flexible language of the Aryans, Sanskrit, which remained an oral tradition for an incredibly long period.

In other respects the Aryans brought about a necessary infusion of vitality and change which the urban life in the Harappan cities could not accomplish, having reached a stage of stagnation in their development. The Aryans pushed east and south, overrunning the earlier inhabitants and clearing the land, first for pasture and then for cultivation. Later, they fought inter-clan wars among themselves for territory, and finally, the great fratricidal war for supreme overlordship of the north. The *Ramayana* epic relates something of their south-east expansion into the sub-continent, while the *Mahabharata* contains an account of the struggle for power.

Since these epics were handed down orally, like heroic ballads today, and were only written down centuries later with many interpolations and variations, they are mythic in character and have assumed the status of religious texts. That is the secret of their all-pervading hold on the Indian imagination, and in particular in moulding Hindu faith and belief. The present-day balladeers of the Thaar claim a very long history for their art, just as the Rajput rulers of the region boast of royal descent from the ruling clans of Aryan times. Although there may be few facts to support either case, the poetic 'truth' contained in such persistent beliefs cannot be denied. It operates as a motivating force in shaping the history and developing the culture of a people.

The inferior greyware pottery attributed to the Aryans has been found in the desert sites near Bhatner (Hanumangarh), a medieval Bhati Rajput capital, before the Bhatis were pushed further west to establish themselves finally, in Jaisalmer. Far more intriguing are the remains of the ochreware at Rangmahal, a dusty little hamlet on the banks of the Ghaggar, about 6 km north east of Suratgarh, a site which local legend attributes to the presence there of 'Sikander Rumi', Alexander of Macedonia. The Greek conqueror never managed to go so far south-west into the sub-continent as Rajasthan, yet the legend endures. Diggings at Rangmahal, however, have unearthed a site of Kushan times and coins of that dynasty and the ochre pottery connected with it, have been discovered. 'Sikander Rumi' is a name familiar to the desert people, who have not heard of the Yu Chei tribe whose rulers held brief sway in the 1st century AD as the Kushan dynasty. This is not suprising as after Alexander many invaders and settlers poured in from the north – the Sakas (Scythians), Kushans, Hunas (Huns) and Gujaras being a few that contributed to the mixed stock of the Thaar.

Out of this rather explosive combination of racial types emerged the Rajputs, who, ignoring all else in their ancestry, harked back to an Aryan *kshatriya*, warrior, origin, and claimed direct descent from Rama of the Suryavansh, solar clan, or Krishna of the Chandravansh, lunar clan. Through a purification rite the Agnivansh, fire-born clan, rose out of the sacred Vedic fire pit at Mount Abu. From these three main branches sprang the thirty-six Rajput martial clans

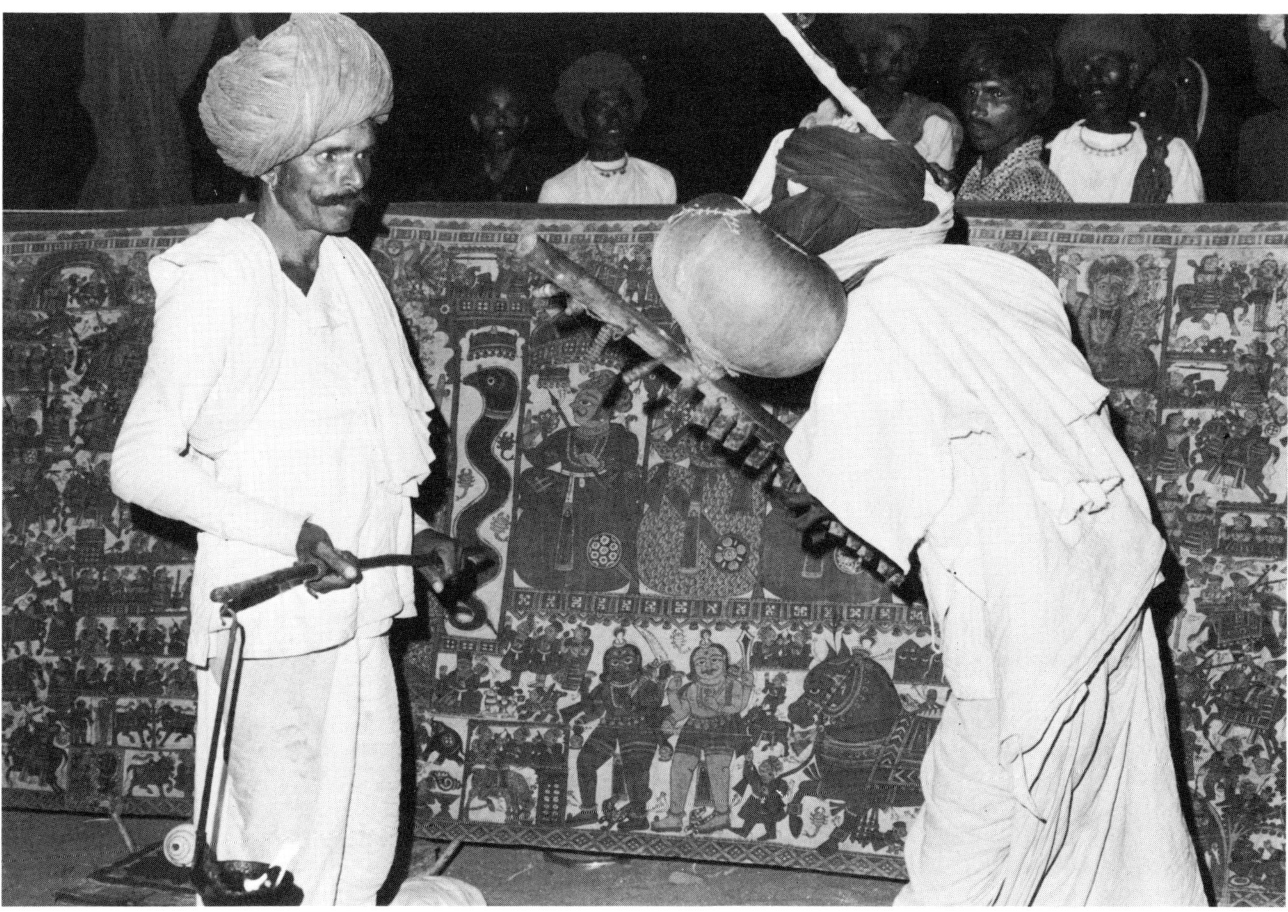

Bhopas reciting the Dev Narayan *parh*, Pushkar.

that were to dominate the Thaar from the 7th century onwards as the ruling caste, till Islam in the 10th century brought fresh waves of invaders from the same regions and through the same passes of the Hindu Kush, to challenge Hindu supremacy.

Warring Kingdoms

Jangaldesh split up into several petty warring kingdoms, and it was only in the 15th century that a semblance of stability was provided by Bikaji Rathor (1444-88), son of Jodha, the Rajput ruler of Jodhpur, in Maroodesh. Raja Jodha had fourteen sons. While most of them were content to accept fiefs bestowed by their father and to serve as vassals of Jodhpur, a few, more adventurous, set about conquering territory for themselves. Conspicuous among these was Bika. Joining forces in 1459 with his uncle Kandhal and a brother, Beda, he mustered three hundred of the most desperate and turbulent members of the clan and stormed through Jangaldesh capturing the strongholds of the Sankhlas and Mohils in a series of lightning raids.

The Rathors were for all practical purposes a raiding party bringing terror to settlements and leaving devastation in their wake. The attack on the Sankhla township of Janglu, south of the present Bikaner, was so severe and the massacre of its inhabitants so ruthless that the Bhati Rajput ruler of Pugal considered it prudent to conciliate the leader by offering Bika a daughter in marriage. Spurred on by this success, Bika determined to consolidate his victories. He sought the blessings of Karni Devi, a Charan woman renowned for her mystic powers and worshipped as an incarnation of the goddess Durga by the martial Jat peasants of the region. Her temple stands at Dashnoke, about 30 km south of Bikaner. The woman blessed Bika and predicted victory. The patronage of their *devi* influenced the six powerful Jat cantons into accepting the suzerainty of the Rathor. They agreed to pay taxes on property and a cess on cultivated land in exchange for his protection against the Bhatis and other traditional enemies.

The kingdom Bika had won was true desert. A cruel land, it bred a savage people. Old trade routes cut across Jangaldesh linking waterhole to waterhole along the routes that had been followed by invaders. Only the tribals and nomadic herdsmen could find their way across the terrain that changed its contours with each raging storm. This was a breeding ground for locusts which, in a cyclic rhythm of years, rose in clouds that blotted out the sun only to descend and devour everything in their path, choking animals, clogging wells, eating clothes off the back of a sleeping man, stripping the earth of all verdure. Tod observed a colony proceeding east from Bikaner 'with a rustling, rushing sound like a distant torrent'. Almost as menacing as the attacks of locusts, and

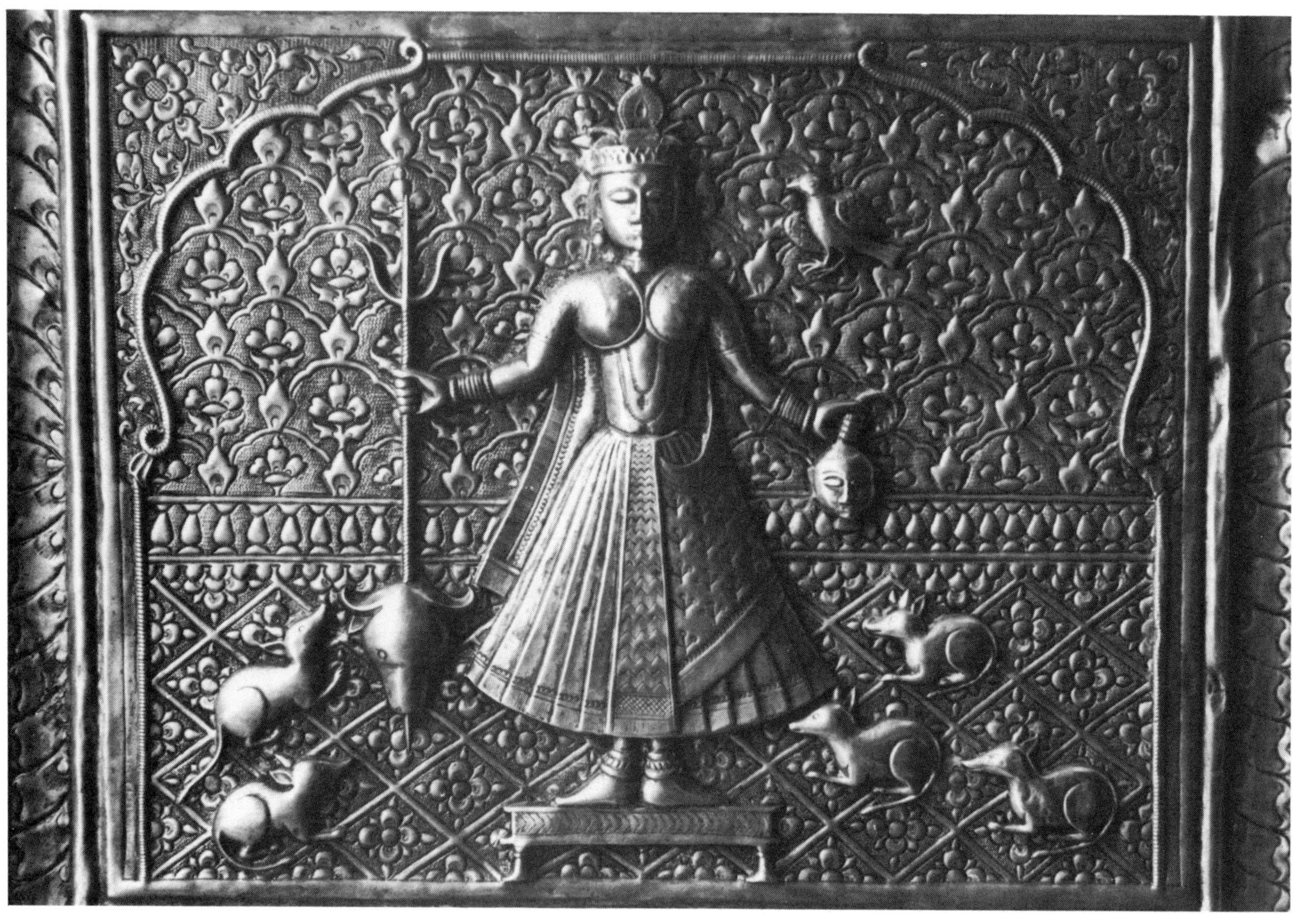

Detail of silver doors showing Karni Devi and the sacred rats

much more frequent, were the raids of marauding robber bands that fell on caravans, stole cattle and plundered settlements. Many of these belonged to clans that claimed an ancestry as age-old as the ruling Rathors, who were merely the most recent visitors in the clash for supremacy. To control these wild plunderers was both a difficult and delicate operation, since the ruler depended on the barbarous fighters to supplement his own contingents in times of war.

Bika's conquests did not stop at Bikaner but extended north, to the areas around the deserted river-beds of the Ghaggar and Hakra. With the help of the Jats he invaded the territory of the Johiyas and added it to his domain. This is the region where the early cities of Kalibangan and Rangmahal lay buried beneath the sand.

Bika's uncle, Kandhal, and his brother Beda were not content to serve under him, but independently made further forays into the hinterland, setting up their own petty states and establishing sub-clans of the Kandhalot Rathors and Bedawat Rathors, the patronymic being used to distinguish their descendants from the parent clan. Although nominal subsidiaries of Bikaner, these princes often defied the ruler and proved troublesome when a tyrant made demands they considered unwarranted. The Rao of Bikaner needed to enhance his prestige and bolster his fighting power in order to keep these unruly vassals in line. The opportunity came during the reign of Rao Rai Singh (1571-1611).

Bikaner was, in turn, subordinated to the ruler at Jodhpur, from where Rathor power stemmed. During Raja Maldeo's reign (1532-62 or 68), Emperor Akbar subdued that mighty prince of Jodhpur, and one of the measures he took to curb him was to recognise Rai Singh of Bikaner as an independent ruler and to add Nagor to Bikaner territory. Akbar's recognition of Rai Singh as a ruler in his own right, gave Bikaner the required support to rival Jodhpur for supremacy in the desert.

At home, this Mughal backing brought Bikaner the requisite authority to overawe local chieftains. Rai Singh further strengthened the tie by a marriage alliance between his daughter and Akbar's heir, Prince Salim, afterwards the Emperor Jehangir.

The graph of this imperial connection and the fluctuating fortunes of the Rathors of Bikaner can be traced in the building of Junagarh, the old fort. Its construction was begun by Rai Singh and continued with additions, embellishments and renovations through the reigns that followed in the next four hundred years.

Junagarh: History in Stone

When Bika built his *Bikaji-ri-tekri* (1488) it was the typical, rather primitive mud-and-rubble desert fortress commanding a strategic position on a ridge,

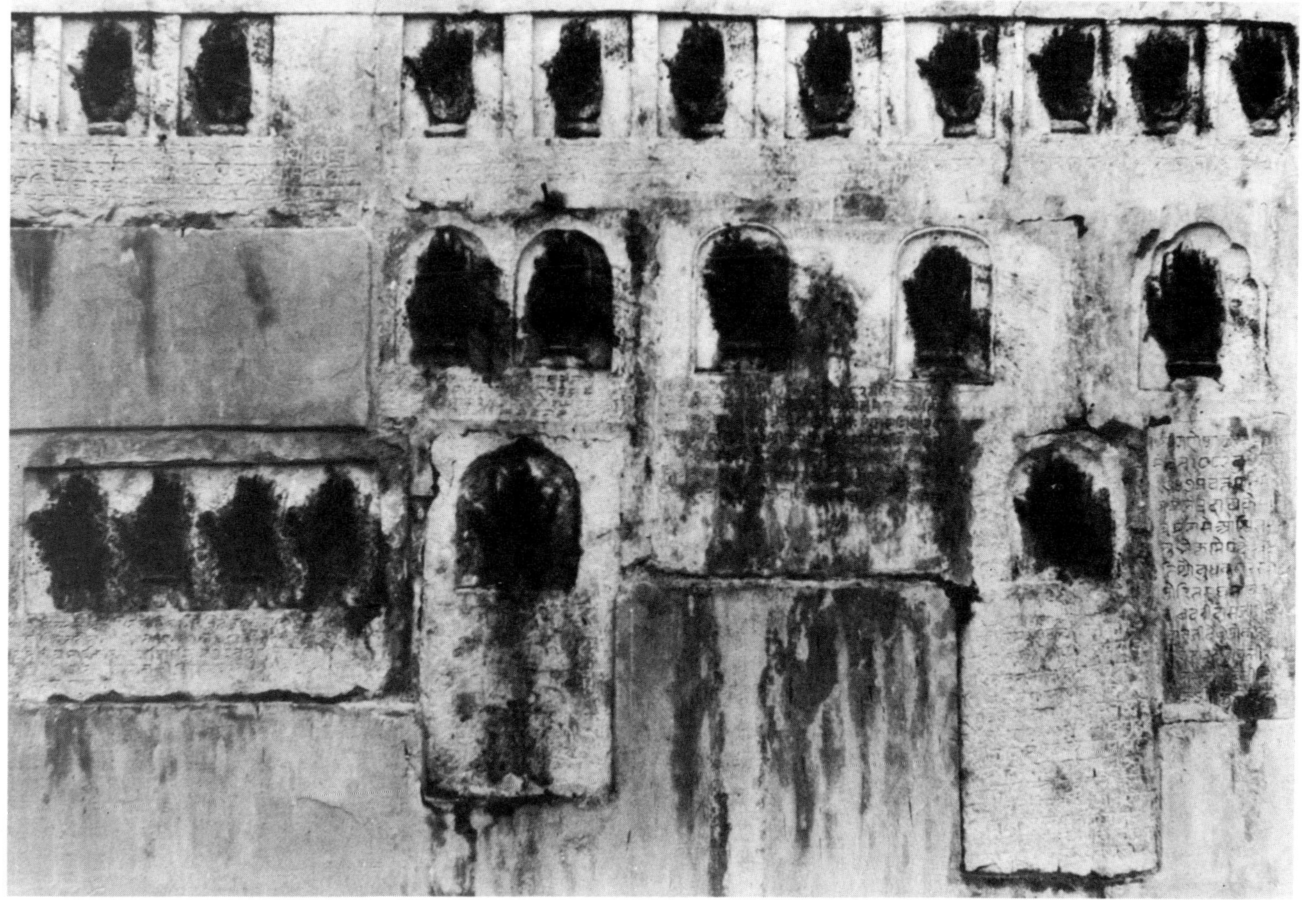

Sati handprints at Junagarh, Bikaner

at the southern end of the present old city. The Lakshmi Narain temple and a few broken ramparts are all that remain of it.

A century later, in 1588, his descendant Rai Singh laid the foundations of Junagarh on a slight rise north of the fortified city and opposite the earlier citadel.

One of the senior generals of the Emperor Akbar, Rai Singh had been exposed to the refinements of a glittering and cultivated court. A man of soaring ambition with the necessary drive and intelligence to accomplish his ends, he played a prominent role commanding the imperial forces in campaigns in the Deccan, Kabul and Gujarat. The Rathor contingents led by princes of his family contributed largely to the success of these wars. The reward or blood-price for such services was the *mansab*, rank, of 5000, the highest that could be held by any Mughal grandee, and the grant of the valuable fiefs of Kathiawar and Surat, in Gujarat.

During these years Rai Singh absorbed many fresh ideas and brought back rich treasures including miniature paintings and icons, as part of the legitimate loot. The revenue from the Gujarat fiefs resulted in an immense increase in the revenue of the Bikaner prince. He engaged expert artists and craftsmen, and attracted scholars, poets and musicians to his court with lavish gifts. He was mainly influenced by the art and architecture of the Sultanate period and by the Deccani-Hindu and Gujarat-Rajput schools. These styles are apparent in the early sections of Junagarh. The impressive citadel, as seen today, is surrounded by a moat nine metres wide and eight deep. The curtain wall surrounds the entire enclosure which is in the shape of a quadrangle. The ramparts, nine metres broad, are interspersed with thirty-seven bastions. There are two entrances, the earlier one to the east, the later to the west. The fort that Rai Singh raised was square, with nine bastions on each side. It was extended later by subsequent rulers. The early portions were built of the yellow Jaisalmer limestone which was transported across three hundred kilometres of desert terrain to Bikaner. Later with the discovery of limestone quarries at Khari, this expensive material was replaced by the deep pink stone of the region.

Rai Singh's fortifications have slightly sloping walls, a modification of the style of the Khiljis and Tughlaqs, with bastions. The ramparts have battlements which are less prominent versions of those found in the Sultanate period. The entrance to the east is Suraj Pol, the Sun Gate, which is flanked by two lifesize stone elephants. Within the gate is inset a black stone inscribed with an eulogy in Sanskrit tracing the genealogy of the Rathor clan back to Jaipul of Kanauj, and through him to Sri Ram Chander of the Suryavansh. Above the gate is the gallery for the *naggara*, drums, between balconies in the purest Gujarati-Rajput style of the 16th century.

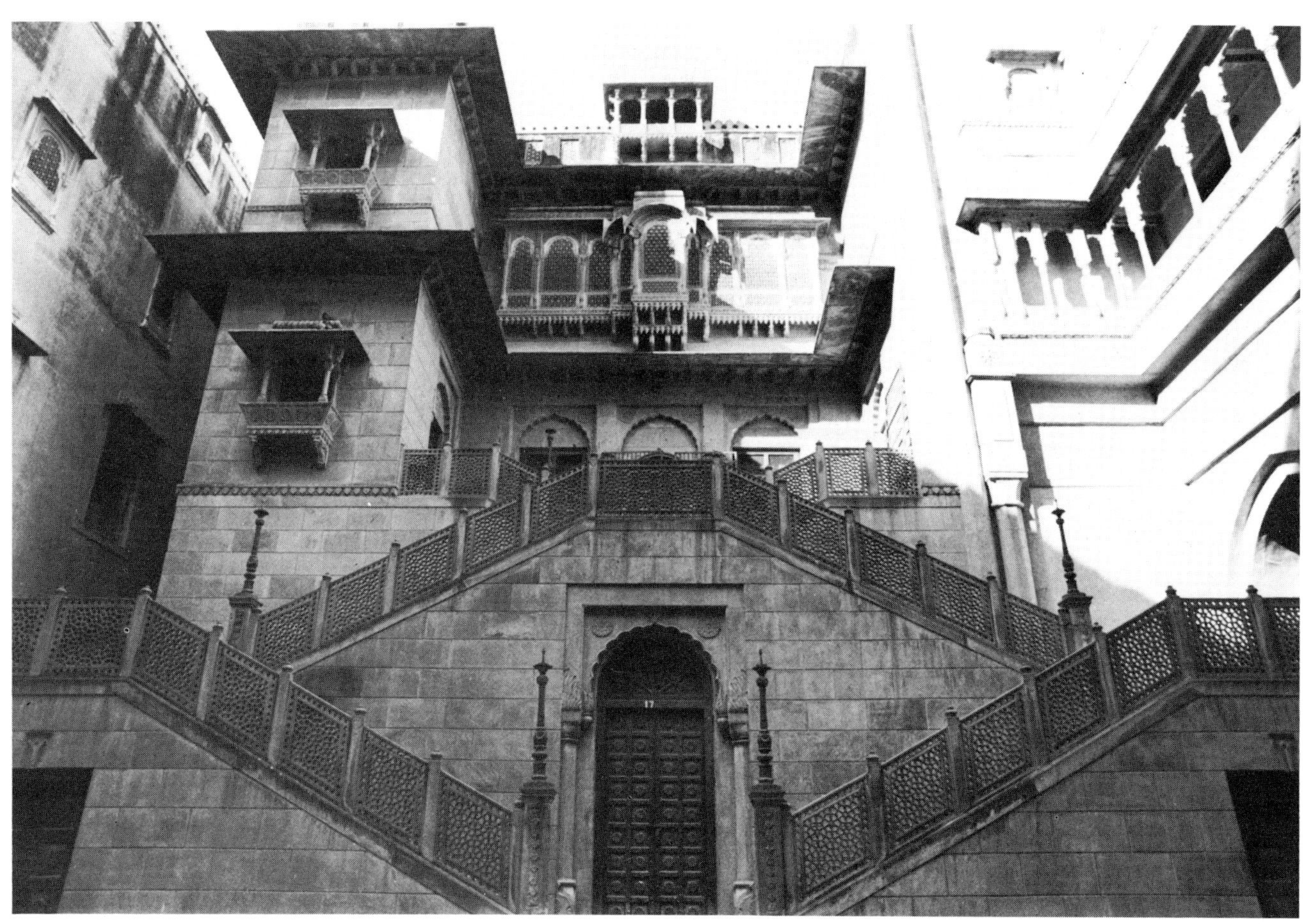

The double-staircase at Junagarh

Ivory inlay in wood; detail of door, Junagarh.

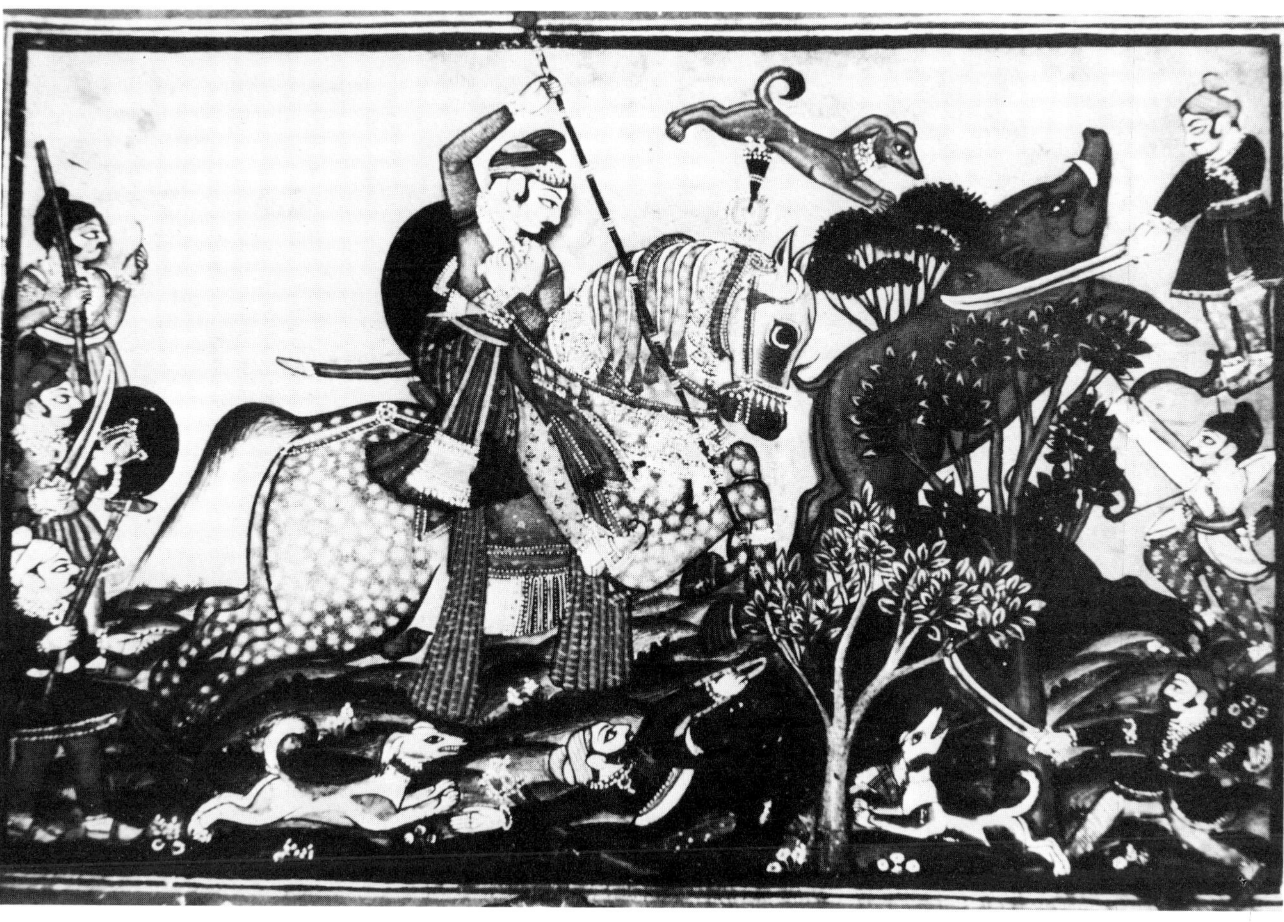

Royal hunt. Miniature painting.

Girl awaiting her lover. Rajasthani miniature.

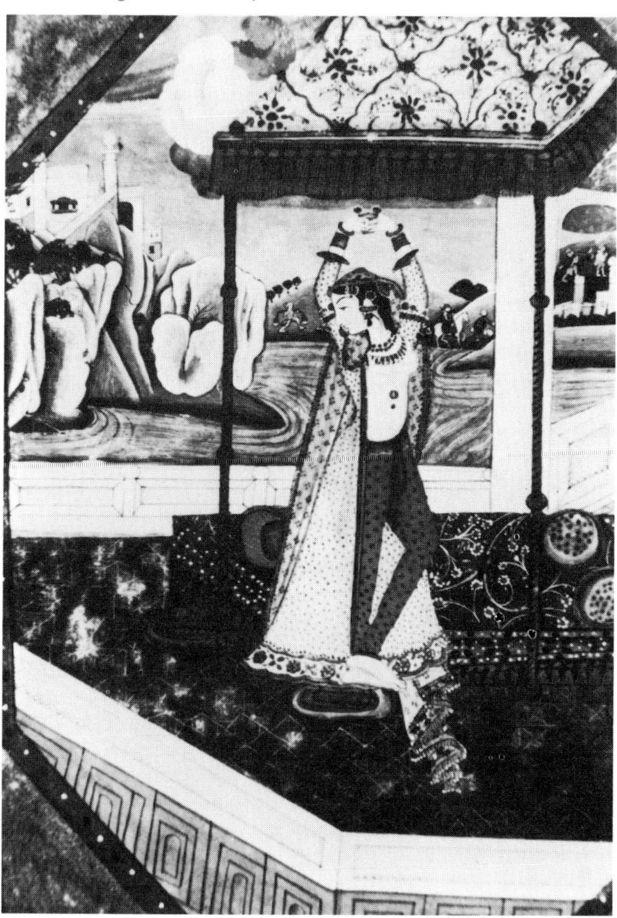

Three further gates, Fateh Pol, Daulat Pol and Karan Pol protect the palaces which lie south of the court. On the facade of Daulat Pol are handprints of *satis*, a poignant reminder of widowed queens who followed their husbands on the final journey to the royal cremation grounds at Devi Kund.

A ramp leads up through Karan Pol into a red sandstone court. The slender columns have shafts about fourteen metres in height cut from single stones. This court with its white marble pavilion set in a tank was probably inspired by the style of Fatehpur Sikri. The marble was brought from Makrana, north of Ajmer. Karan Mahal (1690), also on the south side, was influenced by Shah Jehan's Red Fort at Delhi and built to resemble its Divan-e-Aam, except that the *pietra dura* of the original is here replaced by fine paintings on polished plaster, as the desert kings could not afford the inlay of semi-precious stones in marble.

The elegant gallery and small enclosures of Phool Mahal, Flower Palace, and Chandra Mahal, Moon Palace, form part of the original living chambers of Rai Singh, but the delicate flower and trellis painted designs that cover the walls and ceiling of the former, and the inset mirror work of the latter, were carried out many years later by Maharaja Anup Singh (1674-98). All these living quarters face south, looking out on the public gardens and the city. This exposure ensured protection from the sun and caught the monsoon breezes.

Anup Mahal, a durbar hall of noble proportions, was built by Anup Singh who very likely was also responsible for completing the Karan Mahal begun by his father. This prince had been brought up almost entirely at the Mughal court and typified all that was best in the fusion of Mughal and Rajput cultures. He was commander of the fort at Aurangabad in the Deccan and appointed Governor of Adoni by the Emperor Aurangzeb. The most important ruler after Rai Singh, during his reign Bikaner became a refuge for painters, poets, musicians and scholars seeking the patronage which was denied them at Delhi because of Aurangzeb's puritancial outlook and increasingly bigoted policies. Anup Singh was a Sanskrit scholar and an astronomer, and added south Indian bronzes, Persian, Turkish and Deccani miniatures and a vast number of Mughal carpets and weapons to the royal treasury. Anup Mahal as conceived by him was a chaste, white marble pavilion. It was completely changed in character by a later ruler, Gaj Singh (1745-87), to suit his more opulent taste. The wall surface was covered with elaborate mouldings in the adhesive local clay, the raised designs picked out in gold on a painted crimson ground and the whole area varnished or lacquered. The fluted pillars and arches were coloured to match. A carpet in similar design and hues was woven by the craftsmen of Jaipur. The result is a rich, almost oppressive ornamentation which reveals the Rajput taste of the day.

During the gradual break-up of the Mughal Empire following Aurangzeb's death, the Rajput rulers of the Thaar enjoyed a period of greater independence. Freed from the restraints of the classic imperial style, their natural ebullience, and the more human and playful elements of the folk idiom began to reassert themselves. The former is seen in the lavishness of Anup Mahal and the extravagance of Gaj Mahal, where an elaborate gilded swing, one of the few items of personal furniture still on view, is typical of the uncontrolled love of glitter and ostentation. The folk elements are found in the charming painted panels of the doors of Sur Mahal, which depict intimate zenana scenes of queens and princesses, a refined expression of Rajput folk art.

Unfortunately the period of revival did not last long, and alien Western influences began to percolate into the desert kingdoms with the coming of the British. Chhattar Mahal, built by Dungar Singh (1872-87) is a roof-top pavilion with a tented ceiling painted like a canopy, bordered by a frieze of Raslila figures showing Krishna dancing with the gopis. The wall panels are set with English pottery tiles in imitation Chinese blue-and-white ware, a fashion favoured by the Victorians and adopted by the Rajputs during a period of confused cultural values and political uncertainty.

By the end of the 19th century, the labyrinthine pile of Junagarh with its Rajput-Mughal public halls and its maze of zenana apartments no longer served the purpose of the Bikaner court which had to conform to the requirements of a different era ushered in by the new rulers. Once more an adjustment in style and function had to be made. But this time there was no fusion. The foreign element was far too outlandish to mix. Maharaja Ganga Singh, brought up by British tutors and guided by Political Agents of the Raj, was a product of these influences. He built the new palace, Lalgarh, north of Junagarh, and abandoned the old palace. However, the retainers, descendants and dependents of former princes continue to reside in the old fort, which is now a protected monument.

Ganga Singh was a good example of a ruling prince during the period of the Raj. Intelligent and farsighted, he built hospitals and schools for his subjects, completed the railway link with Bikaner in 1912 and a couple of years later brought to the city the benefits of electricity and piped water. The Ganganagar Canal was started in 1927 during his reign. Cement-lined in its initial stages, this canal has now been extended to form the Greater Rajasthan Canal which, when completed will stretch right up to Jaisalmer and turn the area along its banks into a fertile granary.

Ganga Singh led the Concord of Princes at the Durbar in 1911, and signed the Treaty of Versailles on behalf of the Princes of India. He is still remembered with affection by the people of his state.

4 Jangaldesh: The Wilderness II

Baori Forest-dwellers: The Hunters Hunted

In a corner of the public gardens opposite the old fort stands a modest two-roomed building. This is the office of the Forest Department, and it could not have had a more appropriate setting than under the tall trees surrounded by well-trimmed lawns. We made our way there to obtain a permit to visit Gajner, the game sanctuary that lies 32 km west of Bikaner.

Walking into the enclosure, we were stopped abruptly by a horrifying sight. Propped up against the iron pailings, like crucifed victims, were the bleeding carcasses of a dozen freshly killed deer. A ferment of flies around the animals and the stench of putrefying flesh mocked the fragrant green of the manicured lawns. Two forest rangers stood on guard in front of the fence, and on the ground to one side was laid out as for military inspection an incredible armoury of sinister implements: a long, antiquated gun, slender and delicate to look at, bows and arrows; a malignant assortment of spears, chains, traps and tongs; a skillet; knives, choppers, ropes, bamboo poles and bundles of rags, all stained with blood, age and use. The deer had been slain by poachers, we were informed. Some had been shot, others trapped and brutally done to death. The corpses, we could see, were of animals recently slaughtered. The sight, revolting to all the senses at once, roused us to a frenzy of indignation.

One of the guards pointed to a corner behind the forest hut. There, twitching with fear, huddled together were the perpetrators of this macabre crime: two men, a woman with a babe in arms, and a little child of about three or four, who burrowed further into the tattered shreds of his mother's clothes to escape our gaze, and stared back at us with a bewildered look. I felt a helpless draining of emotion which left me weak with pity. Who could look at the butchered innocent creatures of the wild on the one hand, and the panic-striken, famished 'wretched of the earth' on the other, and dare to pass judgement? What should stir one's conscience more: the massacre of animals by people driven to despair by poverty, or the degradation of human beings by a callous society? For the confusion and terror of these dazed hunters seemed part of a familiar pattern of history, that filled one with shame and anguish at their predicament. At no time were the issues of the struggle for survival between man and animal more blatantly put than in the stupefying spectacle that confronted us.

The poachers were a family of Baoris, a forest people who eke out a miserable existence now that the depleted wooded areas in the desert are rapidly disappearing. During the time of the Raj the Baoris were one of the many groups lumped together by the British and administered under the Criminal Tribes of India Act. This Act covered communities that were ostracised by rural societies as 'untouchables', and possibly were of mixed tribal origin. They lived by anti-social practices such as theft or burglary. The regulations restricted their movement and controlled their activities. The Baoris of the desert claim Rajput descent, as so many castes in Rajasthan do, in an attempt to make a place for themselves in the rigid caste set-up. A suitably plausible and romantic legend is related to substantiate this claim.

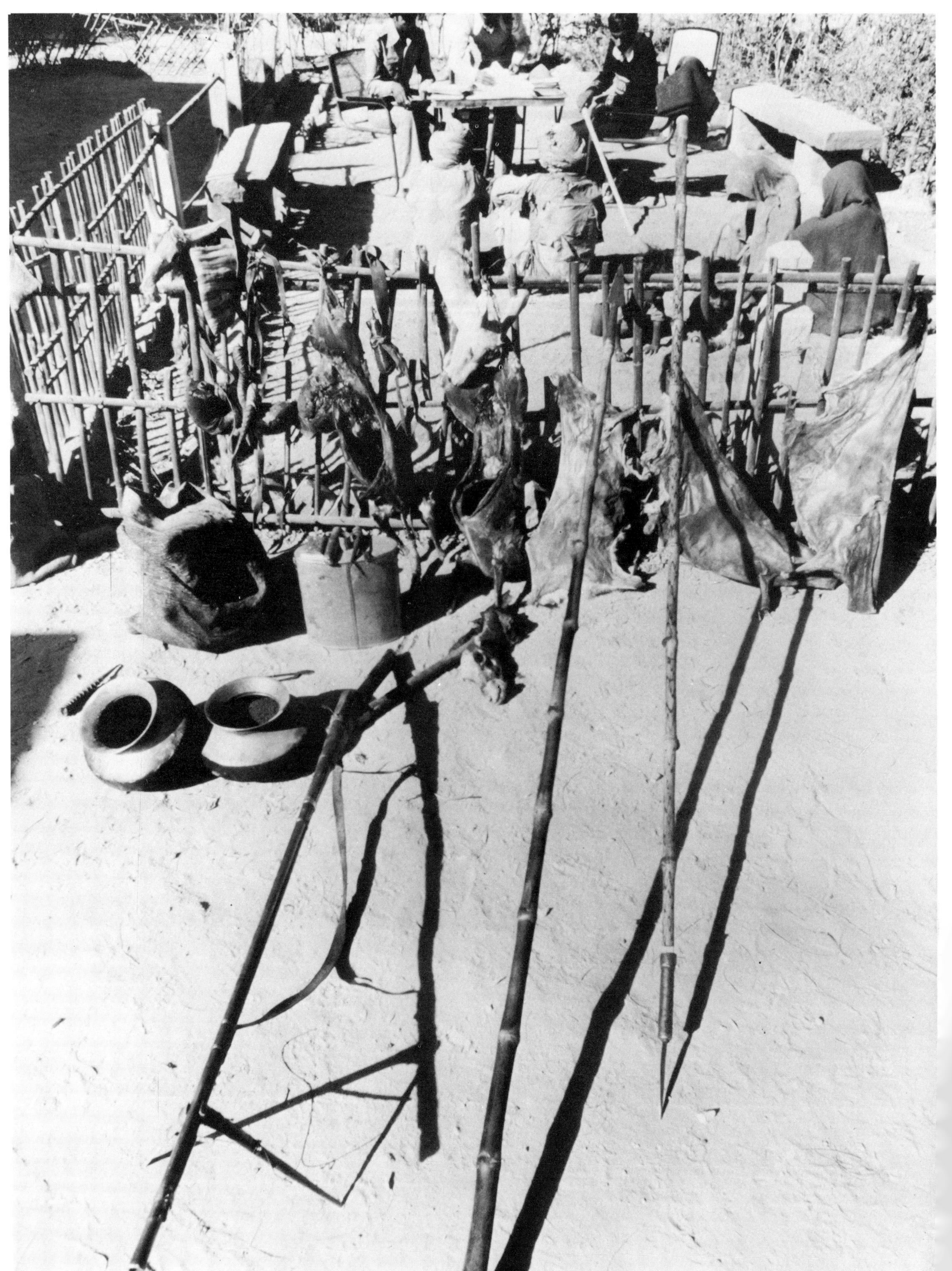

Poachers being interrogated

A long time ago, when the Mughals ruled at Delhi, a Rajput princess was travelling to the capital with an escort of armed guards to join the imperial harem. While passing through the desert on her journey, the princess got down at a tank to wash and refresh herself. While she was doing so, a Rajput girl from the neighbouring village came to fetch water. Meeting the princess and learning who she was, the village lass upbraided her for submitting to the shameful fate of concubinage in the harem of a Muslim ruler. Had she been in a similar situation, she declared, she would have preferred to kill herself rather than to have been the cause of such a stain on Rajput honour. The poor princess was so upset by the young girl's outburst, that she threw herself into the water and was drowned.

Alarmed by the suicide of the noblewoman entrusted to their care, the Rajput soldiers were too frightened to return to their home-town to convey the distressing news. Nor could they complete their journey to Delhi without their precious charge. The local villagers refused to have anything to do with the strangers. Compelled by these circumstances, the escort lived in the forest near the tank, and made their living by looting unsuspecting travellers and hunting wild animals. Because of this they were known as *Baoriwalas*, those who live by the *baori*, tank, or simply as Baoris.

On the basis of this legend the Baoris add the name of a Rajput clan to their own caste, and designate themselves, for instance, as Bhati Baori or Chauhan Baori. In the former state of Bikaner, the Baoris were found to be a very useful class of people, and were not treated as criminals. They were expert hunters and knew the forest region well, and so were employed by the princes as trackers, guides and beaters for the royal hunts organised by the rulers to entertain important guests. This practice was kept up till very recently, and invitations to the hunting parties of the Bikaner Maharaja were the most sought after of winter holidays among the Viceroy's entourage. Guests often included members of the British royal family.

The village people also found useful employment for the Baoris, retaining them as watchmen to guard their homes and fields on the principle of 'set a thief to catch a thief'. Because of this service they were called *chowkidars*, wardens. The Baoris performed their duties well, but only guaranteed to protect the village that employed them, and considered themselves free to burgle neighbouring hamlets with impunity. A clan would claim as its own, a particular territory of about ten to fifty villages. Within this area they were held responsible for any thefts that occurred and, if they were unable to trace the culprits, had to make good the loss. Any expeditions they conducted for nefarious purposes had to lie beyond the villages under their protection. The curious nature of their double life lent them the glamour that attaches to underworld heroes:

Hail! Baori brave,
bringing booty from afar,
rich and greatly feared.
We, your supplicants,
sing your praises.
Hail! Baori brave.

Since they are considered beyond the pale of caste society, Brahmin priests do not perform their religious ceremonies; these are conducted by Naths, a mendicant order. The Baoris are followers of Randevji, a medieval hero-saint, who did not believe in caste and so attracted Hindu, Muslim and 'untouchable' followers. The Baoris worship the mother goddess, Bechradevi, as their clan deity and, like many other low caste groups, bury their dead.

The Criminal Tribes Act has been abolished throughout India, and the Baoris are now designated as belonging to the Scheduled Castes. This change of name has not resulted in any improvement in their condition. In fact, in Jangaldesh where they performed many useful services, their economic and social position has deteriorated. Attempts have been made to settle them on land, and some families have adapted their way of life to the demands of agriculture under unrewarding desert conditions. In the village of Rangmahal, for example, there are ten Baori families that are now cultivators against whom no complaints of anti-social behaviour have ever been made. In Borunda village, there are some thirty Baori families. They are employed mainly as labourers in limestone quarries. But to supplement their earnings many Baoris resort to hunting rabbit, deer and other small game in the scrub around the villages. Their skill in trapping and hunting is unfortunately exploited by urban dealers who instigate them to poach. Deer of many species – *chinkara*, black buck, *nilgai*, the blue bull, the pelt of the desert fox, jackal and rabbit, and the skins of snakes and lizards are some of the items in demand by leather merchants and furriers. The risk is entirely that of the poor Baori, as the real culprits – the middlemen and traders – seldom get caught. The guards told us that the Baori will never reveal the identity of his employer even under 'third degree' methods of the police. The Baori will suffer a prison sentence willingly, so long as he can keep his urban contact a secret. For the connection can be maintained through another member of his family or group, whereas once a Baori has been known to betray his keeper, his source of income will be lost forever. When a woman is involved, her small children accompany her to prison.

The Baoris cannot understand why they should not be allowed to hunt wild animals, since hunting has been their legitimate occupation for centuries, towards which they have developed their skills. Nor do the settled, exacting occupations of agriculture or manual labour seem to them viable alternatives. The family we saw in Bikaner was patently impoverished,

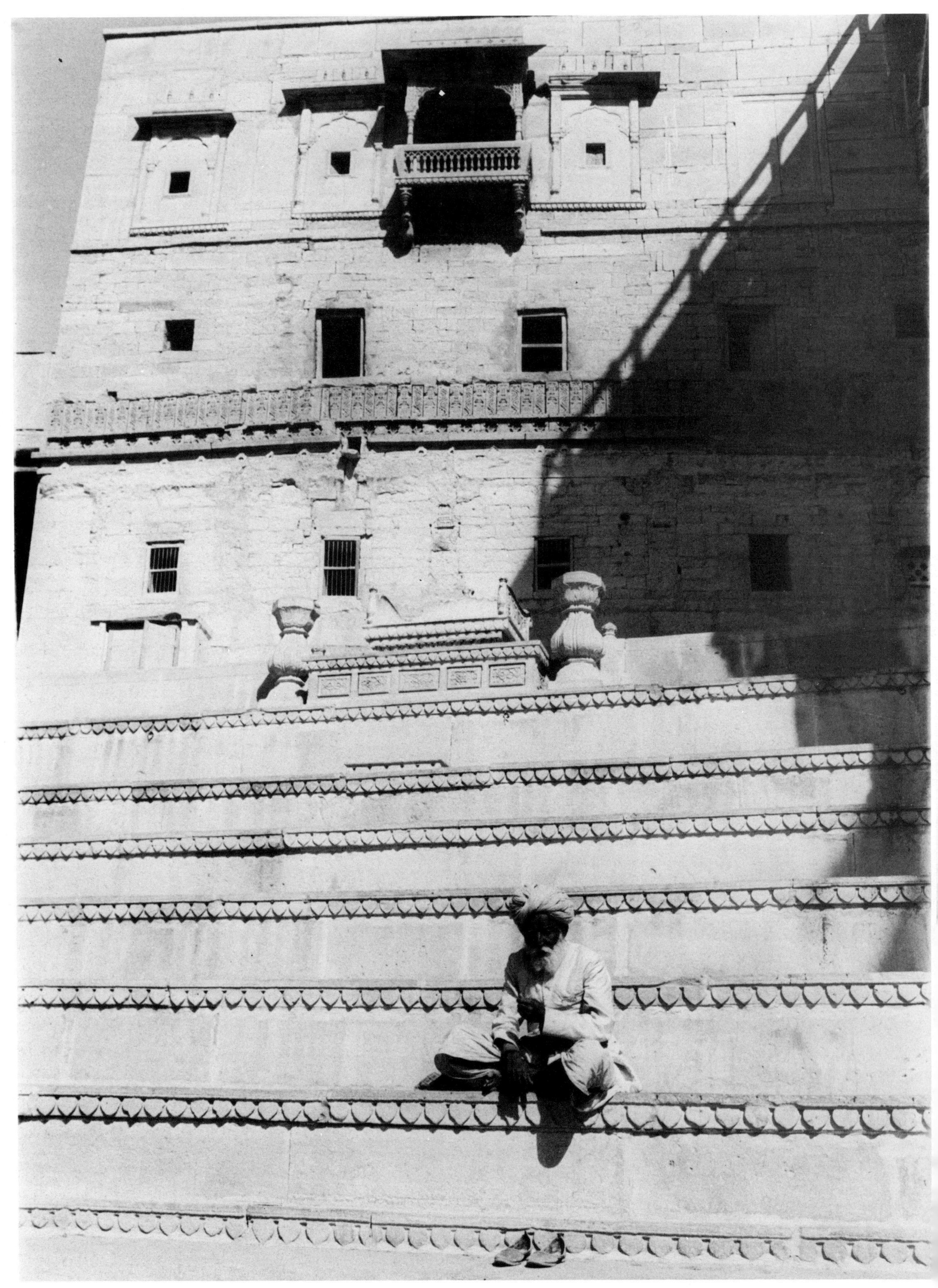

Marble throne in the Great Court, Jaisalmer Fort.

ignorant and devoid of any means to better its lot. A resort to their hereditary occupation, however risky, must seem to them the only solution in their frantic struggle for existence. In the meantime the illegal trade in skins and furs continues to flourish, and our wildlife is seriously threatened with extinction.

Interlude at Gajner

The hour of *bhairavi*. The dark of night had slipped away as the earth tipped imperceptibly towards the east. Overhead the stars flickered faintly in a sky robbed of its velvet richness. Birds murmured to themselves in the branches as they rustled out of sleep, giving hint of the first signs of daybreak – not yet, but soon. The chill, quiet air seemed to hold suspended those haunting minor notes of *bhairavi* that gently tug a cord of silk through the mind's listening ear.

The moment was lost in the cough and splutter of the reluctant engine as the jonga warmed up and we lurched out towards Gajner sanctuary, once the hunting preserve of the rulers of Bikaner. A herd of camels like appliqued silhouettes against the unfolding horizon, held us up as they loped across the road with casual disdain. Camels are not to be bullied by motor horns, nor to be hurried, nor deterred from their purpose. Cars, trucks and jongas must respect their right of way.

The bleak, stony ground gradually crumbled into soft reddish earth, and the terrain, no longer flat, was broken by small undulating mounds of rock and mud. The hard scrub and brush were interspersed with a few trees. the bristly *keekar*, the spirit-haunted *ber*, and the lugubrious *pilu*, relieved by the soothing green of *neem* and *peepal*. The presence of these large deciduous trees indicated a constant source of water. We were soon at Gajner.

Peacocks, tame as household pets, were pecking the grain that had been scattered for them around a shrine outside the sanctuary, while nimble-footed pigeons wove patterns around them. The drive led straight to the bereft hunting-lodge which had once echoed with the laughter and bustle of royal shooting parties. A tracery of tangled weeds whispered of prosperous times, long passed. Along the shallow steps large urns with drooping ferns stood in funerary silence.

The steps disappeared into the lake. The surface shimmered in cold ripples as a light breeze teased the water. A heron stalked past with priestly gait as we watched the ducks bob down for fish. From the farther bank the boom-boom of a crow-pheasant alternated with the thin high call of the pariah kite. Drongos and fly-catchers, like black and green paper darts, flashed low over the water, snapping up insects, and once a drongo dipped dangerously to scoop a drop from the lake.

We scanned the skies anxiously for Gajner's famous avian visitor, the Imperial Sand Grouse. By one of those unexplained miracles of nature, these winter migrants wing their way from distant arctic regions to make of this modest retreat their winter resort. The first flocks alight in late September, after the rains, and pack up for home in February or March, in time for the breeding season. The sand grouse is a game bird, and the Imperial Sand Grouse is said to please the most fastidious palate. Hence the popularity of the royal shoots at Gajner where success was gauged by the scale of slaughter inflicted by a single gun.

The grouse pay an early morning call at the lake and once again as the sun goes down, sheltering from the heat of the day among the bare rocks where their muted colouring blends into the background. In a folk song on the bird called *tilor*, the sand-grouse is described:

> *Her white and yellow flecked wings*
> *merge with the grass.*
> *She sits still as a dried-up cow-pat*
> *as Holva the hawk circles overhead.*

Grouse are at their most attractive in flight when their barred wings catch the sun. This distinctive feature must make them an easy target for hunters. We were held spellbound by several flocks which settled in front of us, and then we wandered into the woods beyond the hunting lodge.

In the small but thick jungle around the lake we came across wild boar, *nilgai* and *chinkara* within a few furlongs of the lodge. The birds were a delight. Friendly peacocks craned their necks for morsels; droves of wary partridge scuttled nervously as school children through the scrub; tree-pies trailed their long tails in and out of the low branches; blue and pied kingfishers swooped down on small fry in the shallows; hoopoes and woodpeckers in bristled concentration tap-tapped for grubs, and tiny sunbirds dazzled the eyes with iridescent flashes from their glossy wings.

We meandered slowly along the winding trails of the sanctuary to where the black buck roams free in the wide space cleft here and there by deep ravines. The herds in these parts are small. We did not see more than five or six does at a time, with a buck or two in attendance. At the Tal Chhappar Sanctuary where the open spaces are much more extensive, these herds are very large, often over fifty animals running together. The black buck is an exclusively Indian creature and is the most elegant of antelopes. The strong black and white mask gives it a dramatic appearance, and its spiralling horns, as long as the animal is tall, add a crowning touch of masculine virility. No wonder it became the symbol of the absent lover in those Rajput miniature paintings where a wistful young maiden is shown caressing a handsome buck or garlanding it with flowers. In poetry this creature is the confidante of the lonesome girl who pines for her lover and confides her secrets to her incelibate four-footed companion.

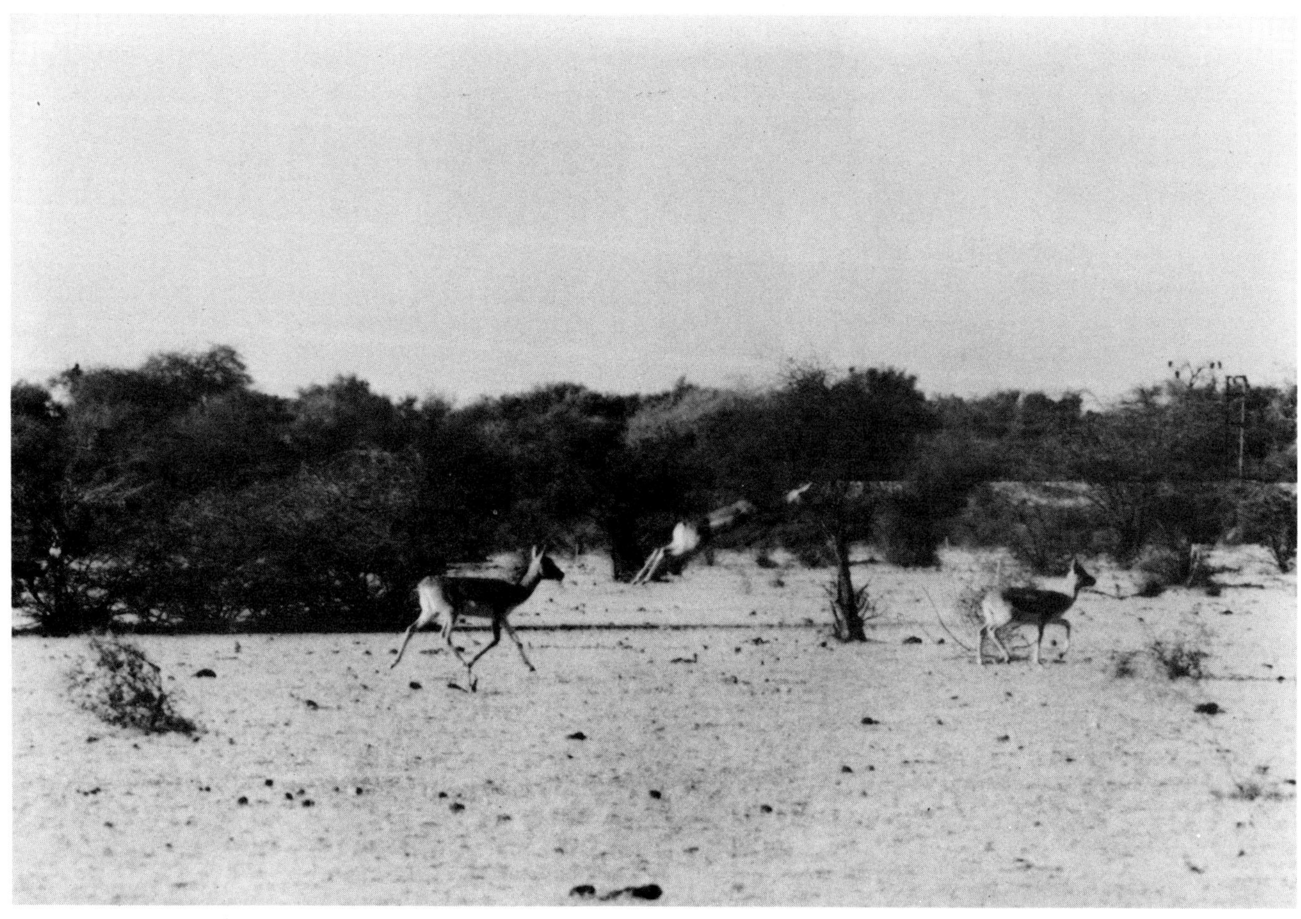

Leaping doe at Gajner sanctuary

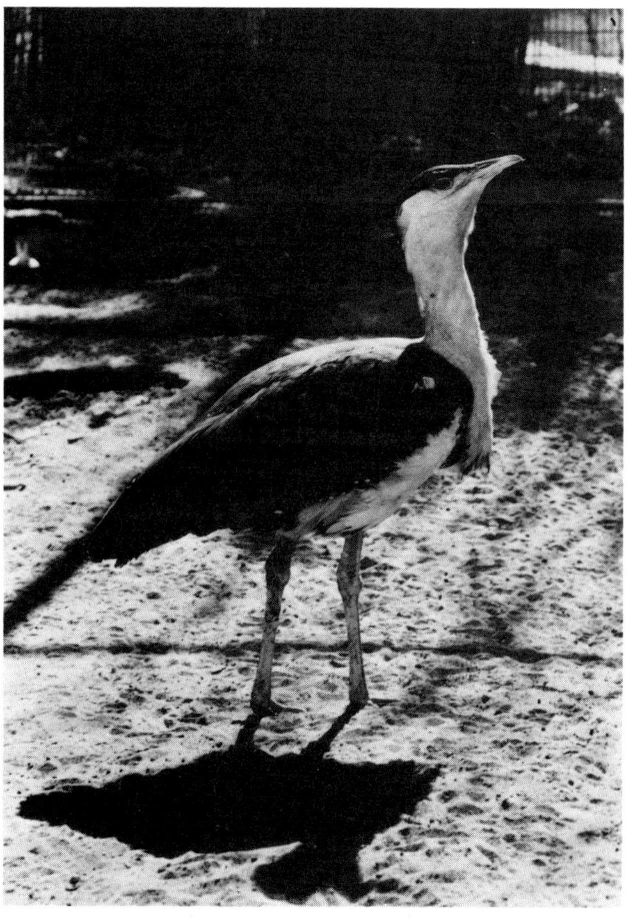

Great Indian Bustard

In former times the black buck was the quarry of the celebrated hunting cheetahs, trained to bring down this fleetest of long-distance runners of the antelope species. It is claimed that the black buck can attain a speed of sixty kilometres per hour and maintain it over a distance of ten kilometres without pause. Hooded and leashed, cheetahs used to be drawn in bullock carts accompanied by their trainers, and let loose close to a herd. Godfrey Charles Mundy, describing a cheetah hunt in 1827 in his *Pen & Pencil Sketches*, says that the carts carrying the cheetahs were drawn up within a hundred metres of a herd of deer. The swift cheetah could attain top speed almost at first bound. Many miniature paintings show these animals at a hunt. Cheetahs are now extinct in India, and if the black buck is to be found only in restricted numbers, that small blessing is due to the protection offered it by the Bishnoi community. It is not so much hunters that threaten the buck these days as the inexorable encroachment by human beings on its living space.

I had hoped, in vain, to catch a glimpse of the Great Indian Bustard in the wild. The only one we did see was a captive in the Bikaner gardens. These handsome birds stand about a metre in height and can weigh up to twenty kilogrammes. A desert dweller, the bustard feeds off grass seeds, insects, locusts, lizards and beetles and can survive on the sap contained in the long-stemmed *sewan* grass. Despite its size, it makes good eating, for which reason it has been consistently hunted by snipers who drive out in jeeps at dusk, when the birds emerge to feed. Although the bustard is a good runner, it stands no chance against motorised gunmen, and as a result is almost extinct. It is fully protected by law, but in the interior of the Thaar few laws are effectively enforced. In a touching Rajasthan folk song about the bustard, called *gooran*, the bird complains:

> *O ruthless man,*
> *why do you hunt me?*
> *I live in the jungle,*
> *but the hunter has found me.*
> *My heart beats fast.*
> *O hunter, leave me to my wild delights.*

In the same song, a young girl welcomes the *gooran*:

> *The* gooran *has arrived in my country;*
> *he has turned it into a land of song;*
> *he moves like a swan and sways like a deer;*
> *his eyes gleam in the night.*
>
> Gooran *has a beak like a writing quill;*
> *his head is like the bitter cucumber.*
> 'Gooran, *come to my home;*
> *my lover is away;*
> *like you he returns only in the rains.*
> Come to my home, O Gooran.
>
> '*Make a lovely sound with your splendid wings.*
> *I will put up a swing*
> *on the branches of a tree,*
> *and spread a carpet of berries*
> *for you to eat.*
>
> '*Gooran, the peacock has begun to sing* raga malhar;
> *the clouds of* bhadon *are thundering,*
> *and the lightning glitters.*
> Rain drops echo the strains of malhar.
>
> '*Come soon, O Gooran, and bring your friend* Tilor.
> *For with you will arrive my lover;*
> *for him I have spread the fresh green couch.*'

By a ravine we startled a desert fox out of its slumber. It was the mating season for foxes and in a gully some distance away, we surprised a courting couple who snarled at our rude intrusion before disappearing into the scrub. A wild boar snuffled up towards us, appraised the jonga with beady eyes and decided to give the hard-boned interloper a wide berth. We sat under some shady bushes to have a snack, but the torrid sun which had harried the jungle creatures into cover sent us sizzling home to Bikaner. On the way back, a camel lay sprawled across the road, quite dead. It had obviously been knocked down by a speeding truck that had not honoured the unwritten code of the desert, by which camels unquestionably have right of way.

Kathputli: the Puppet Play

'Peepeeha-peep-peep', the shrill whistle of the puppet-player welcomed us to our bungalow at Bikaner. With his tin trunk packed with his entire collection of dolls, he had come a long way to meet us. An early *Puranic* treatise tells of a young princess who, lonely in the cold marble splendour of the palace courtyards, created out of flowers and twigs, little dolls that moved and walked, talked and sang and even flew through the air at her bidding. These almost live companions, spun out the maiden's fantasies and filled her days with laughter.

This is perhaps one of the earliest textual references to puppets in India, which claims to be the original home of this art.

Puppet theatre in this country pre-dates human theatre proper and has bequeathed to it a significant term – *Sutradhara*, the 'manipulator of strings' who, according to the poetics of the classical Sanskrit drama, is the controller of a theatrical performance, initiator, conductor and commentator, like the Greek Chorus, and the vital link between actor and audience.

Shadow puppets, enormous, man-size leather figures in full colour, or more humble black-and-white affairs like medieval wood-cuts, rod and glove puppets in every conceivable medium, shape and dimension testify to an incredibly rich tradition of this art. But perhaps the best known are the marionettes of Rajasthan called *Kathputli*, and their popularity stems from the indefatigable enterprise of the nomadic puppeteers, the Barlai Bhaats of the Thaar.

My childhood memories sparkle with the excitement roused by these itinerant players when we heard their high, squeaking whistle in the streets of Lahore many years before Partition. They have reached the remotest regions of the sub-continent through the centuries. Fanny Parks saw a play of puppets and acrobats, in 1835, at the home of Colonel Gardner at Khasgange, near Allahabad. She was not impressed by the performance:

> A *putli-nach* was afterwards brought forward. I was surprised to see natives young and old so eager and fond of this absurdity, until Colonel Gardner said, 'The natives are madly fond of the *putli-nach*; it is all the English have left them of their former glory. You see, represented by puppets, Shahjahan and all his court and Durbar: one puppet is brought forward, and the manager, whilst it bows to the audience, relates the whole history of the minister whom it represents, giving a true account of his pedigree, riches, influence etc. At this moment, standing behind my chair, at a salary of four rupees a month, is a lineal

descendant of one of the first lords in the Court of Shahjahan. The managers of the show mix up infinite wit with their relation of events, and sarcasms on the English.' After this explanation, I could see the reason of the fondness of the old natives for this puppet-show, which before, in my ignorance, I had not comprehended. (Vol. I, p.394)

In 1837 Emma Roberts records in her *Scenes and Characteristics of Hindostan*:

The popular evening entertainment for children in Calcutta, juvenile balls not yet being established, is an exhibition of fantoccini which goes by the name of *kat pootlee nautch*. The showmen are of various grades and exhibit their puppets at different prices, according to the richness of their scenery and decorations. A large room in the interior is selected for the place of representation; a sheet stretched across between two pillars, and reaching within three feet of the ground, conceals the living performer from view; there is a back scene behind this proscenium, generally representing the exterior of a palace of silver, and the entertainment commences with preparations for a grand *durbar*, or levee, in which European ladies and gentlemen are introduced. The puppets are of a very grotesque and barbarous description inferior to the generality of Indian handy-works, but they are exceedingly well-managed, and perform all their evolutions with great precision. Sofas and chairs brought in for the company, who are seen coming to court, some on horseback, some on elephants, and some in carriages; their descent from these conveyances is very dexterously achieved; and the whole harliquinade of fighting, dancing, tiger-hunting, and alligator-slaying goes off with great eclat. The audience, however, forms the most attractive part of the spectacle. The youngest babies occupy the front row, seated on the ground or in the laps of their nurses, who look very picturesque in the Eastern attitude, half-shadowed by their long flowing veils; beyond these scattered groups, small armchairs are placed, filled with little gentry capable of taking care of themselves, and behind them, upon sofas, the mammas and a few female friends are seated, the rest of the room being crowded with servants, male and female, equally delighted with the *baba logue* at the exploits of the wooden performers. (Vol I, p.328)

These two accounts written within two years of each other, about a hundred and fifty years ago, together give a fairly accurate description of the *Kathputli*. The show staged in Colonel Gardner's home seems to have conformed closely to the original play, which is actually about a Rajput prince, Amar Singh Rathor of Nagaur, idealised as the epitome of Rajput chivalry and valour, who served at the court of the Mughal Emperor, Shah Jehan. The audience at this party being mainly Indians and including members of noble Muslim families, the *Sutradhar* seems to have concentrated on Mughal characters.

In the second account, the clever puppeteer cunningly adapted his play to suit the taste of the English *baba logue* and their fond mammas. He concentrated on sub-plots and incidental comic scenes between stock characters, which form part of a regular performance, and which are introduced as interludes between larger scenes of the main plot of the historical legend. The English types were innovations to suit the occasion. Like the similar characters found in the wall-paintings at Shekhawati, these were often incorporated into the various folk forms during the period of the Raj. Being irrelevant today, they are no longer included in the cast of the puppet play.

The wooden marionettes that Emma Roberts considered 'grotesque' are actually highly stylised figures, and their faces, with large accentuated eyes and bold features, conform to the genre of the folk paintings of the region. The dolls, from about 30 to 45 cm in height, have heads carved from the wood of the local *rohira* tree – a heavy, insect-resisting wood that is hard-wearing. Puppets in many collections have been handed down from father to son for several generations. The body is made of stuffed cloth, and has arms but no legs. The sumptuous costumes cover the trunk and trail down over the part where the lower limbs should be. The arms have jointed shoulders, elbows and wrists; the head can move horizontally and vertically, and the manipulator can control the movements of these flexible parts in many combinations and variations. The feats of jousting warriors on horseback, or the pirouettes and seductive gestures of court-dancers reveal technical accomplishment of the highest order. Some minor characters do have legs, being for all practical purposes rag dolls, capable of no more than simple up and down movements, like that of the drummer boy who strikes his drum in either a standing or seated position.

In the past the Barlai Bhaats travelled with their families on foot, their bundles of puppets and a few utensils being loaded on donkeys. They would set up a little tent on the village maidan, and erect the stage with a pretty arched proscenium decorated with bold and effective appliqué, usually red and blue motifs on a white background, called the Taj Mahal. The sound of the shrill whistle 'peepeeha-peep-peep' along with a rousing beat on the drum would draw a crowd. Lately the painted tent and arched proscenium have been discarded as being too expensive to maintain, and the puppeteer makes do with a couple of string cots borrowed from a village household. These are stood up vertically and a plain sheet is hung between

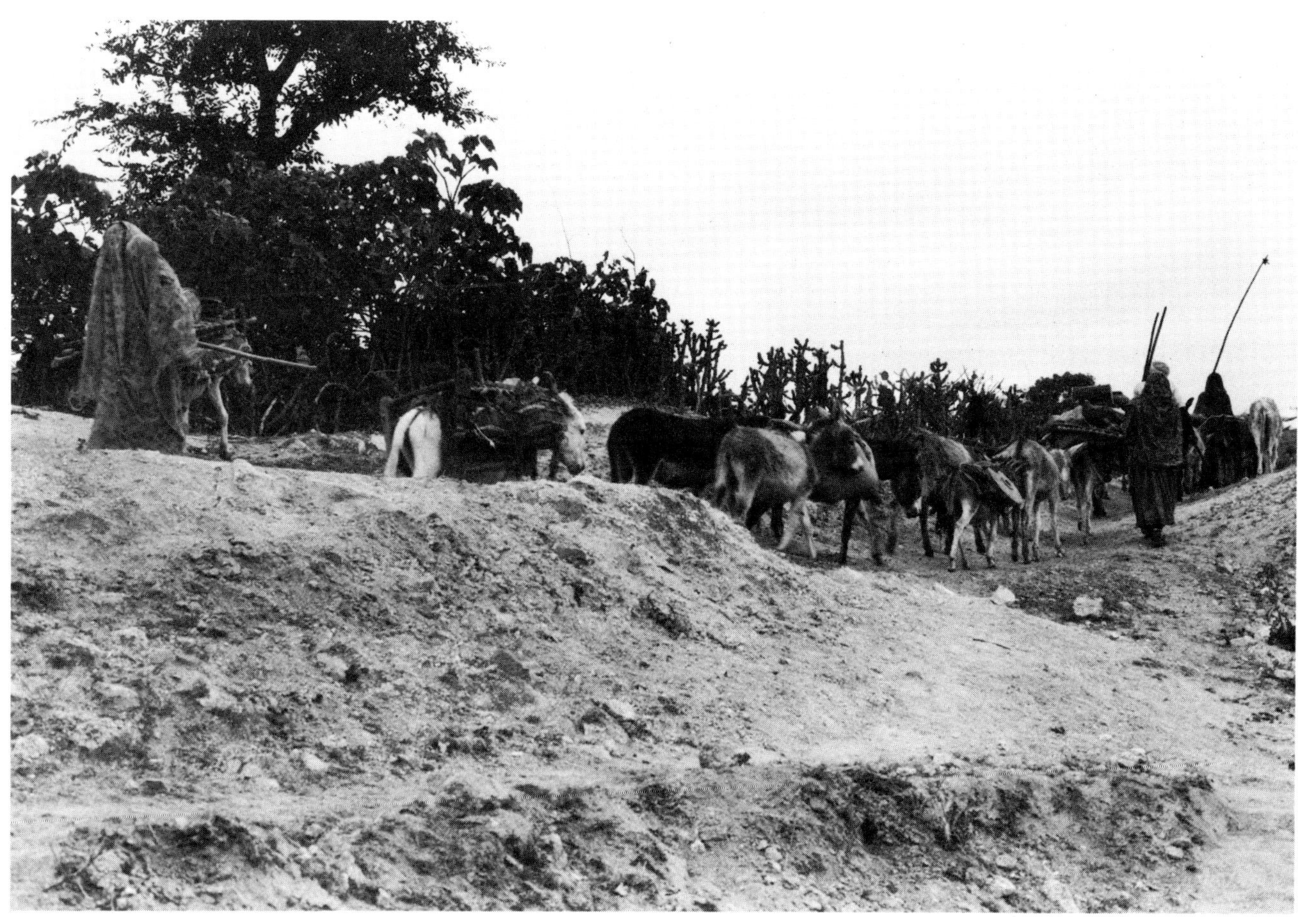

Crossing the desert

them. Hurricane or petromax lanterns illumine the show. Most puppeteers have now no more than a dozen dolls in their collection as the art of carving the dolls has grown increasingly rare; the *rohira* wood and costumes too are beyond the means of the average family. The full set of puppets is of thirty-two characters and ranges from elaborately decked out kings, queens and heroes to clowns and stock characters and, further down the scale, to animals and reptiles.

The story of Amar Singh Rathor is the only one now performed in the repertoire of the Barlai Bhaats. Whether this was always so one cannot tell. Amar Singh was a prince of Jodhpur, son of Raja Gaj Singh who ruled Marwar (1620-38) during the time of the Emperor Shah Jehan. Amar Singh was heir to the Jodhpur throne. A valiant soldier, he had proved successful in many battles, but his rash and arrogant temperament caused great offence to many powerful chieftains who were vassals of the Rathor court. His younger brother, Jaswant Singh, also a seasoned warrior, combined martial prowess with tact and courtesy. He ingratiated himself into the favour of Angooribai, his father's favourite mistress, who wielded influence with the Raja. At the Jodhpur Palace Museum a pair of jewelled slippers that belonged to this courtesan are preserved. Legend has it that these were offered to the lady by the ambitious Jaswant Singh who humbly knelt to place

the slippers on the feet of the woman who could help him place a crown upon his head. He succeeded in getting her to plead his case with the Raja, and when Amar Singh, having got involved in a fracas, was once again in disgrace, Raja Gaj Singh denied him the right of succession and pronounced the sentence of exile on him. He was banished from Jodphur, but given the fief of Nagaur, and Jaswant was proclaimed heir-apparent. Amar Singh thereupon went to the court of the Mughal emperor who employed him in the imperial service.

Here the same imprudent and haughty temper that had lost him his birthright brought about his tragic end. In the Divan-e-Khas at Agra Fort, in the presence of his sovereign, he slew Salabat Khan, Shah Jehan's exacting paymaster-general, and in his blind rage made to strike at the royal person. But his sword struck a pillar and was shattered. He ran amok, maddened as he undoubtedly was by opium, and with his dagger brought down five Mughal noblemen before he was himself killed by his brother-in-law, Arjun Singh Gaur of Bundi. His wife, the Bundi princess, came to Agra to cremate his body and mounted his funeral pyre as *sati*. A mark on a pillar in the Divan-e-Khas is pointed out to visitors as the place where his sword struck. The south gate of the fort is known as 'Amar Singh's Gate'.

Amar Singh became a legend and a people's hero during his lifetime. His death at the imperial court only

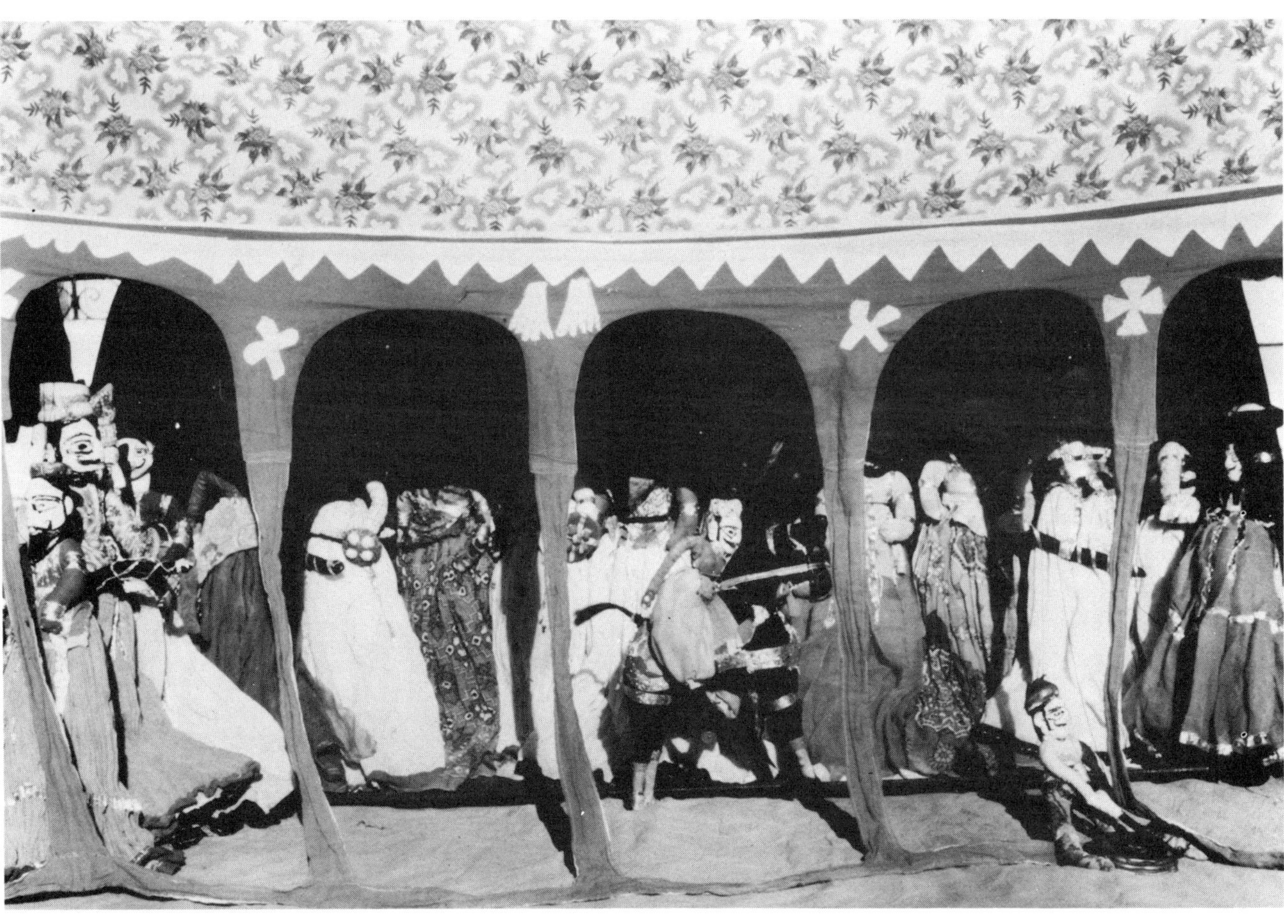

Kathputli puppets: string marionettes

enhanced his prestige in the eyes of the common folk who celebrated him in remembrance as a martyr to Rajput honour. Many forms of traditional theatre enact plays based on his exploits and tragic death.

The performance of *kathputli* hinges on episodes from this story. But its more entertaining scenes are the interludes in which the stock characters appear. We watched the quarrelsome couple *dhobi-dhoban*, washerman and his wife, indulge in another bout of their perpetual conjugal battle, but when the court *durban*, watchman, interfered, with a suggestive leer at the woman, she, true to her marriage vows and provoked by this insult to her virtue, felled him with a single blow, immediately turning to squash her husband's gleeful reaction with a smart rap: one must not let one's menfolk get out of hand.

Jogi-jogan, wandering mendicants, predicted the fortunes of passers-by and promised them the stars above while skilfully picking their pockets below. At this the drummer-boy beat his drum in an excess of zeal and stuck a *bidi*, hand-rolled tobacco leaf, in his mouth, puffing smoke rings at the delighted children in the audience. An inept snake-charmer lost his snake, creating pandemonium among the courtiers and ladies, till the *chobdar*, herald, restored order with his pompous proclamation, announcing the arrival of His Imperial Majesty, and all in the durbar bowed low before his royal presence.

These stock-characters ridicule present-day customs and attitudes, and with satiric comment, point to the social ills that affect the lives of the people. Or, at least, this was their purpose. Unfortunately in recent decades there has been little effort to up-date such acts effectively, and there are few contemporary references in the current staging of Rajasthani puppets. This function has been taken over by the films and television, while the traditional purveyors of mass entertainment have clung on to the faded glamour and tinsel of historical romance.

In the summer of 1980 a troupe of Barlai Bhaat puppeteers was invited to an international festival of puppetry in Washington. They were overwhelmed by the technical advances in the art, as they saw them in performances of troupes from the United States, the U.S.S.R., Czechoslovakia, Japan and Australia. Many of these were stupendous displays of expertise in mechanical devices, computerised lighting and music effects, stunningly beautiful sets and costumes, and sophistication of themes and narrative techniques. What the Bhaats had to offer in return was a glimpse of the beginnings of the art of puppetry: a simple village entertainment, the itinerant family of puppeteers setting up their tent on the village green, while the shrill 'peepeeha-peep-peep' summoned the rural folk to a show of the dancing dolls. The exchange was touching and meaningful, and perhaps a revelation to both.

The Miracle Men of Nokhamandi

The harvest moon of auspicious Kartik had dwindled and died. Now, till the fine, chiselled crescent showed itself again and rounded into the cold, full face of the Agrahayana moon, a bleak, unpropitious period would ensue. We had chosen the wrong time to travel into the hinterland of the desert. No weddings could be solemnised, no ceremonies performed, no rituals take place during the *andher paksh*, the dark half of the month.

Vivek was disappointed. There would be no *barat*, marriage procession; no gaudy *toran*, tinsel paper decorations hung over doorways on festive occasions, no boisterous revelry to liven his day's work, and break the monotony of 'shooting' forts, temples, palaces – monuments mostly empty of life and many in ruins. Nor would we come across those inscrutable, somewhat sinister, rituals taking place around the frequent wayside shrines that are found on the outskirts of villages, or standing in primeval stillness under the protective shade of a *peepal* tree.

On an earlier trip Vivek had accompanied Kothari to the sacred fair at Pushkar near Ajmer, held during the *ujala paksh*, the bright half of the month of Kartik (November). They had gone on to many neighbouring places in search of shrines along the byways. It had been an exciting venture. He had witnessed strange rites in which the *bhopa*, oracle, invoked the spirit of the deity which entered his body, seen the exorcising of spirits by god-men in trance, and the amazing cures effected by them. He had not only watched these scenes with a mixture of awe and incredulity, but he had photographed them. However, we were to have no such luck now, because during the *andher paksh*, we were informed, the deities could not be summoned.

Driving to Dashnoke, a few kilometres out of Bikaner, to visit the temple of Karni Devi, titular head of the rulers of Bikaner, we learnt that further on, at Nokha, there was a practising *bhopa* who might be of interest to us. Would he perform during this unfavourable half of the month? We were doubtful, but decided to take our chance.

Outside Nokha, which is the familiar nondescript mofussil city one finds in the districts, we were directed to Nokhamandi, the neighbouring grain market. The mean streets soon opened into bracing countryside, and neat village huts replaced the squalid brick and asbestos constructions of the urbanised township. The approach of our jonga stirred a cluster of clamorous urchins who sprang out of the dust, like mushrooms after a sudden shower, and escorted us to the hut of the *bhopa*. He was surprisingly a high-caste Rajput. *Bhopas* can belong to any caste, since they are individuals who have the gift of direct communion with spirits or gods, a power not confined to any particular caste or community. To our dismay we found our miracle-man racked with a cough and laid up in bed, divine connections notwithstanding. But word had spread of the intriguing nature of our visit, and within minutes a friendly official offered to take us to a settlement of Bhil tribals in another part of the city. They were said to have a renowned *bhopa* in their midst. But luck continued to be against us, and the Bhil *bhopa* was away at a nearby village to perform a rite of exorcism for a sick woman. But we had been able to glean one significant piece of information: namely, that such rites were indeed taking place, even during this dark period.

We were about to turn back to Bikaner when we were led on to a Meghwal colony at the farther end of Nokhamandi. Here our luck turned and, though at first reluctant to meet us, the *bhopa* finally made his appearance and agreed to perform for a modest fee. Actually, mistaking our station-wagon for a police jeep, he had hidden himself in a haystack when he saw it draw up. But our unofficial status having restored his faith, he asked us to return at sundown, an hour later, to enable him to get his group together and make the necessary preparations.

Night falls with disconcerting abruptness in the desert after the sun has set and the temperature registers a sharp drop. The deep purple-black canopy of the sky sparkled with stars. We sat by the fire that had been lit in front of the shrine to Kalika Devi, deity of the Meghwai *siddhnaths*, to whom the night's performance was dedicated. The musty, acrid odour of smouldering cow-dung cakes hung in the air about us. *Siddhnaths* are those who have developed certain mystic or psychic powers through ritual practices consecrated to their presiding deity.

Lunaraiji Meghwal was the chief *siddhnath bhopa*. Bone-lean and tall, his deeply furrowed face looked like a hurried artist's sketch drawn with bold strokes. The features stood out strongly, without the niggling effects of detail. He was dressed in a full-length pleated coat of scarlet muslin over his everyday garments, with a belt of large round bells about his waist, while small bells, *ghungroo*, circled his ankles. He claimed to be of the seventh generation in his family of performing *bhopas*. His son, a young man in his twenties, was his chief assistant.

The evening began with a prayer to Kalika Devi, and an invocatory hymn of praise. Five men played on drums. Attracted by their call, a crowd of men and boys from the neighbourhood gradually collected. Lunaraiji then installed a huge metal *trishul*, trident of Lord Shiva, in front of the shrine.

The drumming built up to a vibrant crescendo in rapid tempo. The drummers sang as the *bhopa* took up a sword and, dancing before the shrine, dedicated it to the goddess. His son, one of the drummers, now stepped forward, seized the sword, unsheathed it, swung it menacingly above his head, and swiftly drew its sharp edge against his tongue while he knelt on the sand. Blood trickled down the side of the sword, to the audible horror of the spectators. Vivek's camera

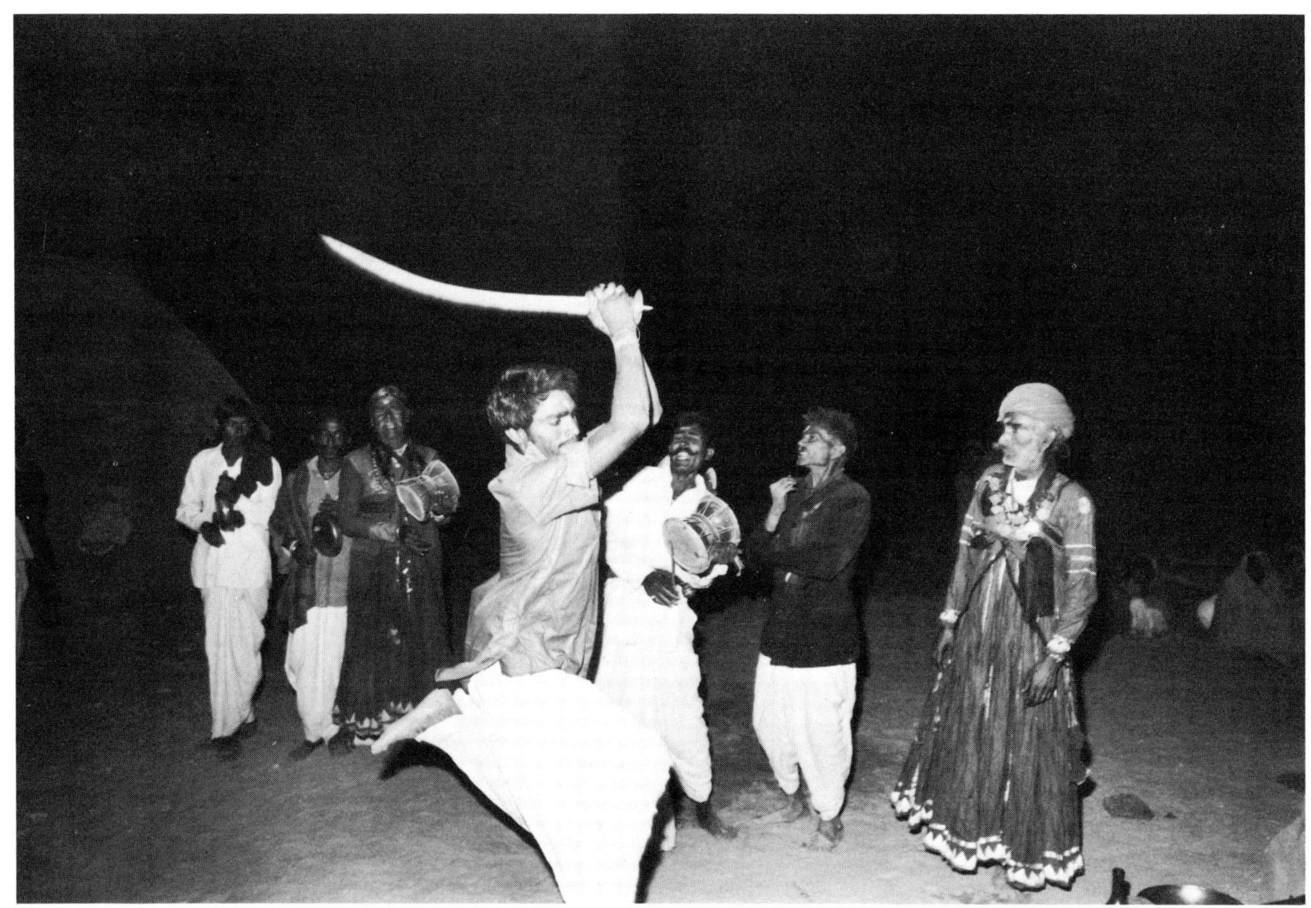

Warming up for daring feats

Lunaji bhopa piercing himself with a trident

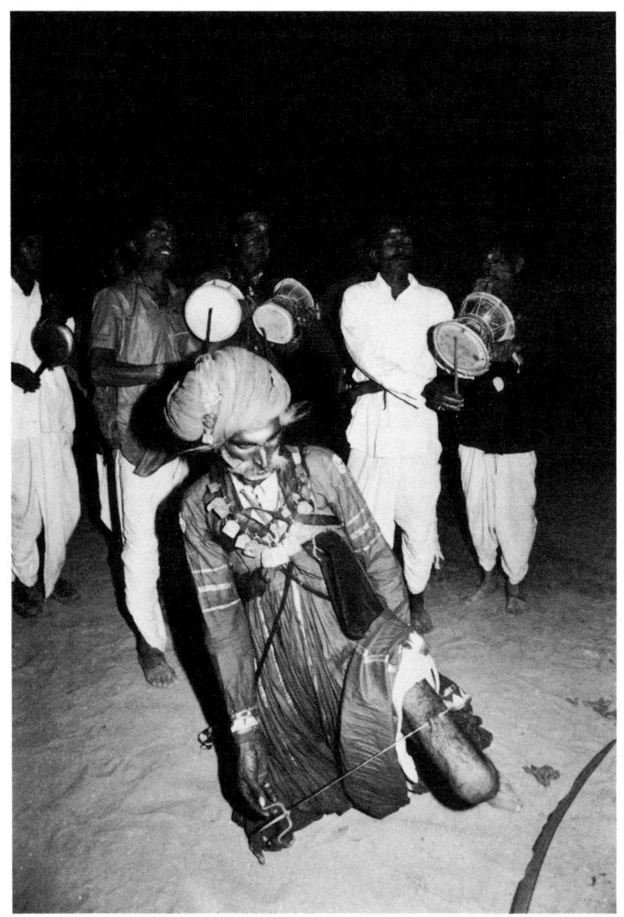

clicked and flashed and clicked again. I turned my eyes away, sickened at the spectacle. Then with almost casual nonchalance, the young man raised the sword, ceremoniously placed it near the *trishul*, rejoined the drummers, and took part in the playing and singing as before.

Now Lunaraiji stepped forward and suddenly spun around in a series of whirling turns that set the pleats of his red coat flying around with such force that he appeared to be surrounded by a circle of fire. Then with a quick flick of the wrist he snatched up the sword without losing momentum and, still spinning, gyrated into the centre of the arena. Two men now moved out of the circle of drummers, and knelt on either side of Lunaraiji. He stopped in the middle of a turn and handed them the sword. They held it at each end, the razor edge facing upwards. Luna turned about, mounted on the sword, steadying himself with his hands on the shoulders of the two men. They got up, and Luna stood upright, his full weight now pressing on the blade, arms outstretched to maintain his balance. In the glow of the fire and the dim oil lamps, the erect, wiry figure of the *siddhnath* in the red coat, with widespread arms, looked like a monstrous totem effigy suddenly come alive to the rhythmic throb of the pounding drums.

Feats, each more daring than the last, followed in rapid succession. Luna swallowed a double-edged, whip-thin rapier; he pierced his tongue with a sharp knife; he tossed burning embers into his mouth as though they were delectable sugar-candy. And the son in his turn dusted his hands with ash, picked red-hot chains strung on an iron ring out of the fire of crackling dung cakes. He dipped the chains in a cauldron of oil, making them sizzle and blaze even more furiously, Then dog-like, on all fours, he opened his mouth and seized, one after the other, a series of white-hot iron spheres, each the size of a cricket ball. An intense concentration cast its spell on the performers.

A youth took up a short-handled trident and pierced his cheeks with it. Lunaraiji thrust a sword through his thigh; an elderly *bhopa*, also dressed in a flowing red robe, danced ecstatically round the small arena with a flaming iron ring that bound his head.

Between these acts of endurance and self-inflicted torture, the performers sang, played on the drums, and danced before the shrine. It was difficult to restrain the excited children from falling into the fire as they pushed forward to get a closer look. The women who had gathered imperceptibly formed a group on the farther side, and their acute cries of fascinated horror punctuated the performance.

The show lasted for almost three hours. Finally, with a prayer in praise of Kala Bhairoji, another local deity, it came to a close. A tray of sugar comfits was passed round the audience as *prasad*, blessed offering.

It was nearing midnight when we started the drive back to Bikaner. We were tense, deeply disturbed, our nerves taut. Not even the friendly farewell of *bhopaji* could dispel the sense of uneasiness that gripped us. What we had witnessed was surely not a mystic rite. Nor was it a magician's sleight-of-hand show. As far as we could judge, it had been a straightforward, highly skilled professional performance, by men who must have spent years in perfecting their acts. None of the performers had actually been in a trance, for although the evening had begun with an invocation to the goddess, it was apparent that the men were alert, concentrated and completely in control of themselves. They had performed 'cold', as we were unable to provide them the warm comfort of even a tot of local brew, since Nokha was a 'dry' area, and the Meghwals were not willing to run the risk of drawing any untoward attention to themselves. They were already embroiled in an unpleasant dispute over the land on which their settlement was situated, and this was probably the reason why the *bhopa* had hidden in the haystack when our vehicle stopped outside his hut.

How then were they able to perform such feats and remain unscathed? Lunaraiji's leg showed no trace of wounds; no blisters covered his son's hands which grasped those blazing chains, nor were his teeth damaged by the red-hot iron balls. He had sung as lustily as the others immediately after slashing his tongue with the razor-sharp sword, and when the second old *bhopa* had danced with the flaming ring round his head, his companions had jokingly remarked 'The live-stock will have to find a new home now', (referring to lice) and he had joined in the laughter against himself.

Our reaction to the performance was difficult to analyse. Apart from being overwhelmed by the incredible skill and endurance of the performers, the nature of the feats had created in us a sense of uneasiness and revulsion we could not easily dispel. Relief was sought in discussion. The visual immediacy had to be smothered in a flurry of words. Speech lent distance to events witnessed in spell-bound silence; it sought to rationalise the incomprehensible; it strove to grasp through the mind what had bludgeoned the senses.

In purely theatrical terms it had been a masterly show. The commanding figures of the two elderly *bhopas*, in their vivid red coats, with bells on their person and heavy ornaments about their arms and necks, had dominated the arena. The grave invocation, the ceremonial installation of the menacing trident, the opening crescendo of staccato drums, all had contrived to create an atmosphere of heightened suspense and expectancy. The manly poise and confidence of the performers; the smooth, uninterrupted flow of act into dance into drumming maintained a current of contact between actor and audience. An occasional casual remark or humorous exchange eased the tension before it became unbearable. Then the insistent drums built it up once more for the next climactic feat.

I was doubtful whether the technique of dramatic presentation had been deliberately planned and executed. It all seemed so spontaneous and effortless as to discount any possibility of conscious design. The pattern was obviously the result of generations of practice. The stark and naked power of the performance held attention in a vice, while the blood-letting invested it with an air of sacrificial ritual.

How or why the feats had acquired their peculiarly violent and disturbing elements was uncertain. The performing *bhopas* as a class were said to possess *shakti*, an inner power or strength bestowed as a mark of grace by the goddess Kalika Devi, whom they venerated. Under her protection they believe they can suffer no harm, neither by fire nor from sharp weapons. The acts were perhaps a demonstration of this divine grace.

Radha in the Wilderness

Mere chance took us to our first desert fair. Driving from Bikaner to Nokha, we had to slow down to allow a stream of camel carts to cross over to a rutted track that led into the wild. A thin stooped figure approached; the pinched looks and myopic eyes peering through thick spectacles proclaimed the 'village schoolmaster' even before he introduced himself, asked if we were going to the fair and, if so,

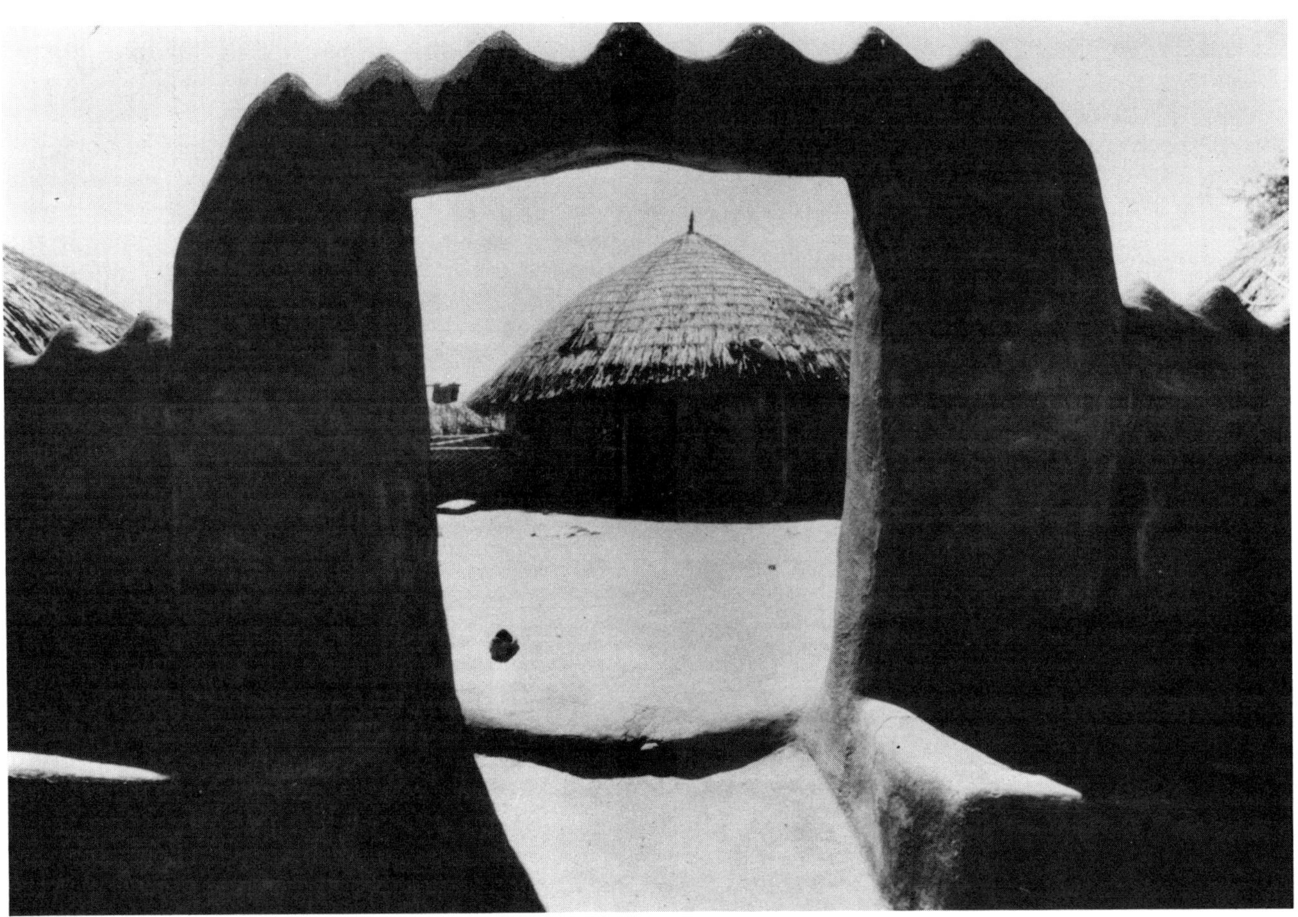

Fort-like entrance to a Bishnoi desert homestead

would we give him a lift. This was the first we had heard of the fair, but we assured him that it was indeed our destination and he would be very welcome as our guide.

We joined the slow moving carts at the end of the queue, and, eager to match up to his new vocation, our hitch-hiker poured out an incessant flood of information. We discovered that we were on our way to Mukam, burial place of the 15th century religious reformer, Jambeshwarji, the revered saint of the Bishnoi community. Much of what we were told by our loquacious companion was later confirmed by official sources.

According to the Political Administration Report of the Rajputana States of 1875-76, Jambeshwarji, or Jambhaji as he is more popularly called, was born at Peepasar village near Bikaner in 1451, of Rajput parents of the Panwar clan. The boy was deaf, and as this precluded a martial career, he used to work as his father's herdsman. He displayed miraculous powers when still quite young. One day while Rao Duda of Merta was passing through Peepasar after he had lost Merta in a battle, he came across Jambha who with a sign of his hands would call his cattle to the well to drink by turns. Impressed by this peformance, the Rao followed Jambha who had led off his herd, but although the Rao was on horseback he found he could not overtake him. Dismounting, Duda approached the herdsman on foot and caught up with him. He saluted

him with reverence and asked the young man to bless him and help him retrieve his lost kingdomn. Jambha who had so far been dumb, now spoke, blessed the Rajput, and gave him a piece of wood roughly in the shape of a sword, as a talisman. Duda left, and won back Merta. Jambha was now acknowledged as a saint.

In the same year, 1486, there was a great famine in Bikaner, and the Jat peasants were preparing to migrate, but Jambhaji told them that if they became his followers, he would protect and provide for them. This group formed the first disciples of the saint. He taught them the twenty-nine principles from which the sect derives its name: *Bis* – twenty, *noi* – nine. These included reverence for all forms of life, monogamy, complete abstinence from liquor, tobacco and opium, and also such enlightened practices as the preservation of trees, and the filtering of water before use for drinking or washing. He forbade the gelding of bulls, a very cruel procedure in those times, and, under the influence of Islam, decreed burial for the dead. Children were to be buried near the threshold of the homestead, an early Central Asian practice.

The saint accepted converts from all religious communities and castes. He dug a tank near Phalodi and founded a village called after him. But he died at a place near Peepasar where he had gone to preach. Although he had expressed a wish to be buried at

Jambha, his disciples interred him where he had passed away, at the village known as Mukam, 'abode'. A shrine has been built over the grave which is a place of pilgrimage, a fair being held anually on the 15th of the dark month of Chaitra (March). And this we were now going to attend.

The schoolmaster recounted an interesting legend concerning the relations of the Rathors of Bikaner with Jambhaji. Rao Bika, founder of Bikaner, went to pay his respects to the saint who blessed him and prophesied a rule of four hundred and fifty years for his dynasty. Rao Bika reported this to his uncle, Kandhal. The senior Rajput was not pleased and went himself to Jambhaji to demand an explanation. The saint was in meditation when the Rao arrived. The impatient Rajput pushed the brazier of incense towards the saint to rouse him from his reverie. Jambhaji opened his eyes, beheld the Rao, understood the purpose of his visit and murmured, 'Take fifty years, more or less, but of trial and tribulation,' and promptly withdrew into meditation. Curiously enough it was in 1459 that Bika and Kandhal set about conquering Bikaner. By the Instrument of Accession, the princes of Indian states agreed to merge their principalities into the Republic of India, and the state of Greater Rajasthan was inaugurated in March 1949. The Rathors, the schoolmaster declared with belligerent triumph, had held Bikaner ten years short of the prophesied period.

The Bishnois later developed into a sect which no longer was open to converts. They still follow extremely strict rules, and do not accept food or water from any other caste, nor do they marry into any other community. With time the Quranic insertions in their marriage ceremony have been dropped. They worship Jambhaji as an incarnation of Lord Vishnu, but remain distinct from other Vaishnavite Hindus. According to our guide the Bishnois were secretive and exclusive in their habits. This was because originally they followed the Scythian practice of the priest-stud who had access to every married woman, but was sacrificed after a set period, in a fertility rite. This last revelation evoked in me a response of startled disbelief. I have not been able to verify this piece of information, and it may well be a misrepresentation of the Bishnois by caste Hindus who resent the distance maintained by this non-conforming group.

Strict vegetarians, the Bishnois have been responsible for preserving the wild life of their region. The deer is sacred to them, as are birds, and in territory where hunting and hawking were major pastimes of ruling princes, their determined stand against the slaughter of all forms of wildlife was respected even by those inveterate hunters, the Rajputs. The *khejra*, a tree common in the desert, is held sacred by the Bishnois, as its flower and fruit are used for food in times of famine, and its leaves and bark are fed to cattle.

A grant by Maharaja Takhat Singh of Jodhpur dated 1844 states

> 'It is hereby ordered that in the villages of the Bishnois, cutting of Khejra within the limits of these villages in banned. Shikar (game) is also prohibited. If anyone cuts green Khejra or plays (sic!) Shikar he shall be punished by the State.'

In the recent past, an Arab sheikh was granted permission by the local government to hunt that rare bird, the Great Indian Bustard. A public outcry throughout the country forced the administration to withdraw the sanction. The Bishnois, however, were wise ecologists long before it became fashionable to be so.

The shrine of the saint is an unpretentious, double storeyed, whitewashed building on a mound around which the camel carts had gathered. We were swept up the steps leading to the sacred place by a throng of laughing, chattering pilgrims. We bought paper cones filled with grain to scatter to the pigeons, the traditional offering to Jambhaji. The air was a-flutter with feathers, and the sound of bird-wing made a paean of praise to the saint.

Food and sweet stalls lined a dusty lane which trailed into the village. Beyond these were the major attraction of the fair: the blanket-sellers. Rough in texture, with a rustic charm, the warm coverlets were in dramatic patterns – black ground with a green and red border; all-over checks in emerald and Indian pink; grey base with edges in black and red stripes. And it was to buy some of these that our voluble mentor had made his journey.

The fair was small, and confined as it was to the community, it had the character of a family get-together. Despite all the school-master had said to the contrary, we found the Bishnois friendly and open. The girls were a merry and saucy lot. They enjoyed posing for photographs, and were artlessly curious about the young men of our party. I am afraid their attention did not include our guide, which is probably what had soured his views on the community through the years! Not only were these girls exceptionally pretty, but the men folk too were strikingly handsome. If this was the result of selective breeding, as our friend had furtively hinted, the practice seemed more than justified by the results.

We came to know more about these beautiful people in Barmer district in Maroodesh, into which their villages also extended.

In the hamlet of Ranasar near Dhorimanna, we were invited to the home of Ramkishan Bishnoi. He is a *gayan*, that is, one of the priests of the community, who sings in its temples and performs religious ceremonies.

Ramkishan's homestead was actually a cluster of huts surrounded by a protecting wall. One entered through an imposing arched gateway like the portals of a small fort, with a crenellated top. The walls were of mud and cowdung thicky plastered over a base of

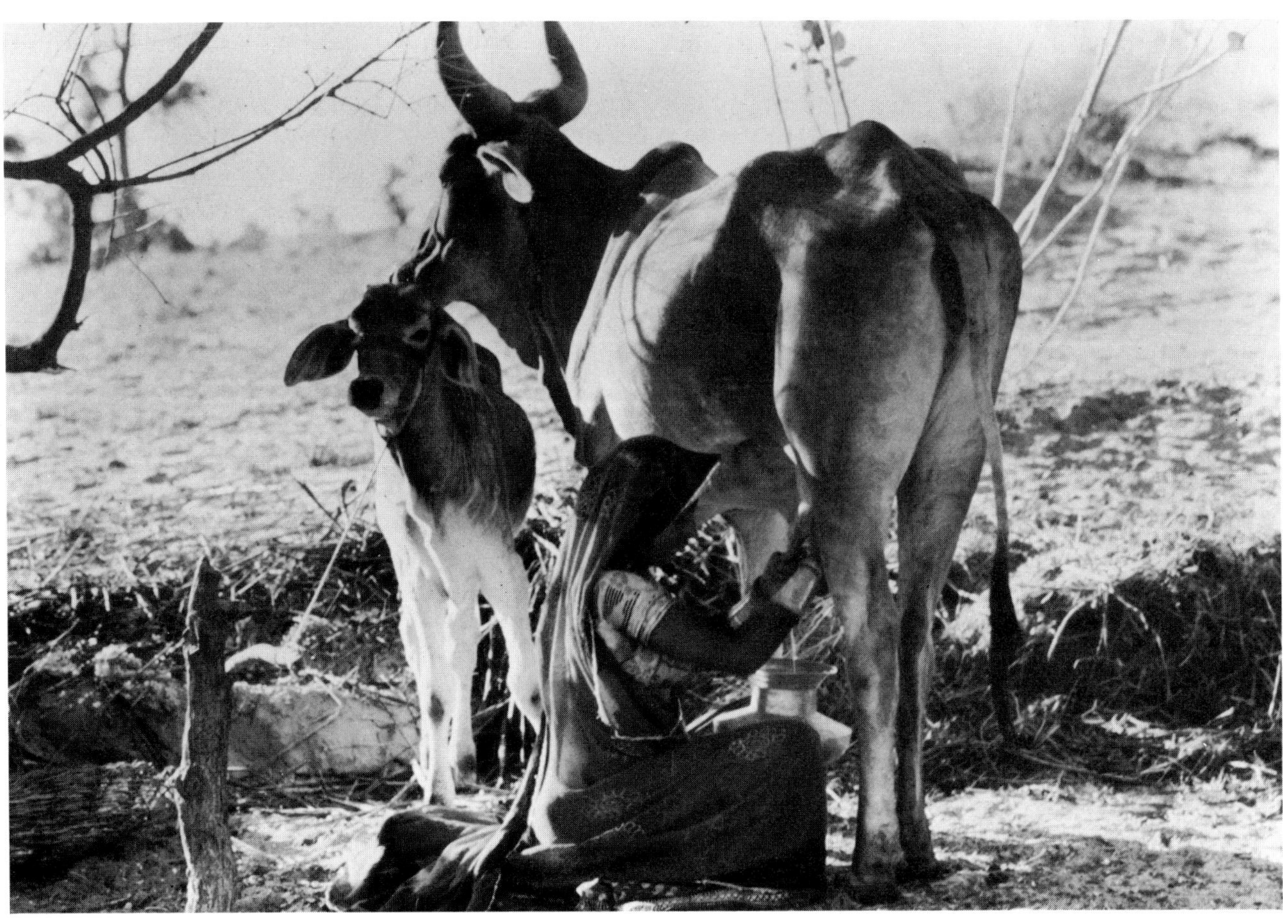

Mira at her daily chores

thorn bushes. The final layer of mud was laid on smooth and decorated with bands of white lime and terracotta.

Rural dwellings in Jangal and Maroodesh differ from the flat-roofed homes in Marh. Thorn and scrub which are plentiful in these parts are used as building material.

When a villager sets about constructing a *jhonpa*, the round hut which is the living space, he fixes a nail in the centre of the site. To this he attaches a string and marks out the circumference, usually on the basis of a diameter of six to seven metres. The walls have a foundation of thirty to sixty centimetres, and stand approximately two metres in height. The conical roof is supported by a central pillar, a simple, straight tree-trunk, occasionally carved. The beams, which radiate from this, lean on slim wooden pillars around the outer edge. The roof is thatched with local materials.

Inside, the walls are plastered with lime, and often adorned with colourful folk motifs. Niches for lamps, or as shelves for small objects, are provided in the walls. The mud floor is treated with a coat of straw and cow dung, beaten and rubbed till it glistens. There is only one door, but no windows, the air circulating through the gap between the overhanging roofs and the walls. The furniture comprises a few string cots and low wooden stools. This simple structure offers shelter from the elements and uncluttered space for sparse living. Inexpensive to build and easy to maintain, its very starkness lends it dignity and charm. The rectangular huts, *pindhwas*, have thatched and gabled roofs. They are used as guest-houses or as store-rooms, kitchens, or occasionally as cattle sheds. Inside, along one wall, is a built-in, plastered, storage space. In the courtyard are several large grain bins called *kothis*, which resemble enormous earthen jars. Ramkishan's wife, a comely, dignified person, brought us cups of tea as we sat listening to her husband sing. Their grandson, a naughty, sprightly lad of two with large, bright eyes, attracted by the cameras, nagged his grandmother till she dressed him up in a new shirt and capped him with a big white turban so that he could have his 'photo' taken. His mother, Mira, the daughter of the house, had been busy milking the cow to provide fresh milk for our tea. When she entered, her beauty stunned us into silence. Radha herself seemed to have stepped into the hut:

Who was the artificer at her creation?
Was it the moon, bestowing its own charm?
Was it the graceful month of Spring, itself
Compact with love, a garden full of flowers?
(Kalidasa)

Blissfully unaware of the impression she had created, our rustic nymph seated herself on the ground with a swirl of her skirt that billowed and settled about her like a vivid red blossom. Mira was eager to know all about us. She tossed a lively barrage of questions at Kothari who had a busy time interpreting them for us, and translating back to her. Her nimble wit assessed his role neatly. She dubbed him 'Vakil Sahib', Mr. Lawyer, since members of this profession are well-known to litigious villagers, and their manner of interpreting law, usually to their own advantage.

Rural people express themselves in casual conversation in a startling poetic idiom, so spontaneous and evocative, so musical in cadence, as to put to shame the stereotyped commonplaces of the educated town-dweller. After submitting the three women of our party to an unabashed scrutiny, Mira turned to Kothari and said 'Vakil Sahib, why have you brought these ladybirds to our poor village? The hot winds will blow the bloom off their wings!'

Kothari tried to defend us by explaining that the 'ladybirds' in question were in fact women who worked very hard to earn their living.

'Will they come and work alongside me?' she rejoined, unconvinced of our worth. 'How will the strutting peahens adjust to my gait? I am the sparrow that picks the grain from under their arched necks. When it rains, the peahen lowers her bedraggled tail under the upturned cart; the sparrow chirps merrily in the eaves.'

Indeed we came off shabbily by comparison. This sparrow fetched water from the well, milked the cows, churned the butter, plastered the floor, decorated the huts, cooked, scrubbed, polished, washed clothes she herself had embroidered, looked after her two children, helped her mother cut and sew, gathered wood for fuel, made cow-dung cakes for the kindling, sifted grain and helped in the fields when the need arose. And with all that it was she who stood out as a resplendent bird of paradise and we the common sparrows. Her sarcasm was not lost on us, but so telling was it that it evoked admiration and laughter rather than resentment.

Had this sharp-witted young beauty the opportunities of education and training she would undoubtedly have put them to good advantage. Her intelligence and liveliness of mind and the grace and winning charm of her physical presence were assets few women could match. It was only natural that her remarks should be touched with a slight tinge of envy. They expressed the vehement longing for a life beyond the drudgery of daily chores. We were moved by her unuttered yearnings.

Mira's mother supplemented the family income by tailoring for local customers, and worked her sewing machine with deft skill. Her only son, Mira's brother, was a sickly lad of sixteen whose ill-health was his parents' chief concern. The boy had been treated for tuberculosis, but the disease had not been eradicated. There had been a recurrence of symptoms. Ramkishan planned to take him again to the hospital at Barmer.

With such confidences we had been admitted into the very heart of the family and the problem that threw its shadow over their existence. Ramkishan, sober and discerning, was a man of some substance and standing. While he was prepared to spend time and money to salvage the health of his only son, he was faced with hard decisions: how could his wife manage the cattle and look after the fields alone? Mira might help while she was there, but she would soon have to return to husband's home. Hired labour was difficult to come by since landless workers are drawn to the towns. Relatives might lend a hand but had their own problems to attend to. Ramkishan was realistic. Would his son's health, however improved, be equal to the hard tasks he would normally be expected to assume? Would he recover sufficiently to be able to marry and raise a family? Or to look after the parents in their old age? His schooling had been interrupted by his prolonged illness and, in getting a local job that required the rudiments of education, he stood no chance against the boys of his age who had completed their schooling.

This brief visit gave us an insight into some of the problems of rural families, specially in the interior. Nothing, for instance, could have demonstrated the rationale of the resistance of village communities to such programmes as family planning, as the predicament of this household. We realised also that the legislation giving daughters equal rights in family landholdings and property proved impractical, as it could lead to fragmentation of ancestral land, and still more litigation between sons and sons-in-law. Besides, this would not automatically mitigate the crippling burden of the dowry system. Desert communities by and large have ignored this law, and have also resisted the campaign for smaller families.

The Bishnois are a progressive-minded community and where opportunities are available have benefitted economically and socially. Their women are more forward and independent than others, and with education or vocational training would be more than a match for girls from Brahmin or Marwari families, who do educate their daughters. Unfortunately, concentrated as they are in remote desert regions, beyond the reach of the common amenities of medicine and education, they suffer from grave disadvantages not of their making. The tragic situation of the two talented and intelligent young people in this one family brought such problems painfully close to one.

The Legend of the Seven Sisters

Who are they, these seven virgins? There they stand beside their brother Bhairon, little maids all in a row, chaste and inviolate. We see them incised on a sacred tablet out in the open amidst outcrops of rock; we find them moulded in bas relief on a clay plaque enclosed in a toy-size temple under a *pilu* tree. We recognise them embossed on a silver pendant worn round the

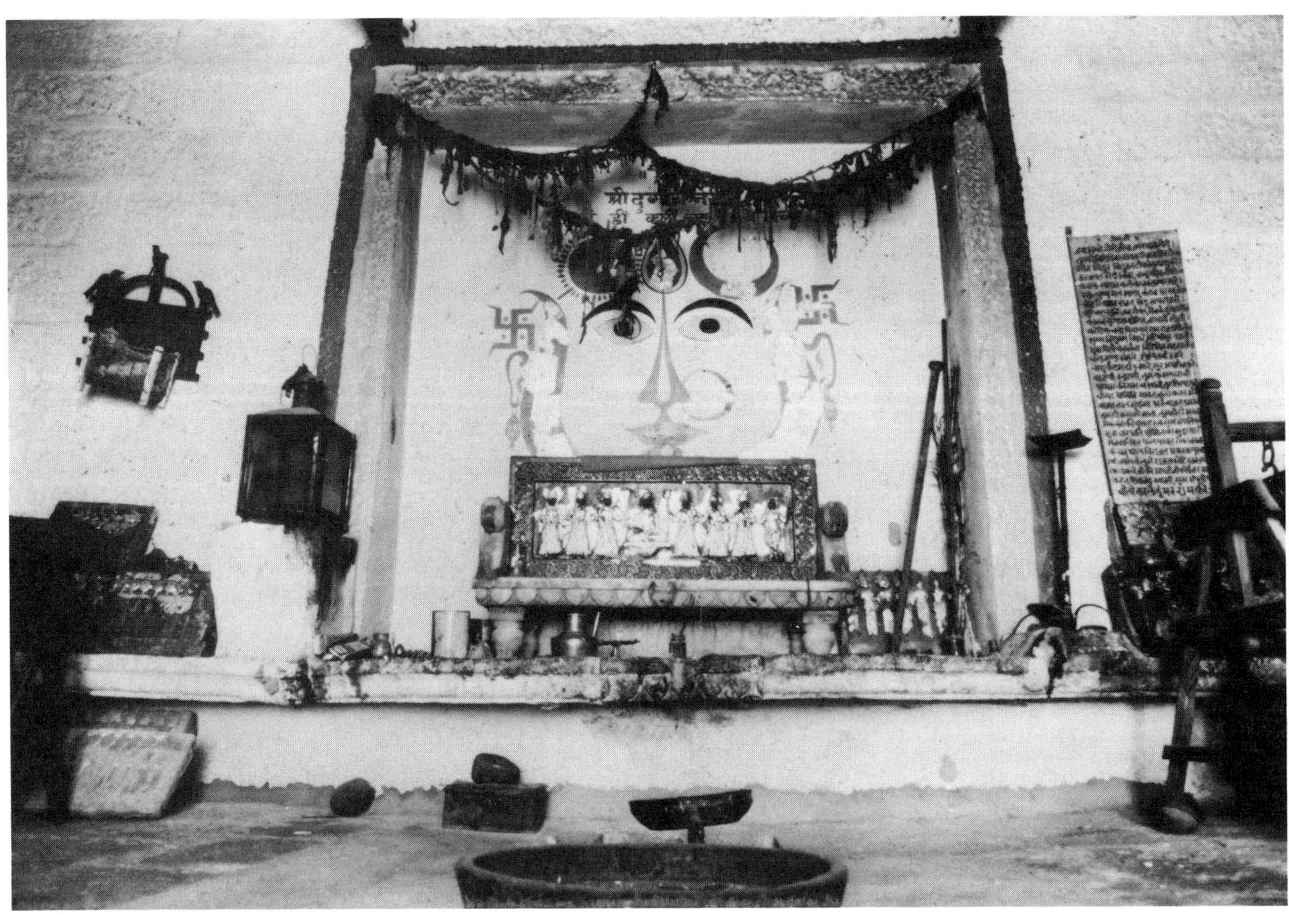

Temple to Kalikadevi, one of seven sisters known as the *bayasar*.

neck by a nomad herdsman. They appear embroidered in appliqué on a wall-hanging in a humble tribal hut; or as crude drawings in white limechalk on a rough surface of earth or carved in wood, dextrously and with many delicate refinements, to be placed above a doorway to bless the home.

How old are they, these ageless damsels, no longer girls, not yet women? They are worshipped, collectively or individually, as incarnations of Durga, but they surely are manifestations of a far earlier concept of *shakti*, activated energy, than Shiva's consort of terrible beauty. They require no celestial union to enhance their status, no male counterpart to circumscribe or share their powers. The sisters belong to an early age in which the female principle was paramount, and the womb, fecund or inviolate, was the dark centre from where the life-force emanated in pulsing waves of light. Bhairon, their brother, is not a protector but a companion, sometimes wilful, often mischievous, occasionally an embarrassment.

The story of the seven virgins, no doubt updated down the centuries, relates their adventures in the Thaar.

Deep in the desert lived a Charan who had seven daughters and a son. He was the pious devotee of a *devi* to whose distant shrine he made an annual pilgrimage on foot. When his wife died, the Charan did not wish to leave his children unprotected. His daughters were young, pure and very beautiful, and he was concerned for their safety. So he took them and his son with him on his next journey. They came to Hakra where they stopped. In order to protect his chaste and lovely girls, he locked them every day in a room and left Bhairon to stand on guard. As soon as it was dark, the girls would ask their brother to release them, and they would run down to the river to bath and play.

One night the ruler of the kingdom happened to see them sporting in the moonlight, and, enamoured of their beauty, demanded that the Charan send one of the girls to his harem. Alarmed and incensed at this indignity, the Charan fled the city with his children. When they came to the river, no boatman would row them across for fear of the raja's wrath. The maidens ran into the stream, and stooped to drink. At their touch, the waters parted, and the family made good their escape.

Many were the miracles worked by the young *devis* on their difficult flight through the desert. At Thanot they met a poor woman, and, being famished, they begged her for food. Destitute as she herself was, the woman was touched by their plight and gave them the few dry crusts she had. They thanked her, ate the food and blessed her before they left. The woman found to her surprise that the bread had been miraculously restored to her. She then realised the divine nature of

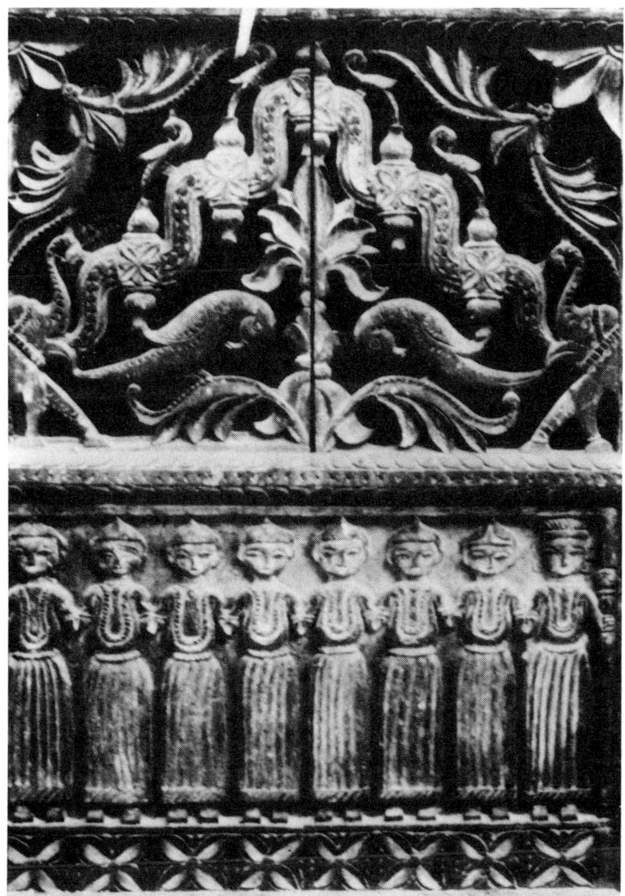

Woodcarving of the seven sisters and their brother

the wayfarers she had succoured.

This exhausting and tedious nomadic existence came very hard on Bhairon and, hoping to ease the situation by having at least some sustenance on tap, he stole a buffalo at Ghantiali village. When the owner came to the *devis* and complained of his loss to the eldest virgin, she pronounced a curse on the thief, and behold! a great *naga*, king cobra, attacked Bhairon and bit him. When she saw her brother writhing in his death agony, the *devi* relented and effected a miraculous cure.

After many such adventures, the maidens finally reached Jaisalmer and sought an audience with the king. The sentry at the gate refused to admit them, but no mere mortal could thwart the *devis* and they were soon in the raja's presence. He gave them leave to settle in his kingdom, although he did not become a devotee. The seven sisters and their brother then took up residence in his domain, and their main shrines are found in various places. The eldest sister settled in Barmer, at Pugal village (not to be confused with Pugal in Bikaner); another at Timera, where she rid the inhabitants of a dreaded demon; at Kala Dungar was Kalikadevi, whose followers perform the same rites as those observed by the Siddhnath Mehgwals of Nokhamandi; other shrines are at Tegi, Thanot and Ghantiali. Bhairon, weary of wandering, decided to make Jaisalmer his permanent home, and his main shrine is at Barha Bagh, near the cenotaphs of

the royal family. There is no further mention of the loving, distracted father whose role seemed over once the daughters were established as *devis*, their purity untouched. The seventh shrine is at Bhadriyarai, off the road from Jaisalmer to Pokharan, and it was here that we went to pay out respects to the seven virgins.

The Bhadriyadevi temple, perched upon a flat rock on a fair eminence, is a recent construction, white-washed outside, and with coloured tiles within. A characterless, ugly structure, as so many modern temples are, it is devoid of any atmosphere. Fortunately, the actual shrine of the goddess is behind the temple. Under a dark, bent-over *pilu* tree, its gnarled and twisted trunk hollowed with age, is the *devi's* sanctum. The *pilu* is an evergreen; its leaves are like black-green fingers thickly bunched together. It has a forbidding, sinister presence, but its ability to survive the harshest desert conditions, and its dense shade endear it to the people of the Thaar. This particular specimen was one of the largest I had seen. Because of its cramped location behind the temple, one could get no view of its crown, and to stand under it was to enter an eerie, spectral world. An enormous waterpot lay near the hollow at the base of the trunk, and a pair of drums hung from a branch.

On one side were stacked together several stone tablets, carved with the familiar figures of the seven sisters and their brother. Some of the carvings were as primitive as a child's drawing: round head, a triangle beneath, for the skirted body, three dots to serve as eyes and nose, a line for the mouth, small, L-shaped lines for the feet. Bhairon differed in that his body was square, with two legs showing below. Other tablets of more refined artistry displayed the maidens in graceful postures, their bodies adorned with necklaces, bracelets and anklets, their veils and skirts enlivened with elegant patterns. But the faces were identical: expressionless, almost to abstraction. Vermilion *tilak* marks were smeared on the stone, without much care as to their placement, as each devotee with slovenly haphazard zeal left her indelible mark. On the branches above these images hung streamers of red muslin, strips torn from the bright veils of brides who had come for the virgins' blessings for a happy married life. There was something poignant and distressing about the wooden cradles, like toy beds for dolls, offered by barren women begging for the boon of a child. Some of these were fitted with little pillows and coverlets. What tender love and anguished prayers must have gone into the stitching of this tiny bedding! Two or three cradles had been hung up between the lower branches of the drooping *pilu* and they swayed gently as though blessed with their precious burden.

The space around the shrine was strewn with curling tendrils of hair, the first soft shavings from the heads of male infants, brought here for their name-giving ceremony by grateful mothers whose prayers had been answered.

Nearby stood a weathered hutment, barred and locked. Against its wall were propped a few finely carved wood doorframes with the forms of the seven sisters hewn in low relief, while tablets, plaques and a profusion of images littered the floor. Obviously offerings invoking the goddesses' blessings, or in gratitude for them, they represented several centuries of ritual art, practised by craftsmen moved by the elemental urge to propagate the species. Out of the flinty, unyielding earth, out of the maternal darkness beneath the tree, emerged these seven sylvan creatures and their single male companion, to draw into their presence from the remotest corners of the desert, multitudes of human beings trailing their hopes behind them. The tree brooded upon their hunger, sighed over their prayers, cradled their dreams in its swaying branches. Silent as the place was, and empty of people, its air seemed heavy with an eternal lament.

On days held sacred to the virgins, the *bhopas*, oracles of Bhadriyadevi, are in attendance. Devotees who desire some particular blessing or wish to ask questions of the *devi,* go to the *bhopa* to intercede on their behalf.

The spirit of the goddess speaks through the oracle in his trance, and the petitioner receives the answer. The *devis* are not distant, inaccessible spirits for those who have faith in them. Pilgrims will often harry, scold or cajole the goddesses in intimate and direct terms. They believe that the sisters, having lived and suffered as they do, must understand their plight, and should be told off if their treatment seems unfair.

As we were leaving, the priest told us that in an underground cave below the shrine lived a hermit who had been there for seven years. He had undertaken a vow of silence and he lived on two bowls of curds offered him by pilgrims or local villagers. It was suspected that he was of noble birth, a fugitive from one of those complicated feuds that frequently lead to violence and sudden death. He was an educated man. Occasionally he wrote answers to questions the curious sent him along with his meagre diet. Would we like to question him? But what questions can be put to one who has judged his own actions and imposed on himself the severest of penalties: solitary confinement? He had withdrawn into his world, and we now withdrew into ours, leaving him in the protective care of the *devi* of Bhadriyarai.

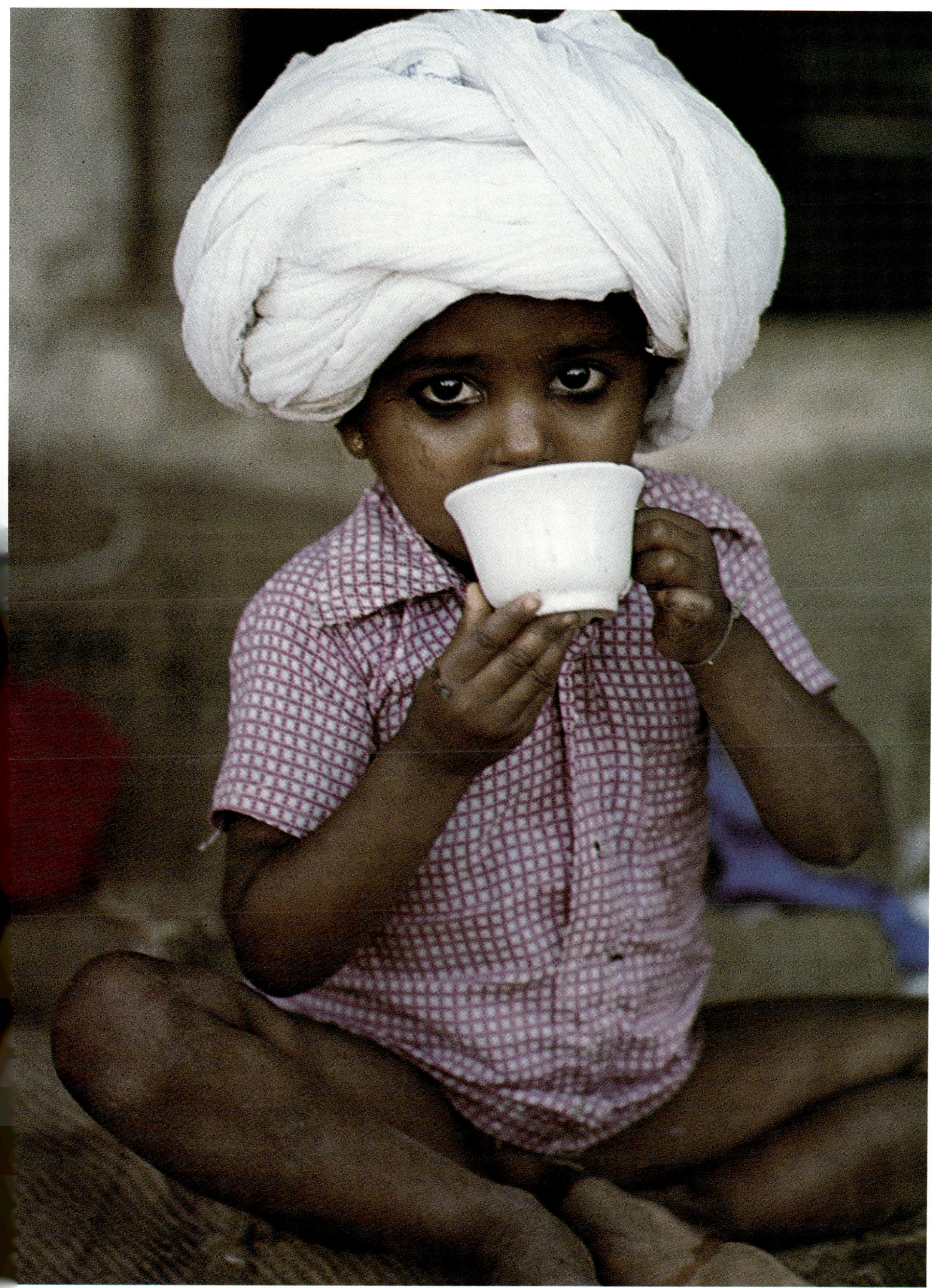

Bishnoi boy, Mira's son.

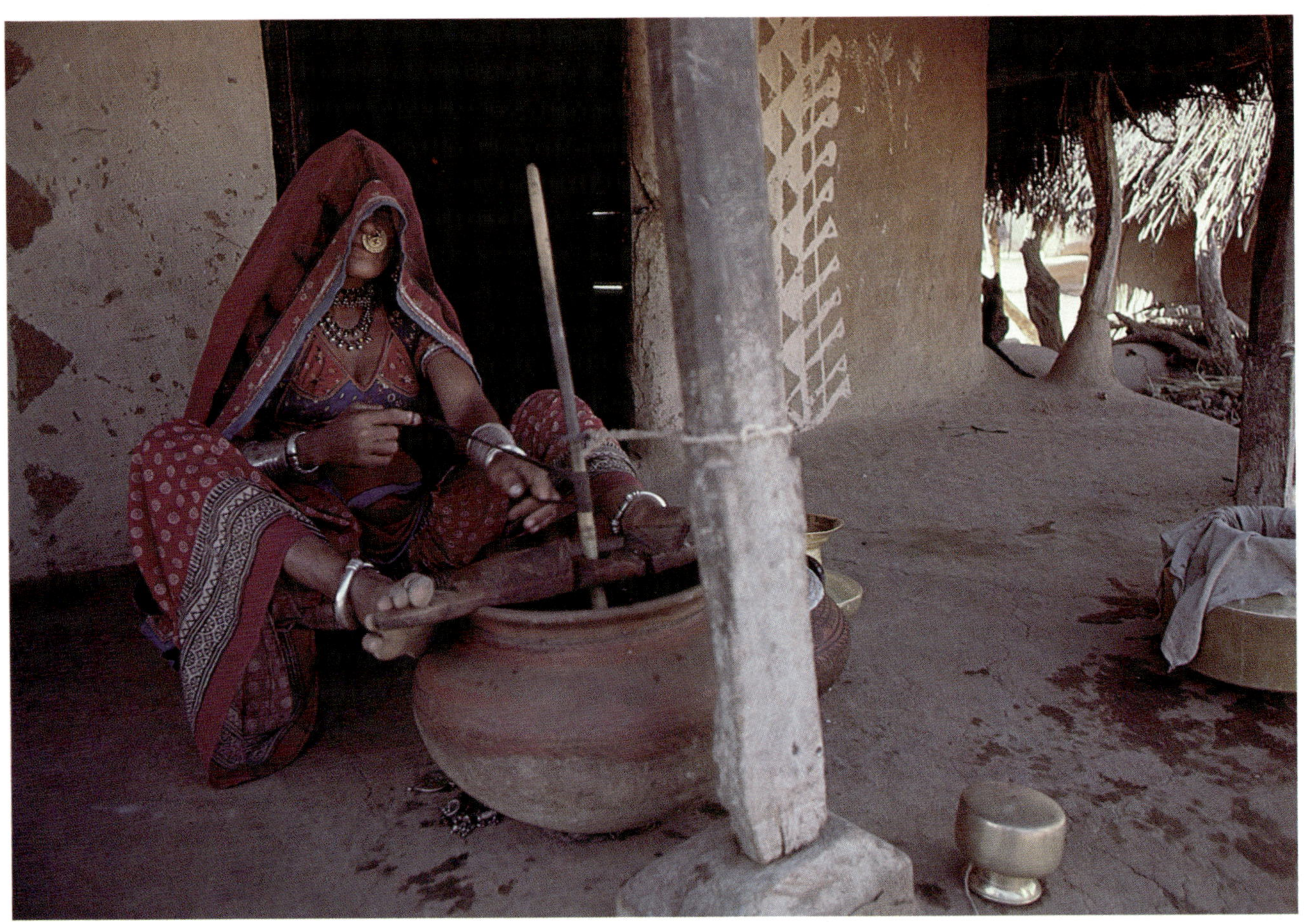

Bishnoi woman, Mira's mother, churning butter.

Votive horses at the Ramdevra shrine

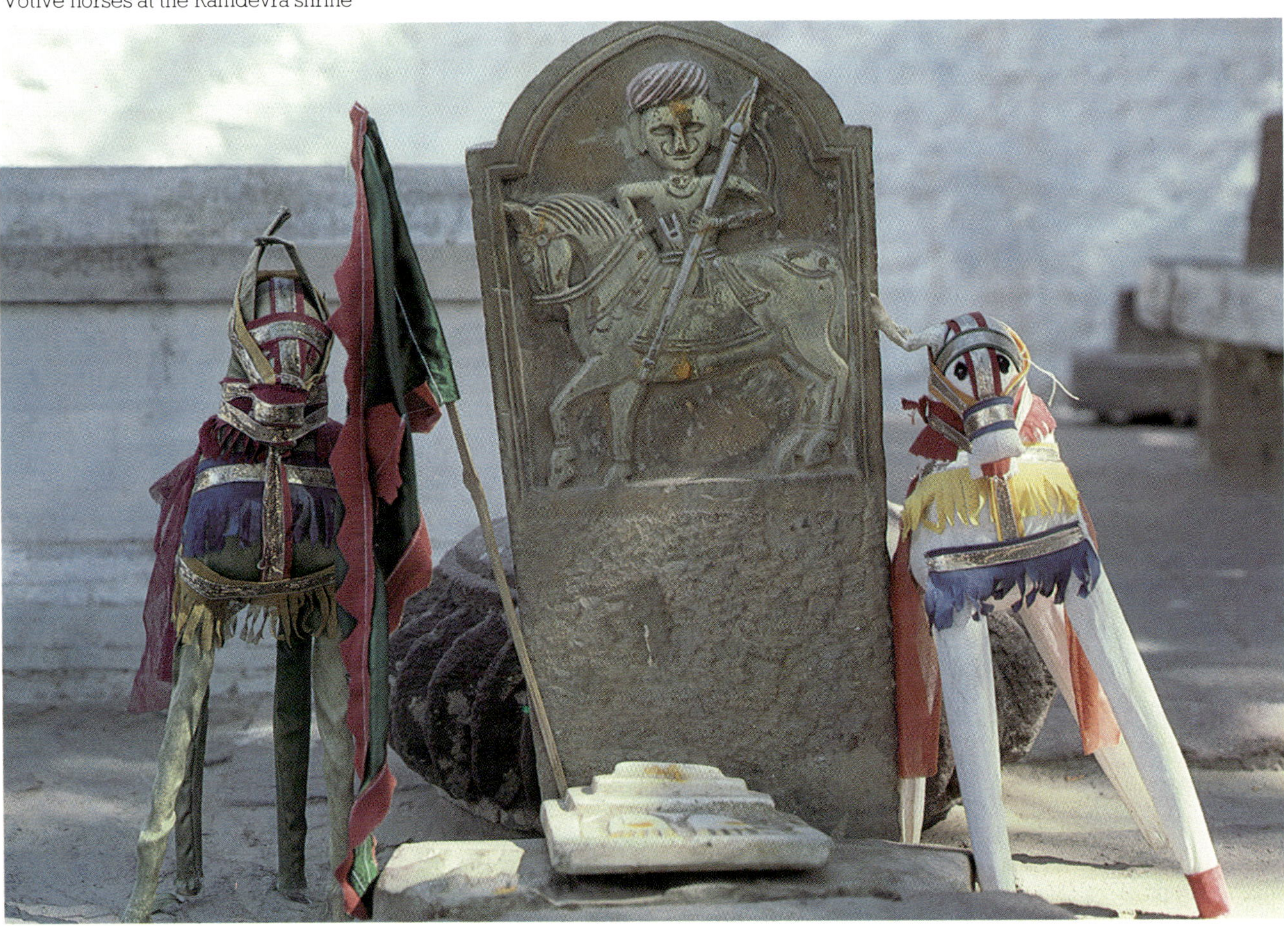

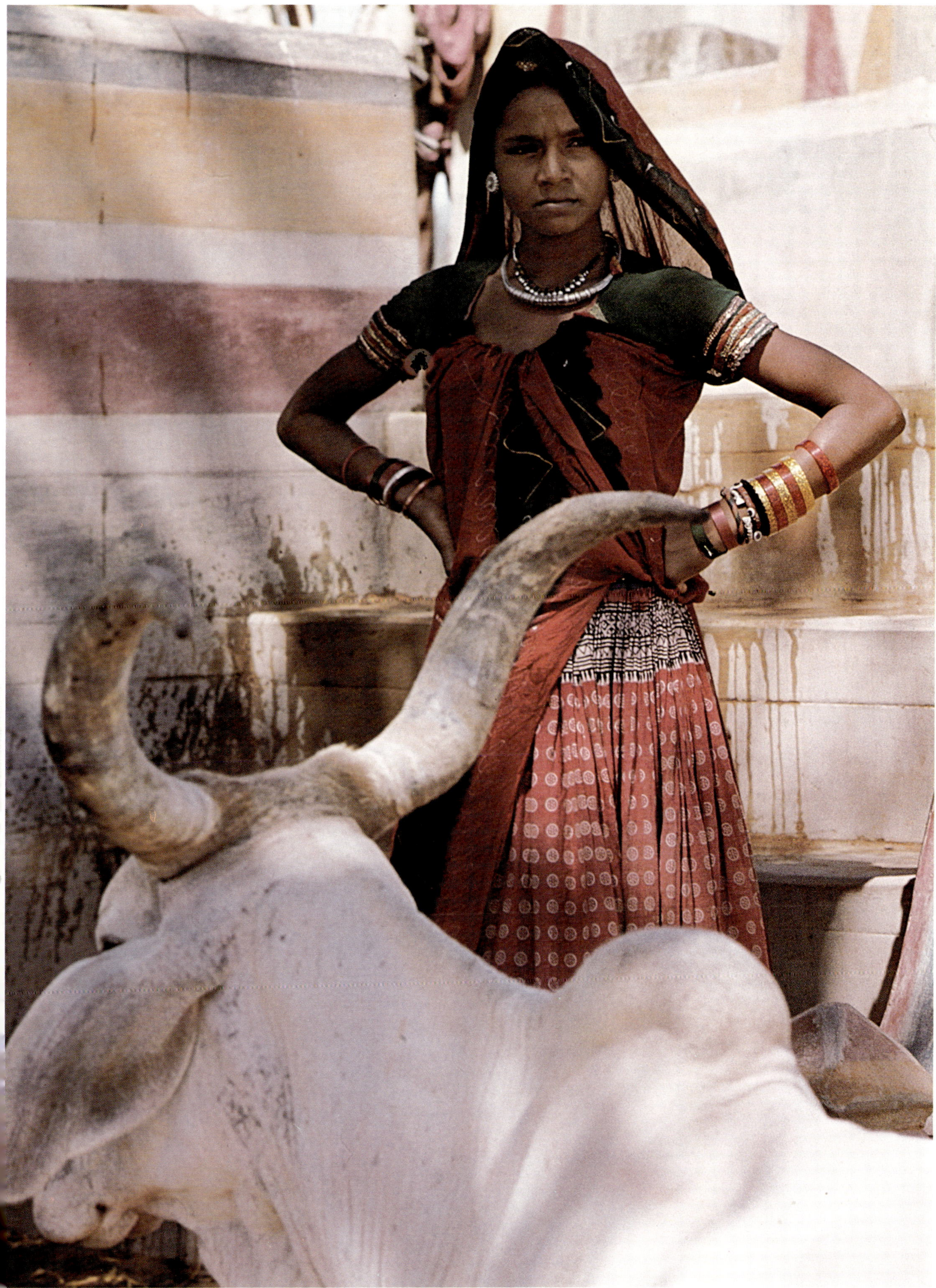

Mira, Bishnoi girl.

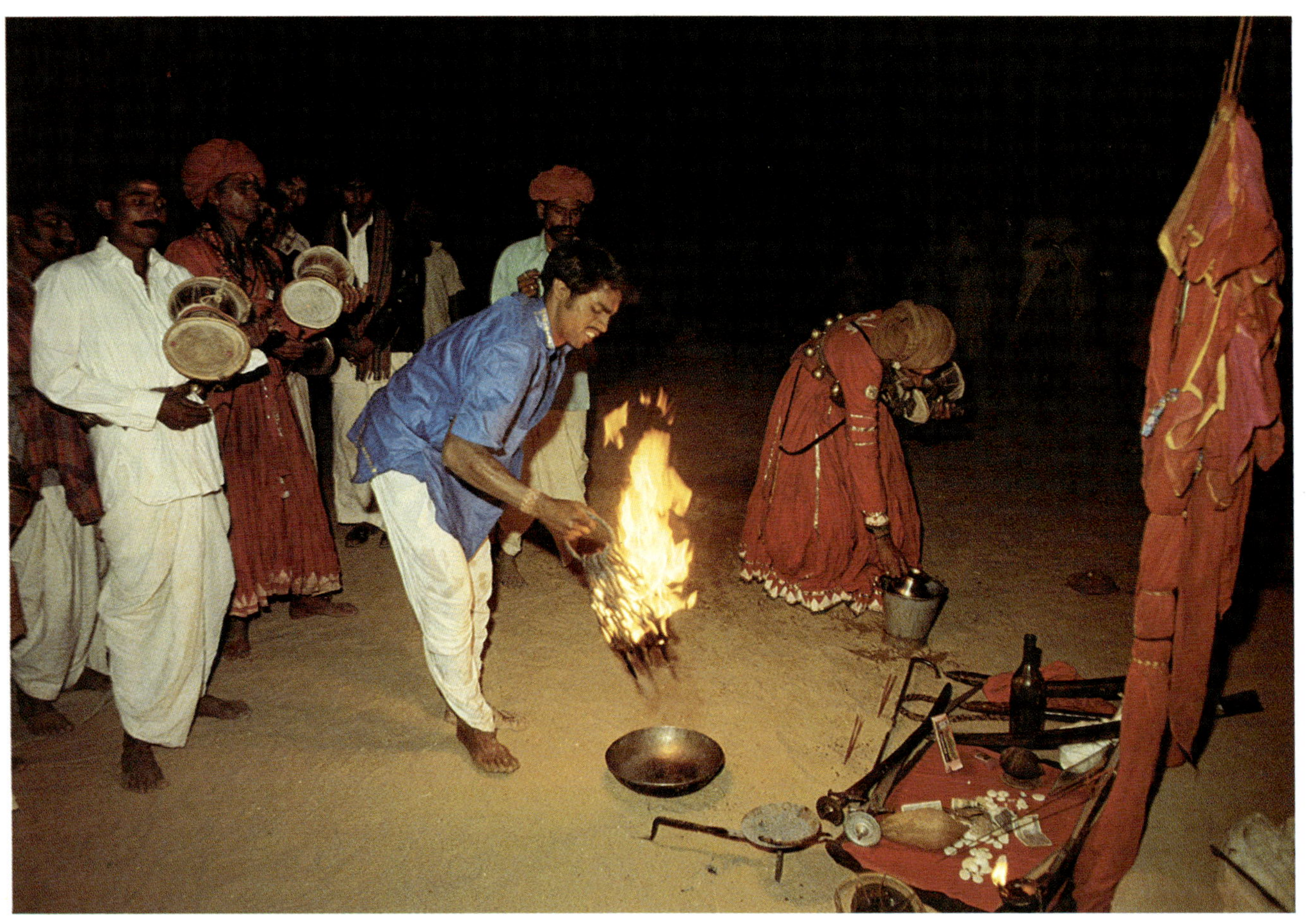

Siddhnaths offering the dedicatory prayer before a ritual performance. Nokhamandi.

Desert burial. A child's bier.

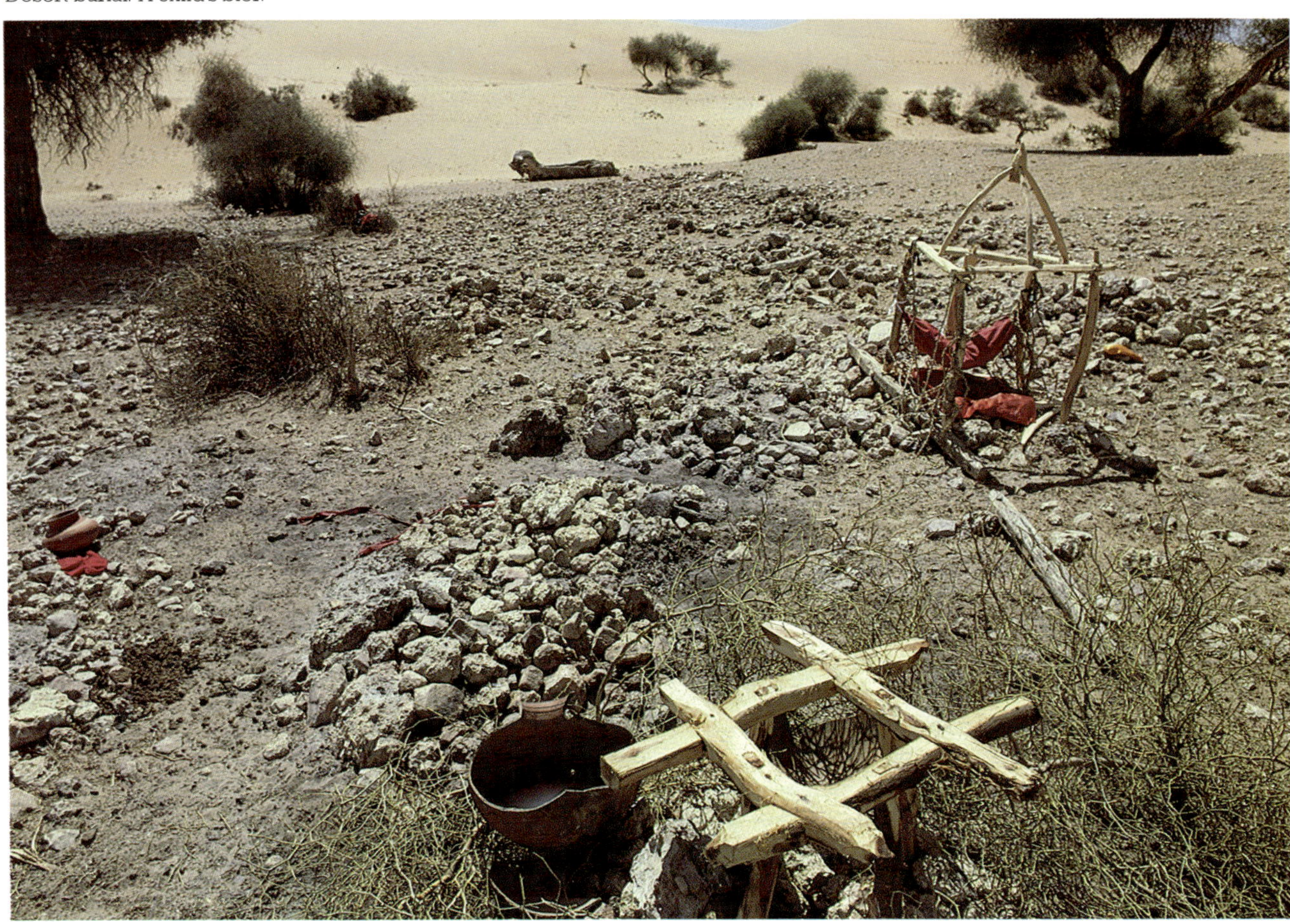

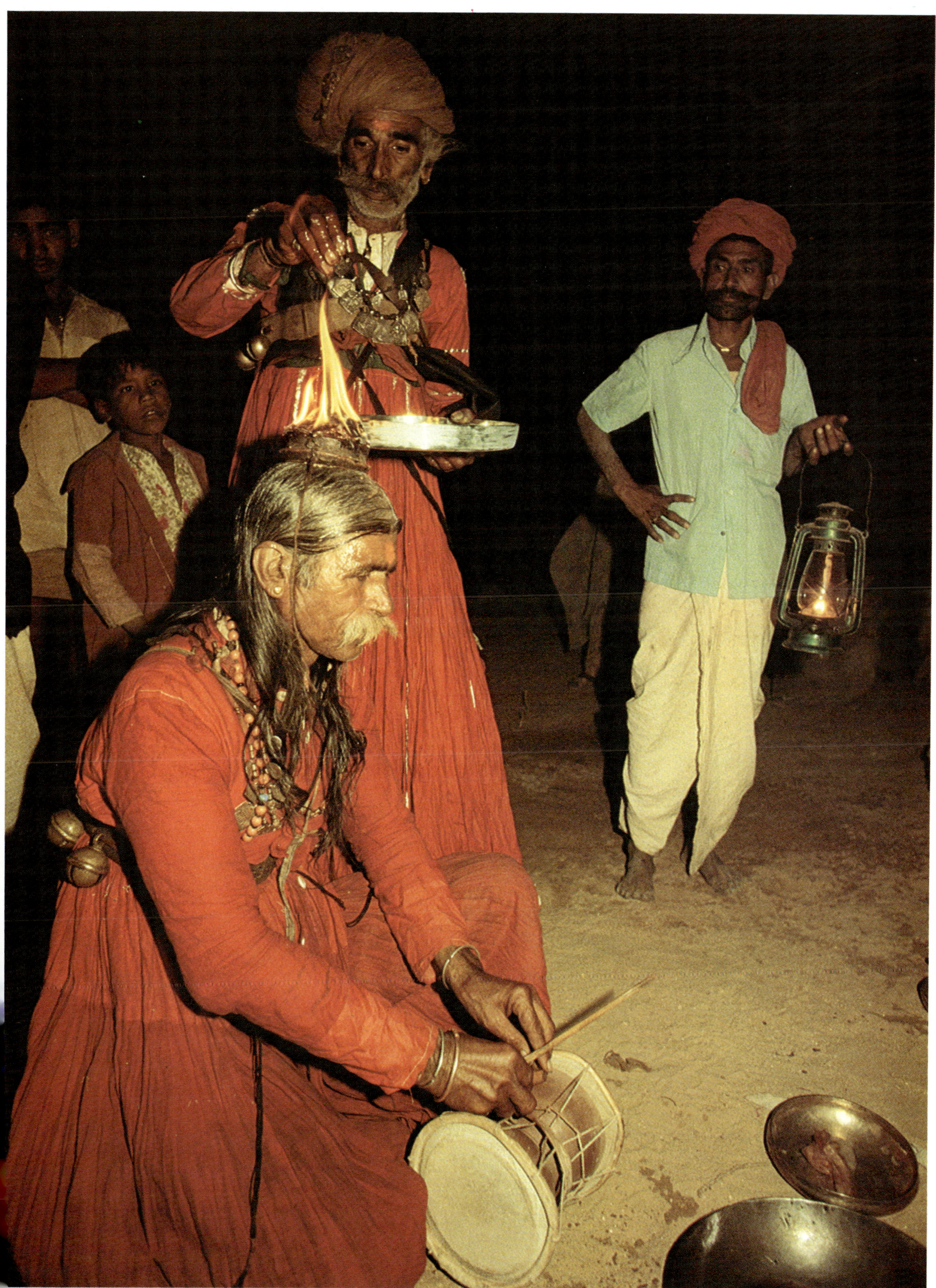

Siddhnath dancing with a burning circlet on his head

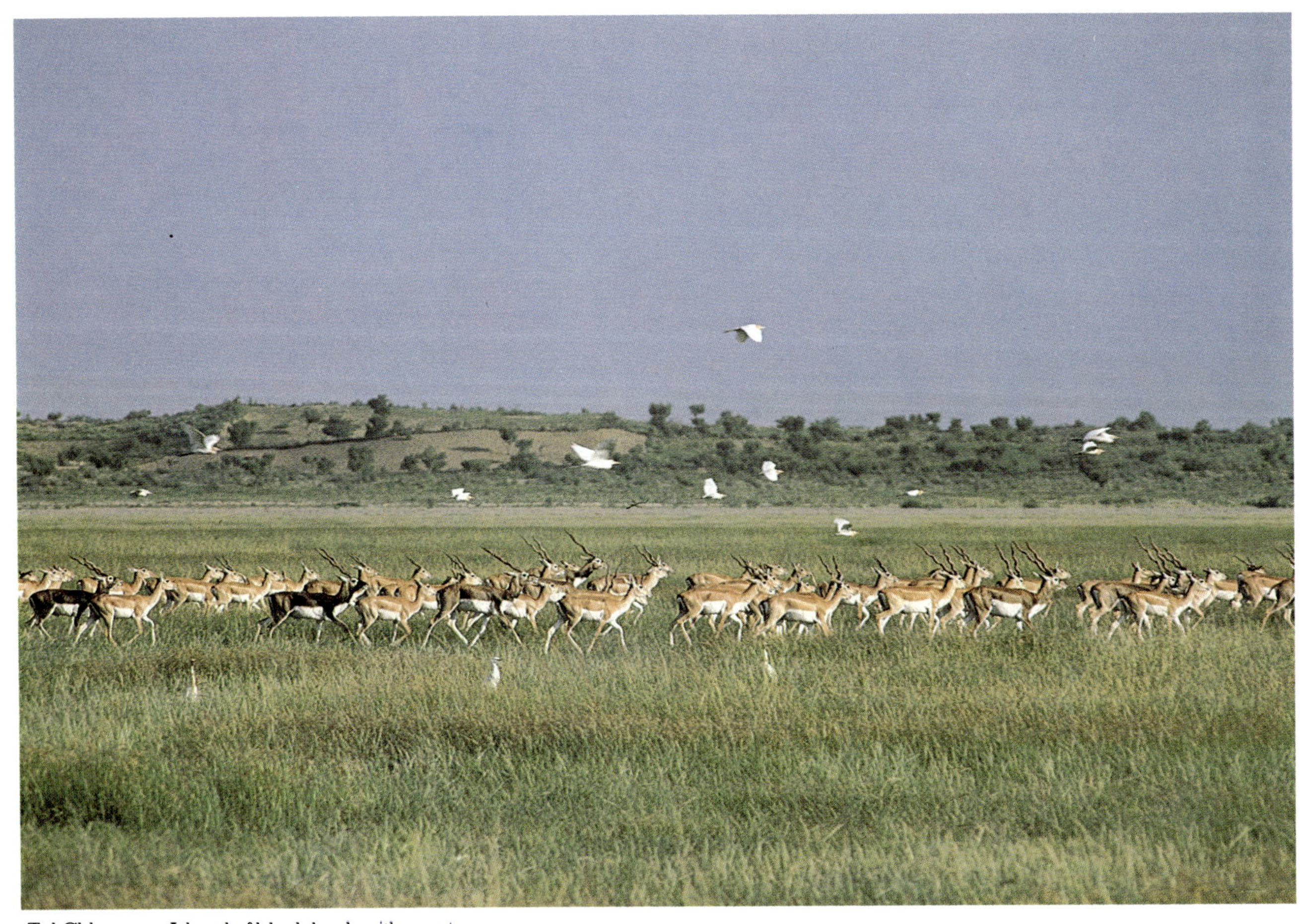

Tal Chhappar. A herd of black buck with egrets.

Street scene, Jaisalmer.

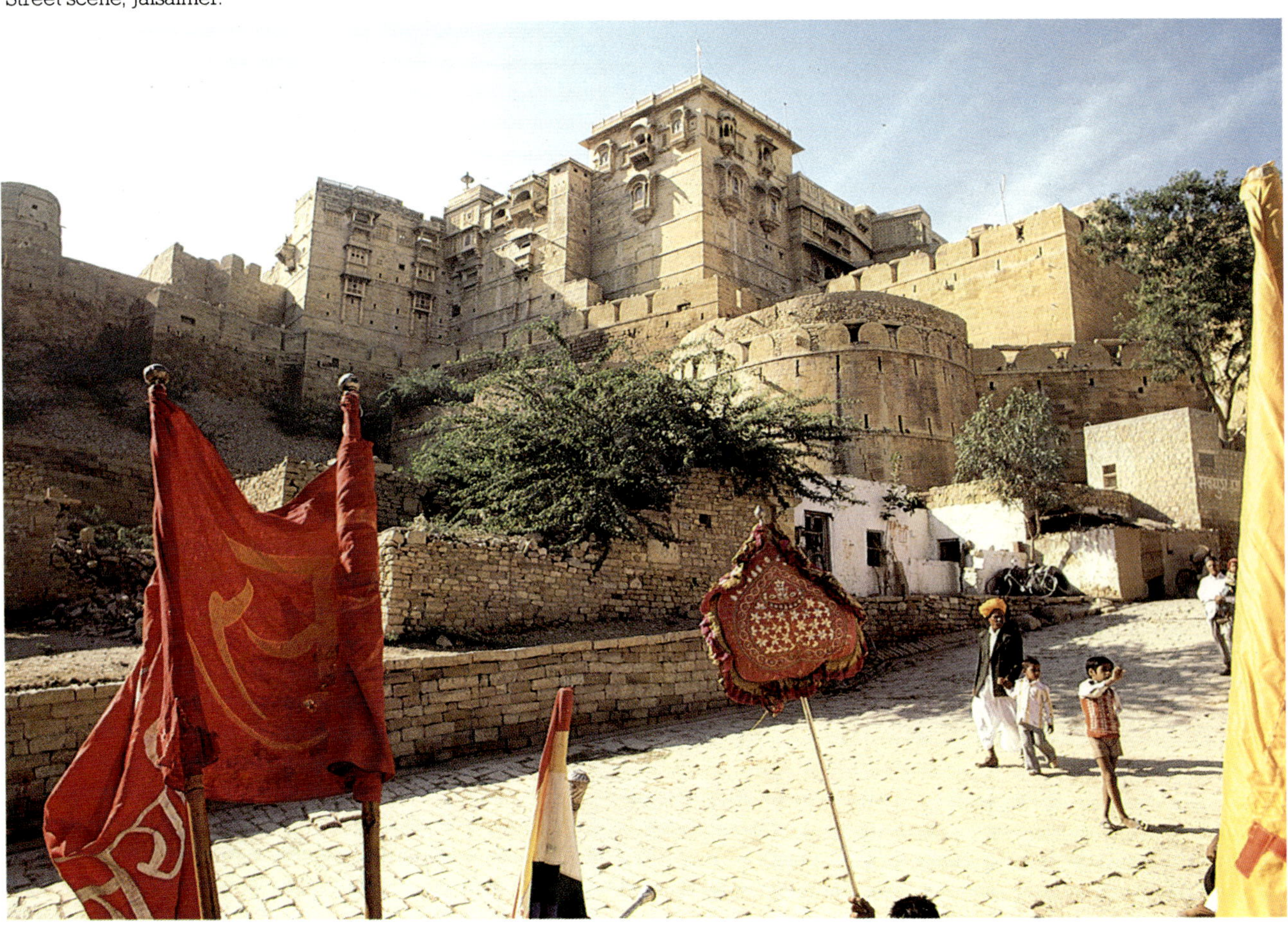

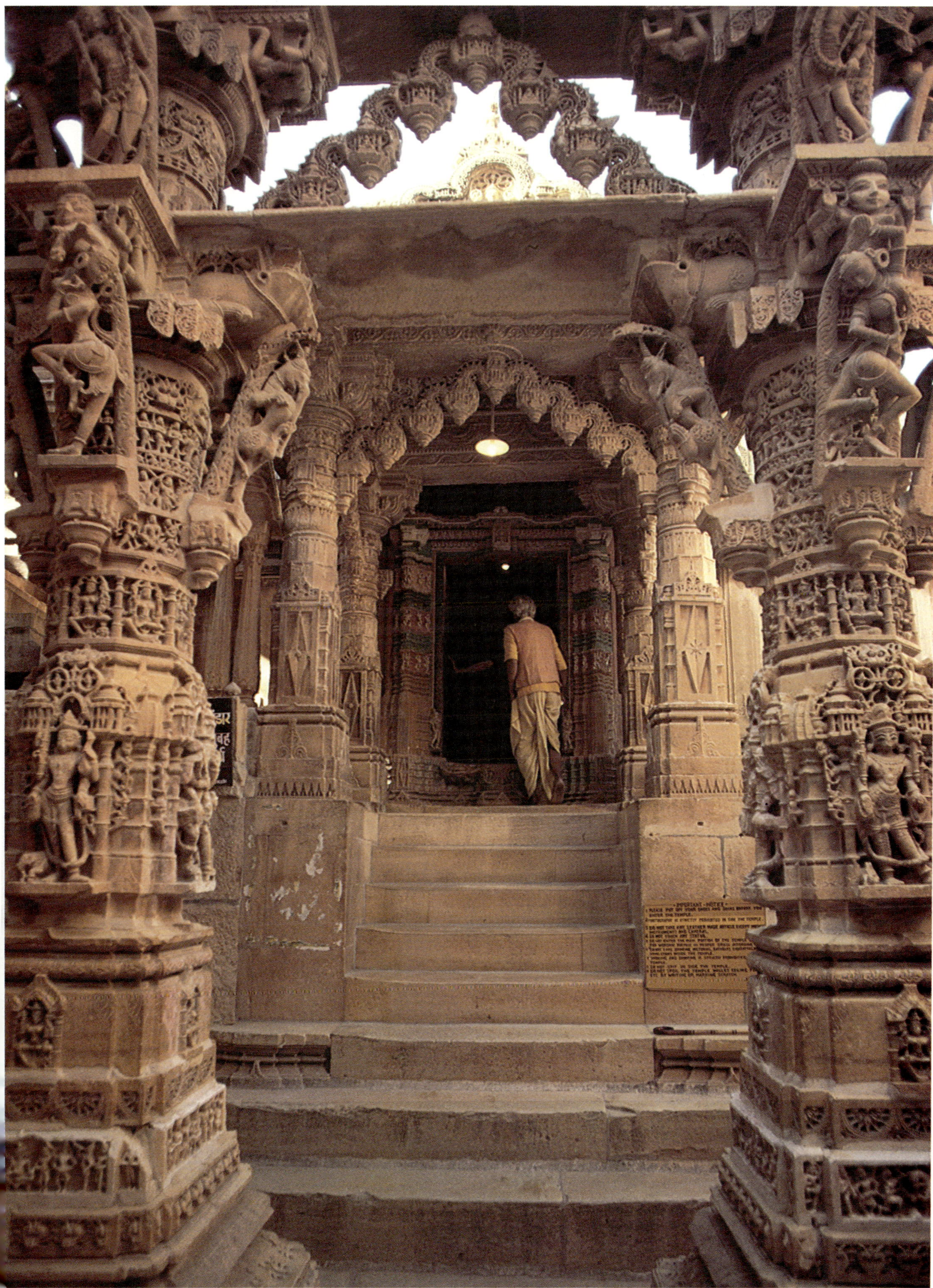

Entrance to a Jain temple, Jaisalmer.

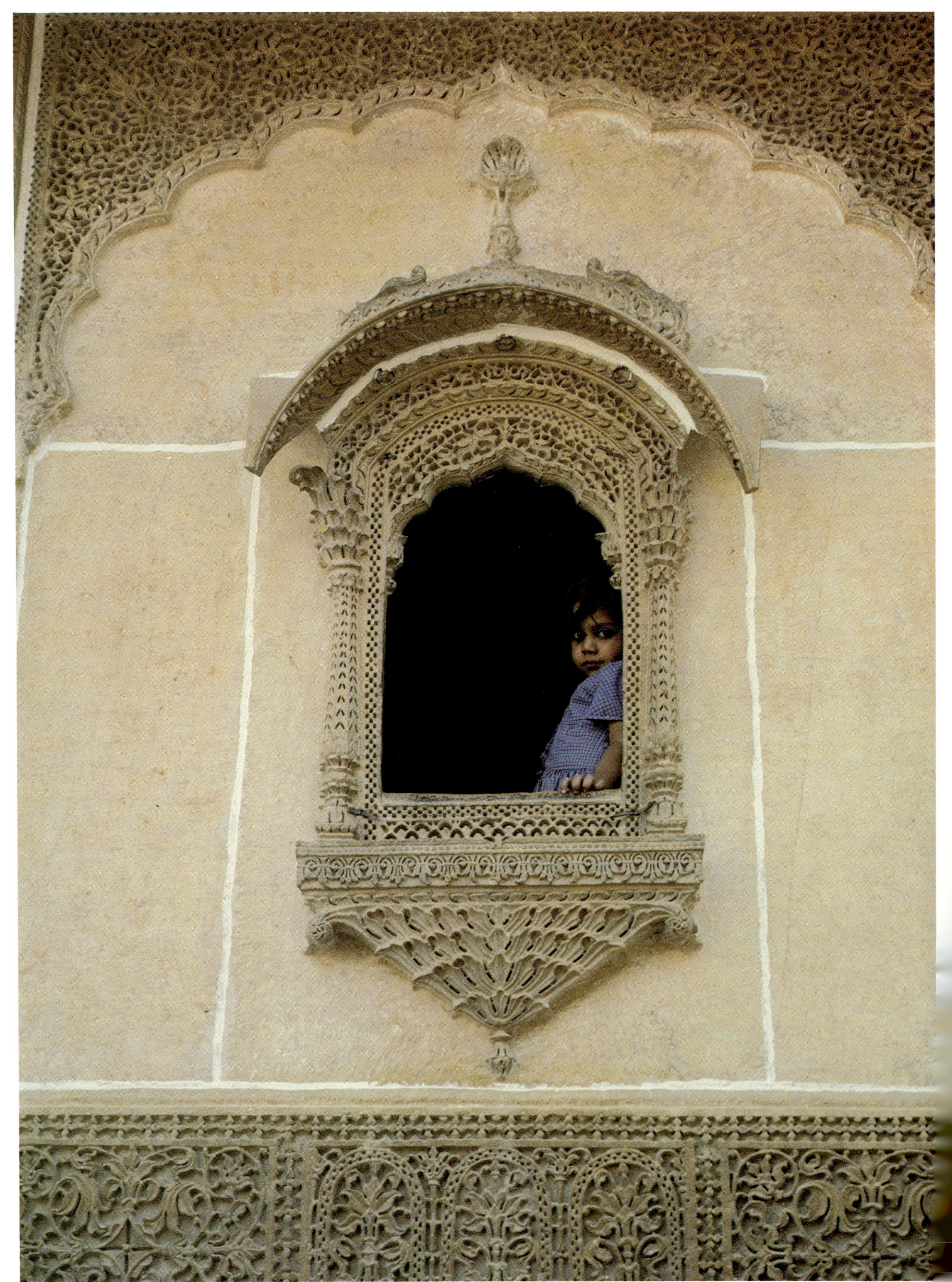

Nathmalji *haveli*, Jaisalmer. Detail of a window.

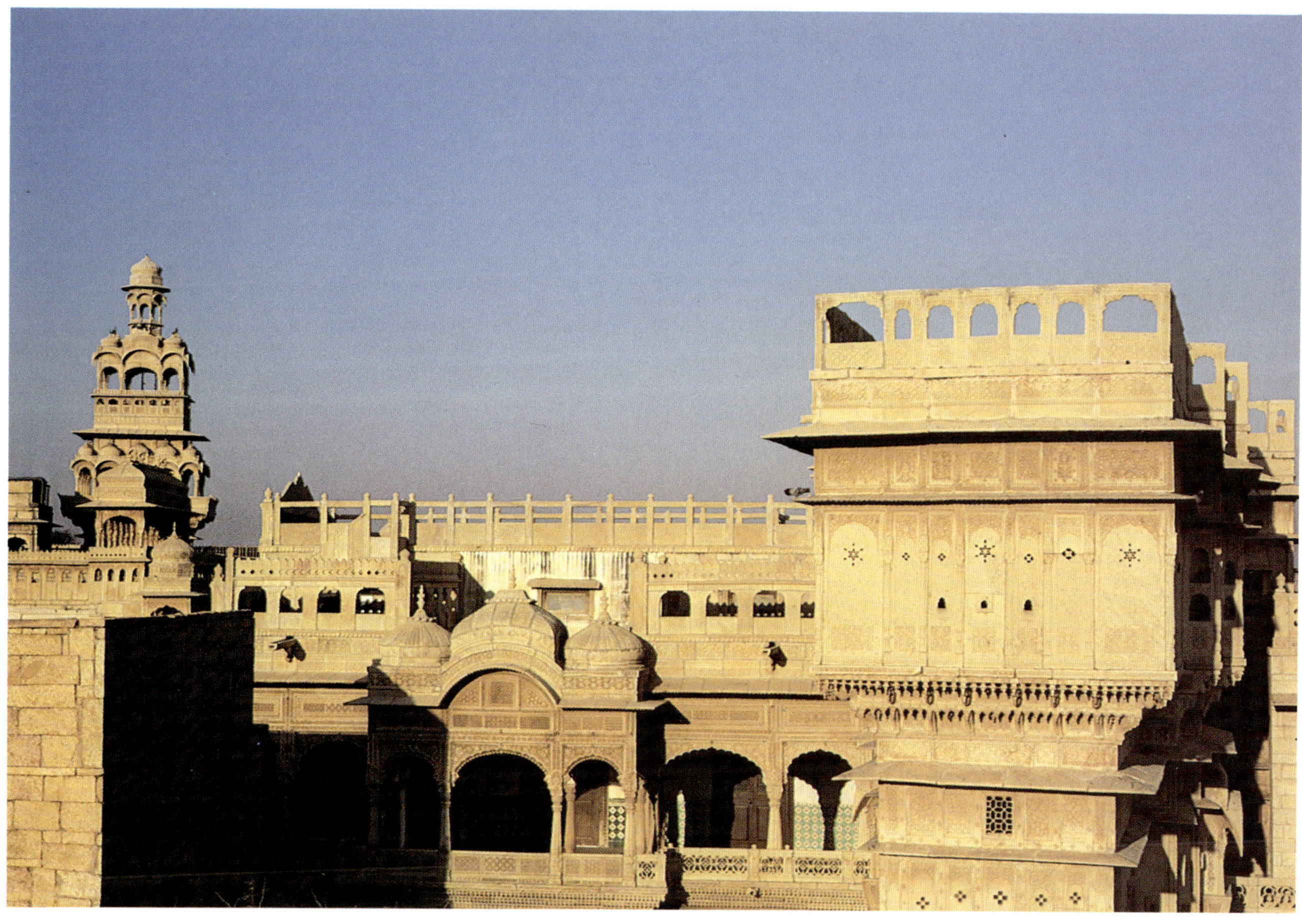

Tazia Tower and Badal Mahal, Jaisalmer.

Khadim, an oasis of green, in the desert

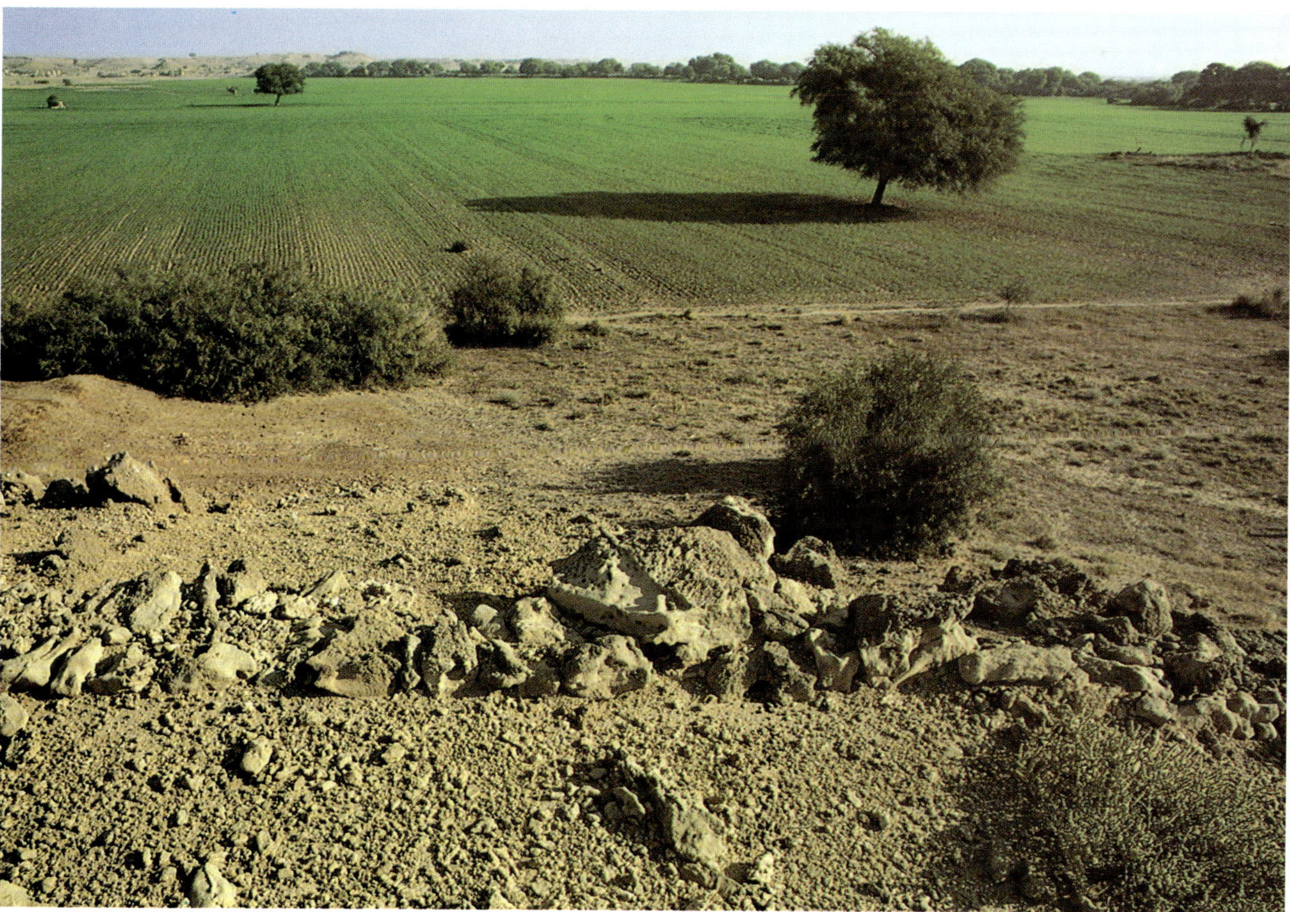

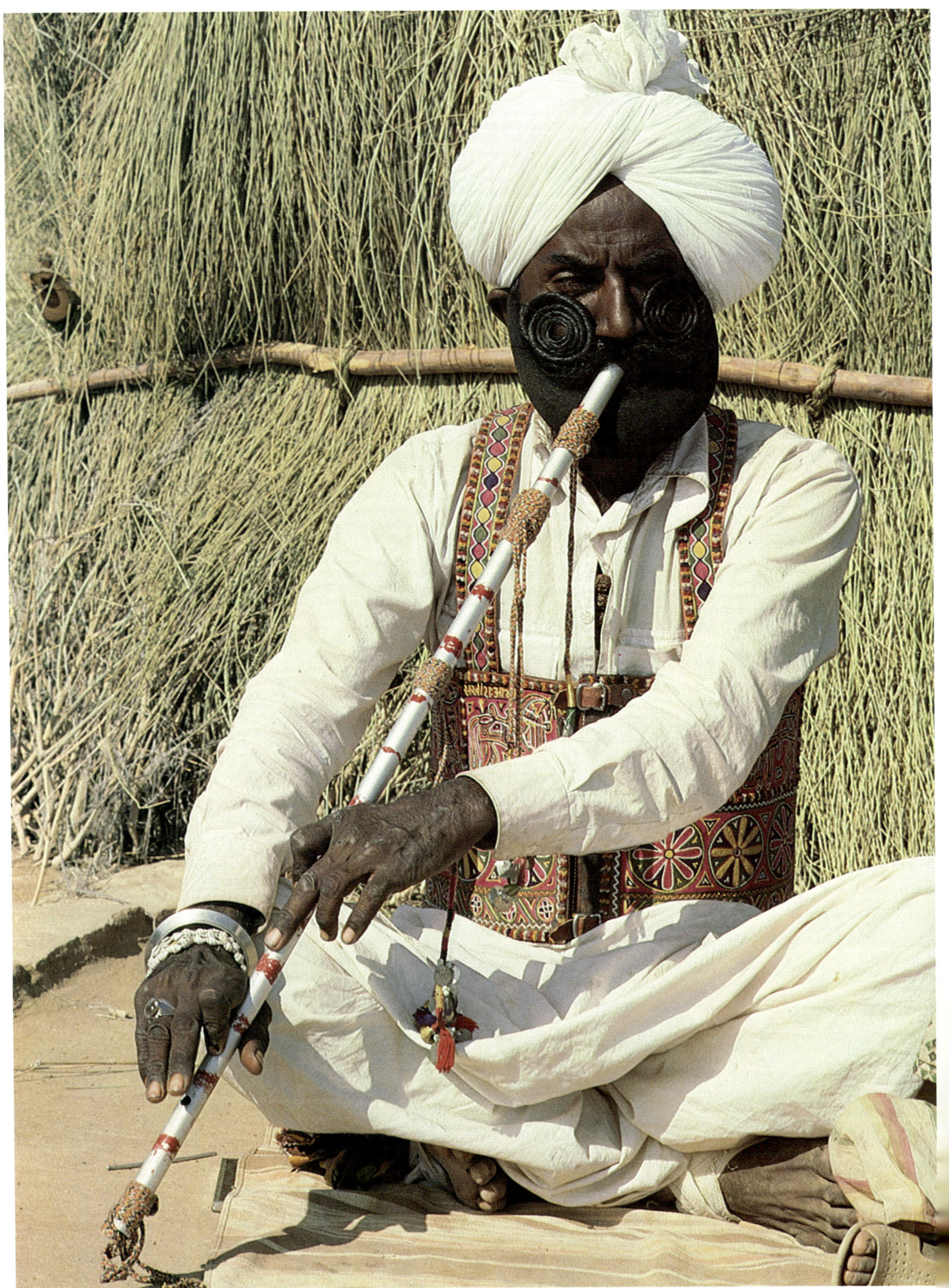

Karna Ram, Bhil, playing the *narh*.

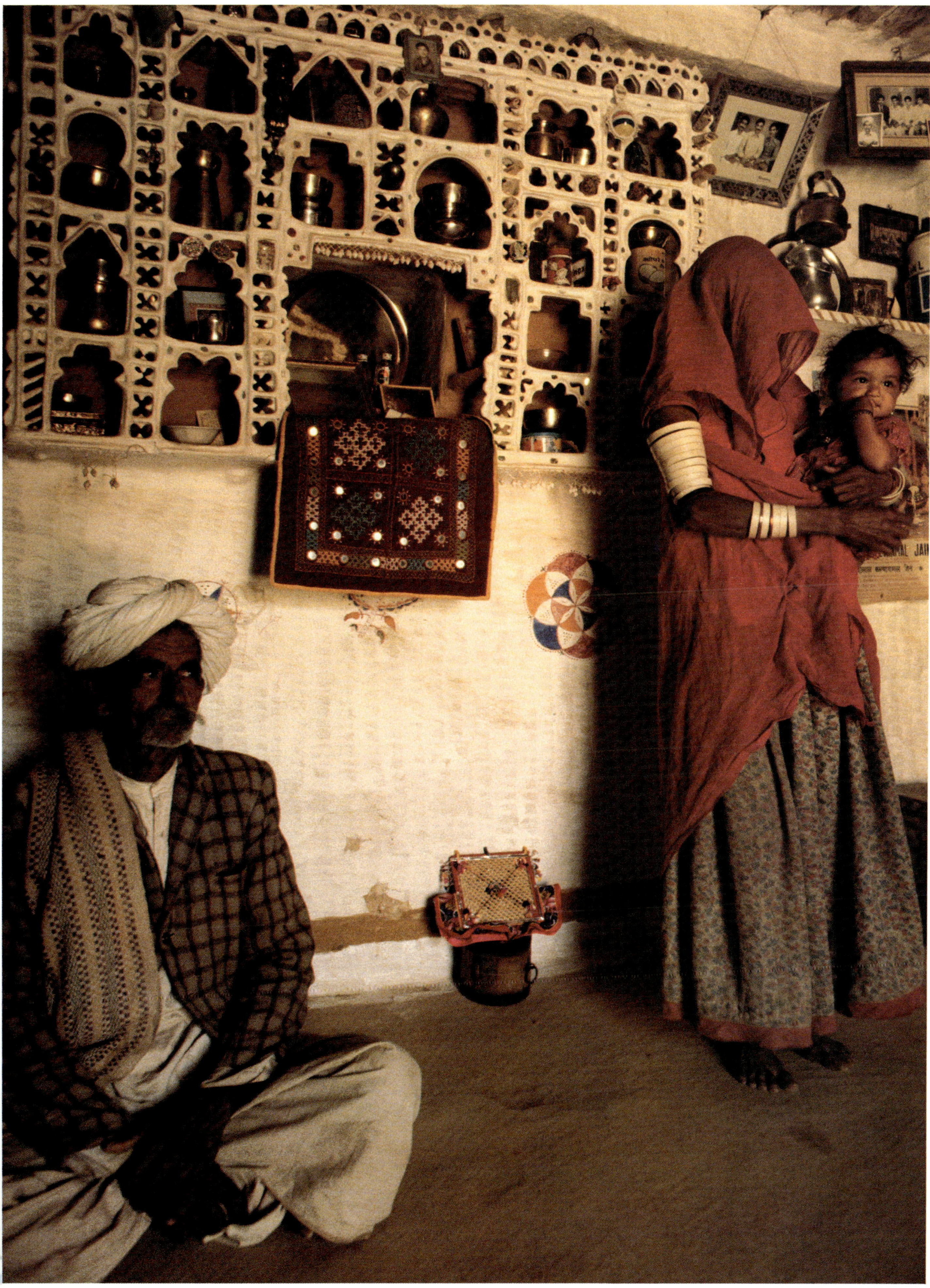
Interior of a home showing storage space

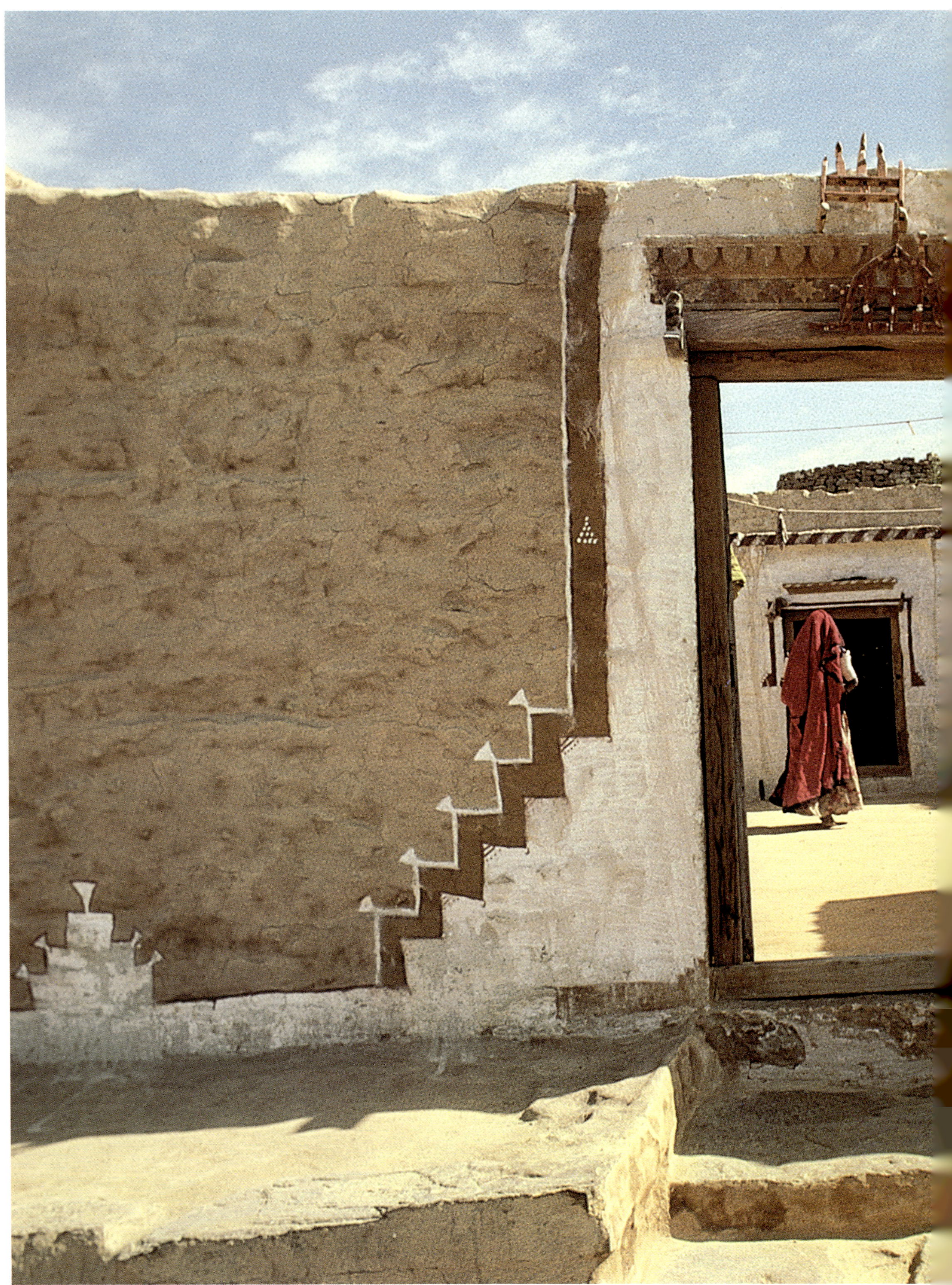

Kanoi. Entrance to a village home.

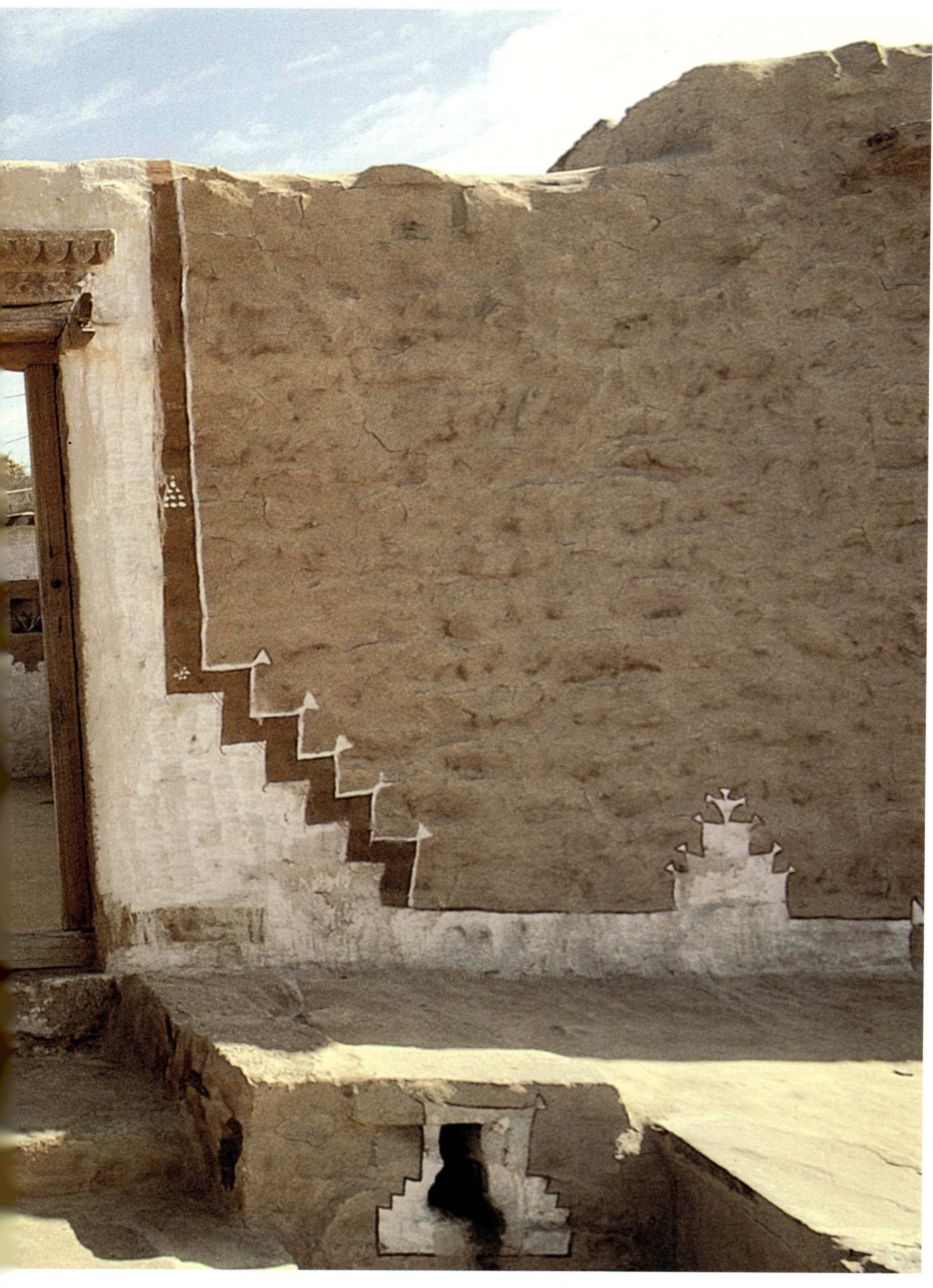

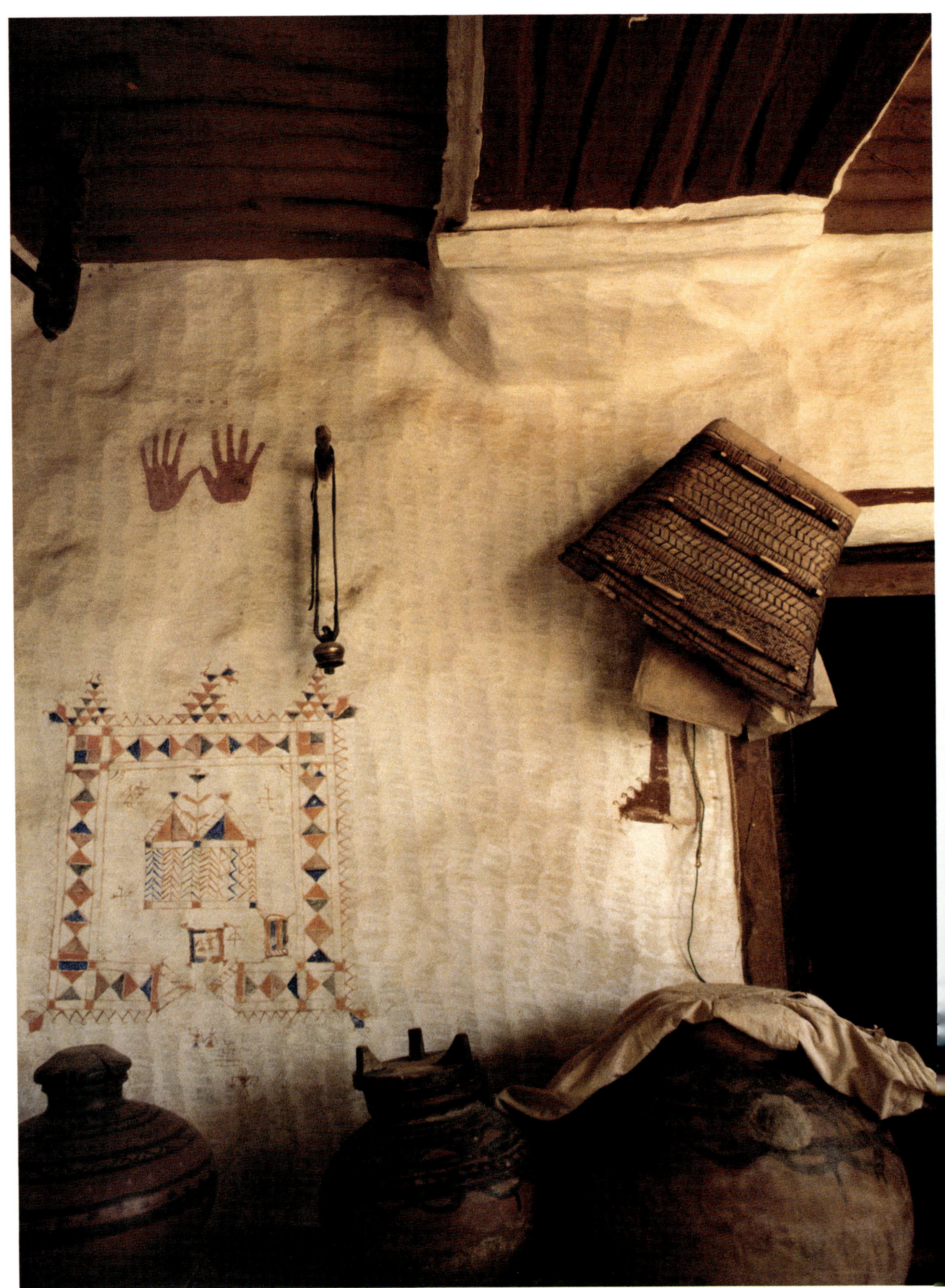

Wall painting and decoration, Kanoi.

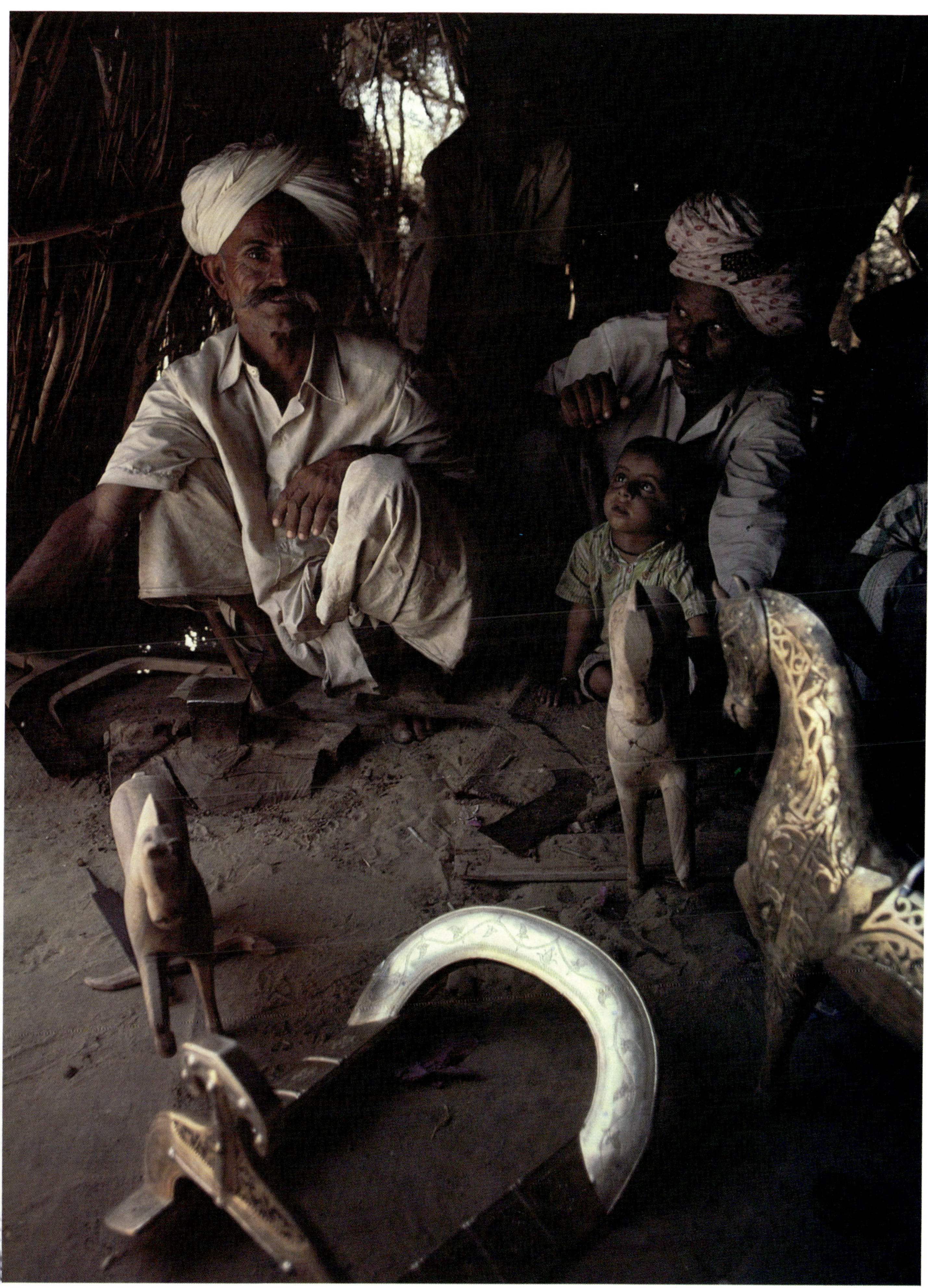

Desert craftsmen making horses, wood with brass overlay.

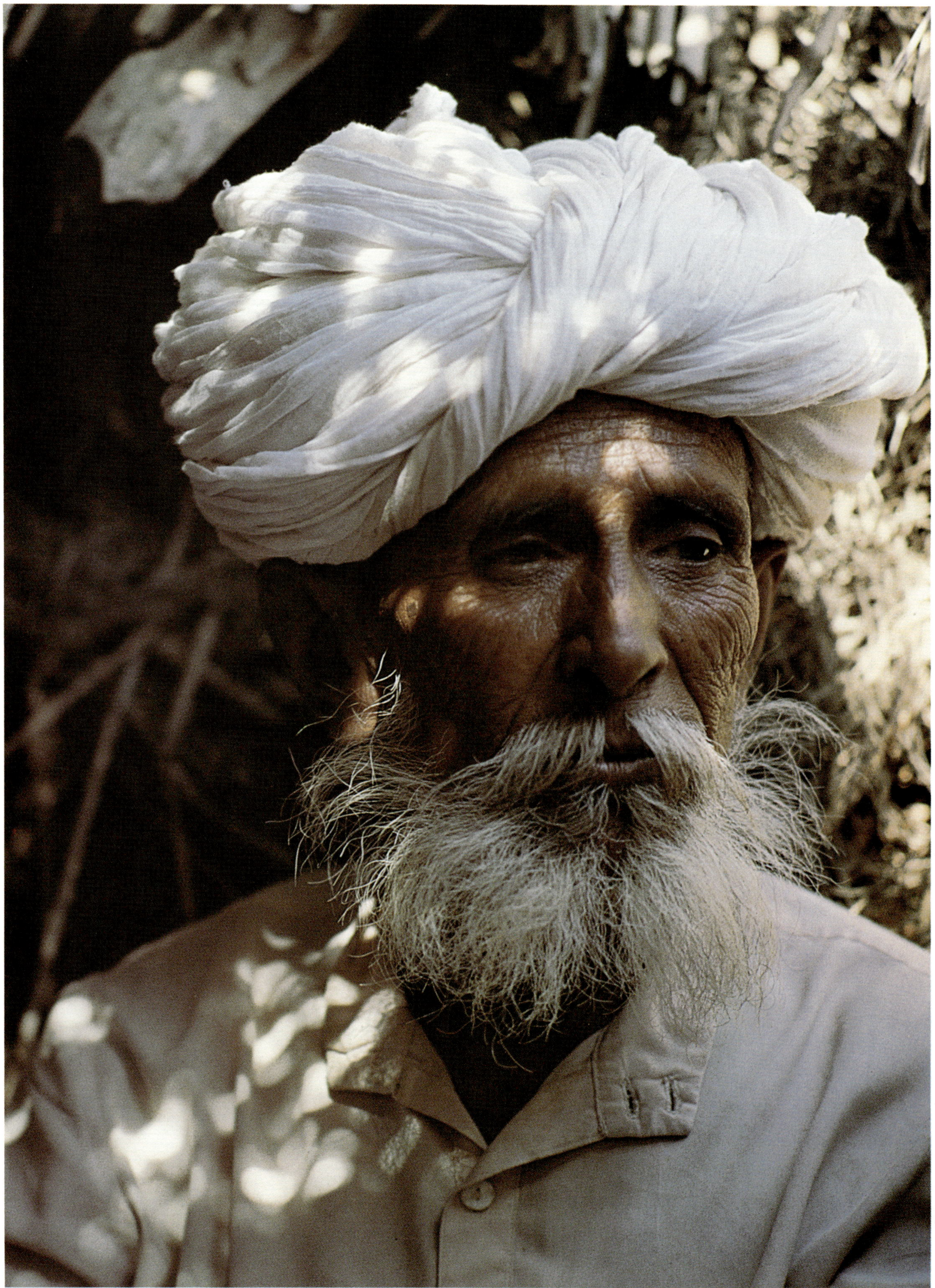

A desert *sutar*

5 Marh: The Rock I

This was once an ocean bed. The waters rolled in from the west and spent their force against a mountain wall that stood higher than any range we now know. The uneasy masses heaved, shifted, broke apart. The earth swallowed itself in gargantuan gulps, and as it spewed itself out in lava, flame and rock, the ocean was sucked in. The mountains that were, disappeared, while far, far to the north, the mountains that are, rose up. The Tethys Ocean of the Palaeozoic Age was no more; the Himalayas were born. The shattered spine of the Aravallis, like some monstrous, pre-historic skeleton, lay half-buried, scattered across the land, showing scarred and tortured ribs in the crags, scarps and rugged outcrops found south-west and north-east of this geologic cemetery. Beyond these weathered remnants, to the west stretched the floor of what was once the ocean bed, and is now an expanse of wind-driven, wind-fluted jurassic limestone known as Marh, the rock.

In the middle of Marh, on one of the rocks that gives the region its name, stands the legendary desert fortress of Jaisalmer.

In the aeons between the death of the ocean and the buoyant rise of the juvenile Himalayas that still continue their upward thrust in periodic upheavals, this region of petrified rock has experienced cataclysmic changes. It has frozen in several ice ages and, in between, has burgeoned in semi-tropical forest or sprouted in green savannah till, during the last inter-glacial period, the winds took over, the sun came home, and the desert prevailed.

Today at Aakal, just 17km east of Jaisalmer, one can stand on a bare mound of yellow, brown and red rock, sparkling with bits of mica, and touch with unbelieving fingertips the petrified tree-trunk of some tropical giant that stood rooted here one hundred and eighty million years ago. These fossilised trunks are now protected by iron grids to prevent them being chipped off by eager collectors who set them in platinum or gold and sell them as talismans, the next-best thing to a bit of moon rock.

When the native states signed the Instrument of Accession in 1949, and surrendered power to the newly formed government of independent India, Jaisalmer was the least known of the kingdoms of Rajasthan. It had been hedged round with tales of horror: of death by sinking into sand drifts; of dunes littered with the bones of travellers who had lost their way and perished of thirst; of dacoits and smugglers' gangs who ruthlessly killed all strangers in their territory. It was rumoured that in the early days of the Raj, when the British Political Agent wished to visit Jaisalmer, the Rawal's camel-mounted, formidably armed escort would meet his party at the boundaries of the state, and conduct them by such a circuitous way that no one could recall the route to the fortress city.

Jaisalmer had not always been so cut off from contact with the rest of the country. Isolated though it was by the surrounding desert, it lay on the path of an ancient caravan route of the spice trade, and was a major halting-place for traders from Africa, Arabia, Iran and Central Asia, who came through the passes of Zabulistan and Baluchistan, down via Tatta or Multan, across the Indus to Jaisalmer, on their way east to Imperial Delhi, or south to Gujarat. The revenue of the

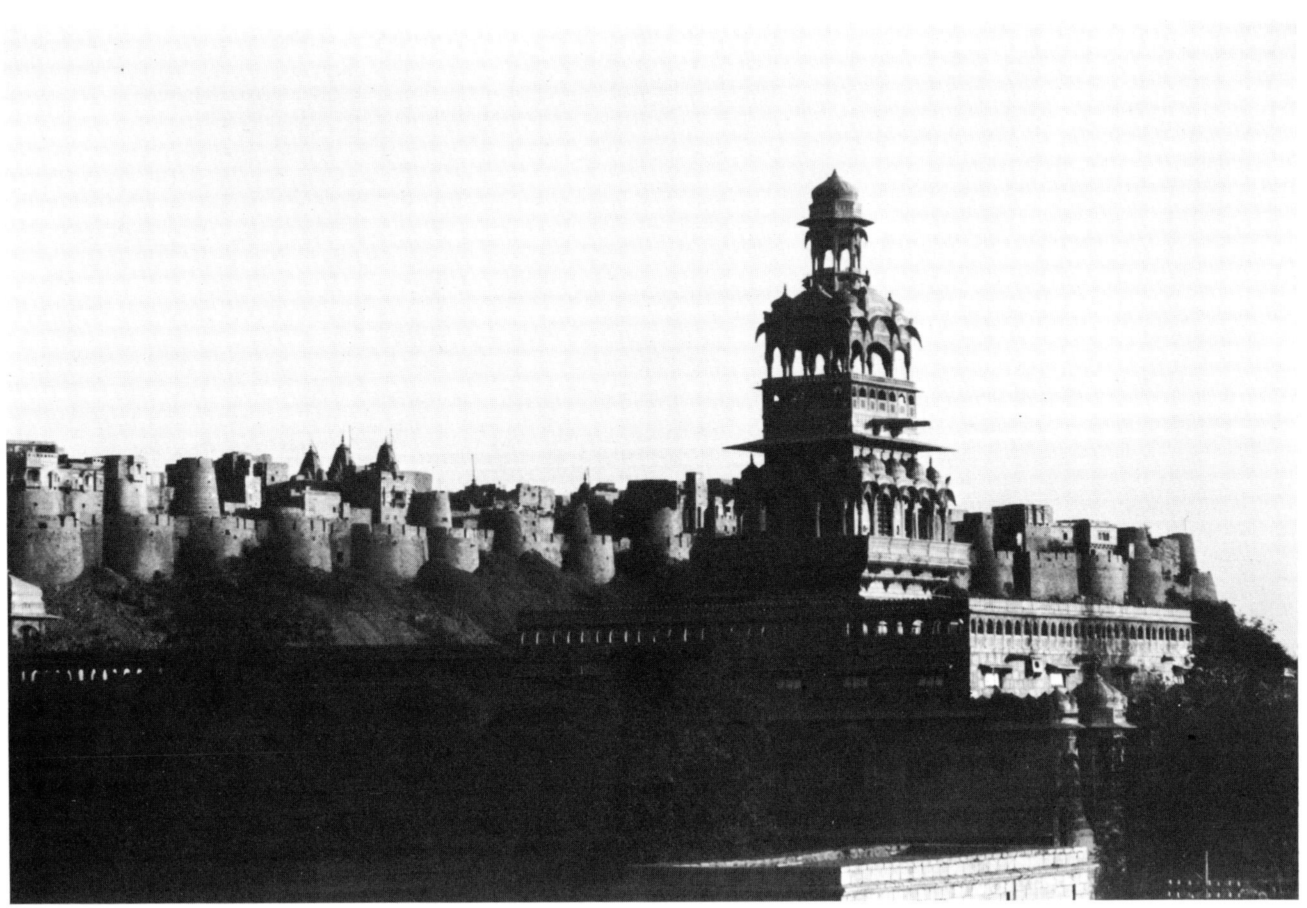

Jaisalmer fort

Jaisalmer rulers derived mainly from taxes levied on the caravans, while the local Marwari merchant-bankers built up immense fortunes through trade and usury. Once the port of Bombay was established in the 18th century and trade diverted to the seas, this perilous and immensely taxing overland route lost its importance, and Jaisalmer its lifeline with the interior. Its remoteness was further accentuated with the coming of the railways at the beginning of the 20th century, which did away with the caravan trade, except in the inaccessible regions of the Thaar.

In contrast to the enterprising ruler of Bikaner, Jaisalmer refused to permit the laying of the railway line within the state. In fact the ruler hoped to protect Jaisalmer from any outside influence, and up to the time of Independence, no strangers were allowed into the fortified city without permits, while his own people were able to leave or return only with his express authority.

So Jaisalmer dwindled and almost disappeared from view into the storm-swept dunes of the Thaar, till it became a sort of mirage in the memory, a recurrent nightmare of an unknowable, terrifying landscape where rock and sky fused under the fiery sun, which was eclipsed periodically by swift winds that raised an eerie howl, made shrill by the gritty swirl of aeolian sand.

There is an old rhyme,

Horse of wood,
legs of stone,
a frame of iron
will get you
to Jaisalmer, alone.

The people of Jaisalmer were held in awe by all other desert dwellers. They were said to walk forty kilometres a day, subsisting on a handful of parched gram and a cup of water, and to continue thus for three weeks on end. When a band of these hardy people entered a town, the citizens barred their doors, shut their windows, and spoke in whispers, for they feared the dread marauders, known as the wolf packs of the Marh.

The rulers of this audacious people were the Bhati Rajputs. They believed they were the direct descendants of the ancient Yadavs, a Chandravansh, lunar, clan, and hence the 'children of Hari', Lord Krishna. Born of the moon, their diaspora had been prolonged, for their homeland Dwarika had been submerged by the seas a thousand years before Christ, and their numbers scattered. Beyond the Hindu Kush they gathered, living in turbulent exile, till they returned to the sub-continent to win territory by force of arms, and to set up their early desert capitals at Bhatner, Thanot, Derawar, Lodurva and finally, in fulfilment of an ancient prophesy by Lord Krishna, in the citadel of Jaisalmer which they raised on *tricuta*, the triple-peaked hill, in 1156.

The country they had conquered was a desolate expanse, a lunar landscape of drifting sand-dunes and jurassic rock that held the secrets of the sea locked in its smouldering heart.

At Kharagarh on a plateau between shallow ravines barely 10km west of Jaisalmer gape the ruins of the forsaken township of the Paliwal Brahmins. The stones of the desolate city sit sulking in the noonday sun. A few pitted sandstone pillars lean drunkenly, on the verge of collapse, holding themselves up with drugged obstinacy. Beyond them brood roofless walls of houses abandoned by residents as though in a hurry to be gone. We rambled through the silent streets, over crumbling steps, in by an ominous doorway into bat-haunted rooms, out through a broken window, kicking over sherds of water-pots by an empty blackened hearth, picking up bits of yellow sandstone. And interred in these stones lay the visible evidence of a much earlier historical transformation – signs of ocean life: the pearly glow of embedded sea-shells, of fish forms etched delicately into the soft gold rubble; of a mollusc fully preserved, which we zealously hoarded, to add to the collection of the museum at Borunda.

We had been anxious to arrive at the Jaisalmer fort before the sun set. But our diversion to Ramdevra delayed us. The red disc had slipped below the rim of the horizon, and by the time we reached the point where a turn in the road brings the fort into view, the sun's brief afterglow, which had streaked the sky in tremendous orange and yellow beams, as though from a colossal searchlight, was abruptly extinguished. Against a smudged violet backdrop the fort crouched in the darkling twilight, a gigantic predatory beast, awaiting the shroud of midnight before making its murderous leap. Even so it must have waited in the past, glowering with sinister intent, before it unleashed the savage hordes that seethed restlessly within its walls. Through its massive portals the opium-maddened, howling horsemen had thundered across this forlorn landscape on yet another of their ravaging raids.

I felt the sharp stab of a splinter of fear, as though I had stepped barefoot on a *babul* thorn. I had come here often by this very approach, but Jaisalmer had never before revealed this secret malignant visage. By the time we drove up to the local rest-house, the street lights had come on one by one, and all along the outer ramparts of the fortress their dim glow smeared the lower levels of the rock with a touch of blood, leaving its upper ridges and the fort itself in the dark. High above us, within the fortified city, a blue light of the Jain temple spire seemed to float on the immense heavens, a single, lost star. For the first time I was glad we were spending the night in the drab, commonplace rest-house, and not within the smothering embrace of those encircling ramparts.

Next morning we saw a cultivated *khadim* at Rupsi village. The refreshing green of the wheat fields appeared like a miracle in the middle of the arid land. Rupsi must have been another of the abandoned villages of the Paliwals but, unlike the ruined Kharagarh, it had been taken over by peasants who maintained the same system of cultivation that the Paliwals had so successfully employed.

Paliwal Brahmins were considered the finest agriculturists of the desert. They migrated in the 12th century from Pali near Jodhpur district, their original home, from where they were driven out by the treachery of their Rathor allies. In the desert their chief means of sustenance was the cultivation of the *khadims*. These shallow troughs are formed between the sand dunes, where water collects during the rainy season and gradually seeps into the absorbent ground. The diligence of the Paliwals transformed these moisture-retaining troughs into oases of green fertility. They built embankments round the catchment area, dug wells often to a depth of 100 metres, and constructed tanks to serve as reservoirs. Kharagarh had been one of the villages bestowed on the Paliwal Brahmins by a grateful ruler who exempted them from taxes. But during the long tyrannical rule of Salim Singh Mohta, a prime minister of Jaisalmer who was in absolute control of state affairs in the first half of the 19th century, the Paliwals were ordered to pay taxes. They pleaded exemption, but when this was refused, they left Jaisalmer in a body and migrated to Bikaner where they were made welcome. Kharagarh was abandoned in this general exodus about the middle of the last century. I believe that Salim Singh tried to coax them back later, but without success.

Rupsi peasants cultivate two major crops, wheat as the *rabi*, winter, and millet as the *kharif*, summer crop. As the rains had failed that year (1979), no *kharif* crop had been possible.

At Kucharee village we were fortunate to see a weaver at work. His wraith-like figure surfaced through shallows of shuttered light like a nostalgic image in a daguerreotype. The loom was being set for the white cotton blanket common in this area, with a broad border in black and red stripes. The village was bare of trees and the mud-houses were flat-topped, the walls smooth, and the doors and windows outlined in white and ochre bands with an occasional geometric pattern of triangles to break the wall-space. The visual impact of the hamlet as a whole was of a spare simplicity of cubes in sand-grey and mud-brown. The few touches of ochre and white had a startling effect against this low-toned background. Kucharee had the intergrated beauty of a three dimensional cubist painting, but it must have been very like purgatory to live in. The sky is usually a washed out leaden grey, and the implacable sun on a landscape shorn of green must turn the mud houses into infernal ovens in the summer. It was difficult to believe that the soothing fields of Rupsi lay just a short distance away.

The Fort of Jaisal

We returned to Jaisalmer at midday, the sun directly overhead. A heat haze rose from the desert floor in shimmering waves above the immense sea of sand. Around the bends of the road the fortress appeared, disappeared, through the dazzling air, a tantalising mirage. Slowly, as the blurred image of a submerged galleon assumes firm substance when the waters are still, the triple-peaked hill took shape. Following the natural curve of the rock, the curtain-wall of the fort undulated in gigantic billows, echoed in the counterpoint of diminutive ripples of sand below. What we had glimpsed as elusive and insubstantial from a distance suddenly assumed a massive, overwhelming presence: the Rock of Jaisal. It is the colour of the fort that makes it unique. The jurassic limestone of the region is a pale yellow that is burnished to a deep rich gold. Wind and sun have created the topaz shades of Jaisalmer. Hewn and sculpted and firmly embedded in its setting of stone, the edifice seems to glow like a majestic gem under the resplendent sun.

Jaisal had chosen the site of his new capital with great care. Not only is *tricuta* the highest of the rock-hills around, but its flat-topped triangular shape, rising in a gradual slope south-east to north-west, gives the lofty extremity a vantage point for surveying the countryside. The palace stands at this highest spot surrounded by formidable double ramparts, about a hundred metres above the market-place and township which nestles within the outer fortified walls. The inner ramparts protect the royal enclosure, so that this vulnerable core of the fort could be sealed off from the city if the need arose. The approach is barred by a series of four protecting gates.

The heart of the upper complex is the great Central Court facing the palace. A grand flight of marble steps on the left leads up to a white marble throne.

There the Rawal held court, granted public audience, or attended religious ceremonies. Between the throne and the palace wall is an old, disused well with a rusted iron cover, known as Jaisal's well. The legend on the founding of the fort centres round this primordial source of water.

It is related that, during his search for a strategic site, Jaisal visited an old ascetic called Eesul, who lived on *tricuta* beside a spring reputed to be a hallowed site of the epic age. The saint told Jaisal that his *karma* had brought him to the right spot, because *tricuta* had been a place of pilgrimage since the days of Krishna who had come here with the Pandava hero, Arjuna, after the great *Mahabharata* war had ended. They had joined the ritual sacrifice conducted by the sage Kaga, who lived on this hill by the natural spring. After the rites were over, the thirsty Arjuna drank from the fountain and remarked that the water was brackish, whereupon Krishna smote the rock and a stream of sweet water gushed out. Krishna then prophesied that in the distant future, during the 'dark age', a descendant of the Yadav clan would rule at *tricuta*. It

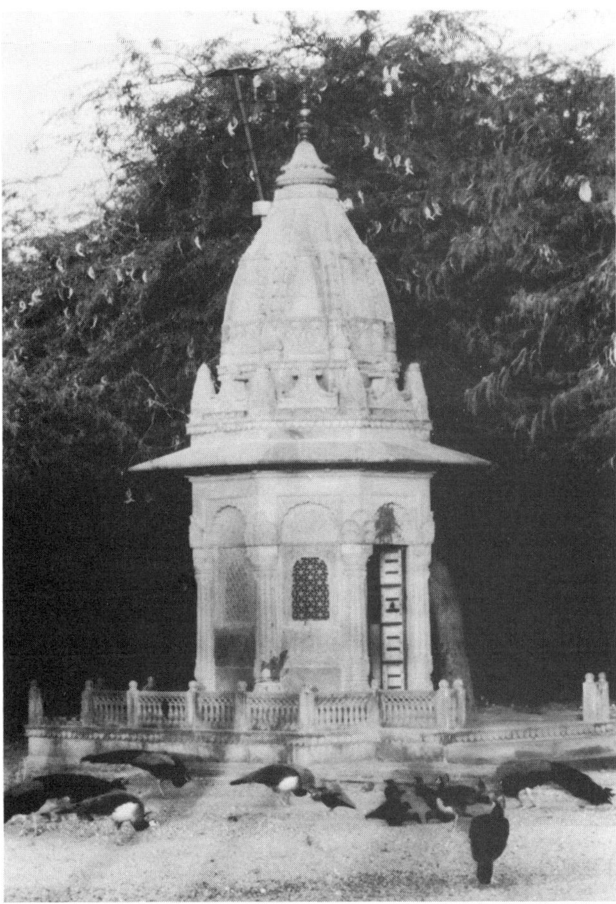

Peacocks, crows and pigeons at a small temple

is said that Eesul showed Jaisal a stone inscribed with this prophecy.

Jaisal's well marks the place where the spring flowed at Krishna's bidding. In use for many years, the well is now dry, but the stone inscription, alas, has never been found.

To the right of the throne is the temple to Bhavani, the goddess Kali in her terrible form as Destroyer. After offering sacrifice and prayers to the goddess, the Bhati warriors used to set out for battle, or more frequently, on one of their marauding raids. Opposite the temple is the entrance to the Great Court. The paved road, wide enough for four horsemen riding abreast, winds between buildings on the hill-side on the one hand, and the high inner protecting wall on the other, through Hava Pol, Gate of the Winds, the enormous Suraj Pol, the Sun Gate, past the Akai Pol and the Ganesh Pol, till it reaches the lower city.

Several years ago an English friend had accompanied us to Jaisalmer. After visting the palace he had withdrawn into a silence which lasted for many hours, lying on a cot in his room, staring at the flies on the ceiling. When he finally roused himself from his stupor, he confessed that he had been unbearably oppressed by the atmosphere of the fort, the stones of which seemed to reek of blood. I sympathised, for I had felt a similar sense of stifling horror in the streets of Florence where the forbidding palaces of the Gelphs and Ghibellines seemed to exude the cruelty and terror of their blood-soaked history.

This fort too has known barbaric times, which is not surprising considering the life-style of its brigand rulers. When Jaisal had first decided to fulfil the prediction by founding the city, the hermit Eesul had warned him that the stronghold would be sacked two and a half times. The Bhaats, balladeers of the Bhati Rajputs, love to recite the heroic epics which tell of the consummation of this augury. These highly exaggerated and colourful accounts were not written down, but memorised and sung in a form of traditional oral poetry distinguished by its rhythmic style, known as *dingal*. The tradition was handed down from father to son in the families of the Bhaats attached to the Rajput courts.

Legend tells of the first sack which took place in the reign of Alauddin Khilji (1295-1315) as a result of a foolhardy raid by the Bhati Rajputs on the royal baggage-train carrying tribute to Delhi from Tatta. In reprisal, the Sultan sent an army which besieged Jaisalmer for seven long years. During this period the fighting was desultory while the Muslims attempted to starve out the defenders. One of the young Rajput princes, Ratansi, became quite friendly with Nawab Mahboob Khan, the commander of the besieging army. Between skirmishes, the two antagonists would meet under a tree to play a game of chess. On one occasion, finding the younger brother of the commander ill, the chivalrous Rajput offered him the hospitality of the fort and conveyed the sick man inside. In the meantime the Khan had decided to lift the siege. As luck would have it, his brother, having observed that conditions in the Rajput citadel were indeed critical, pressed for a final assault on his return to camp. The Muslim army decided to attack, and made preparations. The Rawal reproached Ratansi for his over-friendly gesture to the enemy, the bitter price of which would now have to be paid. The food and water stocks were so low that the fastness could no longer hold out.

The signal for *johar*, that most awesome of all Rajput rites, was given. On the marble steps and in the Great Court, the women and children were immolated by fire or put to the sword. After this dreadful slaughter, the warriors, dressed in sacred saffron, threw open the gates of the fort and rode out to meet their death. Before he left for the battle, Prince Ratansi sent his two young sons under escort to his friend Mahboob Khan, with a request that the boys entrusted to his care be brought up in their own faith. His trust was not misplaced. Although the fort was stormed and laid waste and the city deserted for some years, the two Rajput princes grew up at the court at Delhi. When Gharsi, the elder of the two, had proved his mettle in the service of the Muslim Khan, Jaisalmer was restored to him, and the Bhatis occupied it once more.

The second sack occurred during the intervening years, between the first *johar* and Gharsi's restoration. A branch of the Bhati Rajputs under the command of a headstrong prince named Dudha tried to restore the city to some semblance of life and order. Unable to resist the temptation, Dudha raided the camp of the Tughlaq Sultan, Ferozeshah, at Anasagar lake near Ajmer, making off with the horses of the royal stable. The stronghold was once again overrun by the Delhi ruler, and the *johar* repeated.

The half-sack referred to in the prophecy is explained by an incident that took place during the reign of Rawal Lunkaran in the 16th century. A friendly Pathan named Amir Ali tried to capture the citadel by an oft-repeated ruse. He ostensibly made a request for the begums of his family to pay a visit to the ranis of the Rawal, but actually filled the palanquins with armed warriors. A fight took place, during which Rawal Lunkaran, rather prematurely as it happened, put to death several of the Rajput queens with his own sword to prevent their being carried off by the Pathans. But the intruders were beaten off and Amir Ali captured and slain.

The dates as chronicled by the bards are confused, as usual, and the names of the Muslim rulers often incorrectly given. This is not unexpected in purely oral records. Since Alauddin was a long-remembered and powerful sultan, he is occasionally held responsible for deeds well before his time or after he was safely entombed. Similarly, raids subsequent to the brief but unforgettable incursion of the dreaded Taimur Leng (1398) were laid at his door. Occasionally a corroborative date from the written chronicles of the meticulous Muslim historians helps to pin-point an event. The real worth of the Bhaat's traditional accounts is not in their factual accuracy, as in their poetic validity. They provide revealing insights into the prevailing social order and the complex systems of values. The recounted incidents are not so much historical narrative as they are parables and allegories exemplifying an intricate and punctilious code of behaviour at all levels of the corporate hierarchy. Besides capturing the spirit of the times, they evoke the vast hinterland of meaning and belief, the invisible web of impulses which transforms conduct into instinct.

Bardic legends are mainly concerned with the incessant struggle of the Bhatis against the encroaching Rathor Rajputs of Jodhpur and Bikaner. It is an endless saga of reprisals and revenge in which forts were captured and lost with montonous regularity. What these conflicts meant to the unfortunate inhabitants, the bards do not recount. They blandly tell of wells choked with sand to render them unusable, villages and towns razed to the ground, warriors taken prisoner, and citizens looted or put to death. While deeds of valour, according to the bards, were the exclusive prerogative of the martial Rajputs, the fact is that the people of the desert learnt to live hard, to protect themselves as best they could, to take advantage of whatever conditions offered, and to deal with the fortunes of war in the

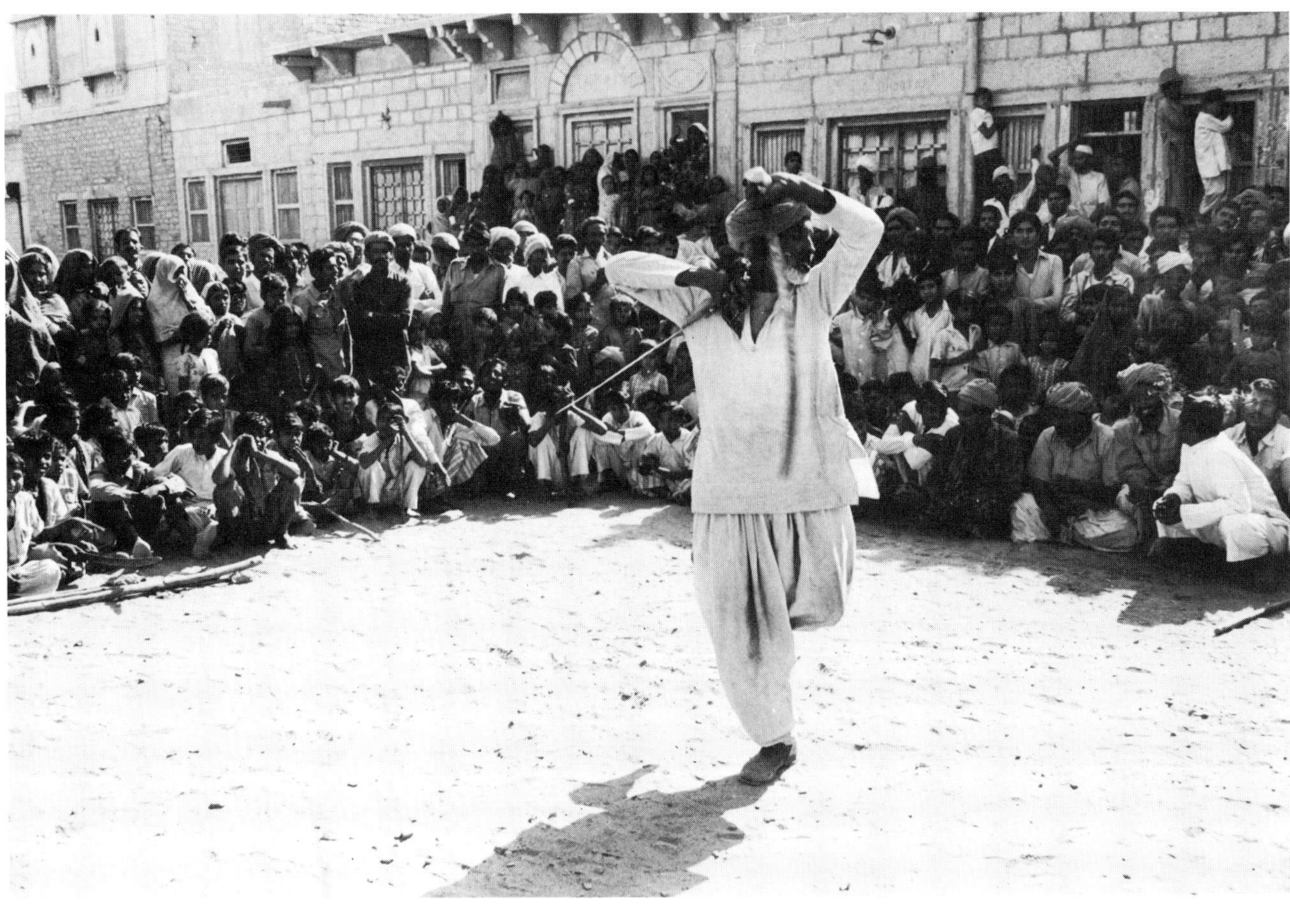

Moharram ceremonial performance in Manik Chowk

same way as they faced the calamities of their barren environment. They developed a stubborn resignation and spare frugality that are still the most outstanding traits in their character.

With the establishment of Mughal power in Delhi during the reign of the Emperor Akbar (1156-1605), the Rajput kingdoms one by one came under imperial suzerainty. Despite its remote location, Jaisalmer was no exception. The Rawal paid the stipulated tribute demanded by the emperor. Princesses of the Bhati clan were sent to the royal harem as royal consorts. Bhati soldiers formed contingents employed in the wars of Mughal expansion, and several Rawals of Jaisalmer served as generals commanding the imperial forces of their overlord. The contact with the Mughal court and the lavish gifts of a grateful sovereign stabilised the position of the Bhatis in the desert. The uncouth brigands of an earlier time benefitted from contact with a cultivated court. These material gains, augmented by loot as the legitimate bounty of triumphant battles, made them powerful rulers of their kingdom.

Manik Chowk: Past and Present

Beyond Ganesh Pol the road fans out into the wide sloping expanse of Manik Chowk, the main market square. In the centre of the Chowk is an old water-trough. It is not very large but it remains the favourite watering-place for animals that live or work inside the

fort. I have watched the instinctive protocol of creatures around the trough, without the interference of humans. Camels take precedence invariably. They thrust between the waiting cattle and donkeys to imbibe long draughts, necks stretched down to the water, front legs straddled wide. Donkeys come low in this unquestioned hierarchy. They stand by with meek patience, eyes half closed against the glare, while the free-roaming bulls and staid cows with calves drink noisily, huffing and snorting between deep intakes.

One seldom sees horses here, though mounted Rajputs must have clattered through this square often in the past, fully caparisoned, riding to battle in formation, pennants flying from their lances. The enormous kettle-drums of war were hoisted on the best of camels, one on each side, the drummers beating out the ominous, rousing roll, rallying the citizens. They thronged the square to urge the martial procession on with throbbing excitement, the women chanting *bhajans* as they scattered flowers on the passing cavaliers, and the men joining in the blood-chilling battle-cry of the Bhatis, 'Jai Bhavani!', their voices quickened with an underlying note of fear for on the outcome of each battle depended the lives of their women and children and the security of their few worldly possessions. Although the Rajputs were the fighting class and professional warriors, it was up to the citizens of such an isolated stronghold to defend

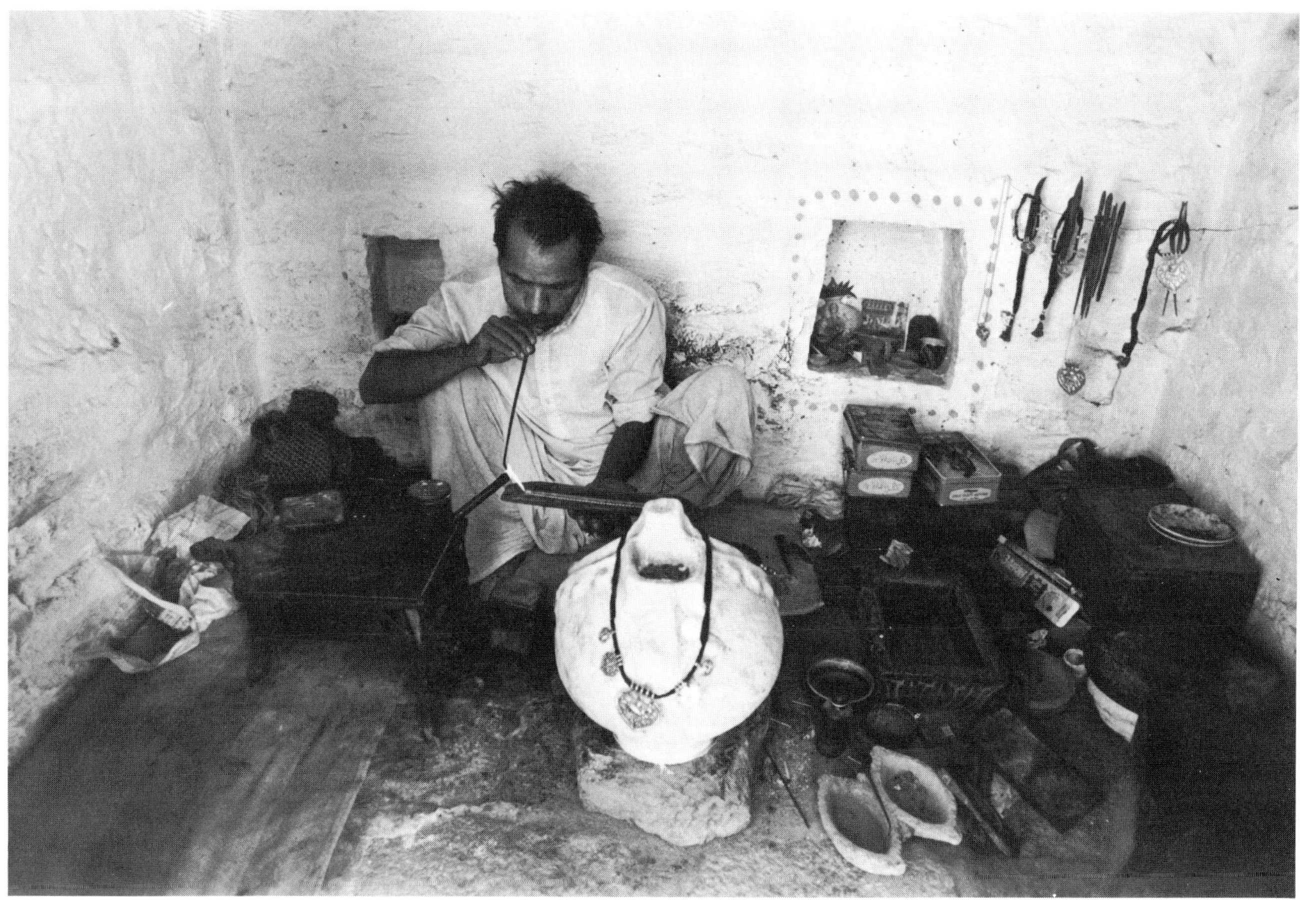

Silversmith in Jaisalmer

their individual homes and families. Most men went armed, as they often do today. Even the Marwari merchant class who profess the Jain faith of total *ahimsa*, non-violence, are strict vegetarians, and fanatical about taking animal or insect life, were skilled in the use of sword and dagger which they effectively used to protect their wealth and their women folk. But the weaker sex were not to be outdone, for the women of Jaisalmer are celebrated in song and story as much for their beauty as for their physical prowess and their bold, aggressive spirit.

Beyond the trough, a row of vegetable sellers sit on the ground with their produce heaped in front of them. The scarlet of the chillies warns of their pungent sting, plump purple brinjals roll against a pile of dark green spinach. Half a pumpkin, opaque seeds lining its warm golden-yellow belly, lies exposed to the dust, as the vendor weighs the cut portion for a customer in hand-held scales, her extended arm covered from wrist to elbow with glass bangles and silver bracelets, and above that, right up to the armpit, with cream-coloured ivory arm-bands.

Across the road the barrow-men tend their moveable stalls. Some sell sweets, fruits, second-hand garments. Others display items of hardware: penknives, screw-drivers, nails, chains, locks, hooks and hammers. Cyclists jostle with the crowds around the fruit-stalls and make their purchases without bothering to dismount. A camel nuzzles a bunch of bananas on a barrow, across my shoulder, before striding on, nose in air, leaving water dribbling down my neck. A sacred bull gives me a decisive shove which lands me in the open drain, where I lose a slipper. The huge beast pilfers a bunch of spinach, and with the nonchalance of an absolute monarch resumes its royal peregrinations. Children scoot past like buzzing beetles on home-made wheel-carts. Dodging between the bullock carts and camels, a scooter splutters past, while the sudden appearance of a car laden with tourists, or a noisy jeep bulging with officials on their rounds, makes everyone skip aside for safety. We take refuge in a tea-shop, where I am consoled by the thought that embroidered Rajasthani slippers are easily procured round the corner. The radio blares out film songs in ear-splitting decibels from a loudspeaker fitted above the shop, a philanthropic device contributed by several petty traders for the general entertainment of their fellowmen. Manik Chowk is as clangorous and manic as any other Indian bazaar, but with a difference.

All one's ramblings here are punctuated by echoes from the past. Images of the square, as it must have been, intrude into the present, superimposed as a sort of double image on the mind's eye, in a continuous montage. The petty hawkers and vendors dissolve into the powerful merchants and intrepid travellers from distant lands and, in place of the handful of wilting vegetables or barrows of fruit and hardware, appear, in a succession of vivid close-ups, the luscious dates of Basra, the large sultanas and plump raisins from the vineyards of Chaman, dried figs and apricots that retain the sharp flavour of the orchard-gardens of Isphahan, walnuts, hazel-nuts, almonds and those enticing pistachio nuts, glimpsed through shells agape, from which the delicious sweet, *piste-ki-laus*, was made. Here were piled carpets from Herat, fur-lined jerkins from Kabul, superb swords and scimitars from Damascus, with their finely chased blades, and casks of the perfumed wines of Shiraz. Spirited Arab steeds were brought from far away Balkh; hapless captive slaves from Turkestan and Abyssinia, and those legendary red-haired, green-eyed Circassian houris abducted from unknown mountain kingdoms, who fetched fabulous prices and were the pride of the harems of Hindustan.

Jaisalmer was a brief haven on the long, tortuous route to the distant cities of the eastern plains. The caravans camped outside the fort walls, and while the merchants and traders made financial deals with the shrewd Marwari bankers of the city, travellers replenished their provisions and rested their animals. Scholars and divines passed through on visits to the exalted Mughal ruler of the day, carrying with them rare manuscripts. Occasionaly a Turkish or Persian princess made the long, endless journey to the royal harem at Delhi, escorted by a special mounted guard and accompanied by her fair companions, maid-servants and slave girls from her parental home which she never again would see.

On their return, these extensive caravans took back with them the lustrous gold and silver brocades of Benares; bales of sprigged gossamer muslins of Murshidabad that have bequeathed their name, *chheent*, chintz, to an alien tongue; indigo to dye the cloaks of royalty; saffron, cloves, cardamom, black pepper, cinnamon and all the exotic fragrant herbs of the East were transported through, along with the rare musk, aromatic gums, attar, antimony, precious gems, ivory, sandalwood, opium, monkeys and peacocks for the wealthy who lived in lands far beyond the Fertile Crescent.

There are other centres in the Thaar that were busy marts in earlier ages, but none is so redolent of the past. Confined within its fortified ramparts, located in the sequestered desert with no rival over a wide radius, Jaisalmer is unique in retaining its medieval atmosphere, and Manik Chowk evokes most vividly in its sounds and sights and smells the secrets of this lost world from its past.

This Chowk is the apex of the lower township. The major roads from the four gates of the citadel lead up to it, and these in turn are connected with each other by cramped lanes, roughly following a grid plan. Upper balconies of houses on either side almost touch on top, providing deep shade for pedestrians below. The different castes and communities live in localised ghettos, with the simple lime-washed, mud and rubble huts of the poor packed close between large, imposing *havelis* built of the local ochre stone. The conditions that dictated the distinctive features of the architecture were imposed by the environment and life-style of the people. These were: protection from the encroaching desert, the blistering heat and frequent sandstorms; the limitation of space; and the need for safety. Although such conditions prevail throughout the Thaar, the considered response to them is not demonstrated with such clarity as in the tightly knit community living at Jaisalmer. To avoid heat and dust, walls are thick, ventilation is through small, narrow apertures, protected by latticed screens to ensure through passage for the slightest whiff of breeze. The single door at street level is necessary, as much for keeping out sun and sand, as for ensuring the safety of the inmates.

Inside the *havelis*, in the familiar immemorial style, small rooms surround the central courtyard. This inner court is the multi-purpose living-room of the traditional Indian home. It ensures the privacy so essential in a densely built-up area. It is here that women cook, wash, sun-dry vegetables, or sift grain in the mornings; spin or sew in the afternoons, while the little children use the space as their playground. In the evenings the family gathers together for the last meal of the day, and during the long summer months sleeps out in the cool of the desert night under the stars.

The distinguishing beauty of the *havelis* of Jaisalmer is in their renowned carved facades. The art of the *silavats*, stone carvers, has not attained such excellence anywhere else. The intricacies of the art of carving in India are said to stem from the early use of wood for building and ornamentation. This has been translated here into the more enduring material of yellow sandstone, with no less finesse or delicacy of effect. The mellow tints of the Jaisalmer stone, when cut, chiselled and incised, are more appealing than the cold white tracery of marble we see in the celebrated screen at the Taj Mahal, although it may be heresy to say so. The ornate decoration of wall-space around doors and pillars serves a purpose beyond the aesthetic, for it subdues the glare, while sunlight filtering through the fine screens casts soft, honey-toned shadows.

Patwon-ki-haveli, the mansion of the Patwas, is considered to be the finest of the *havelis*, and is certainly the largest and most elaborate of them. The Patwas were a wealthy family trading in *zari* and *badla*, the gold and silver threads used in brocades and embroidery. They soon expanded their business to include the lucrative trade in opium, and acted as revenue contractors and bankers. In the late 18th century, Guman Chand Patwa was reputed to have a chain of three hundred centres extending between Afghanistan and China. It was during his lifetime that his five sons first began to build this distinguished *haveli*, and its construction, begun in 1800, took over

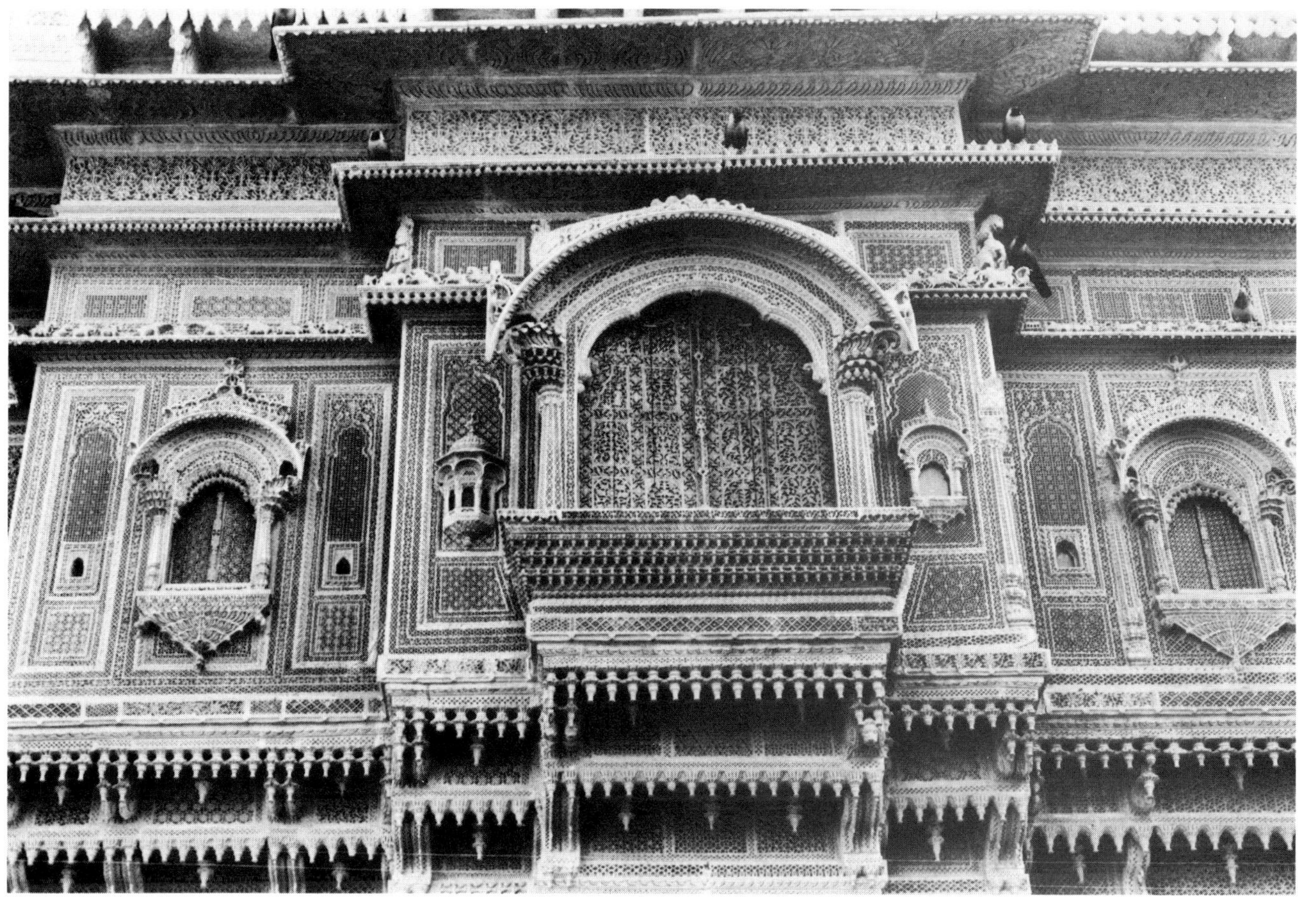

Intricate facade of Pathwon *haveli*

fifty years to complete. The mansion stands in a cul-de-sac, and is actually a series of five, separate self-contained establishments which are interconnnected. The lofty arched entrance that spans the lane separates the domain of this wealthy family from the rest of the street, giving it the seclusion of status. This building is now a protected monument, as is the fortress as a whole.

I have always preferred the modest but also more cohesive and compact of the mansions, which is Nathmaliji-ki-haveli. This is still the home of the descendants of Nathmalji, who was prime minister of the state in the latter part of the 19th century. It was also the last of the great *havelis*.

The entire front wall is composed of huge boulders, instead of the usual cut and dressed stone. On the inside these rocks have been left in a raw state, giving the rooms a captivating, unfinished look. In contrast, the outside surface has been covered with matchless fine carving. The craftsmen who fashioned this consummate masterpiece of the stone-carver's art were two brothers, Hathu and Lallu. One worked on the right side of the facade, the other the left. With studied purpose, each artist made minute modifications in design, so that although the whole gives a completely harmonious impression, the patterns on either side are variegated in detail.

Another impressive *haveli* is Moti Mahal, Pearl Palace, the mansion of the tyrant, Salim Singh Mohta.

Its conspicuous features are the upper storey that projects in cantilever fashion, supported on carved stone brackets, and the multiple little blue cupolas that cap its roof. It is not a large house, in fact it appears modest for Jaisalmer's big bogey-man who is still remembered for his rapacious greed. He finally succeeded in impoverishing the whole state by driving away all the wealthy merchants and the industrious Paliwal farmers, poisoning several princes of the ruling house, and destroying in this manner the economy and stability of Jaisalmer. In the end, his own family migrated to Hyderabad, and the *haveli* now houses the shops of petty traders.

What gives the architecture of Jaisalmer its homogeneous character is an underlying uniformity of workmanship and design. This was achieved by the busy factories of stone carving that came into being during the hectic years of construction. Here stone was cut, dressed and hewn to certain set proportions, and certain types of patterns became a tradition with particular families of artist-masons. When building a *haveli* a person could buy individual units of windows, doors, balconies, brackets and pillars, all conforming as to size and style – an early system of standardised prefabrication. It was only the very wealthy, such as Nathmalji, who could afford the services of individual artists.

The *silavats* of Jaisalmer who built for the royal family the Jawahar Mahal, Jewel Palace, which stands

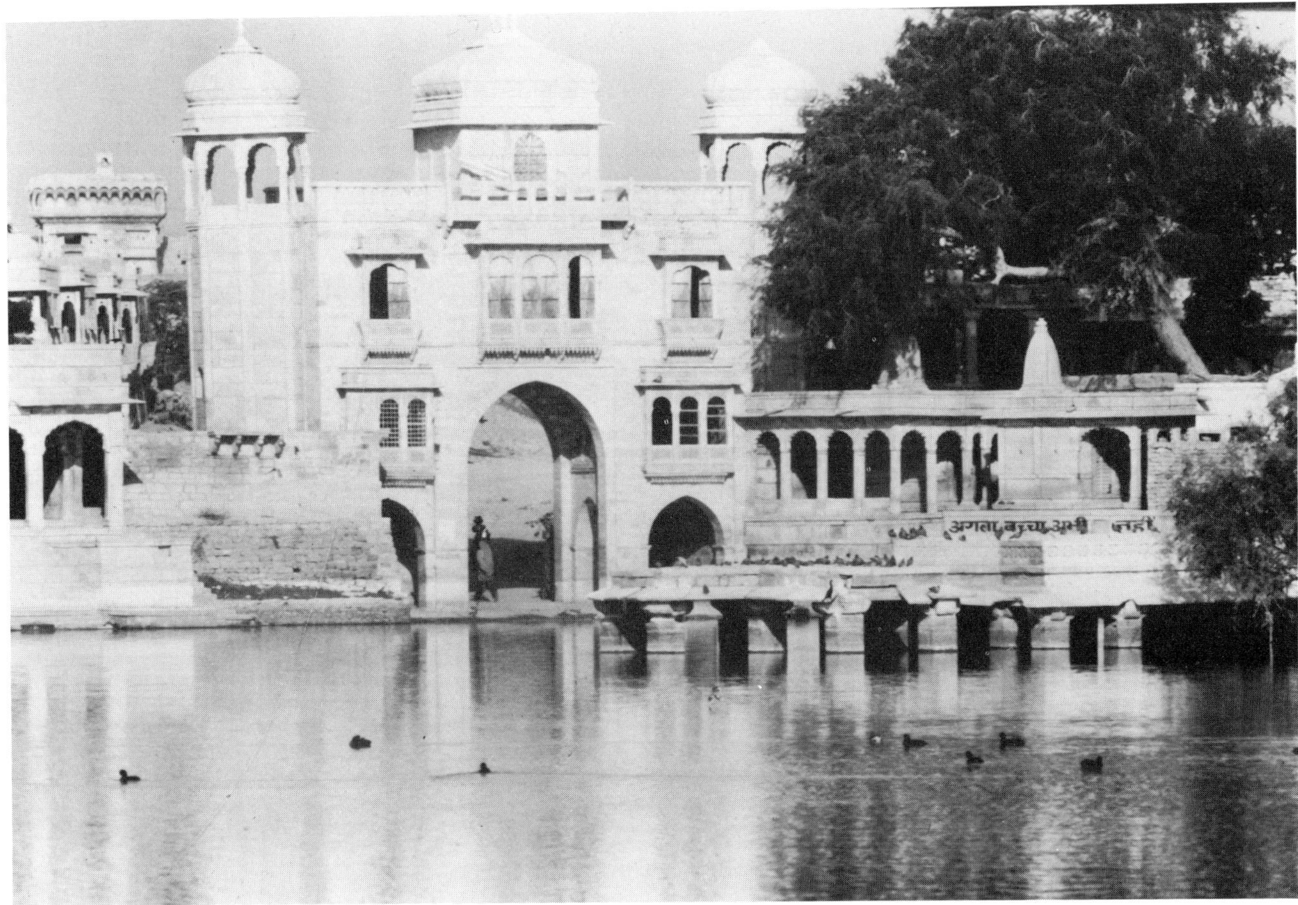

The gateway of Tila, Gadsisar, Jaisalmer.

outside the fortified city to the south-east, also gave it a final touch of elegance. They proffered as a gift to their royal patron the Tazia Tower in the Badal Mahal, Cloud Palace. This extraordinary structure is like no other in India. It is built in the shape of a *tazia*, the delicate, split bamboo, paper and tinsel ornamented replica of a bier, which is carried in procession during the Muharram period of mourning. It thus acquired an exotic, pagoda-like look. The gift became a parting gesture, as in 1947 with the partition of the country at Independence, the Muslim stone carvers migrated to Pakistan. The family of the ex-ruler of the state still resides in Jawahar Mahal.

In the light of the dying day, the tower, around which pigeons fluttered, undecided where to roost, looked like a smudged *sumi-e* study. The lanes, by now, were empty, as the citizens of the fort eat their evening meal at sundown. It was too early for us to turn in, so we strolled down to Gadsisar, to listen to the sound of water. 'Pee-aao' 'Pee-aao!' Beloved, come! invited the peacock in its plangent dischord which sounds so sweet to Indian ears. A pale half-moon led the way.

Gadsisar Lake and a Courtesan's Gift

Gadsisar lies beyond the Tazia Tower south-east of the fort and is a fairly large rain-water lake fortified with man-made embankments. It is entered on the north bank through an arched gateway and open pavilion, beyond which steps lead down to the water. This is known as Tilon-ri-Pol or the Gateway of Teela. She was a captivating, accomplished courtesan who belonged to Hyderabad in Sindh. During the season of rains she used to visit Jaisalmer where she was welcomed as a favourite of the ruling prince. Magnanimous and compassionate by nature, and perhaps wishing to gain respectability through a charitable act, Teela built the gateway to the tank and the bathing ghats for women and children. This benevolent gesture was resented by the ladies of the royal family. They considered it an insult to enter the precincts of Gadsisar through the gateway built by a woman of dubious social standing, and insisted that the Rawal pull it down. But Teela was a match for their machinations. She immediately installed an icon of Sri Satya Narayan in an upper chamber of the gateway and had it consecrated as a temple by a Brahmin priest. Not even the Rawal could desecrate a temple, and so the useful attractive gateway has remained. But the ladies of the royal household always avoided this entrance.

In the early morning and late evening, water birds gather at the lake. It is a pretty sight to watch the rush of coot as they tread water, wings flapping as they rise in the air. Or to follow a flight of herons, slowly circling, till they settle like drifting snowflakes upon the rocking waves. Egrets ride the water-buffaloes that graze on the banks, skilfully keeping their perch when their mounts wallow blissfully in the oozing shallows for a long siesta.

Gadsisar used to be the only source of water for the fort in times of drought, when the wells dried up. One of the major achievements of the state was to pipe water from the lake up to the fort in 1942. But though it is barely a generation since water has been laid on, a pronounced change can already be seen in the life and manners of the citizens. People have grown self-contained, aloof and indifferent. In the old days, in times of drought calamity brought a great sense of closeness and belonging to the community. They would all go to Gadsisar for their allotted ration of water. The Rawal would be present to see that fair distribution was made and would himself share in the general distress. Now the complaint is that the installation of the piped water system has made everyone live in his own private yard and ignore the joys and sorrows of his neighbours. In many subtle ways the benefits of civilisation have eroded established patterns of culture, though its advantages cannot be discounted.

Immortal Lovers: Moomal-Mahendru

The most enchanting of the many versions of the Moomal-Mahendru legend tells of the princess's residence at Moomal-ri-mehri, the Palace of Moomal, on the banks of the seasonal stream Kak, near Lodurva, where they still point out the remains of the once celebrated site. The princess was a spirited and independent-minded young woman of unusual accomplishments. Her palace was said to be an entrancing abode where strangers entered at their peril. Moomal and her sister Soomal would sit on the terrace of their mansion and sing hauntingly beautiful songs. Many princes charmed by their voices tried to gain entry to the palace, but not one was able to force his way in.

One day Prince Mahendru of Amarkot was riding by on his swift camel, Cheekal, accompanied by his brother. Beguiled by the wild, enticing song of Moomal, he determined to meet the singer. On entering the palace the young princes were menaced by ferocious beasts that seemed about to pounce on them. Mahendru's brother took fright and turned back, but Mahendru attacked the animals only to find that they were stuffed. He sped up to the terrace to claim his prize, the princess Moomal. She met him with couplets from a song, and he replied in like manner. They fell in love, and every evening Mahendru would come on his camel, spend the night with his love, and leave before dawn to get back to Amarkot as the sun was rising.

These nightly escapades greatly vexed Mahendru's seven wives. As the distracted lover would go to the chamber of his youngest wife on his return, the other six asked her to try and discover where he went. She reported that he came back with his clothes dripping wet, and without a word to her, fell asleep.

They advised her to squeeze a sample of the water from his wet garments. She did this and from the nature of the water they discovered that he crossed the Kak stream. So it must be Moomal he visited, she who was reputed to be an enchantress.

The seven wives then conspired together and bribed his camel keeper to kill Cheekal, which he did. Deprived of his favourite mount, Mahendru had now to resort to an animal which was not as fleet-footed, and so was late for his rendezvous.

Moomal fretted the hours away in despair; there was no sign of her lover. To distract her attention, her sister Soomal dressed herself in male attire and played the absent prince, singing and dancing to comfort her woebegone sister. Worn out with waiting, the two girls fell asleep, their arms around each other, and that is how Mahendru found them when finally he arrived. Mistaking Soomal for a man, he left in disgust, dropping his camel-whip in his anger and confusion.

When Moomal awoke she recognised the whip and realised what must have happened. Night after night she continued to wait for her lover, all in vain. Maddened with longing, she disguised herself as a mendicant singer and set out alone for Amarkot. Spent with hunger and fatigue, she trudged her way to Mahendru's palace, and under its windows she sang of Moomal's steadfast love for her beloved. But Mahendru was too deranged to heed the message of the wayfarer. For many days and nights the slowly weakening voice lifted itself in song, in poignant appeal, till the singing mendicant fell exhausted outside the palace gate. When the guards went to him they discovered it was a young woman and that she was dying.

Too late, the prince of Amarkot was reunited with his beautiful enchantress. She collapsed in his arms. Wild with grief, he died soon after of a broken heart.

They say that since the death of the Princess Moomal, the river Kak has ceased to flow.

What strikes one about this legend is its unadorned simplicity. Here are no tyrannical parents, wicked uncles or cruel villains. The two girls lead uncluttered lives in their charming palace which they have peopled with such cleverly contrived devices as the stuffed animals for their protection. They sing, dance, enact plays and are accomplished, cultivated young ladies of talent. When disaster overtakes Moomal she does not pine and waste away but courageously decides on a course of positive action. She is in fact the embodiment of the ideal Rajput princess, captivating, gifted, laughter-loving, brave and faithful. This is the noble lady of the Nayika series in Rajput miniature paintings – the *Abhisarika Nayika*, the maiden without fear, who ventures out into the dark storm to her clandestine meeting in the jungle, undeterred by the lightning that zig-zags through the ominous sky, the menacing snakes that cross her path, or the savage jungle creatures that peer at her through the dense foliage.

In her happier and lighter moments, Moomal recalls the *Svadhinapatika Nayika*, secure in the ambience of her love, shown in play with her enthralled lover at chess, or at a game of blind man's buff amidst laughing fountains, or enjoying a performance of dancers and acrobats.

But while disguised animals hold no terrors for Mahendru, and he scoffs at them for the harmless illusions they in fact are, he is unable see through Soomal's male guise, and immediately assumes his love has been betrayed – so misleading and tenuous are the ties of love. Unable to rationalise his own dread imaginings, it is left to the woman to make the long pilgrimage to him and knock, as it were, at the doors of his heart. Once again the man is taken in by the woman's disguise, and his overweening self-pity makes him deaf to the promptings of true love. The star-crossed lovers shed all illusions only in death.

The Living Legend of Karna Ram Bhil

To speculate on the life of a legendary princess from the past is one thing, but to meet a legendary hero-deity in the making is quite another. We spent a morning with Karna Ram Bhil whose personal charisma and 'macho' image might well find their final epitaph in a contemporary ballad of Jaisalmer and a hero tablet under a *pilu* tree. Karna is not unaware of the possibilities of such immortal glory. Nor is he averse to the more transient fame that the click of the camera bestows.

A familiar flamboyant figure in the streets of Jaisalmer, with his spectacular height and glistening rose-wood complexion, Karna's moustachios alone could earn him a certain notoriety. They may well aspire to figure in the Guinness Book of Records, as they measure the full length of his arms when uncurled, and when dressed, greased and tightly coiled, they lie like black serpents against his swarthy cheeks. His dark looks are admirably set off by spotless white *dhoti-kurta* and an embroidered waistcoat of intriguing design, fashioned by himself. With a peacock's plume in his white turban and the whole magnificent ensemble finished with the flourish of tasselled flute, sword, dagger and lance, Karna is the tourist's wildest fantasy of the exotic desert desperado conjured up in person.

He had asked us to his home, if such it could be called, because at present he is homeless. Karna is a folk musician, among his other pursuits. He plays the *narh*, a large bamboo flute, primitive in its low murmuring tone, and restricted in its range of notes, but difficult to manipulate. The flautist provides the drone himself by holding a long, sustained tonic, even as he plays the tune on the flute. In effect, he uses his breath in two different ways simultaneously. It is an almost impossible feat, and consequently there are very few *narh* players to be found. Among them Karna is outstanding. His breath control is phenomenal, and his deep bass voice has the resonance of distant thunder gradually fading in, as on a well-controlled sound system. In between playing on the flute, the player recites his narrative, and with Karna the vowels roll like an incantation of a dimly remembered ritual evoked into recall by his guttural utterances.

Karna is by way of being a protégé of Kothari's, at least as far as his skill as a *narh* player is concerned. He has been recorded for the research archives of the Rupayan Sansthan, and it was through this contact that Karna got known to a wider public as being more than what his local reputation holds him to be: a desperate character with a somewhat nervous finger on the trigger of an old-fashioned gun.

Two little children were playing with a pup and a newborn kid in front of a couple of grass-and-bamboo huts. String cots were pulled out for us to sit on, while Karna sat on a rug on the ground. He refused to place himself on the same level as his honoured guests. Cups of tea were sent out to us from the improvised kitchen. He played the *narh* for us, enjoyed posing with his family for photographs, and then sent for a small metal box which he unlocked, to share his treasures with his visitors.

These were an album of photographs and paper cuttings, and an object which he unwrapped from an old cloth. It was a carved wooden piece, armless and badly mutilated, of a female figure. He had found it in the bed of a dried-up tank. Kothari later identified it as being a household goddess that is installed in the home on festive occasions, and on the final day of worship is taken to a nearby source of water for immersion. To Karna the finding of the mother goddess was a sign of good fortune, a token of hope.

'I shall install her in my home,' he declared, reverently wrapping her up again. He turned to discuss his problems with Kothari.

'I am a Bhil, an outcast among outcasts!' Was it the pain, anger and humiliation of an entire people that we sensed in his voice?

The Bhils are possibly the aboriginal inhabitants of this region. They were rulers of the land when it was part of a younger, greener, more fertile earth. Bow and arrow hunters, food gatherers, and slash-and-burn cultivators, the Bhils belong to an early stage in the evolution of human culture. What was remarkable about them was their determined resistance against assimilation by the innumerable intruders and conquerors of the area. We know little of their pre-history; we do not even know their original name. It was the Dravidians who, more than five thousand years ago, called them *Bhila* – the bow – from the weapon that is still so much part of their being that they are never without it, even when it is of little use, now that the forests that were their home have been denuded of trees, and the game they hunted either extinct or protected, depriving them not only of their natural food, but of their whole way of life.

The Bhils are mentioned in both the great epics. In the *Ramayana*, it was a Bhil boatman who rowed the exiled prince, Rama, across the river, and Sharbari, a

Bhil woman, who shared her wild berries with him in the forest. In the *Mahabharata*, a Bhil named Jara by mistake shot Krishna with a poisoned arrow and caused his death.

We know that the Bhils still held a few of their independent jungle strongholds well into the late medieval period, and that the Rajput kingdoms were compelled to arrive at pacts of friendship with these wild, spirited people. Many of their primitive beliefs seeped into the religion of their more highly developed and organised conquerors. Spirit and ancestor worship is widespread among the common people, while the powerful *shakti* cult of Hinduism derives in part from early tribal beliefs in the fertility mother goddess.

Since they continued to resist a settled agricultural life and the amorphous embrace of Hinduism, the Bhils gradually sank to the level of outcasts. They were pushed into the interior of south-east Rajasthan, Gujarat and the jungle tracts of Madhya Pradesh, where they still exist in concentrated areas and retain, to a diminished extent, their tribal identity. In the desert, their numbers dwindled, and they lost all importance. Today the Bhils are termed a Scheduled Tribe and are counted among the many Scheduled Castes of Hindus.

'People dread the Jaisalmeri,' Karna said. 'They are in terror of the Bhils, and I am a Jaisalmeri and a Bhil, so...' he broke off with a booming laugh.

Karna Ram was a farmer with a meagre holding in a desert village. A dispute arose over the land with powerful neighbouring caste-Hindu landlords. He defied them, and after the fracas that followed, escaped, living for years as a hunted man on the edge of the desert.

He was finally caught by the police and imprisoned on a murder charge. While he was in jail, a French film unit, making a documentary on the folk music of Rajasthan, required a *narh* player. Permission from government was obtained, through the good offices of Rupayan Sansthan, to meet and film Karna in prison. Since then Karna has been released on bail. No one knows when the case pending against him will be finally settled.

In the meantime the influential landlords of Karna's village are determined not to allow him to re-occupy his lands. By the code of vendetta that operates in the desert, Karna's life is forfeit to his enemies, whatever the law may decree. Karna is homeless, but by now he has become a celebrity. He plays at government-sponsored desert festivals, and is one of the biggest tourist attractions of the city. The local folk musicians sing the songs of Karna. His photograph in the National Geographic Magazine has spread his fame across many continents.

'It is not what a man is born; it is what he does that matters. And freedom is here,' he declared, pounding his chest.

He apologised for the scanty hospitality he could offer in his improvised huts. He worries about his children.

'They have no home. But when the tourists ask me where I live, I point to the city palace,' he says, with a flourish of his arm in the direction of the fort. 'I tell them my family lives there.' He concludes with a burst of laughter into which we are drawn.

It is impossible to be depressed or disheartened in his presence, impossible to believe that his incredible vitality could be stifled on the gallows or confined within a prison-cell. Whatever his destiny, Karna seems bound for an immortal role. Already the Ballad of Karna Ram Bhil is spreading through the Thaar. Here is a hero-deity in the making.

6 Marh: The Rock II

Sudden Death at Joshi Talao

Khuiala, a village on the Sindh border, attracted us because of its reputed leather craft. But a short diversion off the main road brought us to Joshi Talao, a haunt of some of the larger water birds we had missed at Gadsisar. This small tank is a mere couple of kilometres beyond the south-east fringes of the sprawling city, but is little frequented. The road that leads to it is a deeply rutted dirt-track that lurches drunkenly across a bare, uneven plain.

In the quickening morning light, we could clearly see the trees around the tank in the distance to the right, but the road turned and twisted, here around an outcrop of rock, there past a clump of thorn, in and out in puzzling curves, leading us by false enticements through a maze of devious paths which brought us no closer to our destination. Finally, annoyed and impatient, we abandoned the track altogether and drove cross country straight towards our target. The cooing welcome of wood-doves soothed our ruffled nerves, and snatches of breeze skipping across the water braced the skin on our faces.

It was tranquil by the articifical lake, overhung with trailing branches of *keekar* trees, which drooped across the edge of the broken embankment to shed their tiny green ovals in its waters. On the farther bank a neglected pavilion with a look of impoverished gentility stared at its mocking reflection in the water. The *keekar* trees soughed plaintively above the steep steps, and their minute leaves formed flotillas on the lake's surface, joining and sailing together till the bubbles from a passing aquatic creature burst them apart. Water-bugs skied around the leaves, their lightning spurts streaking threadlike Vs behind them, while the plop-plop of the larger water-flies made rings in the water that cut across the bug tracks, or lost their widening momentum by colliding with the drifting foliage.

In the thin, blue sky, a solitary sparrow hawk wheeled so high that its presence did not disturb the coot and dabchick that bobbed like painted toys in the middle of the lake. But apart from these familiar friends, there were no other water birds.

Except for the occasional frenzied cry, 'Did-you-do-it, did-you-do-it' of the red-wattled lapwing, as it swooped down to the shallows, all was peaceful and calm. This bird is called *Titeeree* because of its weird call, and the name is an onomatopoeic equivalent as apt as the English, by which this handsome but hysterical bird is commonly known.

A peacock flew out of the scrub, alighting briefly on the dome of the pavilion, awaking with the Argus-eyed splendour of its plumage the fanciful past of the ruin it graced. It bent its crested head in kingly fashion before descending to plebian scratching. Then it collected itself and sailed back again into the trees.

Flocks of small *munia* winged across the lake in frenzied bursts. As we watched one of these fly past, there was a sudden whirring sound of panic as the high hovering *shikhara*, pinions held back, dived into the cloud of birds. In a swift manoeuvre it seized one frantic scrap of feathers in its claws, and darted with it into the *keekar* trees behind us.

This sudden experience of death, literally like a bolt from the blue, left us quite shaken. The rest of the flock had flown on in its characteristic dip-flight, as though

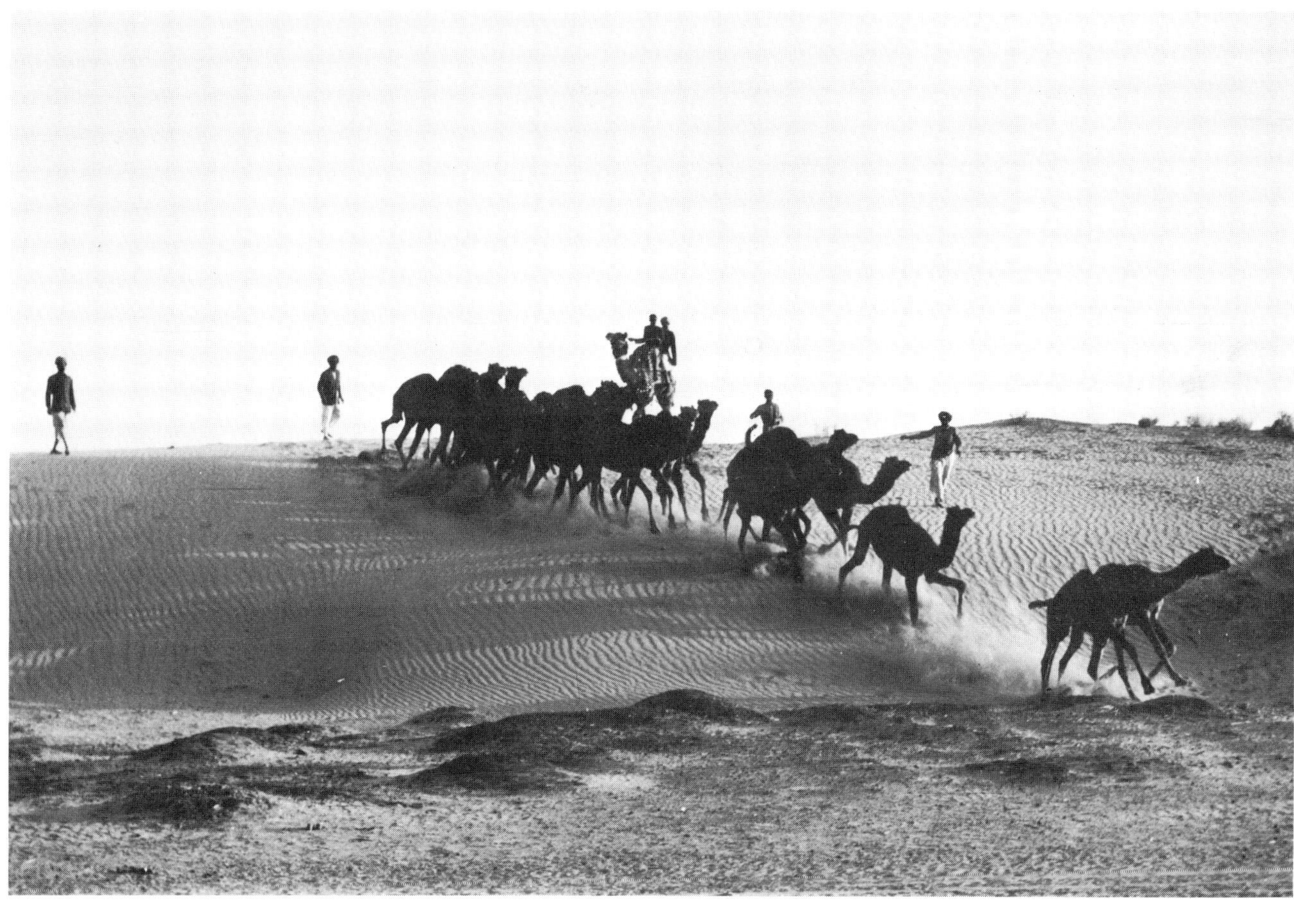

Running down the dunes

unaware of the tragedy befallen one of its members. But for us the idyllic peace of the lake had been shattered. We felt restless and disturbed. As we drove away, the renewed cry of the lapwing 'tit-tit-tit-teeree' carried across the plain like a mournful threnody.

The Sand Dunes of Sam

Forty-one kilometres west of Jaisalmer, the scrub crumbles into the rippling sand dunes of Sam, beckoning with the alluring softness of brown velveteen. Below the dunes, a group of three riding camels loped across the landscape like small craft in an ocean, huddling close for company. As they approached we found them to be splendid animals, decked in colourful trappings, gay and musical as a bridal party. Their riders called out to us in friendly banter and as we stopped to exchange greetings, the beasts looked down on us with supercilious disdain. Our new acquaintances offered us a ride, but nervousness got the better of our romantic inclinations, and we graciously declined.

I have never summoned up enough courage to mount one of these creatures, my sentiments being expressed accurately by the irrepressible Fanny Parks who, in the course of her pilgrimage in search of the picturesque, was extended the same courtesy:

'They were eager I should mount the camel; I thought of Theordore Hook. The hostess said, 'Mr. Hook, will you venture upon an orange?' 'No thank you, Ma'am, I'm afraid I should tumble off!' I declined the elevated position offered me for the same reason.' (Vol. II P.38)

And so did I.

The dunes at Sam extend for about two or three kilometres and rise to a considerable height. Blown into smooth, sensual, feminine curves, the sand is fine and silken-soft under bare feet. Burrowing beetles leave their tracks in obscure designs across the surface like a trail of undecipherable hieroglyphs. Deceptively solid in appearance, these hills of slithering sand are a treacherous death-trap, and often the first step lands one knee-deep into them. Cattle have been known to sink, sucked deeper and deeper as they flounder in the loose-packed mounds. The undulating dunes leave no trace of the tragic event.

The contours of the terrain change in the summer sand-storms, when the fine grains are whipped up in dark, roving funnels that rage across the desert floor like monstrous banshees. The moving columns can be seen approaching from a distance, rising up into the threatening sky. The force at the centre of these terrible whirlwinds is so intense that trees are torn from their roots and carried for long distances, to be strewn in splinters along the path.

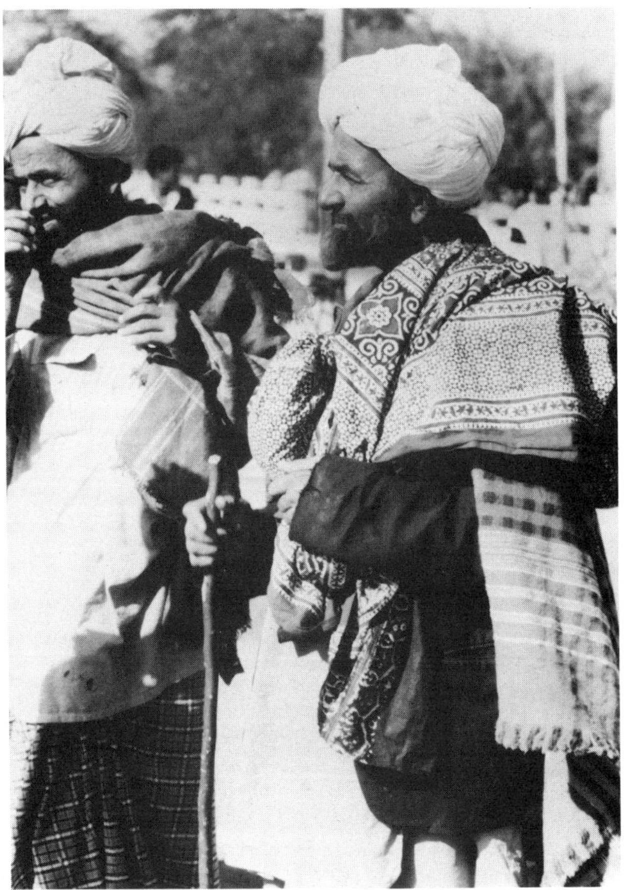
Desert cattle herdsmen wear textiles in bold hand-printed designs

On one occasion, driving towards Jaisalmer from Pokharan at the end of February, we watched a sinister, moving funnel pass swiftly out of sight on the distant western horizon. Although we must have been on the outermost eddy of the current, the wind whipped and sang about our car, adding an extra bounce to its passage, and covering us in a film of powdered dust which blew in through the tightly shut windows. In winter the dunes of Sam lure the traveller with their friendly picture-postcard beauty, but in the sungod's domains are many mansions, and some of the most alluring can prove fatal to the unwary. Venturing too far into these dunes would be a sure way of tempting fate.

The Patriarch of Khuiala

Khuiala is a large settlement for a desert village. It is built on two levels. The lower level boasted a few brick-built houses and the only village store where customers could buy food-grains, maize, wheat and lentils, also salt, oil, jaggery, tea, onions, chillies and a few shrivelled potatoes. Thick hemp ropes hung in coils from wooden rafters, while piles of finer rope made from the local *aak* grass stood against a wall. Some exercise books, rather the worse for want of use, lay in a tin tray jumbled up with packets of highly coloured sweet-drops. Parched gram, sold in miniscule paper cones improvised from old newspapers, was the children's favourite choice.

They mixed the gram with a sprinkling of jaggery and munched this delicacy in lip-smacking competition.

The families in this part of the village were Muslim herdsmen, and seemed fairly prosperous, with a number of camels and large cattle herds. The men were tall, rugged, thick-set as the animals they tended, and handsome. They carried their woollen blankets of green and Indian pink checks with a calculated swagger, and the same sense of confident superiority was reflected in the saddles of their riding camels. These were expensive, made of engraved metal work, with colourful upholstered seats and showy trappings.

These Muslims breed cattle for draught purposes and not as milch cows. A man controls over two hundred head of animals out at pasture. He ranges over a three-day beat, bringing in the herd every third day to the water-hole for watering. The herd recognises the voice of their herder and obey his commands implicity. At his call they come to a halt, or turn and proceed. He can cause a stampede, and herders have been known to use the herd in attacks against marauders or as protection against wild animals. When a bull calf is born it is not allowed to drink milk for a month, but is given small amounts of fodder. As it cannot eat much it grows very thin. Such animals develop a lean but strong muscular body and, as bullocks, are able to fetch the highest prices at cattle fairs.

Their women were not in purdah, except for an occasional veil drawn half across the face, covering with good reason the mouth rather than the eyes, for it was these that reflected every subtle flicker of emotion. The long *kurta*, like a midi-length dress, slit on the sides to above the knees, sheathed the body over tight-fitting pyjamas. The younger men sported skull caps, embroidered with mirror work in bright chain-stitch designs. The needlework on some of these was so fine that I wished to purchase one. But I found that those of the most delicate workmanship were tokens of love, not articles of merchandise: a lifetime's devotion sewn into every stitch in the personal gift of mother to son at the time of marriage.

The upper level of Khuiala was a Meghwal settlement of *chamars*, professional leather workers, whose craft we had specially come to see. But from this point of view our trip was abortive, as they could show us no samples of their skill. Most of the professional handicraft workers are now on contract to government centres or private export firms. As they had just despatched a large consignment of finished work, there was nothing for us to see.

Regrettably the crafts are now geared entirely to the demands of the export and tourist trade. It is almost impossible for individual buyers to purchase items for personal use. For the village craftsmen, this is a traumatic change in function and values. Formerly these leather workers made the local slippers, saddle-bags, waterbottle containers, harness straps

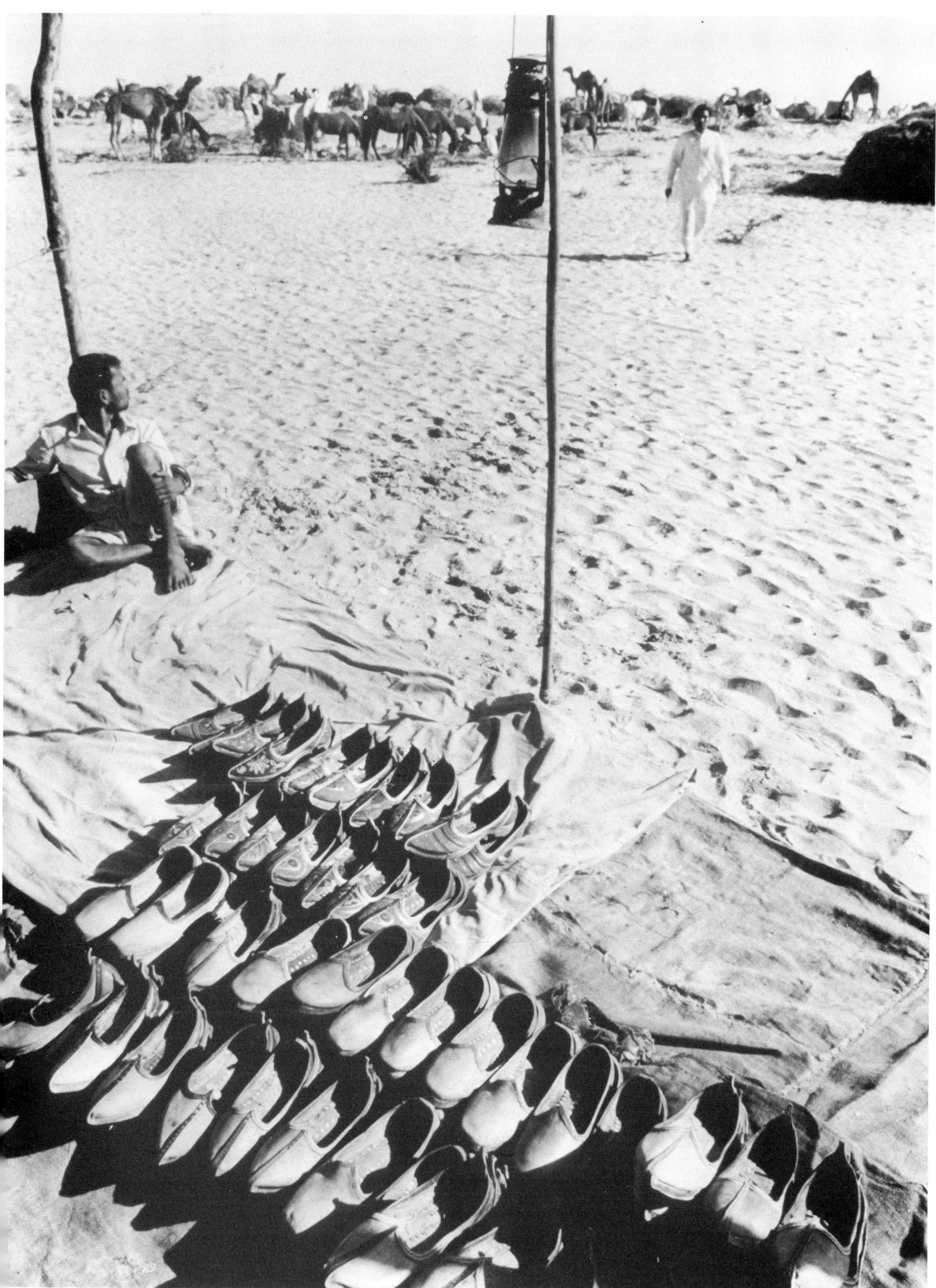

Shoes are often embroidered with traditional motifs in bright colours

and other objects of rural use. Each separate item was embroidered in a time-honoured pattern of coloured threads, sequins, beads, bits of mirror, cowrie shells, occasionally outlined with touches of gold or silver thread for special pieces.

Every design, seeped in nature lore, rural legend and tribal symbol, was in itself a universe of signs and tokens, part of the living dream. Craft shaped the dream into tangible forms, into objects of everyday use, investing each with a sanctity of purpose and meaning. That same craft, torn out of its local context, was now pressed into service to shape alien objects: ladies' handbags, pouches, cigarette cases, embroidered strips for wedge-heeled sandals, cushion covers and the like, for uses the craftsmen cannot conceive and for customers they cannot see. Every piece of the large orders from abroad has to conform as to size, design and colour-scheme. Creativity and individuality have been wrung out of the craft, and the personal relationship between craftsman and customer replaced by a sordid standardisation and cheap substitution which have eroded the very craft they were meant to foster.

The dreary monotony of the assembly-line, the concentration on sections to the neglect of the whole and the tyranny of time schedules have reduced most crafts to meaningless drudgery. The economic gain is dubious. A glut in the market, or an arbitrary change in fashion will seal the fate of workers with no local custom left to fall back on. In the scramble for a quick profit, no one bothers to give thought to problems such as these. This rapacious intrusion is more destructive to traditional patterns of life than seasonal swarms of desert locusts.

A warren of narrow lanes teased their way into the lower settlement. A half-open doorway framed the form of an elderly Muslim woman. Commanding in aspect, still handsome, her height, that in another woman would be an embarrassment, gave her a dignity in old age seldom seen in this harsh land, which transforms women in their thirties into wrinkled crones. The wistful expression of her face gave a hint of reverie, the mind in remoter regions than the eye. I seemed to have drifted into her waking dream, for the smile she gave me was one of recognition, of such warmth and charm that when she spoke her voice sang in echo to her feelings.

'What! Are you leaving without meeting Alam Mian?' she said. 'Alam Mian?' I repeated. My ignorance surprised her, but her voice had no suggestion of reproach in it. Rather was it an invitation, an offering of hospitality to a weary traveller from far away.

Had we not come to photograph Alam Mian?

It appeared that Alam Mian was Khuiala's prize exhibit. Over a hundred years of age, he was once a magnificent figure of a man, more than 7ft in height. Bed-ridden at present, unable to carry the weight of his over-size frame, he sounded like a dying emperor, whose authority, fast dwindling into history, still commanded respect and customary obedience. No one who came to Khuiala could leave without paying him a courtesy call.

The idea of intruding on the privacy of an ailing gentleman who had spent his later years on show, as a freak at fun-fairs, was distasteful to me. So while the woman held me in polite coversation, I left Vivek to be ushered into the august presence to offer due homage on our behalf.

But Alam Mian was delighted to find that he was still a celebrity, and sought after to be photographed. He posed, propped up in bed, with as regal an air as his weak condition would allow him to muster.

His moment of glory had been that historic occasion, the Delhi Durbar of 1911, when he had been included in the Rajputana Contingent. I regretted my overnicety when I realised that for the fading giant such attention was welcome relief in the slow monotony of his declining years, as it revived for him memories of early splendour: the stately Durbar, his meeting with Jawaharlal Nehru years later at Pushkar Fair, his journeys as an itinerant entertainer with his vast following of idolatrous admirers throughout the desert. My thin-skinned partiality for privacy was misplaced. Privacy has no meaning in a desert village, neither prized nor guarded by people whose welfare depends upon a close-knit community life. I had denied myself a rare opportunity, and deprived an old man of the brief pleasure of wandering again in the twilit pastures of nostalgia.

Kanoi: Desert Hospitality

Driving back from Khuiala in the late afternoon, the jonga suddenly swerved off the road and careened over the uneven ground. Since the narrow, poorly tarred tracks in the area were full of deep potholes, this was not in itself an alarming diversion. Instead of running along the route till the vehicle could be guided back on to the road, this time we seemed to be heading straight for the horizon. Obviously our driver, Shankar, had some place other than Jaisalmer in mind. Shankar is himself a desert dweller, and belongs to the arid hinterland, the Sindh border on the Pakistan side. He had migrated to India in the wake of the refugee influx during the 1965 war with Pakistan, along with the entire Hindu population of his village. A dark, well-built, stocky man with fierce Rajput moustaches, Shankar is by caste a *sutar*, wood-carver and carpenter. Many of these craftsmen have taken to professions connected with cars – as mechanics, drivers of buses and trucks, cleaners and so on – skills for which they seem to have a marked aptitude.

Shankar has been driving for a Jodhpur-based transport company for almost fourteen years the same tough, well-weathered, almost invincible army-disposal jonga. He has accompanied the Sansthan team so regularly on its field trips that he is now regarded as one of the seasoned field workers, deeply involved in the task of recording,

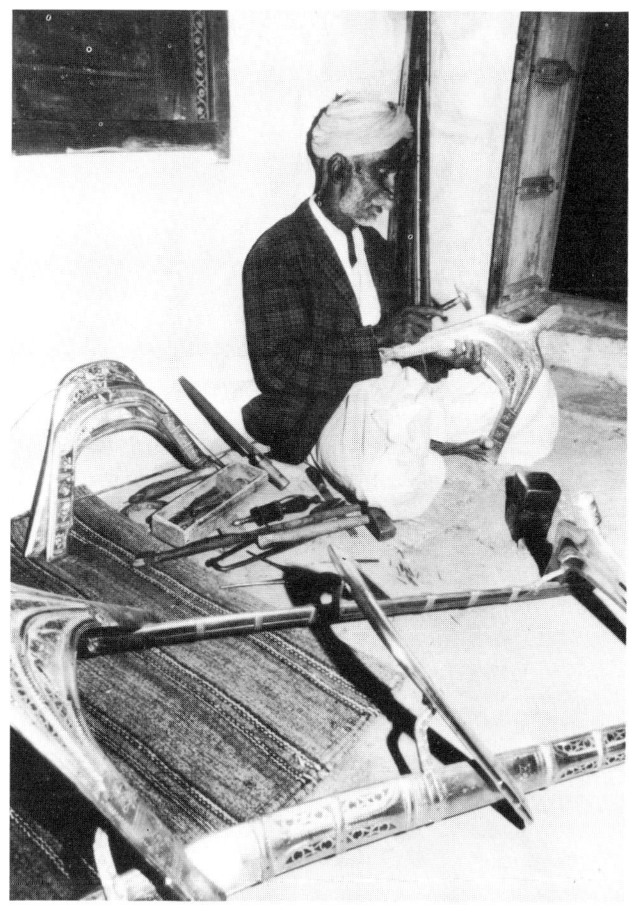

An old carpenter working on a camel saddle

photographing, filming and documenting for studies in ethno-musicology, as any trained member of the group. His knowledge of the desert is uncanny. He is familiar with every hamlet on every route from Barmer to Bikaner. From likely nooks in the inner bazaars, from stray scraps of conversation with chance acquaintances, from bizarre episodes and incidents bordering on fantasy, he ferrets out intriguing bits of information that sometimes provide the last link of a bewildering puzzle in research.

The present hi-jack operation was obviously the beginning of some new adventure.

The jonga dodged between stumps of *sewan* grass, bounced over ruts, scattered fusillades of loose sand as it drove through dry nullahs and brought us to the outskirts of a desert village. The car wove in and out of lanes, scraped the sides of thatched huts, hurled itself over a mound of debris and clattered to a halt.

'My in-laws live here,' explained Shankar with tardy loquacity. 'I could not leave the area without paying them a visit. I met one of them in Jaisalmer last night and the whole clan knows by now that I am here. So I had to come or they would have been offended.'

We understood. One could not displease one's in-laws. And then Shankar's family, whether close blood relations or distant cousins perched on remote twigs on the farthest branches of the ancestral tree, scattered in innumerable hamlets throughout the Thaar, had often proved very handy in a crisis,

helping us to locate elusive folk musicians, providing impromptu meals at odd hours, or replenishing our provisions with home-made bread and savouries. We got out to meet the group of men who now converged on the jonga and engulfed Shankar in a tussle of warm embraces.

A son-in-law, however distantly his wife may be connected, is above all others the most esteemed of guests, and we basked in the lavish hospitality the *sutar* community of Kanoi village extended to Shankar.

The term 'carpenter' as an equivalent for *sutar* is inadequate. The village *sutar* along with the mason is also the rural architect. He is a master craftsman who carves doorways for temples, and niches for the household deity. When these are of mud and plaster, as in the desert where wood is scarce, he moulds and shapes the entrance archways and brackets, and constructs the elaborate shelving system which stores family goods in village homes.

The plan of these houses is simple and uniform. They stand on a mud and plaster plinth about a half-metre high. One enters through a single door into an open courtyard some four metres square. To the left is the kitchen with an open hearth, and an occasional earthen oven. It is a small area covered with a low roof without a door. A sink at ground level has a drain leading out.

Opposite the front door across the courtyard is the living room. It runs the whole width of the enclosure. The ceiling has wooden beams, usually supported by four pillars. Along the main wall of this all-purpose room runs the storage space for utensils. This is the focus and chief beauty of desert interiors. A great deal of care goes into making it practical and aesthetically pleasing. The entire family helps in this task, and the women often put the finishing touches of colour, sometimes covering the mouldings of the compartments with silver paper, inset with bits of multi-coloured glass. Copper pots burnished to a gleam in their niches, act as reflecting surfaces, and at night a single lamp repeatedly mirrored in the tiny glass scraps, is sufficient to light up the whole room.

On one side of the room, between two pillars, stand large storage bins about one or two metres square, made of plaster and mud, some containing grain, others clothes, quilts and blankets. These bins are so arranged as to screen off a section of the room to provide privacy to a young married couple, a welcome luxury in joint-family living.

On the other sides of the courtyard are open verandahs. In one, members of the family rest, or work at household chores. In the other, goats and chickens may be housed, with piles of fodder and feed in a corner. Or if there is no livestock, the men store their tools here: ropes, logs of wood and other items connected with their profession. During the day it also serves as their workroom. Floors throughout the house are plastered with mud mixed with cowdung and straw, beaten flat, then rubbed and polished to a sheen.

From the corners of the flat roof run channels from which the precious rain water drains into the courtyard, to be stored in containers, or an underground tank.

The Kanoi *sutars* specialise in camel saddles. These are worked with mixed metals, sometimes copper and brass, with engraved designs. They are expensive, the prices ranging from six hundred to eighteen hundred rupees for a work of truly skilled craftsmanship. The saddles are sold at the large cattle fairs which are the normal markets for such wares. They may on occasion accept an order from a wealthy customer for a special piece.

Jaisalmer camels are riding mounts, distinguished by their small heads and slender bodies. They are bred for speed and not for carrying heavy loads, as are the sturdier camels of the Bikaner breed. Highly temperamental, they need careful tending and expert handling. A good Jaisalmeri camel fetches a handsome price and fully decked out with metal saddle, embroidered leather bags and elaborate shell and bead straps, an animal represents a fortune of eight thousand rupees or more.

The news that a son-in-law was visiting the community and had brought with him a party of city folk had been spread by the children through Kanoi. The opportunity to meet such rare and odd guests was not to be missed. Gradually, in groups of twos and threes, the village elders began to assemble in the home of Shankar's in-laws. They sat on the raised platform outside the main door on rugs in bright stripes, which showed up as vivid patches of colour against the beaten earth. Such unassuming touches of beauty spoke of an unerring, instinctive aesthetic sense.

The patriarchs waited with the ruminative patience of rural folk, while we quenched our curiosity in all aspects of village life which to them appeared amusing, if not naive. Young men stood around, as etiquette demanded that they should not presume to a place on the rugs unless expressly invited to do so. A few sat on a lower level on the ground, oblivious of the afternoon sun, scrupulous to observe the rules of local custom.

Among the elders was a white-haired, luxuriantly bewhiskered old Bhati Rajput, apparently a person of consequence in the past, but now poorer than the lower-caste *sutars*, whose skills were still in demand in a plebeian age. Rajput chivalry and prowess on the battlefield have no place in the changed social scene. But traditions die hard among people with a rich past, and we noted that the ancient scion was seated with honour in the centre of a rug, the others maintaining a respectful distance, and in discussion deferring politely to his opinion.

Talk ranged over a wide variety of subjects, and questions about the impending elections revealed among the assembly an awareness of the complex issues involved in party politics. With the canny shrewdness of villagers they were quick to seek views, slow to offer their own. They were more forthcoming about the hard times facing the traditional crafts which were driving young men to jobs in urban centres. Though they spoke with mild regret about the passing of the old ways, they seemed to welcome the benefits of the new: roads linking villages, medical centres, teaching facilities, improved water supply and electrification. They appeared to be as progressive-minded and liberal as one could wish. But we have learnt through experience to take such well-turned opinions with reservations. The villager is apt to regard the outsider with suspicion. His polite rejoinders express ideas which he thinks will be acceptable to his guests; pleasant agreement is part of the proffered hospitality. Justifiably, he feels himself under no obligation to reveal his private thoughts on matters that affect him deeply, on values and attitudes that sustain the cohesiveness of a beleaguered community against the inroads of an alien world.

I was the only woman in the party, and was touched by their unobtrusive courtesy to me. They overtly ignored my presence, while they quietly made every effort to provide for my comfort; a cot for me to sit on, a refreshing drink, gentle fanning to dispel the heat from which they saw I suffered. They reacted to my occasional intrusions in the discussion in true courtly fashion: they replied, but without looking at me, directing their responses to one of the more visibly acceptable male visitors.

While we gossiped with the men, the women in time-honoured custom were hard at work, and we were soon treated to an afternoon meal especially cooked for us. They did not join us but continuously served us wheat and millet bread fresh from the oven, a variety of vegetable dishes spiced with herbs and chillies, cool butter milk – and for the men, liberal portions of a potent local *daaru*.

I was amused to see the Rajput dignitary part his moustaches to quaff his drink, an act which was hallowed by tradition, for when the noble warrior of old set out to battle, he did so doubly fortified, on the outside with shining armour, and within with a fiery potation.

So when our ancient stalwart strode out into the blazing sun, he did so with at least that residue of his ancient heritage which no outside influence could pollute. No doubt when this Rajput Falstaff swaggered home, many tender hands would reach out to comfort him against the rigours of another arduous day.

We too, had to be on our way, as Vivek was anxious to be in Jaisalmer before the sun set. I went in to thank our hostess and the girls. Some of the men of the family accompanied me and I was glad to find that in the privacy of their home they dropped their formal manners and joined with the women in questioning me directly about my work and family.

Surya Descendant

To keep an appointment with Surya in the Thaar desert, in whose mansions he reigns supreme from sun-up to sun-down, would seem a simple matter. Yet as we drove away from Kanoi it was apparent that it would be dark before we reached Jaisalmer. The dazzle on the clumps of *sewan* grass had lost its sharp, cutting sheen from which the eyes recoil when the day is young. Apricot-soft, the grasses glowed at the tips, a tender grey-green at root level, where the slanting rays no longer touched them. Shadows under *khejra* and *ber* dissolved their tight, dark fists in violet fingers that splayed across the road. Evening had overtaken us. Sunset was now.

We sauntered into the opaline landscape of sand and grass, shaking the silver-green stalks to watch the pink daubs waver from tip to tip. A hesitant blue returned to the blanched sky and a halo of limegreen rays cradled the heart of the sinking sun. We lingered till this display of colours paled, then gradually faded, and finally meshed into a uniform dusk.

We passed the dunes at Sam, humped like giant pachyderms, somnolent under the first timid stars, and soon, in that uncertain evening light, we drove into Jaisalmer, dusty but elated, and very hungry.

There are places that are indelibly linked in memory with some particular culinary delight. Jaisalmer, unfortunately, is not one of them, and I doubt if I have ever had a decent meal there during any of my several visits. We were repelled by the grimy restaurant at the tourist bungalow, where an unwholesome breakfast of fried eggs in dirty brown petticoats on soggy toast, served by surly waiters, had hastened our departure thence that morning. So it was to the *dhaba* in the fort, which offered vegetarian food, that we now turned.

Experience had taught us the wisdom of eating the same foods as form the staple diet of the local people, as these are apt to be freshly made and more palatable. Almost all the people of the desert are vegetarian, either through religious conviction or from necessity. Meat, when available, is of poor quality, and expensive. So we conformed to native practice.

There is a monastic simplicity about a *dhaba*, an unadorned asceticism, that reduces food, furniture, environment and conversation to the barest minimum. The coarse-grained, rough-hewn tables and the comfortless galley-benches have never known the luxury of polish, except that of age and use. The dun-coloured walls are inhospitable even to flies, and are occasionally redeemed by a strident oleograph, from which the gods in their celestial capers pause to look down on mankind. Here all human aspirations are bent towards the single purpose of combatting hunger with such intentness that no sound is heard except that of earnest mastication: rapid movements of lips and tongues, adam's apples shuttling up and down like frantic dumb-waiters in reverse, the hiss and click of teeth being sucked, dilated nostrils snorting like cattle at a trough, fingers clawing into dishes, and eyes restlessly dancing over the diminishing portions.

And so we sat among sanyasis and hippies, herdsmen and tribals, truck drivers and tradesmen, all, with that one step into the *dhaba*, reduced to so extreme an egalitarian society as to make one yearn at once for the bourgeois comforts of the corrupt.

Discipline here was strictly enforced by the littlest culinary commissar you ever saw — a brazen, pale-faced boy, with spindly legs, piping voice, speedy, peremptory and efficient, degrading the loudmouthed to silence, and needling the timid to speech. His ten fingers dipped at one time into eight tumblers of water, which he set down before as many customers, and dishes were stacked in high-rise tiers upon his arms. Each order given was immediately computerised in his small, round, well-groomed head, with a capacity for instant recall, which at the same time calculated the bills of a dozen separate tables, and yelled the totals to the cadaverous man at the till in a tone which would brook no contradiction.

But the mobile presiding deity of this gastronomic shrine was an ancient crone who rocked her bulk between the customers, wiping the tables with a rag of indeterminate shade, droning out admonishment and advice in a cracked, raucous rumble, as she tumbrilled her way in the wake of her pert, officiating priest, who pointedly ignored her. He obviously ranked higher in the hierarchy of the hostelry, as she merely mopped up after operations, while he planned and directed them.

It had been a long, long day and all I could think of by this time was the luxury of a nice warm bath and so to sleep. But at the tourist bungalow two figures, crouched in the corridor outside our rooms, rose to greet Kothari with rapturous delight. They were the Manganiyar musicians, old Chugga Khan and his young nephew, Anwar. It is as impossible to keep a Manganiyar from singing, whatever the time of day or night, as it is for a mere mortal to do without breathing. In a matter of minutes, our fatigue forgotten, we were sitting entranced, in a remote corner room, swaying to the click of Chugga's *khartal*, castanets, while Anwar Khan sang, full-throated, the verses of Kabir and of the loves of Krishna, till the dark sky lightened to greet another day.

The Manganiyars and their Pure Stream of Music

For five consecutive monsoons, 1968-72, the rains failed in Jaisalmer. These were bitter years of drought. While most parts of Rajasthan received a minimum of rainfall, this district had none. When it did rain finally, during the season of 1973, they say that children of six and seven cried in terror, never having known the heavens to open and pour such

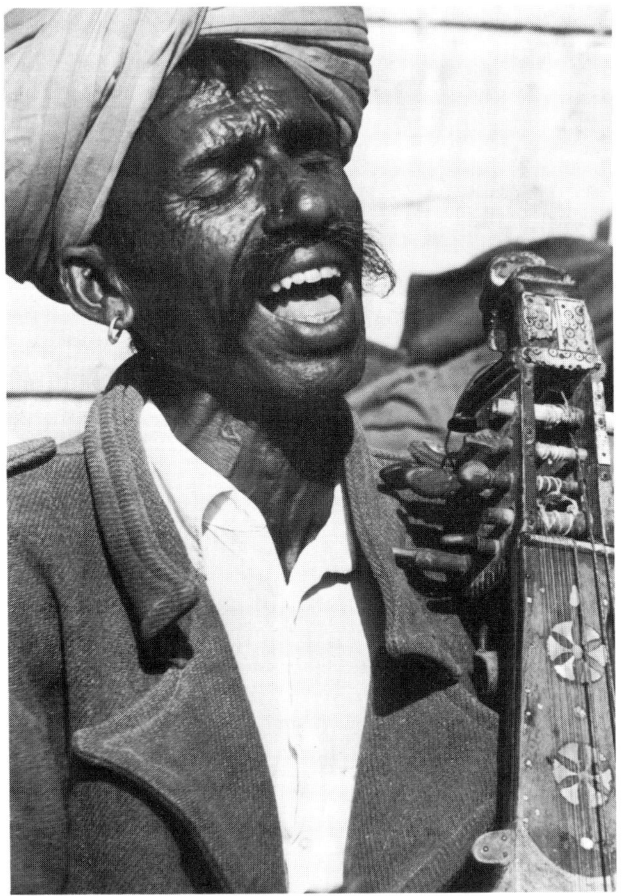

Blind singer

benediction on their innocent heads. It was the prolonged years of aridity that introduced us to the Manganiyar musicians.

The people of the Thaar live with the spectre of lean years looming perpetually over them. Their vigilance never falters. They are sparing during a good season and frugal in a normal one. The state only comes to their aid in a time of famine. Such was the case during the winter of 1972-73 after five successive years of drought. The carefully garnered stores were exhausted, and the people were reduced to eating berries, seeds and barks of trees. Their cattle languished, stumbling to their death in the frantic search for water and food. Compelled by these circumstances, the desert dwellers migrated to work camps set up by the government. Here, in return for stone-breaking, road-building, digging ditches and other manual tasks, they were given a daily pittance that barely enabled them to feed their families.

It was during this crisis that Rupayan Sansthan organised a field camp at Jaisalmer in January 1973, to record the folk musicians of the district. Manual labour was out of the question for these men whose livelihood and talent depend upon hands nimble and dextrous enough to play their instruments. They needed ready cash to buy provisions for the season. The Sansthan was able to help them in this, in exchange for recordings of valuable music for its archives.

Word went out into the interior to say that the Manganiyars should arrive by a particular date. The desert grapevine, swift as the wind, spread to one farflung Manganiyar settlement after another. The man responsible for this extraordinary network of instant communication was Akbar Khan, a humble peon in the municipal office at Jaisalmer. But Akbar also happens to be the son of the last of the great durbar troubadors of the former princely state. His father, at the height of his fame, had been in great demand at the court, where his talent held its own even against sophisticated classical singers at lavish royal functions.

Born into the profession, Akbar had been initiated into a family tradition which had been handed down without a break for eight hundred years. Before he was twelve years old, history had overtaken remote Jaisalmer. India had become an independent republic. The days of princes and kingly durbars were over. Soon the court retainers would be disbanded. The last royal favour the prince of Jaisalmer could confer on his accomplished Manganiyar singer was to help get his son a job. Fortunately, Akbar could read and write, a rare achievement for a boy of his caste. So he gave up his traditional profession, and took to dusting furniture in a dingy government office, and delivering papers. But he was still looked upon as the hereditary chief of his caste. His message carried by word of mouth from village to village, calling upon the best performers of his clan to gather together at Jaisalmer, had the moral force of an edict.

By the time the recording unit had installed itself, about one hundred musicians had mustered in strength, and more were to add to their number in the ensuing week. Over one hundred and fifty musicians in small groups were to be recorded during that mammoth session.

At Jaisalmer, Kothari met us with the news that the dak bungalow had been commandeered for a high-powered team of doctors. We were to be accommodated in a half-finished Jain *dharamsala*, pilgrims' rest-house, which except for a roof over our heads and a tap in the open courtyard, provided no amenities. We were excited about meeting the musicians, who were to be housed in the same place, and could not be bothered about creature comforts.

Many housing sites of the lower middle-class in Indian cities remain incomplete for years on end, and have a ramshackle air about them even before they have been occupied. It seems that the charitable impulse, or the financial resources, or the conclusive will somehow get exhausted midway in the enterprise, and for long years after, an unroofed section, unpaved corridors, unplastered walls, unshuttered doors and windows, and the chaotic litter of building materials give the impression of a place in ruins. And somehow in this exhausted, half-uttered sigh of an edifice, a strange welter of human beings, animals, poultry, even the very sparrows, pigeons, mainas and crows, set up their temporary fixtures for shelter, each according to his need, and to the degree of his ability: make-shift doors, improvised kitchens, battered tin-sheets and tarpaulins for protection overhead – in the belief, apparently, that since life is transient, it is folly to create any form of permanence.

Here, most of the essential functions of human existence are performed under cover of darkness: cots are drawn out or beddings spread under the open sky; ablutions performed and bodies washed as night falls. In the daytime, the greater part of the work, from domestic chores to professional crafts is conducted out of doors. So home is nothing more than a conglomeration of nooks and corners for basic necessities, tin trunks for clothes, bins for storing food, clothes lines for all articles capable of suspension, nails to hang the gods by, the odd sewing machine and bicycle and, for the final bizarre touch, a funnel-horned gramophone. For what is life in India without music?

Whole sectors of cities give the sensation of having barely recovered from a flood or an earthquake, and proclaim their savage defiance of stability. The *dharamshala* in which we now found ourselves was a fitful assertion of this credo.

I do not know in what condition we expected to find the musicians of the famine-ridden Thaar, but we were totally unprepared for the scene that met us. The place was in a ferment of movement and sound and, at the moment of our arrival, keyed to a vibrant pitch of tension.

The Manganiyars numbering about a hundred, were, by any standards, a striking group. They were well above average height, with complexions in every shade of brown, and with the clearcut features characteristic of their community. Dressed in white with turbans of strident hues, they flung their checked or striped blankets across their shoulders with a rakish flamboyance. Vibrant colours, daring black eyes, and the flash of brilliant smiles gave the finishing touches to their innate theatrical swagger. The whine and scraping of instruments being tuned, the rattle of drums, the clearing of throats, and voices breaking into irrepressible ripples and fragments of song made the air thrum around them. I felt a tingling of nerves in the soles of my feet, a spiralling of energy to the top of my head. It was hard to maintain an outward composure, impossible to quell a throb of nervous exhilaration.

While the engineers made their preparations for recording, I was led by Kothari to a comparatively quiet corner where three musicians were waiting. They greeted us respectfully, we sat on the rug in front of them, and with no more ado they burst into song.

It was my first experience of the art of the Manganiyars, and those moments were amongst the most memorable of my life.

I am not a musician, nor a musicologist, but I have, in the course of my work, had the opportunity to listen to every class of performer, of almost every region of the sub-continent, from the ritualistic tribal to the cultivated refinements of the classicist. I was familiar with a wide range of Rajasthani music, including the superb artistry of the Langas of Barmer. But the Manganiyars are quite another class of traditional performers.

Their music is *raga*-based, but these are not the *ragas,* modes, of classical music. Their method of voice production differs from the style of the classical vocalist. It is open-throated and ringing, akin to that of the folk singer. The rhythm, too, is based on set *tala,* cycle beats, which do not conform to the *tala* of classical rhythms but are nevertheless strictly codified, subtle and complex. The main instrument, both for accompaniment and solo performance, is the *kamaicha,* a stringed lute, played with a bow. Percussion accompaniment is provided by a *dhol,* two-faced drum, and *khartal,* two flat pieces of wood, a pair in each hand, struck together like castanets.

The trio that performed for us were Ghazi, lead singer, Luna on the *kamaicha,* and Hakim on the drum. The accompanists also sang. The blending of voices was extraordinarily skilled. Ghazi would begin a phrase which would be taken up by the other two, and even before they had completed it, he would break into the next, with a tumbling ripple of notes or a sudden flourish. Back and forth the voices spun, weaving a tapestry of sound that enmeshed us in its aural web, and which continued tracing its intricate pattern without let or pause, as if it were a dynamic element, once released, impossible to contain.

During the days that followed we lived to the rhythm of music. Recording sessions began early in the morning and continued, after a short midday break, late into the evening. In between and after recordings, much of our time was taken up in conversation with groups of musicians, learning of their background, particular family traditions, transcribing the texts of songs, while Kothari also made detailed notes on the technical aspects of the *raga* and *tala* systems peculiar to the music of the caste.

It was a lesson in adaptability to watch how rapidly these rustic performers adjusted themselves to the requirements of sophisticated electronic equipment. They were, at first, inhibited by the presence of the microphone and sang timidly. When the tape was played back to them, immediately after recording, so that they could hear themselves, they at first were amazed, then amused, laughing spontaneously like children and finally, critical of their own performance. They soon lost their nervousness and sang with their usual verve. Yet the recordings could not capture the full effects of their art, which depends on the visual impact created by these master performers and which differs in the manner of presentation with each

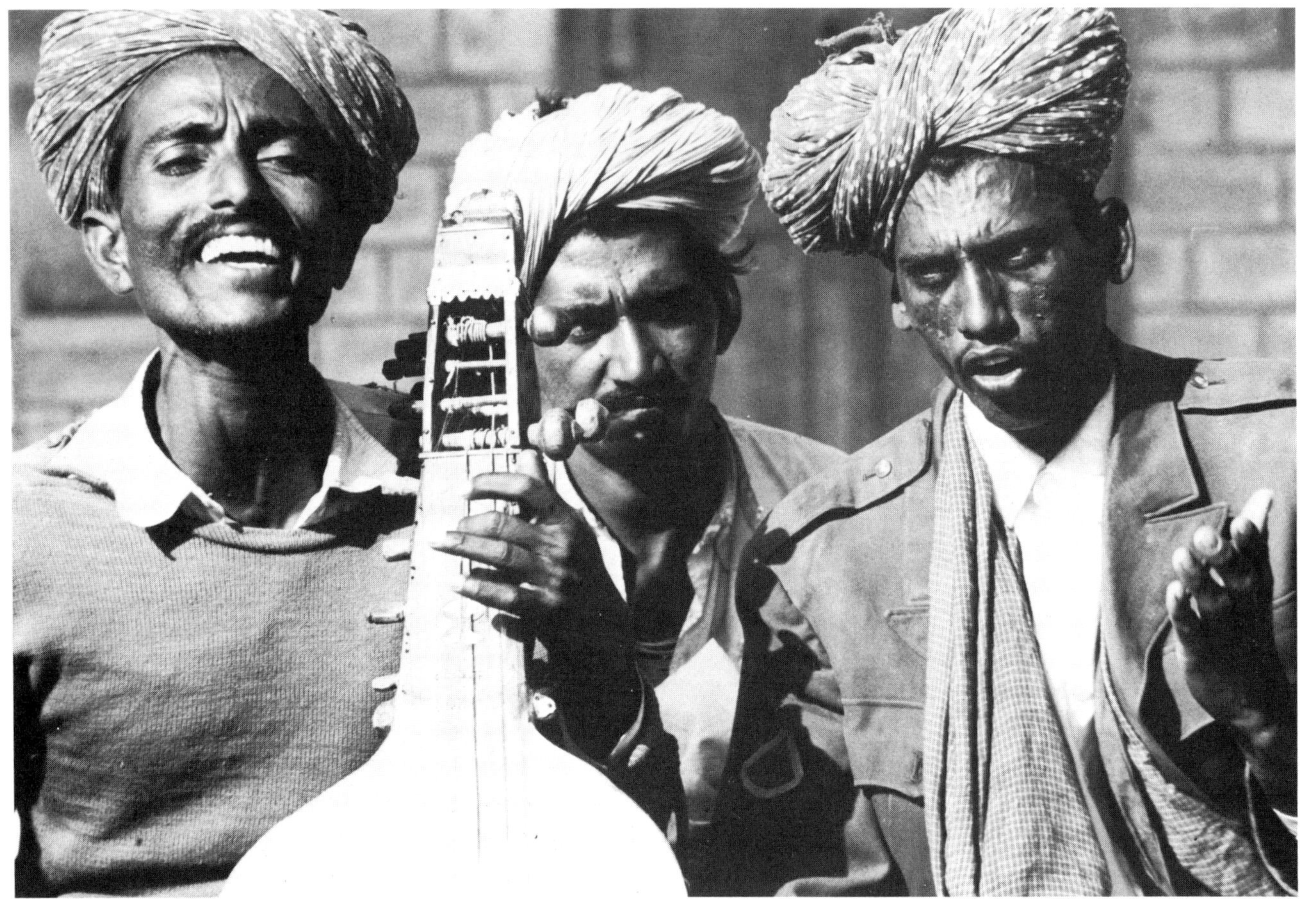

Ghazi accompanied by Luna and Hakim

Manganiyar playing the Jew's harp

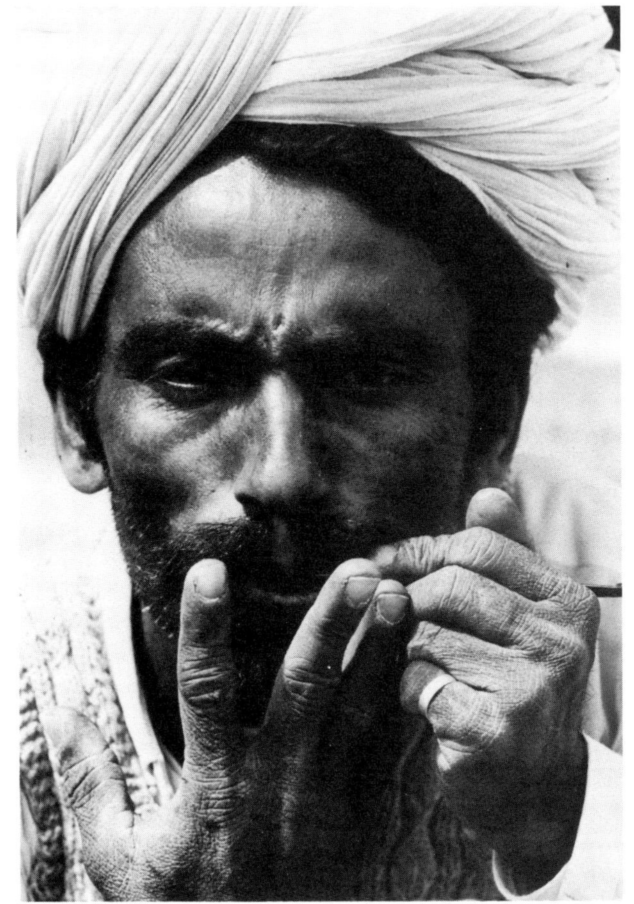

individual artist. When they sang for us after the recording sessions were over, we heard them at their best.

In this group of Manganiyars was the only Bhil, Hakim Ram. Among that effervescent and extrovert crowd he was noticeably subdued and shy. Only when he raised his instrument, the *satara*, double-flute, to his lips, did his eyes glitter, and his face assume the mischievous look of a dusky Pan. The *satara* is made from the thick stems of the gorse bush. This was the first time I had heard of the gorse being put to such practical use. The delicate pink-orange flowers against its soft green spikes makes it a strikingly attractive plant in the sandy landscape. Often growing to a height of four metres, its main branches become woody and strong enough to hollow into flutes.

A singular instrument played by some of the Manganiyars, is the *morchang,* Jew's harp. I have come across two types, one made of bamboo, and the more usual one of metal. Its haunting, melancholic twang barely conceals an undertone of menace. It conjures up visions of desolate distances and rising dust winds, and its unnerving buzz suggests the threatening approach of clouds of locusts. When added as accompaniment to the songs of the Manganiyars, it introduces a note of tension, in contrast to the rousing beat of the *dhol* or the merry, staccato clack of the *khartal*.

Among the outstanding musicians present, perhaps the most distinguished was the *kamaicha* soloist, Sakar Khan. Withdrawn and ruminating by temperament, gentle in manner, he had recently suffered the loss of his mother, and his deep grief isolated him from the rumbustious presence of his companions. His performance of the *aalap* on this instrument, unaccompanied by percussion, led one far beyond the popular, earthy qualities normally associated with folk music, to an emotional intensity which reflected the depth of his sorrow.

Sakar's brother, Pempa, was a totally different character. As friendly as an overgrown bear-cub, he had something of the exhibitionist virtuoso in his playing of the *pungi*, snake-charmer's pipe, as well as the folk *shehnai*, double-reed pipe. But his skill exhibited the effortless ease of the master musician, and his melodic acrobatics brought glamour to instruments distinguished ordinarily by little more than rustic charm.

The *khartal* in the hands of Chugga Khan fluttered with tremulous ecstasy, and with such dramatic flair and precision of timing as to suggest some secret base to his musicianship. It was only years later that I learnt of old Chugga's renown as a vocalist in his earlier days, which explained the firm foundations of his technical skill.

Two young lads, Abu and Omi, about nine years of age, sang together the *marsia*, elegies, of Buleshah. Then there was Mohan Mastana, literally 'beloved ecstatic', whose gnomic charm and vivacity made up for the loss in richness of what was once a mellifluous baritone, now ruined by the effects of chewing tobacco. A blind singer, his eyes curtained, his face deeply pitted with smallpox which had robbed him of his sight, shook us with the passion of his singing that burst from his dark centre like a caged bird into flight.

One day a Bhaat loitered into the *dharamsala*, and gave us a scintillating recitation of *dingal*, the rhythmic oral poetry that enshrines the chronicles of Rajput clans. During this impromptu performance, a colleague from Jodhpur, a Rajput Rathor, gave us an interesting insight into the behaviour of the Bhaats. He explained that the Bhaats have an hereditary right to receive gifts from any member of the clan to which they are attached by tradition, if they recite for them epics of their royal house.

One afternoon the young Rathor, who was in reduced circumstances, had gone to the bazaar for a snack. On the way he was confronted by a Bhaat who, fixing him with hypnotic eyes, burst into a dramatic recitation, extolling the mighty deeds of his victim's ancestors and their bountiful generosity to their bardic retainers. A crowd, excited by this street tamasha, gathered round the two. Unable to escape, the wretched Rathor dug into his pocket, and parted with the last five rupee note which was meant to pay for his lunch. These the Bhaat accepted with the same grandiloquent flattery with which his forefathers had received the gold coins of bygone princes. The Rathor ruefully confessed that whenever he catches sight of a Bhaat in the bazaars of Jodhpur, he dives down the nearest alley to avoid him.

The caste name 'Manganiyar' means 'one who begs', and indicates the low status of these superb artistes in the social hierarchy. This is further borne out by their kinship, *jajmaan*, to the caste of Meghwals, who are considered untouchables, as they are tanners and leather workers by profession. At some time in their history, the Manganiyars became converts to Islam, but this did not prevent their traditional kinship with the Meghwal community. They continue to sing at Meghwal homes on all ritual occasions such as marriage, birth and death, and during seasonal festivals. Religious differences prevent them eating together so the Manganiyars do not eat in the Meghwal homes. But their hosts offer the musicians gifts of grain, clothes and, now, of money.

Despite their conversion, the Manganiyars retain certain Hindu practices. For instance, they observe the laws of exogomy and endogomy in marriage, and do not permit cross-cousin alliances, as is the rule among other Muslims. Music has been the hereditary profession of this community for eight centuries. The Bhati rulers of Jaisalmer retained the finest of these musicians at their court, and Manganiyar minstrels accompanied their royal masters when they went to war. Not only was it the duty of the Manganiyar to entertain the Rajput before and after battle, but it was also customary for the chief Manganiyar to stay by the ruler when he died, to accompany his cortege to the cremation ground, and to remain there day and night, in constant vigil, till the ceremonies for the peace of the departed soul were concluded, and the period of mourning was over.

How or why such a custom prevailed, the Manganiyars could not explain. Kothari stumbled across the practice through sheer chance. He had arranged to record a particular musician. Since the man was on vigil at the *samadhi* of a member of the ruling family, arrangements had to be made for another to take his place before he could be free for his assignment.

The Manganiyars saw nothing incongruous in this custom, by which the Muslim retainer of a Hindu prince kept the final tryst with the departed soul. According to Hindu belief, it is only on the thirteenth day that the connection of the spirit of the dead with the world of the living is finally severed. Perhaps the Rajputs hoped that the divine art of the Manganiyars, which had often helped to comfort them in times of stress in this world, would ease their passing into the next. But these are mere conjectures. The practice is still kept up as a part of the credo of loyal and punctillious community, even in times when the power of the Rajput rulers has crumbled and their glory departed forever.

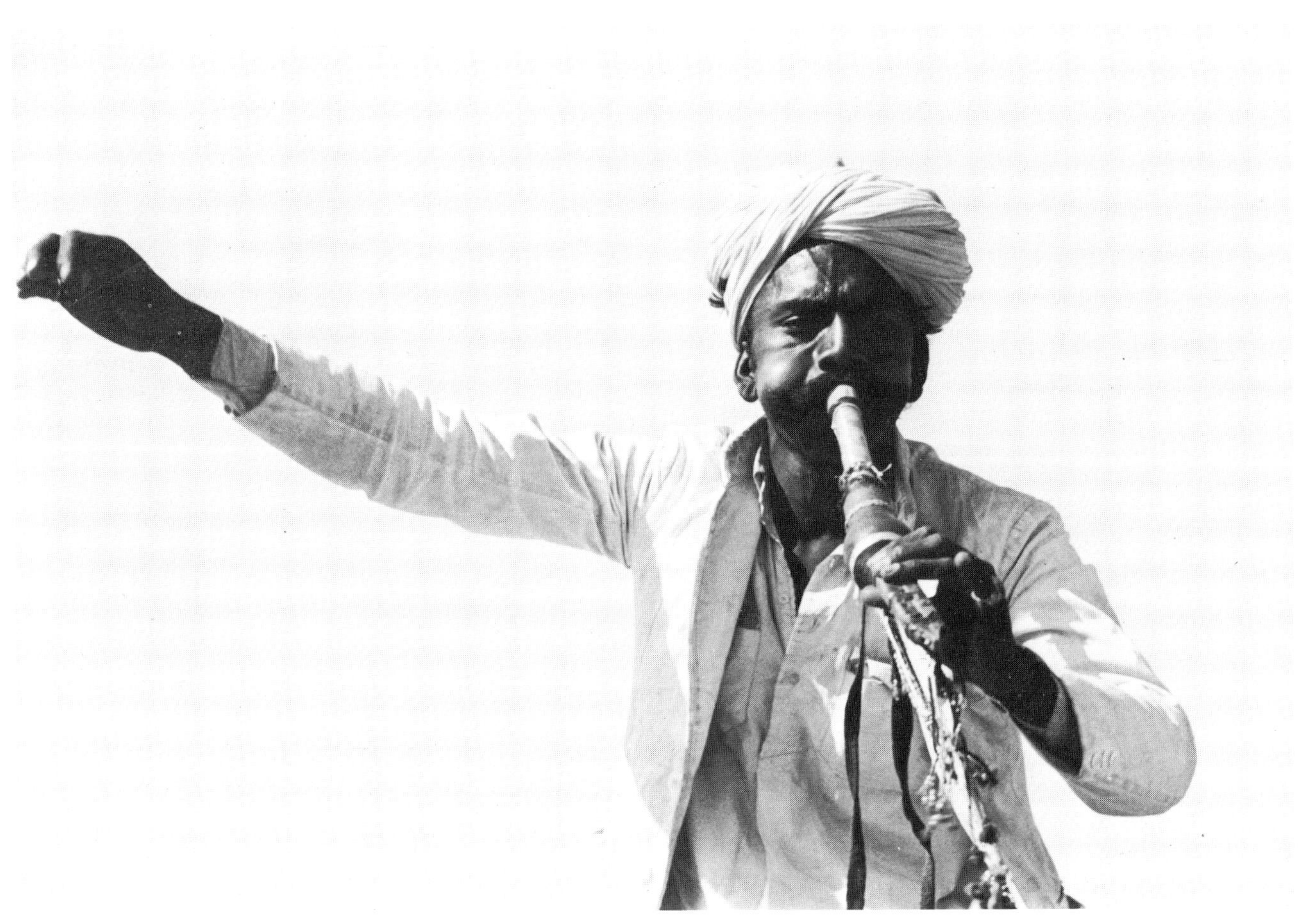

Pempa playing the *pungi*

Keepers of a Sati Shrine

We later learnt of a further connection between the Bhati Rajputs and the Manganiyars. South-west of the fort of Jaisalmer, at a spot where a hundred and fifty years ago a Rajput princess of the Bhati clan had immolated herself, stands a shrine on a raised platform under a *ber*, jujube, tree. Its keepers, incredibly enough, are members of a family of Manganiyars who sing ballads in praise of the princess, light lamps before her tablet, and accept offerings from worshippers towards the upkeep of the site. This curious convention arose out of strange circumstances.

The Bhati princess was one of the many daughters of a Rajput Thakur, a landlord of modest means. One night a wounded Rajput prince sought sanctuary at the home of the Thakur, and perhaps as a return for this favour, the princess demanded that he marry her. He did so, and returned to his estate with his bride. In her new home the princess soon became the target of a whispering campaign due to her familiar behaviour with her husband's younger brother.

When the prince and his brother had gone to fight in a war with a neighbouring state, a messenger brought back from the battle his master's turban. This was the customary manner in which the death of a warrior was announced to the family. On receiving the fatal symbol, the Bhati princess resolved to become *sati*.*

** Sati* means pure and it is believed that the wife who immolates herself on her husband's pyre not only attains redemption for herself, but, through her sacrifice, redeems the sins of her husband. Her act of piety and martyrdom assures her eternal reunion with her lord. To 'commit' *sati* is a misnomer. The phrase came into use after the passing of a law forbidding this inhuman practice. But in its original sense, a woman 'became' *sati*, that is, she took on a new, pure, radiant being. This applied of course to voluntary acceptance, though whether it was ever so is a moot point, the family, social, and religious pressures on the poor widow being tantamount to a decree. To flout such formidable conventions meant facing a future that was no more than a living death. From their earliest years, the girls of Rajput and Brahmin families were brought up to regard *sati* as part of their *dharma*, sacred duty.

The body of the dead soldier was brought home by the Manganiyar who had accompanied his prince to battle. Only then was it discovered the dead man was not the prince himself, but his younger brother. The princess, having gone through all the rites that precede *sati,* and having already given up all hold on life, refused to be turned from her resolve. She declared that the young man had been as a son to her, and that she was determined to become *maha-sati*, great *sati*, one who gives up her life not for a husband but for the redemption of a son. And so she died.

The prince her husband had, it appeared, deliberately sent his turban as a test, to see whether his wife would resolve to end her life on his account. He had expected that she would discover the truth in time and so be saved. By the time he returned, she was dead.

Did the question of her fidelity haunt him ever after? Had she after all preferred to die along with the one she had truly loved? No one will ever be certain. The Manganiyar who had come with the body remained to look after her shrine, and to immortalise her in his songs of praise. Ever after, his descendants have claimed the right to be the keepers of the shrine of the Bhati princess, the *maha-sati*.

It was revealing that the two communities of local Hindus and Muslims should accept as natural and correct the official position of the Manganiyars at the shrine. Since the original Manganiyar had devoted his life to its upkeep, and since his inspired singing had established it as a place of pilgrimage and the *maha-sati* as a local deity, he had earned the right to a hereditary claim which has been respected ever since. The economic significance of this cannot be overlooked. In the quest for a viable means of livelihood every possibility is worth exploring.

Throughout the recording sessions, Akbar, the titular head of the Manganiyars, sat by us, curbing the over-enthusiasm of some, and pointing out those who merited special attention. On the last evening the men insisted that Akbar also perform. He was reluctant, having given up *riaz*, regular practice, since he had taken the job, but finally he agreed to sing provided that he would not be recorded.

In contrast to the tall, handsome members of the clan, Akbar is short and frail, with a sallow face and a toothy smile. His voice was sweet in tone but lacked power. He began with a lilting melody set in a *raga*. The opening phrases held much promise, but he soon faltered. He made another attempt but this time his memory failed him; he just could not recall the words. Finally, after several anguished attempts, he broke down and wept inconsolably. He accused himself of having betrayed his family and the time-honoured tradition of his forefathers; of having thrown away a priceless inheritance for the security of a pittance. It was a poignant moment which reflected a crisis of conscience, not only for himself, but, in anticipation, for his clan. For who could deny that the days of this artistic legacy were indeed numbered?

The reaction of his clansmen was touching in the extreme. In the embarrassed silence that followed, the musicians one by one came to him. Each held a rupee note in his hand, which he ceremonially passed over Akbar's head in a circular movement of blessing, and then deposited it in his lap. This collection Akbar would hold in trust to pay out to other poorer musicians who are *jajmaan* to the Manganiyars, that is, who perform in their homes on formal occasions, and on whom they are dependent for their livelihood. The intricate interdependence of the desert communities was brought sharply home to us by this unexpected event.

Our work now over, we celebrated by treating everyone to a lavish feast of *jalebis* and *laddoos* along with the indispensable cups of hot tea. The men were relaxed and gay, and the younger lads up to all sorts of mischief.

In retrospect, I realise that nothing will ever match the impact of that first exposure to the music of the Manganiyars. It had the intensity of a collective experience and an accumulative effect that was at once aesthetic and emotional.

Added to this was the undoubted contribution of the human situation which had brought about the meeting. On our part, we had come armed in sympathy for artists we knew were in straightened circumstances and to whom we were glad to be able to offer some slight relief, however minimal and inadequate we knew it to be. We had looked forward to hearing good folk music and to adding some worthwhile recordings to the Sansthan's archives, although we were prepared for the eventuality of finding the musicians unable to perform up to their usual standard. We were totally unprepared for the rapport that took place, both on the human and artistic level.

On their part, the Manganiyars had come to Jaisalmer with great expectations. They had grasped, perhaps intuitively, what we had not realised, that this meeting was crucial to the future of their community as professional musicians. Ever since Independence the existing patterns of life in the desert were being eroded. Their former patrons, the Bhati Rajputs, were no longer in a position to retain them and the little they received from their Meghwal *jajmaans* could not by itself, hope to support them. The tragedy of Akbar could overtake all their sons. A unique and wholly unexpected opportunity had now come to them to make a break into the contemporary scene, to find a fresh and wider audience and another avenue of earning through doing what they knew and loved best. As a result they excelled themselves.

To some extent their expectations have been fulfilled through the years. Many of them now broadcast regularly; they perform in festivals of folk music and some of them have travelled to foreign countries to participate in international music gatherings. The Jaisalmer Desert Festival is now an annual winter event that attracts an increasing number of visitors every year. The Manganiyars have been recorded on tape and filmed by Indian and foreign teams. All this has encouraged them to continue in their profession. To help them in this the state offers stipends to promising young boys in Manganiyar families for training, so that they can carry on the tradition. These are hopeful trends, but certain drawbacks have also appeared which may not be simple to counteract.

The major source of earning is for performers to appear in concerts of folk music. These are the festivals organised by private bodies or increasingly, by the tourist department. The audiences at such functions are large, heterogeneous and ignorant. Music that appeals to them is of necessity of the simple, catchy and popular variety. There is a great deal of this type of music in the repertoire of the Manganiyars; it is good and deservedly popular, but it is only part of their art. Unfortunately now, it is monopolising their attention to the detriment of the more serious, *raga*-based music that distinguishes them from other good folk musicians and which is their exclusive preserve. In a way, this is the same predicament that faces the traditional craftsman who is attempting to adjust to new market requirements. The integrity and character of the art gets dissipated through contact with alien influences. The result is usually fatal to the art.

There is no reason why artists of the calibre of Sakar Khan or Ghazi should not be able to improve and extend the range of their music and virtuosity within their own system. The help of trained musicologists and an exposure to the best classical music might revive some of its past glory. The exchange between the Manganiyars and classical music could be of benefit to both.

Late into that last night the Manganiyars continued to sing and play with no hint of fatigue, or flagging of voices. I walked out into the cold, dark courtyard, under an open sky ablaze and crackling with stars, listening in wonder to the sound of their music which seemed to well out of the earth under my feet. I asked myself: from what secret reserve do they draw such strength? How deep are the roots that feed their spirit giving them such a vigorous hold on life? What hidden springs nourish the unquenchable flow of their music which gushes out, to make what is barren, green with beauty?

When I had asked one of them about famine conditions in his village, he smiled and said, 'Three years of drought we can manage; we are used to it. But six years is a little difficult.' I was abashed by the understatement that chided my curiosity, and I could not question him further.

We left at three in the morning. The *dharamsala* was strangely quiet. As we walked out to the waiting car, we were taken aback to find the Manganiyars lined up in two silent rows on either side of the path to the gate, in the biting cold before dawn. We moved slowly past this guard of honour which solemnly greeted us with that ceremonial *namaste* which is traditionally reserved for royalty. We were so moved, we could barely respond. I hurried into the vehicle and stared, unseeing, at the blurred landscape.

7 Maroodesh: Festivals in a Dead Land

Ger Dance

The *rohira* was in bloom. Fields of wheat and *zira* lined the road through the black buck sanctuary beyond Jodhpur, westward to Barmer. South of the road lay the dry bed of the Luni. We crossed the river at Balotra to take a narrow track to the township of Kanana where the annual *ger* dance was to be held.

The day of the spring equinox, Holi, is celebrated throughout the north as a carnival of colours and *ger* is the dance of the season. Kanana lies half buried in sand. Its roads are no more than deep ruts ploughed out by the obdurate passage of bullock and camel carts, hard as rail tracks. During the days of the fair, trucks crammed with merry-makers and buses hired by parties of dancers join the multitudes of carts and carriages lurching their way to the fair.

Kanana is the home of the descendants of a remarkable Rajput nobleman, Durga Dass Rathor. During the days of Maharaja Jaswant Singh of Jodhpur, the Emperor Aurangzeb (1658-1707), last of the grand Mughals, ruled at Delhi. Jaswant was one of Aurangzeb's generals, and had taken part in the campaign against the Maratha ruler Shivaji, but his loyalty to the Mughals was suspect. The Emperor did not trust his Rajput commander, but being unwilling to lose his services, apppointed him Governor of Kabul, demanding that his son and heir Prithvi Singh be held as hostage at the Delhi court. Here the young prince was poisoned, and it was rumoured that it was the Emperor who had had him killed. Broken in spirit, Jaswant Singh died in Kabul. His queen gave birth to a posthumous son, Ajit. Aurangzeb was unwilling to recognise the infant as the heir to the Jodhpur kingdom, unless the child was handed over to him to be brought up at the Mughal court.

The Rathors saw this as a ruse to put an end to their royal house by converting the infant Ajit to Islam. The chief clansman, Durga Dass, smuggled the baby out of his ancestral home and escaped with him into the hills and ravines west of Jodhpur. He concealed the young prince near Siwana, in the caves among the rocks of Haldeshwar, which now are inhabited by a few Raika camel herdsmen and their families. Over a period of thirty years the Rathors kept up a guerrilla war against the Mughal forces which had occupied the citadel of Jodhpur.

For a while Prince Akbar, the rebellious son of Aurangzeb, wishing to usurp the throne, joined Durga Dass. But seeing no hope of defeating his indomitable octogenarian father, Akbar left for Persia entrusting his little daughter to the care of the Rathor. The young Rajput prince and the Mughal princess grew up together in the wilderness under the paternal eye of Durga Dass. But when the Rathor chief realised that a tender relationship threatened to develop between the two young people, he honoured his promise to Prince Akbar, and sent the princess to her grandfather, Aurangzeb, at Delhi.

A few years after the death of the Emperor, the Rathors were able to oust the Mughals from Jodhpur, and Ajit regained the throne of his father. Unfortunately he turned against his benefactor, and banished Durga Dass from the state of Marwar, although the Rathor had dedicated his entire life to the welfare of the ruling family at Jodhpur against the overwhelming might of the Mughals.

Kunwar Sahib, Thakur of Kanana, a direct descendant of Durga Dass Rathor, and the present head of the clan, was our host.

As one approaches Kanana, the township lies sprawled on the left, while on the right stretches a sandy plain. At the far edge of this is an enormous shallow bowl surrounded by broken ridges of hard earth with shrubs and bushes alternating with smooth, wind-moulded dunes. Beyond the bowl, on a raised platform under a grove of *ber* trees is a shrine to Sitalmata. The steps leading up to it are painted candy pink; the shrine itself is white, but the idol was so heaped with garlands of marigolds that nothing of her could be seen. She is usually shown seated astride a donkey.

Sitala (literally 'cold') means small-pox, and Sitalmata, protectress of children, is the goddess. *Sitala* is the name of the disease and also that of the goddess herself. It is believed that small-pox is a visitation of the goddess who inhabits the body of the victim to punish some act of dereliction on the part of the victim, the parents or the community. She must be propitiated with rituals, prayers and offerings. The patient is confined in a darkened room, and the earth around his cot is sprinkled with water soaked in *neem* leaves. Family members may not shave or change their garments till the goddess has departed, that is, till the patient is cured. And when she leaves, the occasion is celebrated with the burning of all the used garments, with ceremonial baths and prayers of thanksgiving, indicating precautionary hygienic measures mixed with superstitious beliefs under the guise of ritual.

Small-pox has been eradicated in the country, through the benevolent blessings of Sitalmata, with a little help, no doubt, from the municipal vaccinator! The goddess now has transferred her domain and extended her compassionate mercy to those suffering from cholera, dysentry, epilepsy and other dread diseases, and with these additions to her kingdom seems in little danger of losing her following.

Carts formed a circle on the rim of the plain, the casual, orderly setting-up of one-night homesteads demonstrating the ingrained discipline and practical sense of nomadic logistics. Flames from cow-dung fires licked the edges of darkness, catching the gleam of bracelets, mirrored embroidery, cooking utensils, and playing on the ruddy faces of children who brought straw and dried twigs for the kindling. Camels settled grudgingly into the dust, and the men unharnessed them with nimble fingers. Unyoked bullocks blundered in tight circles, and eased their necks with apparent relief.

The four-wheeled camel carts served as one-storeyed homes, the underneath a cosy basement for calves, goats, dogs and poultry. The bullock carts with upturned shafts and sloping keels made an encampment of small stockades, each with its own independent existence, but linked to others through sound and movement. Groups of animals shuffled towards the water-trough, with much shoving and mock-serious passes. Women carrying tiers of water-laden pots sauntered through the throng with graceful ease. Between the moving forests of legs of man and beast, dogs wove patterns of their canine world, border skirmishes defining territorial rights. Smoke from the fires rose in thin spirals. Women were making *rotis* on skillets. The smell of fresh baked bread mingled with the pungent odour of dung cakes, and the smoky haze gave a blurred softness to the scene. The children had already discovered the sweet seller and the doll maker. Their high excited voices were raised in demand for these treats for which they could not wait till morning.

In the centre of the bowl a post had been erected. It had a cross-beam which made it look like a crucifix. On it hung a hurricane lantern. Several men came in groups and stamped down the earth around it. They were no doubt dancers testing the arena they were to perform in next morning.

The road we now took wound through the small township up between rows of brick-built houses to a slight rise. Here it opened into a large square, dominating which stood the gateway of Kunwar Sahib's *haveli*.

The arched entrance led into a large courtyard.

Kanwar Sahib mounted on his black horse

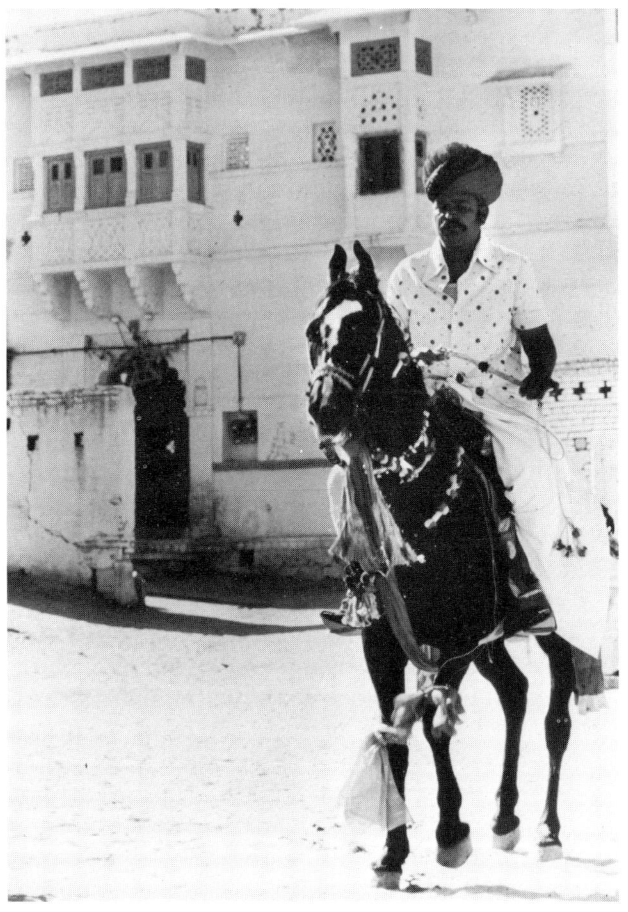

Opposite was the family home of the Thakur. To the left was the guest-house, and on the right steps gave onto a terrace where rich carpets with an elegant arrangement of bright cushions offered us a welcome as princely as in the days of his illustrious ancestor. With thoughtful consideration, tea, cold drinks and a variety of delicious snacks were laid out on low tables for us.

We were greeted with courteous dignity by Kunwar Sahib's son, a handsome young man, and his sister Durga. A lively child of ten, she immediately attached herself to us, and played the hostess with a mature air of concern for our well-being. This adult rectitude was enlivened by sudden bursts of childish high spirits.

No princely household is complete without its retinue of court musicians. And whom should we find among the present company but our ubiquitous Manganiyar friends, Ghazi and Luna. There was also an old *sreemandal* player, and a dreamy-eyed young man whose special skill lay in blowing into a painted waterpot, as an accompaniment to the singer, Ghazi. The *ghara*, pitcher, is a common percussion instrument in many parts of India. It is usually tapped on the sides or struck with the fingers on a membrane stretched over the mouth. But I had never seen it used before by the Manganiyars as an accompaniment. In this case, the mouth was not struck; it was blown into with such skill as to produce a wide range of sibilant notes, as the player knelt and swayed, bent and rocked to the rhythm.

We needed no alarm clock to wake us next morning. Durga was up before the first birds, twittering with excitement at the door of the guest-house. We must get up, the trays of flowers for the *puja* were already set out, the sweets were piled on the brass plates. Hurry! the procession was about to begin.

Arrayed in festive finery, groups of women and children began to trickle in through doorways, down corridors and staircases into the enormous courtyard, then out through the archway into the square. Like regiments of ants resuming their broken ranks, they formed themselves into the procession with an instinctive sense of their place in it. Their sarees and veils and clusters of jewellery made a riot of colour.

A camel with the *naggara*, drums, led the way, followed by Kunwar Sahib mounted on a spirited black horse, which clattered and pranced and proudly arched its neck, aware of its own importance. His son came next, perched more sedately on a camel, flying the *panchranga*, the five-coloured banner, and sailing with unruffled calm through the boisterous throng. Women carrying trays of flowers and sweets sang as they walked to the temple. The sun spangled their faces with tossing reflections like slivers of light from water. Their eyes darted like fish in the aqueous gold of their veils. Children with large staring eyes blackened with kohl skipped and shrieked with excitement. From balconies, doorways and rooftops, ecstatic women yelled their greeting, and joined in with snatches of the processional chant. We formed the rear-guard, and all along the route, from every alley people surged in, forming eddies of movement in the larger stream, singing and laughing, till the entire population of Kanana became part of a frothing rivulet of colour and music and movement, coursing down to the sandy maidan.

This barren space had suddenly blossomed into an expansive tossing field of poppy-red, marigold and saffron. We passed by the stalls of swords and sticks, daggers and knives and paused by a bevy of giggling girls surrounding a bangle-seller

The procession came to a halt at the shrine at the edge of the bowl. The sanctum appeared withdrawn, absorbed in its tree-shadowed silence. Up the pink steps tripped the girls in yellow, green and orange, bearing their shining brass trays, to offer flowers and sweets and their song of praise. Then suddenly the cry went up, 'Sitalmata ki jai!' Hail to the mother goddess!

Kunwar Sahib held up his hand. His words were lost in the excited tumult of the crowd. His hand came down, and the drumming began.

At this signal the crowd slowly fell back, forming a circle round the night's crucifix and, pushing their way through the press of bodies, the dancers appeared. A group came in from the right, dressed in

Actor in make-up for his role as Rama in the *Swang* of the *Ramayana*

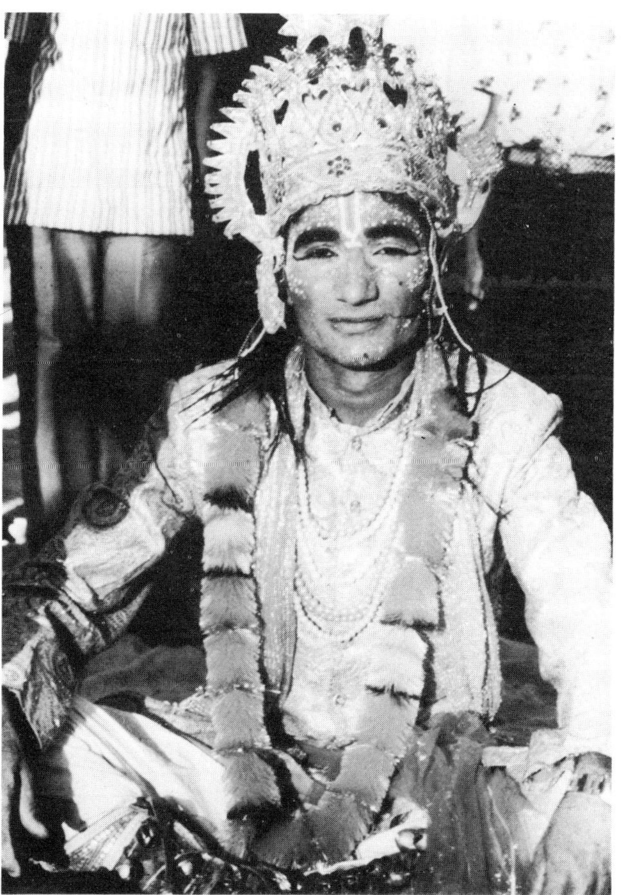

red, with saffron turbans and crimson cummerbunds, and as the lead dancer stepped into the arena, a second drummer added an echoing beat to the first. Answering the double beat of the drums, the dancer moved, his feet picking up the rhythm, his shoulders swaying, the throb of the drum seeming to ripple through his body. Forty dancers followed their leader and as each one stepped into the circle, he responded to the drum with his whole being.

Now a second team pressed forward from the opposite side, in white coats, flaunting blue-green peacock feathers in turbans of red. And suddenly, as though they had erupted out of the earth, a third group leapt into sight, scattering the laughing, cheering crowds further back, tumbling the children into the end stalls that marked the edge of the maidan.

Batteries of drummers took up the rhythm, working variations of intricate beats within the basic cycle. Gradually the groups of dancers formed into separate circles, each around a nucleus of two or three drummers. There were one, two, three, four, five, six circles of dancers, composed of forty to fifty members in each, and each gyrating to the beat of its drummers. The *ger* is a circular dance performed by men.* The dancers wear a long, ankle-length coat over tight-fitting trousers. The coat crosses over the chest and is fastened at the waist, from which the voluminous circular skirt falls in pleats. A cummerbund is wound round the waist. The skirt made of home-spun cotton is so wide and heavy that, in walking, the dancer has to carry it draped over a stick. The weight and swirl of the enormous skirt gives the dancer the necessary balance while executing the intricate movements of the dance. He turns around himself as the earth turns on its axis, and he circles around the arena as the planets orbit the sun. The skirts fan out like flowers opening in sunlight, and as the dancers change from a clockwise to an anti-clockwise turn, the skirts of forty, fifty, a hundred dancers whirl about the legs and thwack like a whiplash across the beat of the drum.

The dancers start with slow and simple movements. The drum coaxes, nudges, leads them on. The body of the dancer seems to unfold, expand. The steps, at first light and staccato, slowly build up to a steady, throbbing rhythm, as firm as the drummers' beat. The arms take on fluidity as, with a flourish, silk handkerchiefs appear.

Sharp turns of the wrist flick these to the drum beat, and they flutter in the sunshine as though the hands of the dancers had burst into tapering flames.

The drummers incite the dancers on, circling in the centre, closing in on the spinning forms, leaping at them like possessed demons, their eyes aswim with the intoxicating rhythm.

Now from their cummerbunds the dancers draw short wooden batons, and the rhythm of the drums is augmented by the click of the sticks. The circling movements never cease, the sticks strike to the right, strike to the left, strike above the head, and then, when least expected, miss a beat, only to take it up again in a movement above, to meet the stick of the dancer with a click to the left and a click to the right. These patterns become more involved and rapid with the rising tempo of the drumbeat. They are discernible though not predictable, for they vary in innumerable combinations. Finally the dancers produce swords from their cummerbunds, and the drumming builds up to a rousing crescendo.

At first the crowds were attracted to the circle of scarlet-clad dancers. Then their attention was divided between these and the team in white, as they spun and whirled. Finally, they drifted towards the third group, drawn by the hypnotic intensity of the drumming, the precision of the movements, the blood-tingling verve of the performance. Who were these dancers? They wore no spectacular pleated skirts, nor did they flaunt peacock feathers in their turbans. They were dressed in white cotton *dhotis* with short black waistcoats over white smocks. But how superbly their steps were synchronised. What supple grace was in their movement, what energy vibrated through the measured thud of the feet, the toss of the head, the twirl of the limbs, and agility of the leaps, the rippling of power through the bending bodies. These were the Jat Chaudhiris of Jhalmand, and they were the finest dancers at the fair.

All day the dancers whirled and spun. All day the drums throbbed. The children ran off to watch a group of *Swang* players performing the *Ramayana*, but scampered back to the dance arena. Girls wandered to nearby stalls to look at trinkets, but were soon lured back by the insistent drums. Customers lingered among the foodstalls, but not for long, for the drums pulled them back into the hypnotic centre of the dance.

The sun was low in the sky, the stalls were lit with the glow of oil lamps. Someone had lighted the hurricane lanterns that hung on the posts in the centre of each whirling circle, while the dancers danced on. It was as though they were caught in an unending motion like the rotation of the earth, the movement of the heavenly constellations, the cycle of the seasons, the beat of their own hearts. The world was awhirl.

---

* The phrase *ger khelna* literally means 'to play the *ger*', a complicated game with *dandis*, short batons.

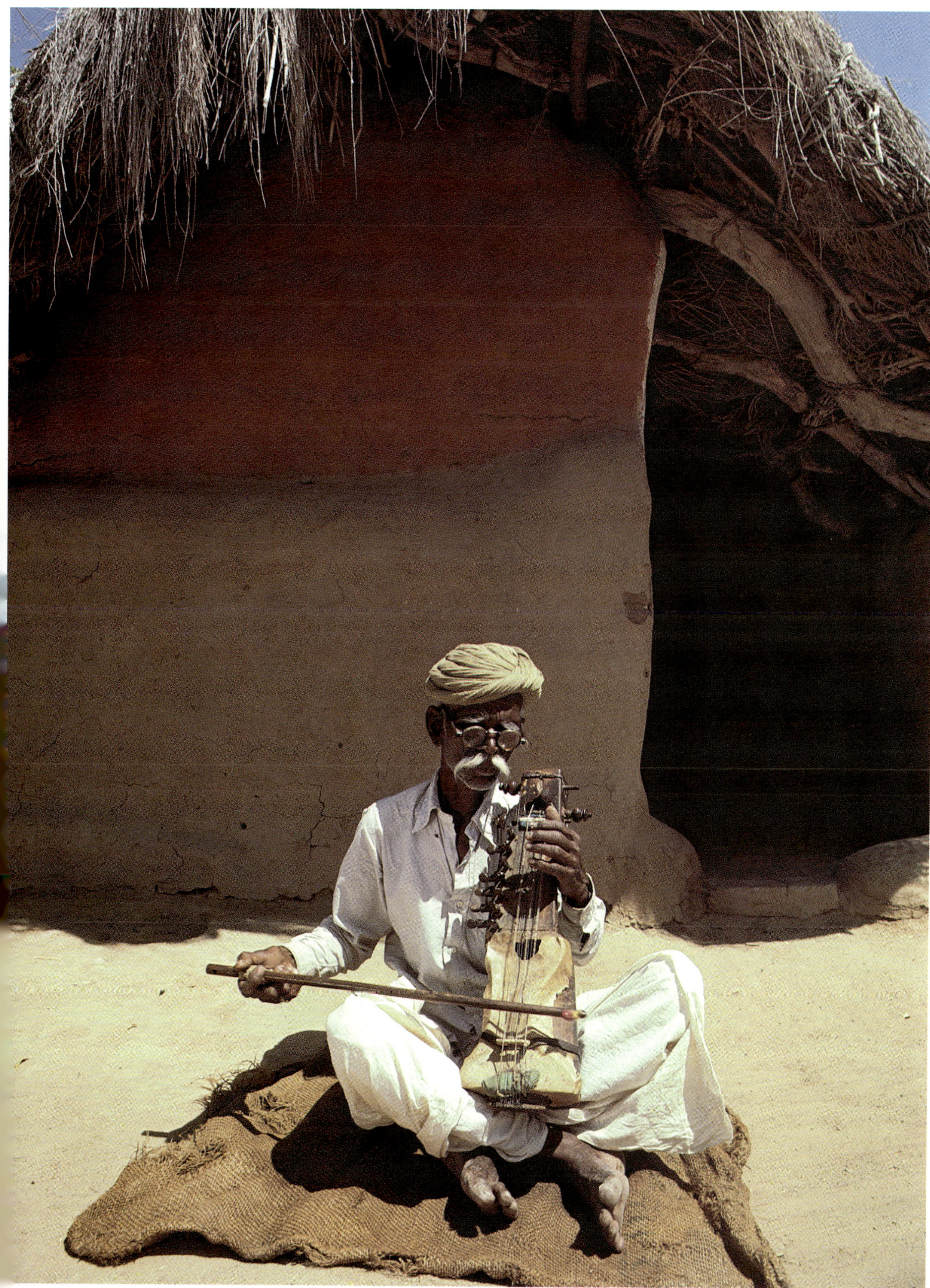

Old Dholi *sarangi*-player

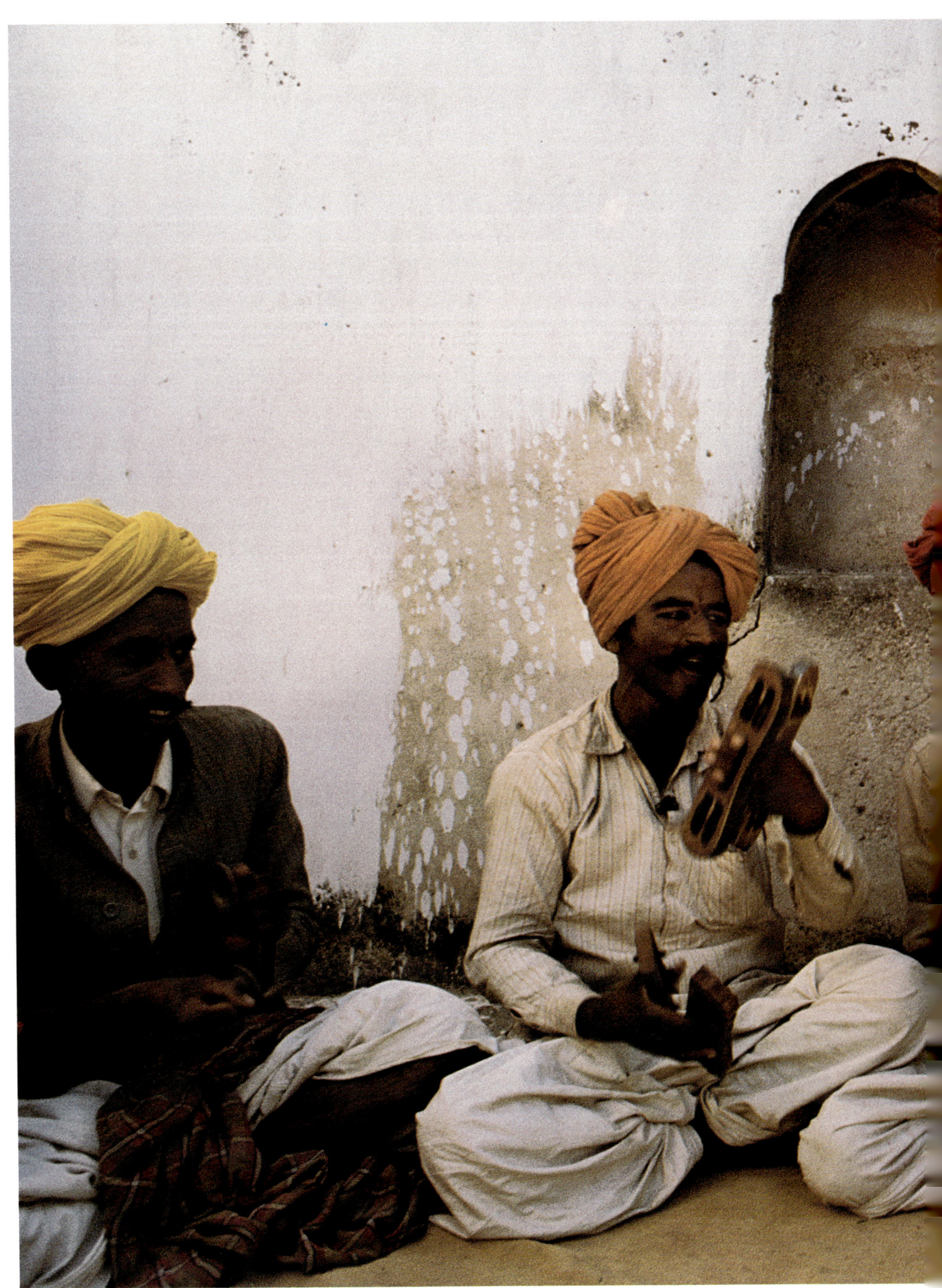
Manganiyar musician, playing the *gharra*, at Kanana fair.

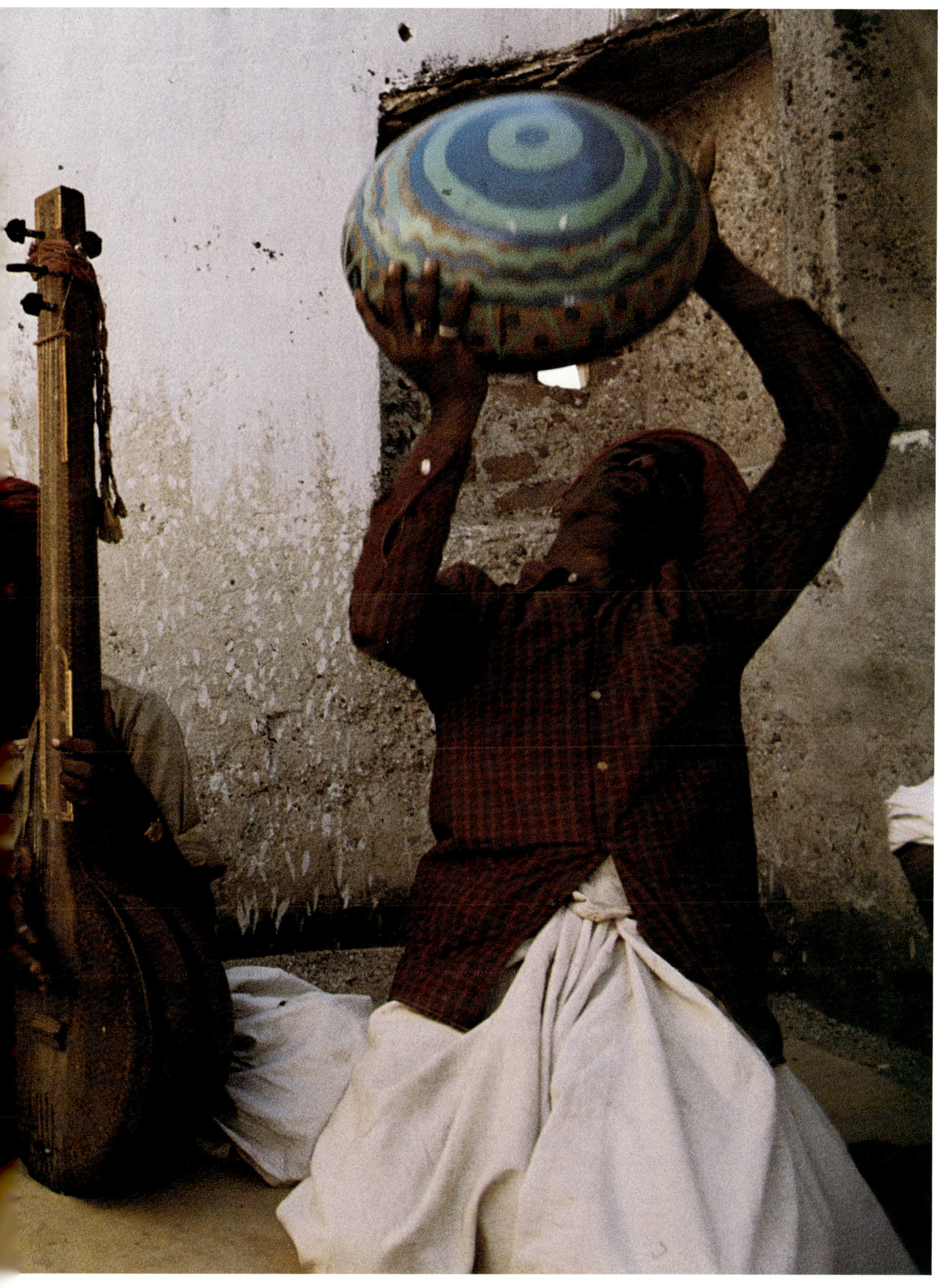

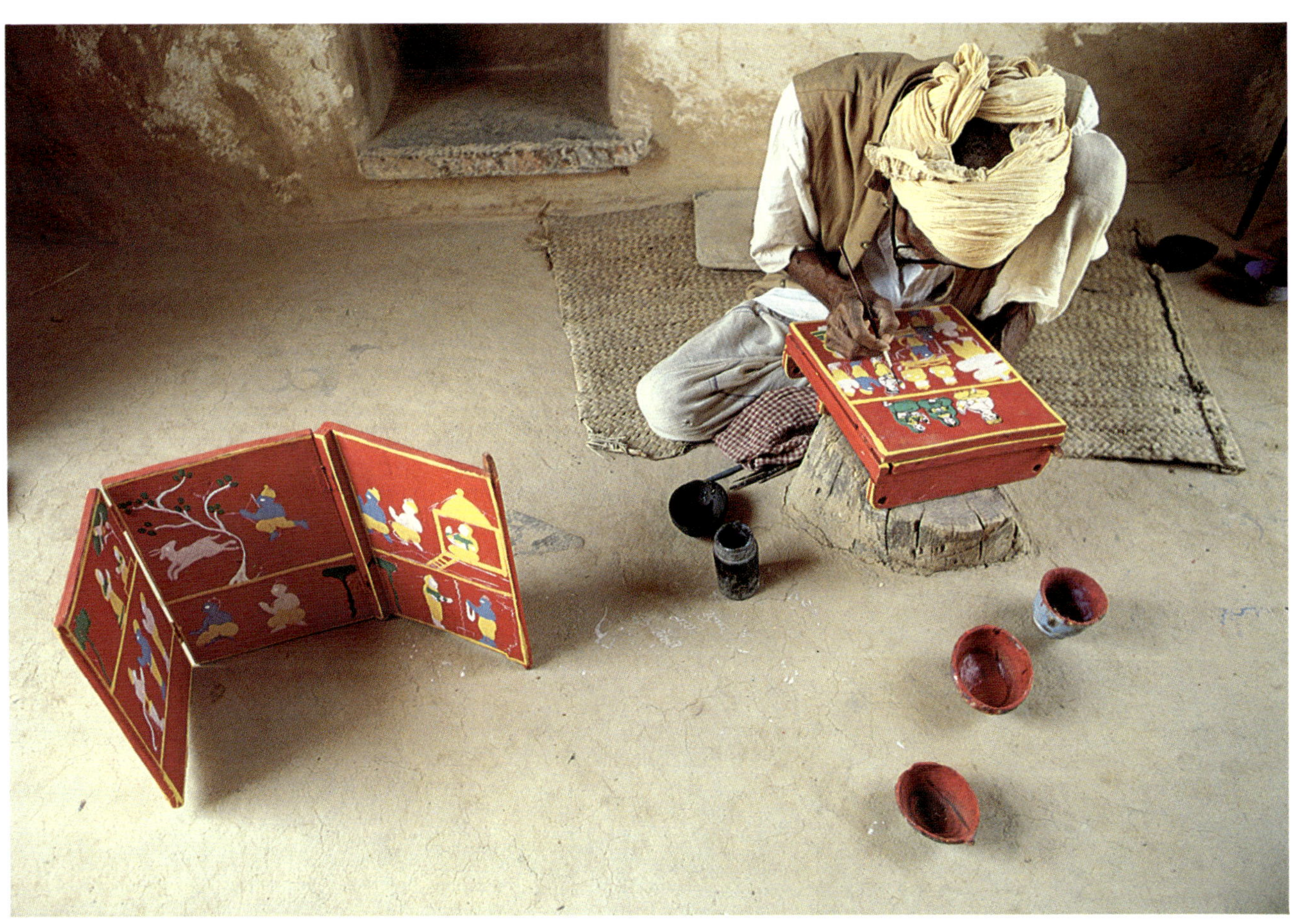

Painter at work on a *kavadh*, a painted cupboard.

Bathing in the sacred lake, Pushkar.

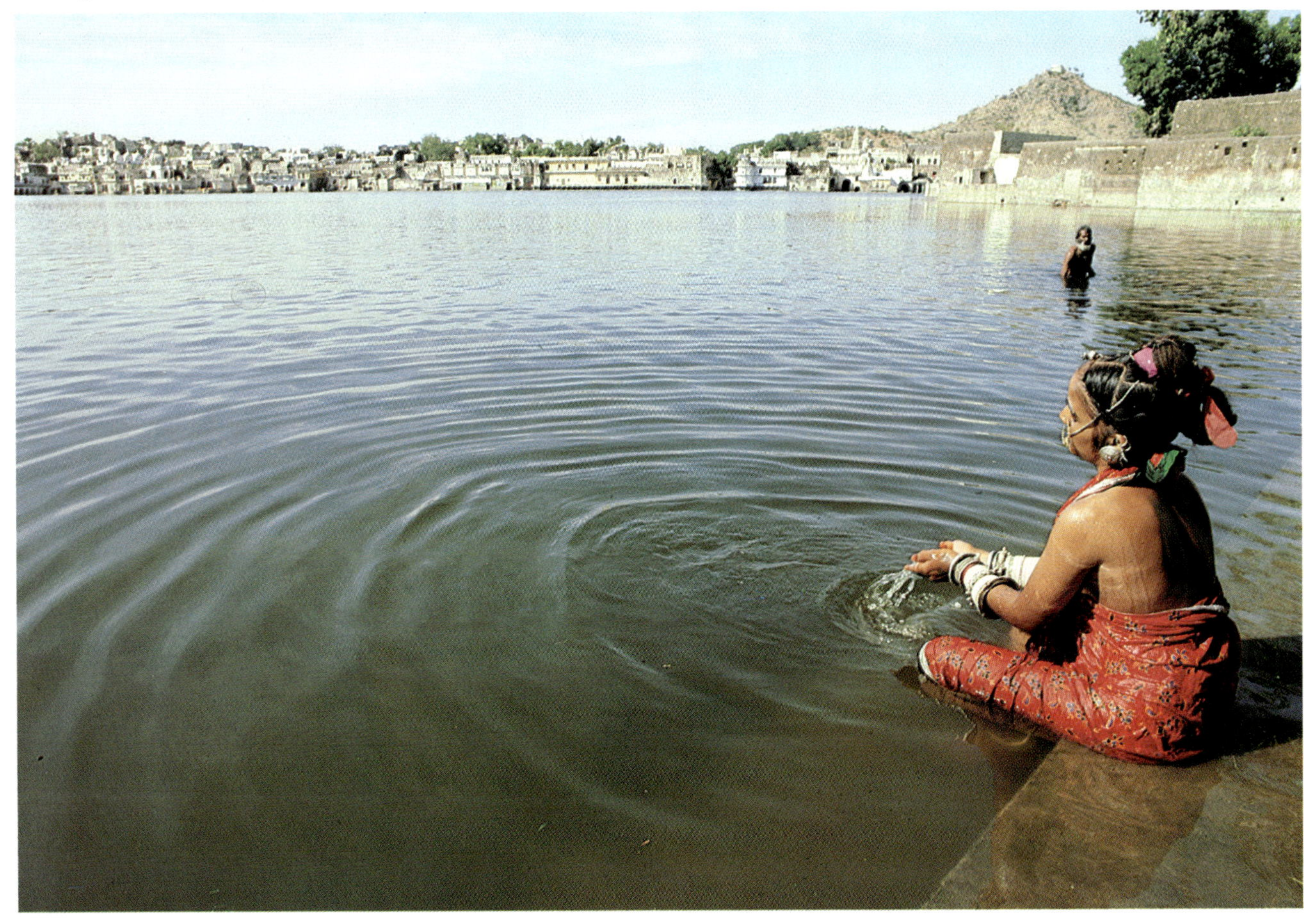

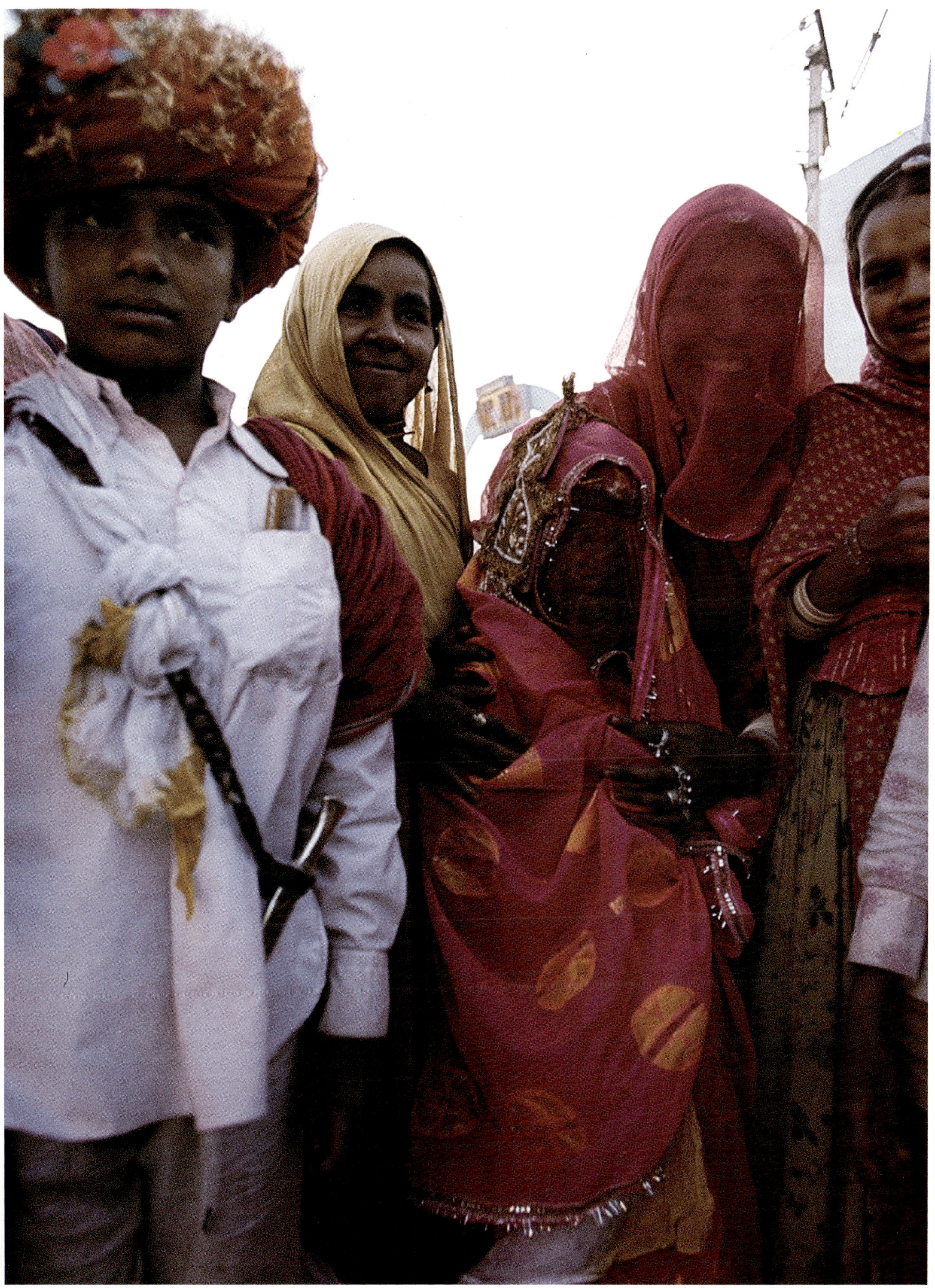

Child bride and groom at Balotra

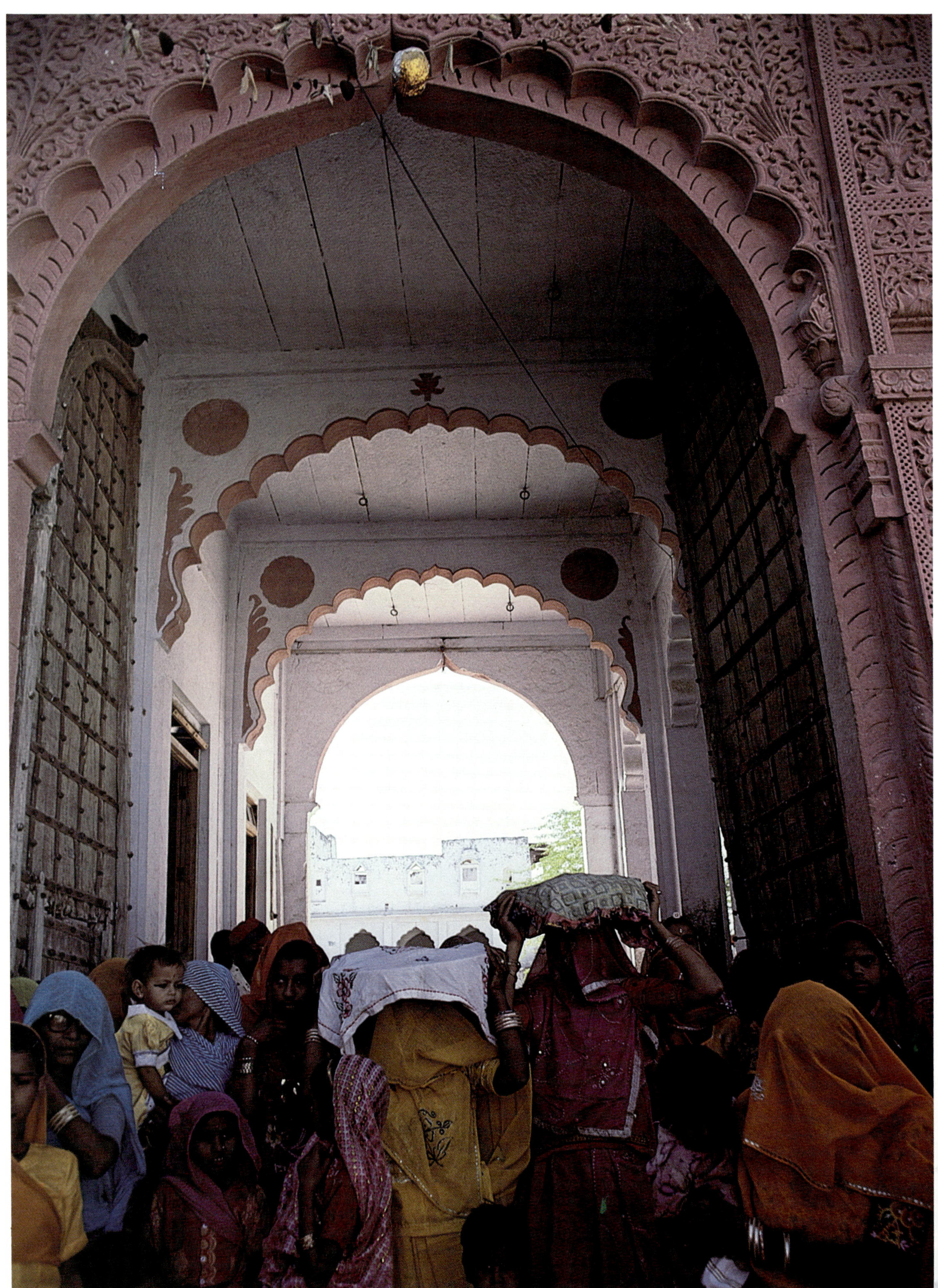

The procession during the Ger festival, Kanana.

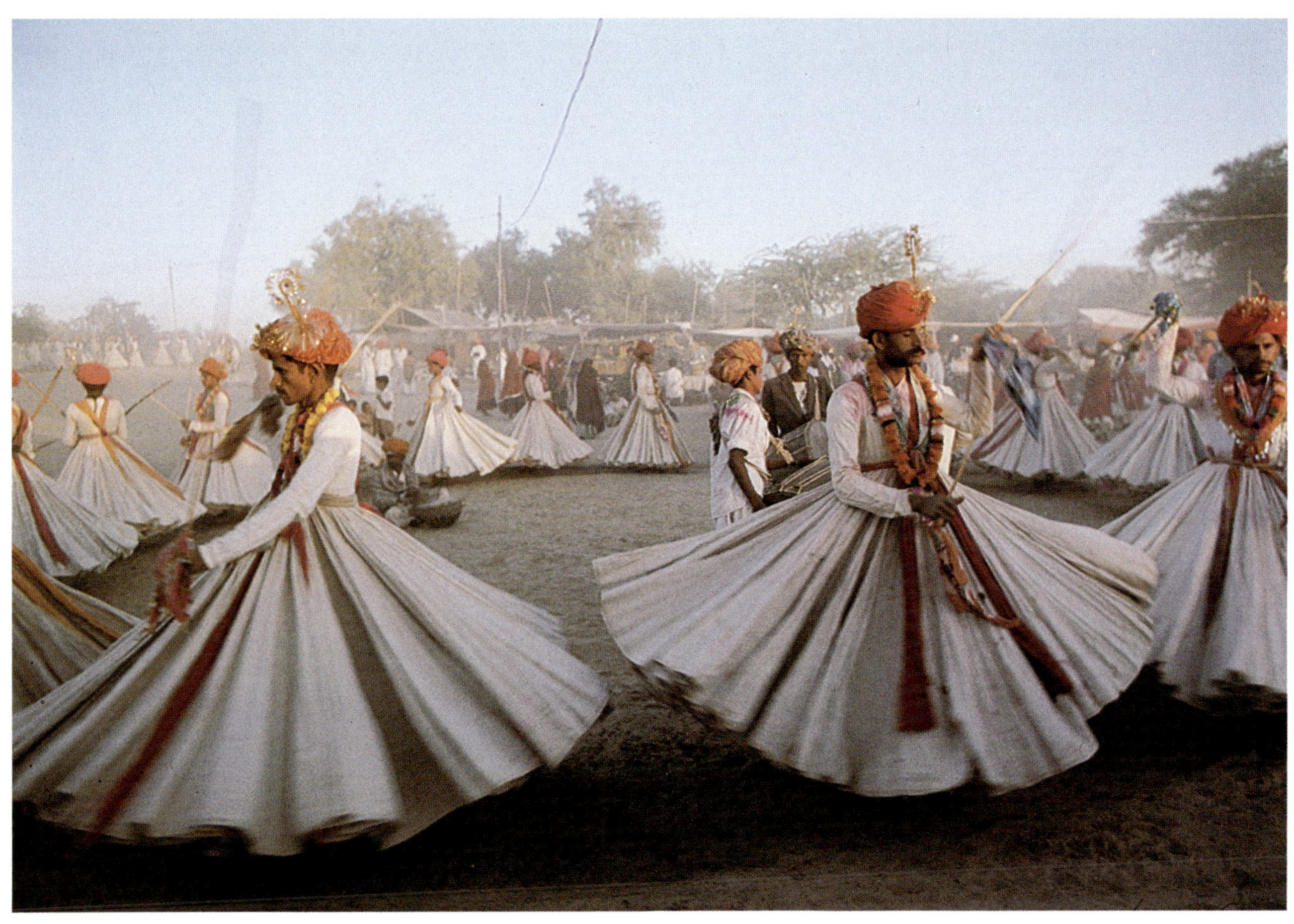

Ger dancers, Kanana.

Close-up of a dancer

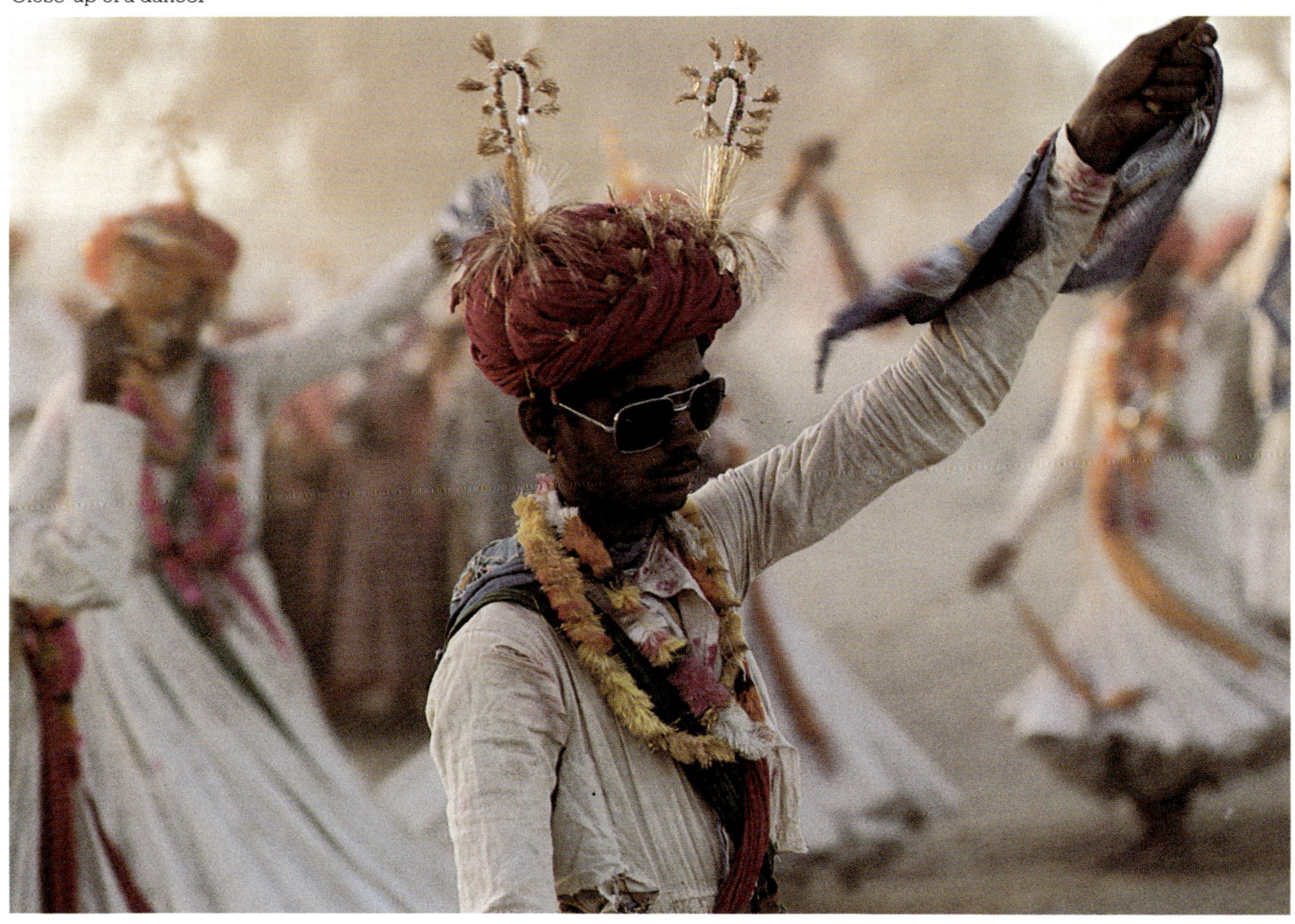

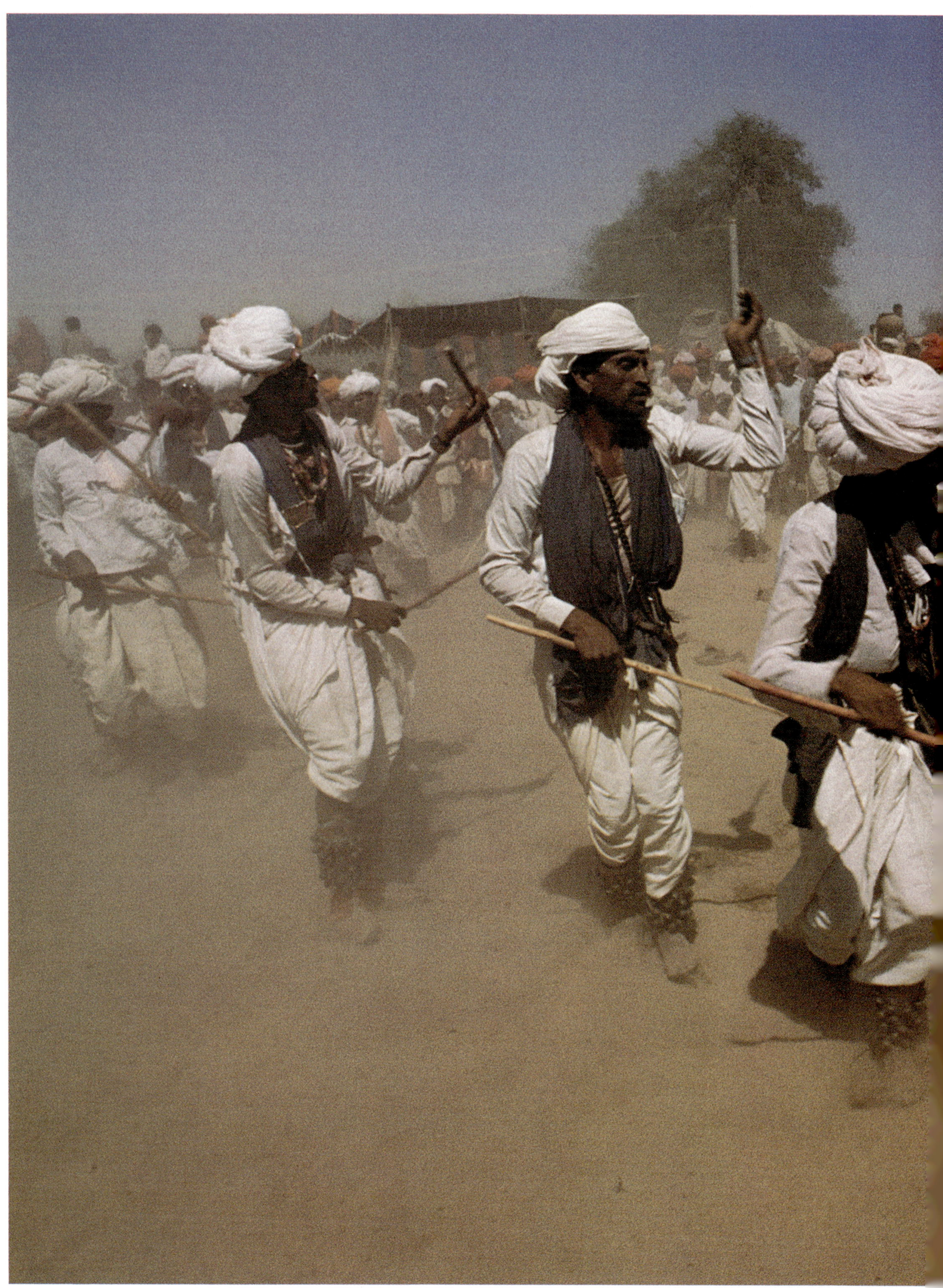

The prize-winning team. Ger dance festival, Kanana.

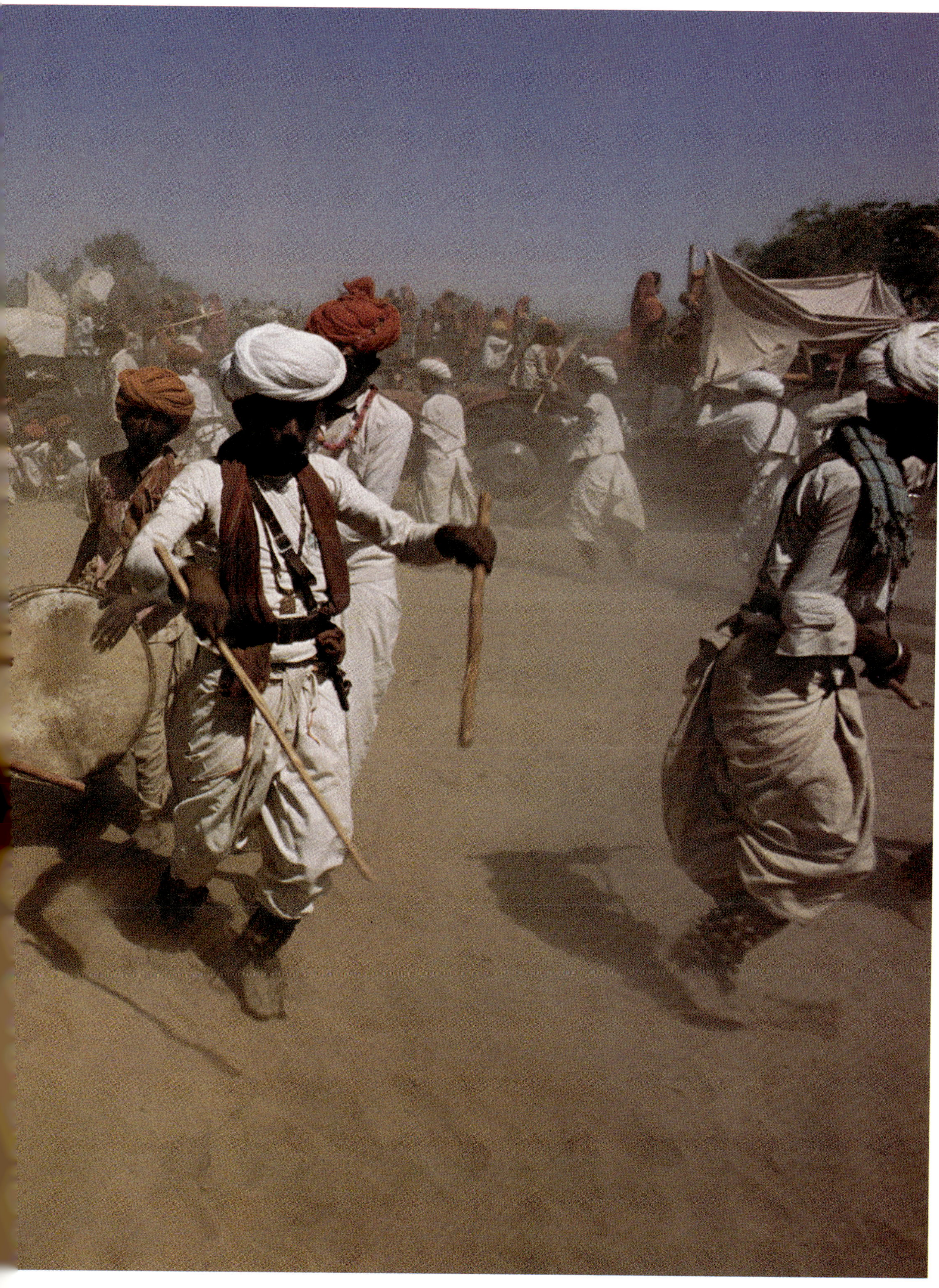

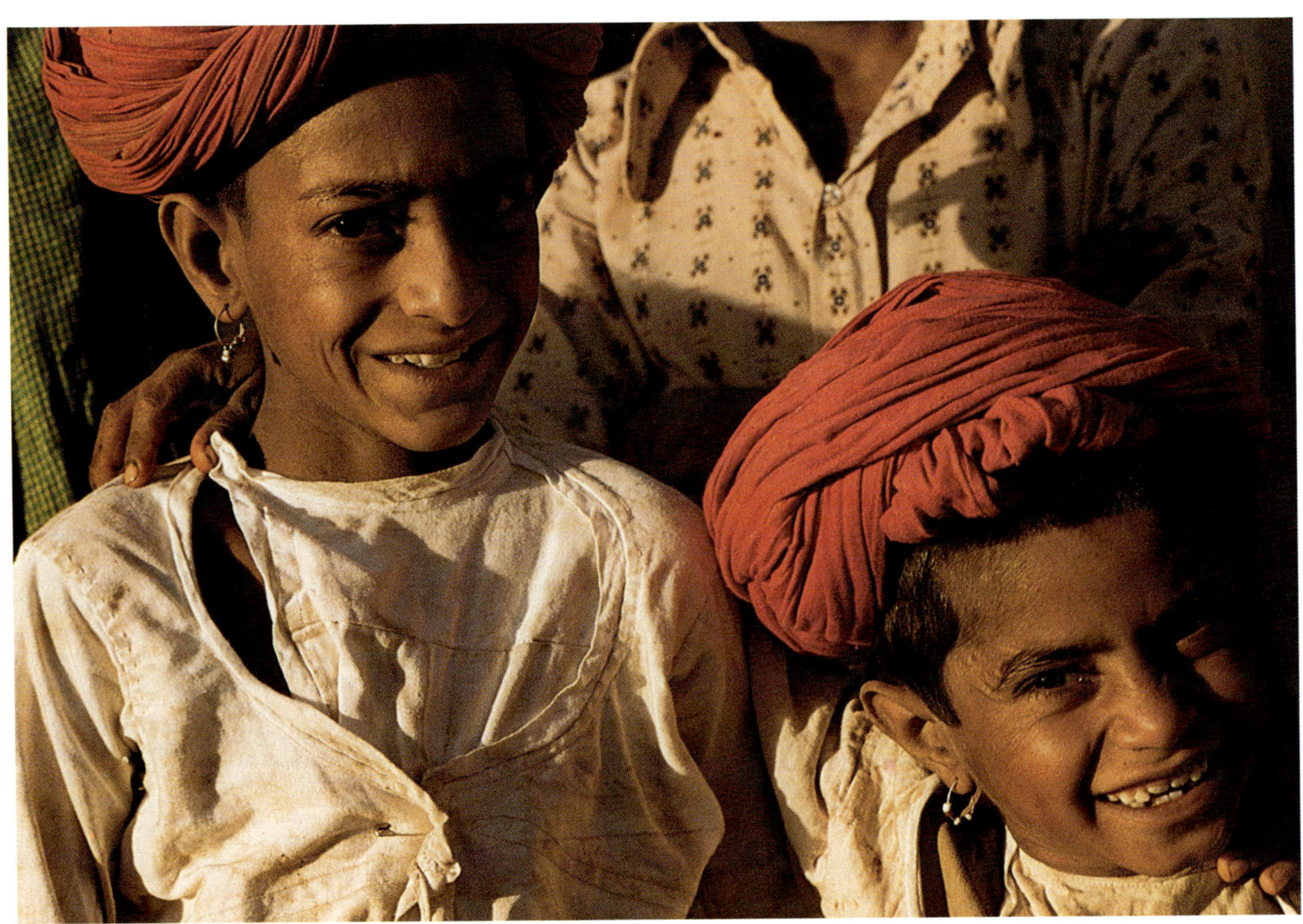

Raika boys watching the dance

Bishnoi woman showing jewellery

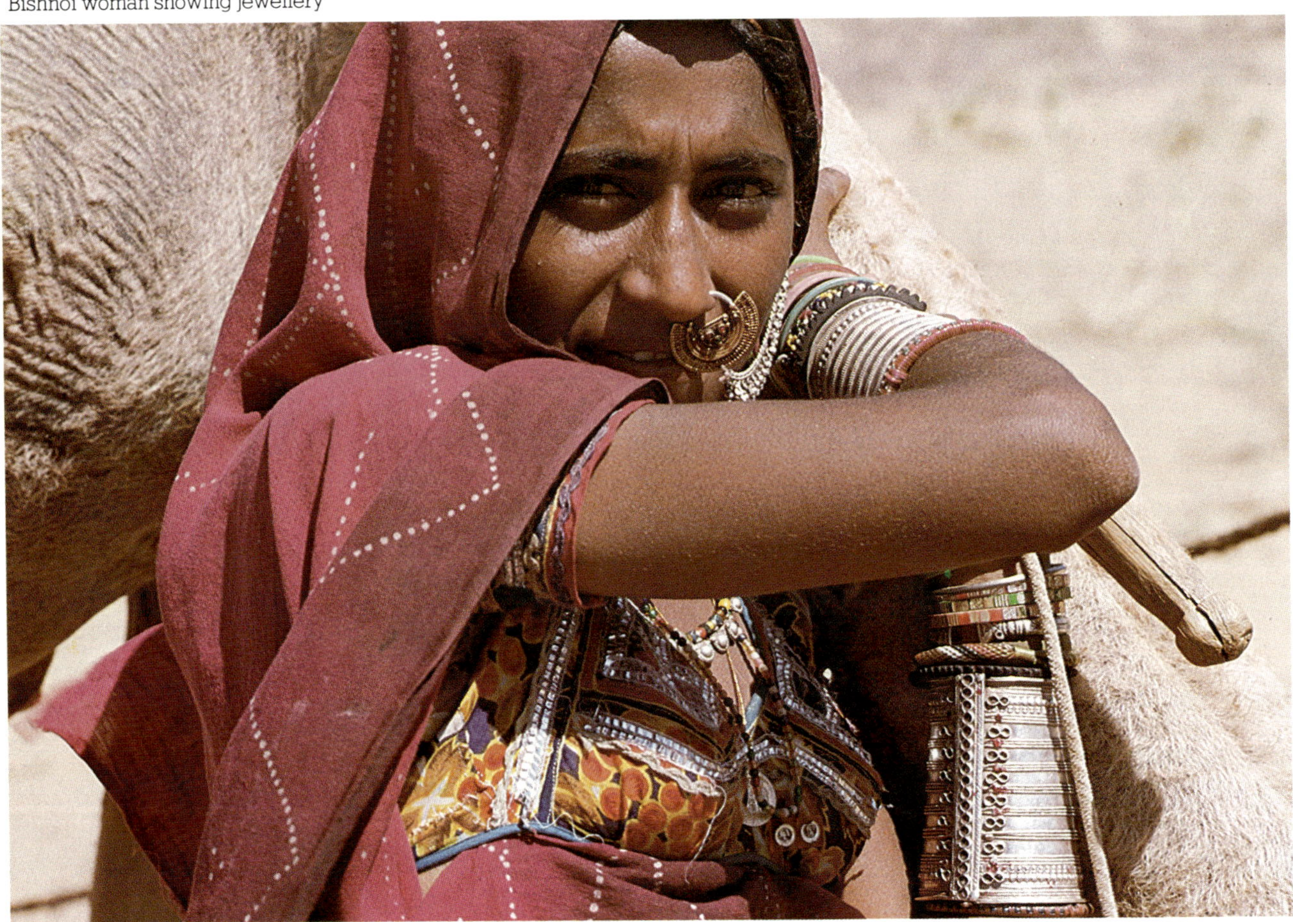

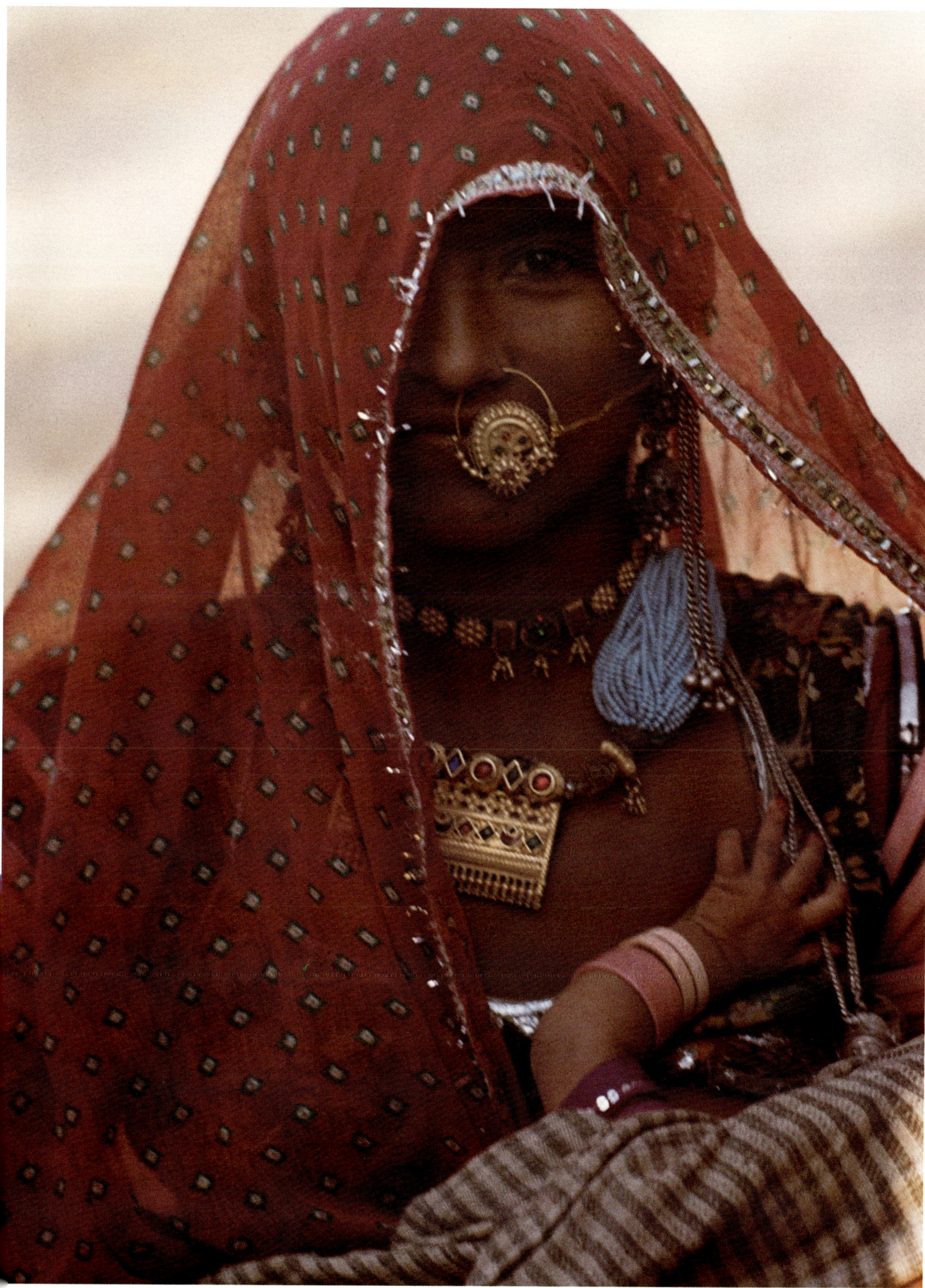

Mother and child at the fair

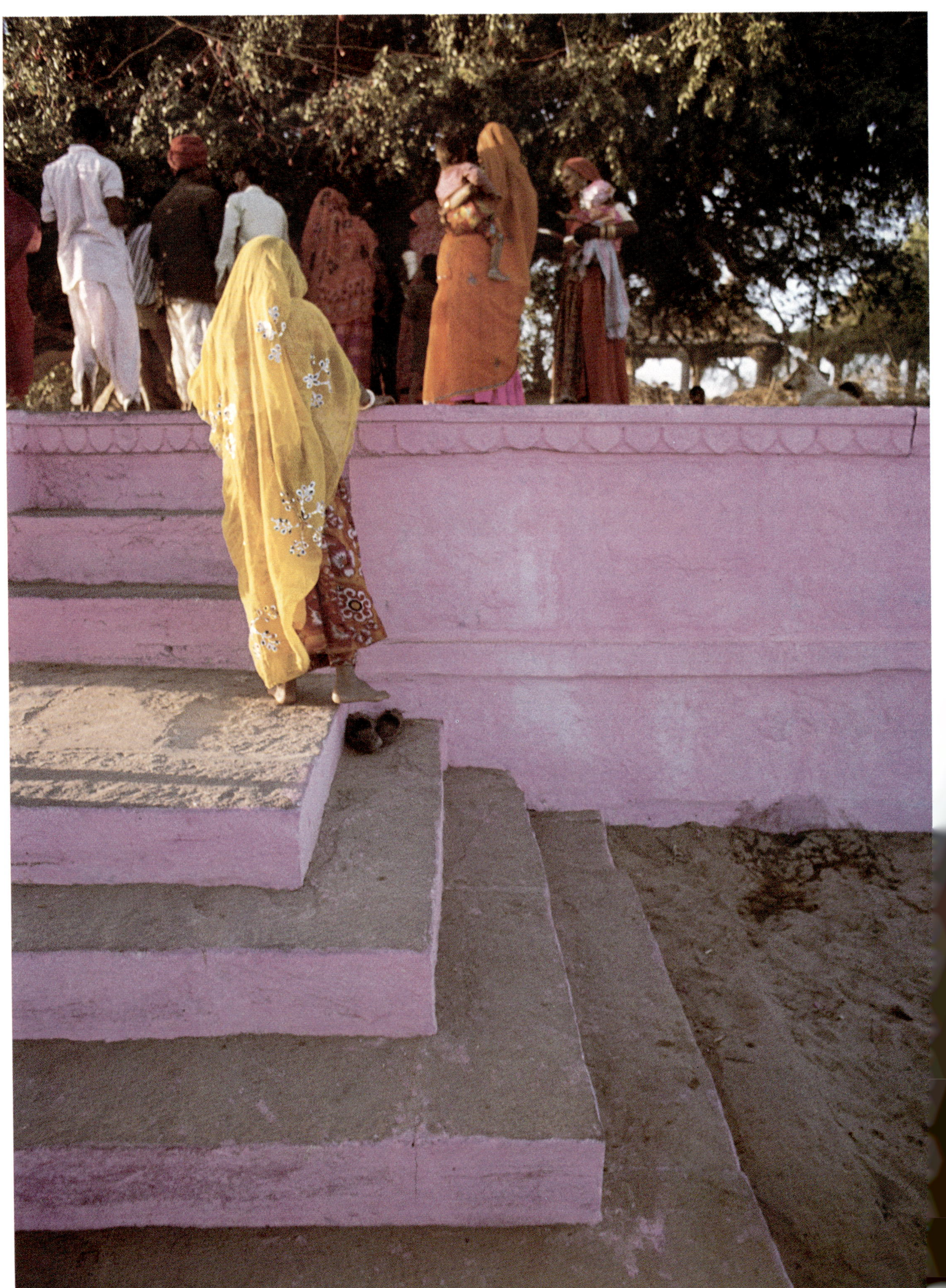

Sitalmata temple, Kanana.

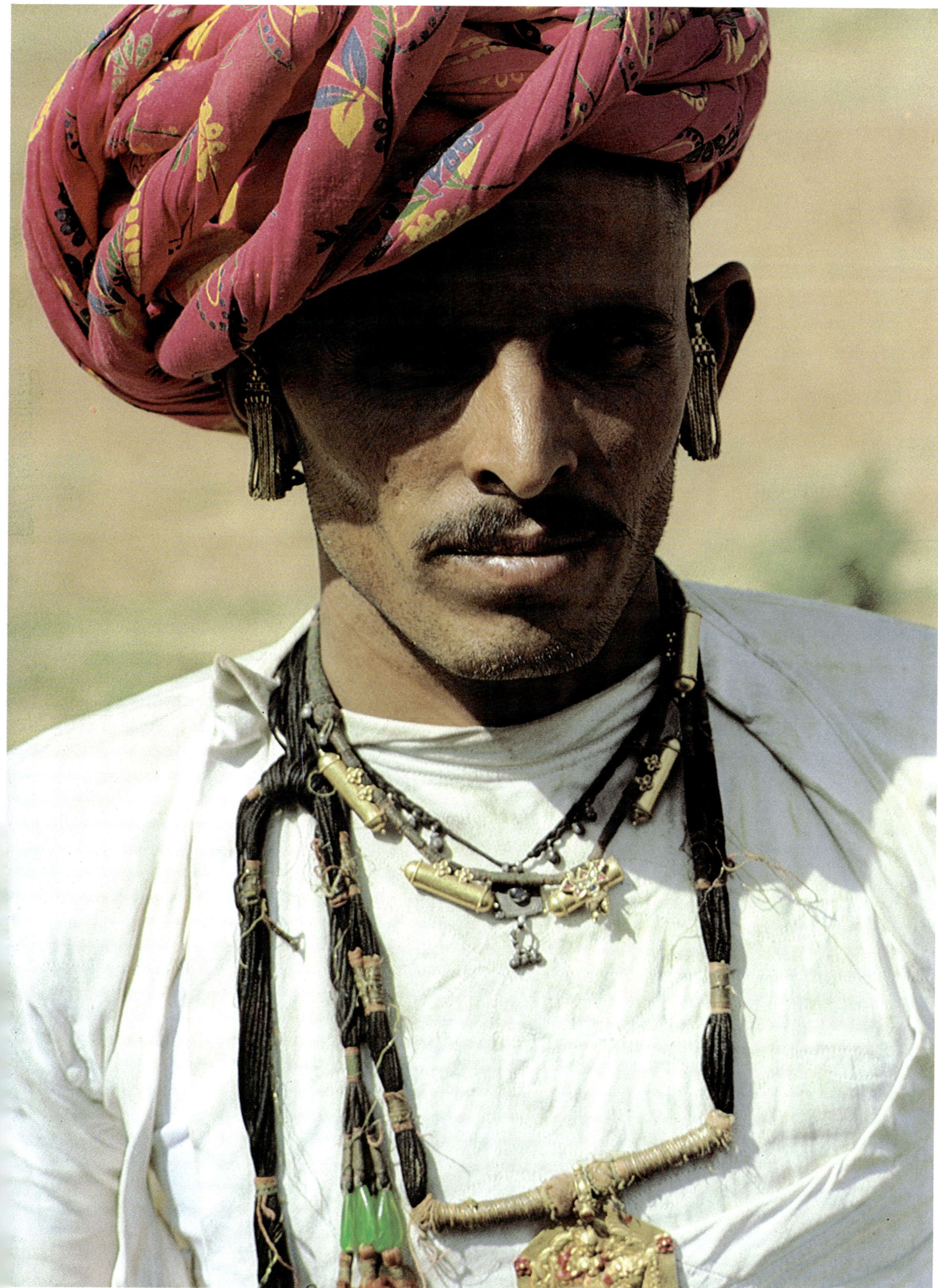

Raika herdsman wearing typical ornaments

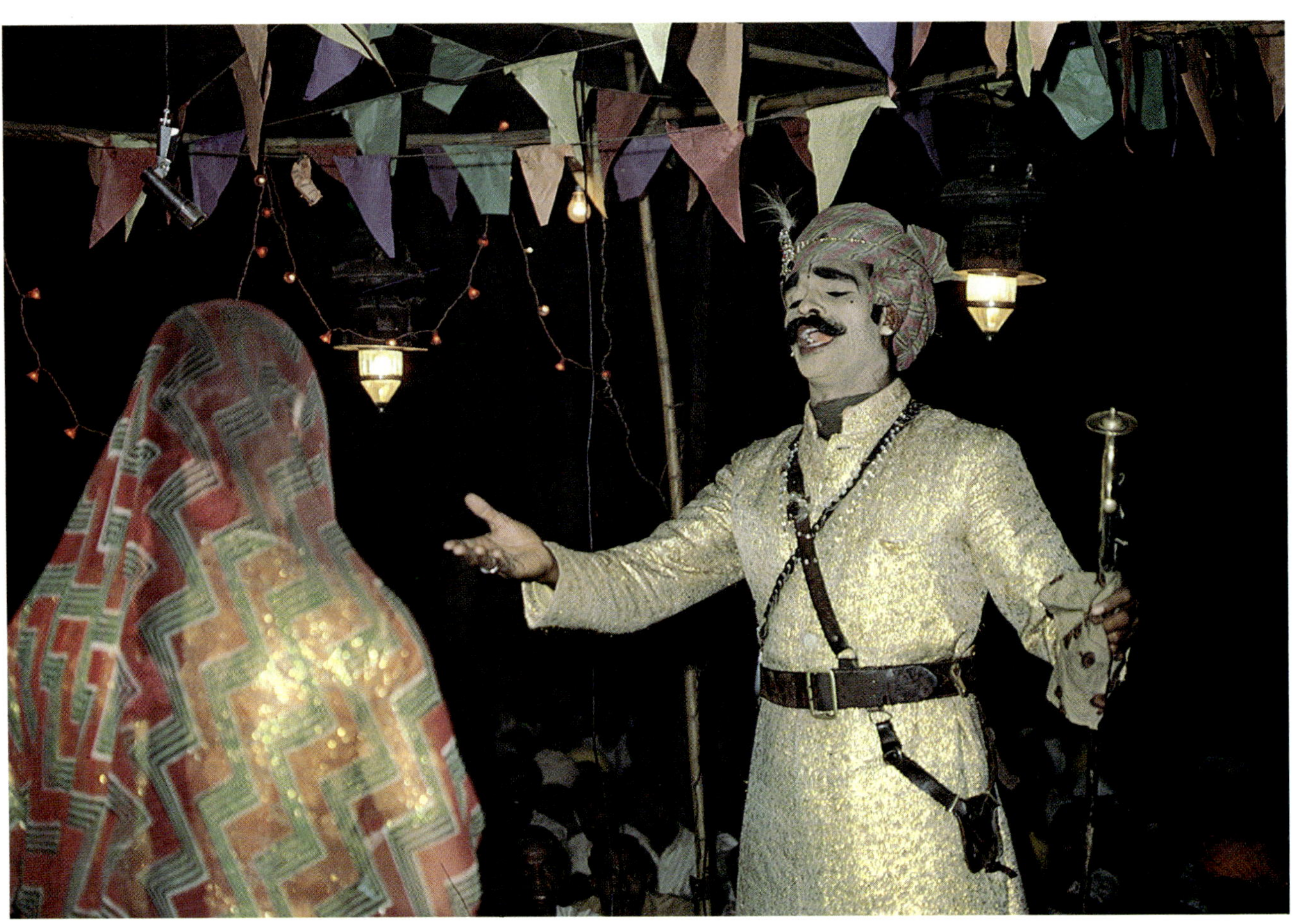

Khyal performance of traditional theatre at Tilwara cattle fair

A sweet-stall at Tilwara

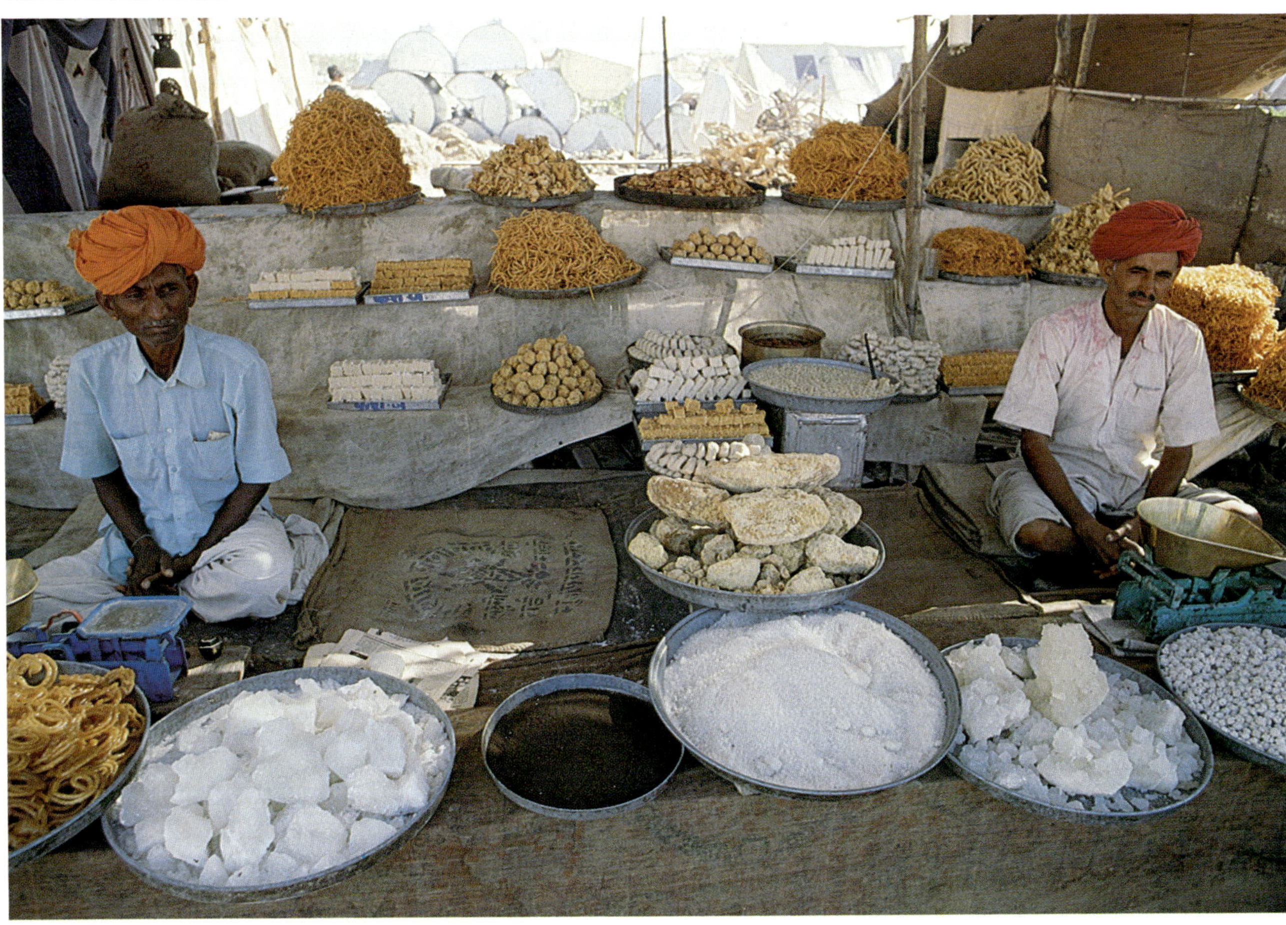

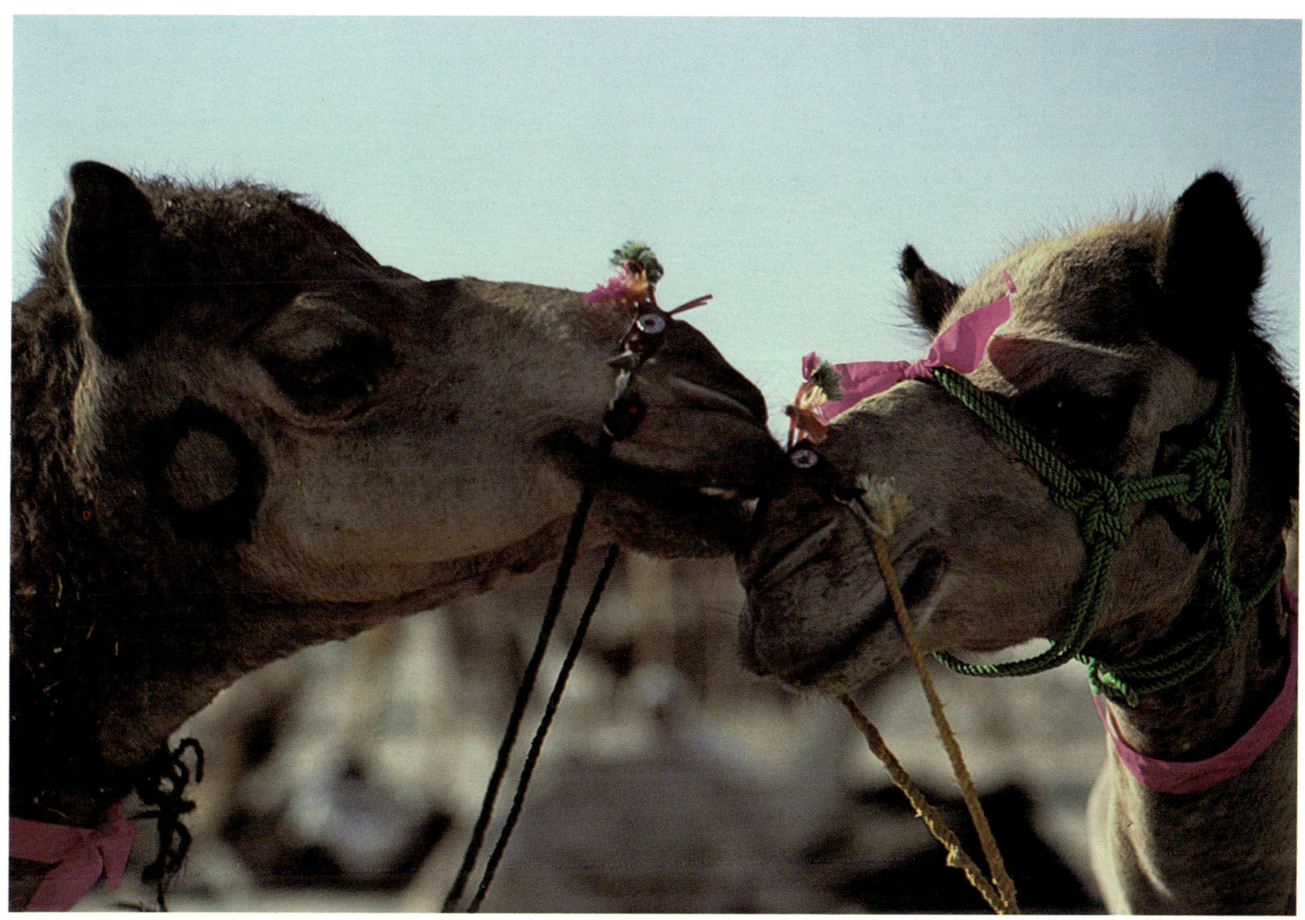

Desert love

Horses on trial runs

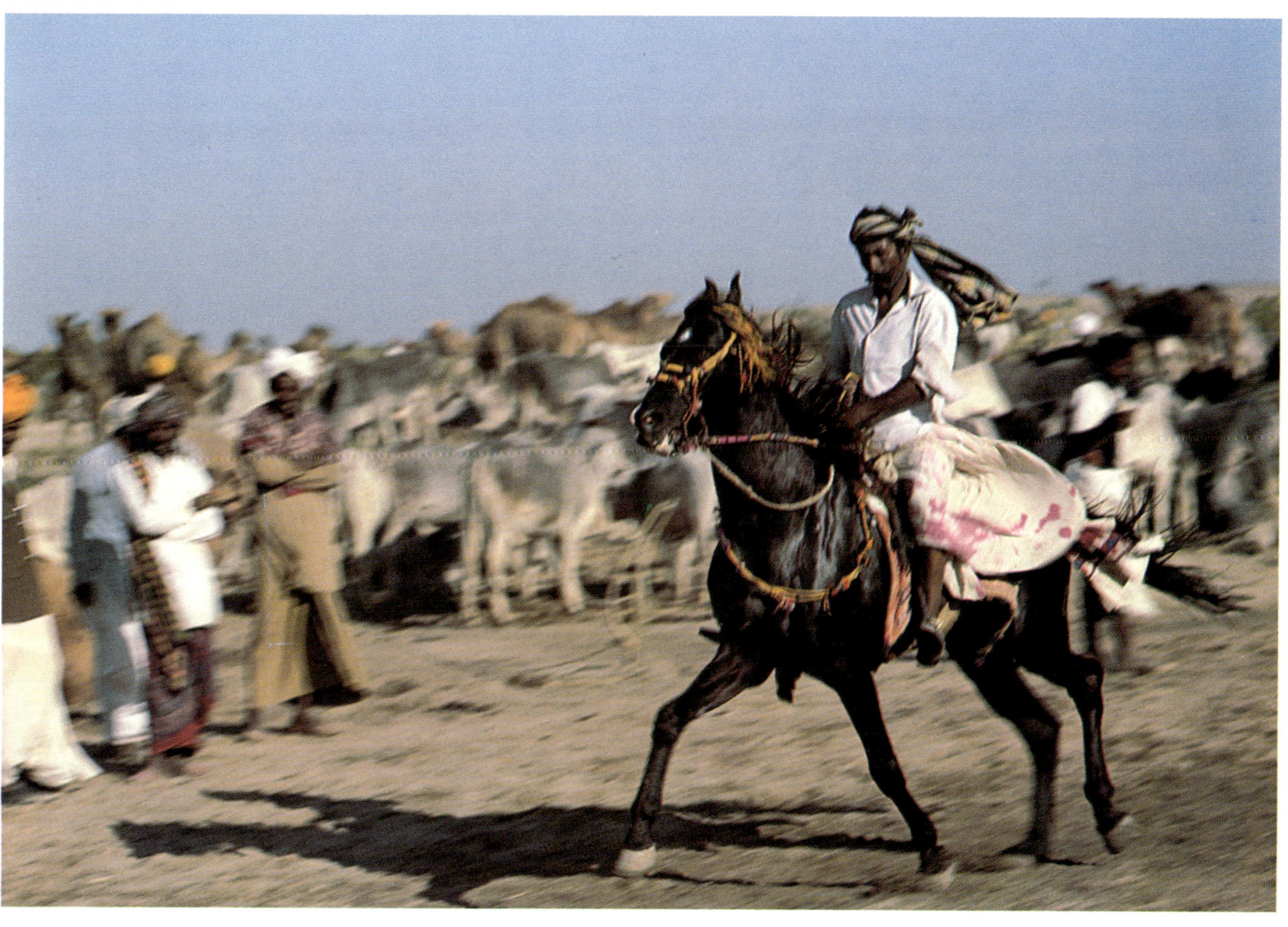

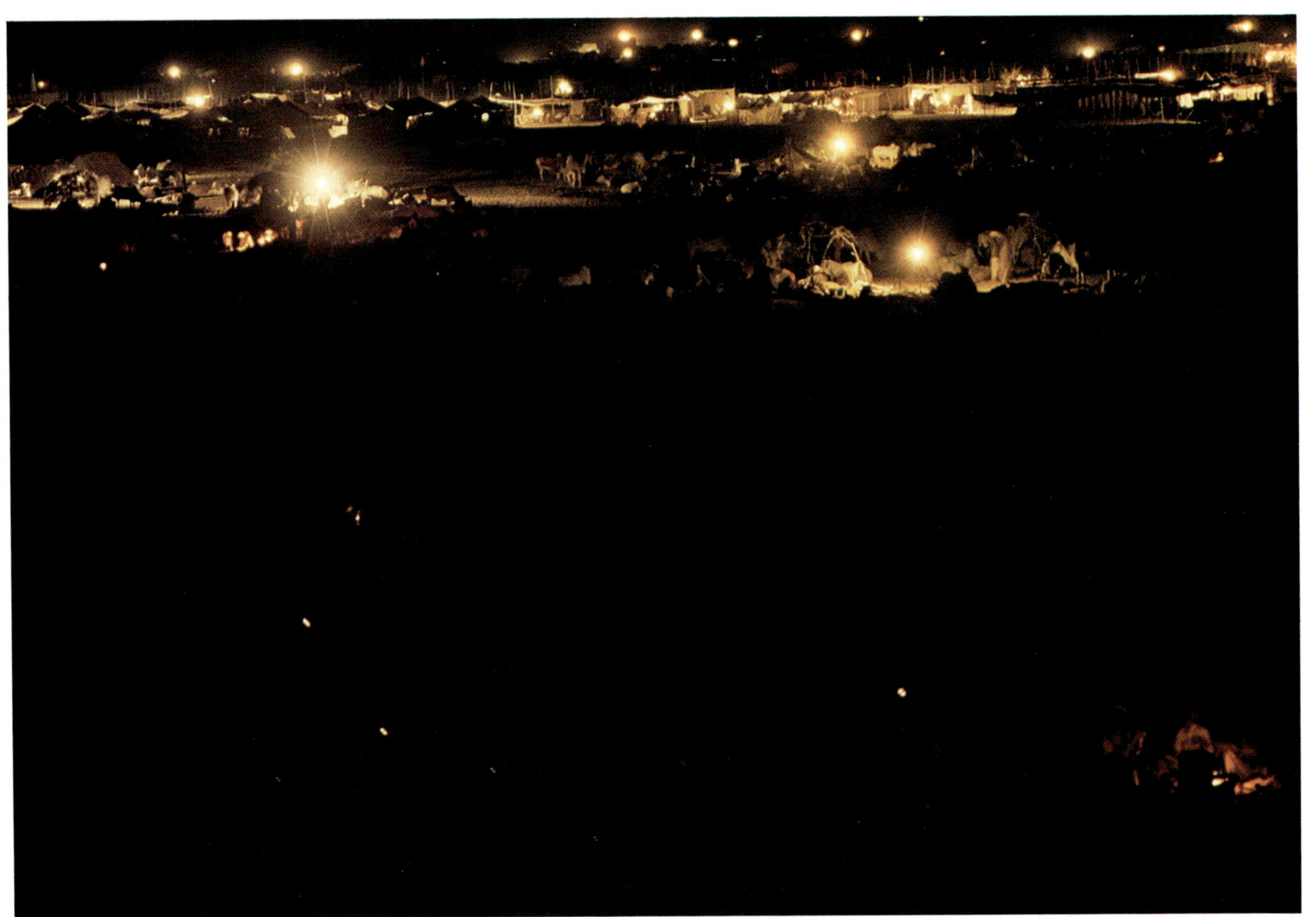

Tilwara by night

Of Birth and Marriage

Old towns, when their importance dwindles, take on the odour and aspect of decaying flowers. Rose petals turning brown, crumple and fray at the edges, the centre withers, rots and spills apart. Even so, Balotra. We drove through, wearing blinkers, en route to the splendid cattle-fair at Tilwara and had no thought to spare for the sad fate of disintegrating towns. But Balotra was not so dead that it could not arrest our flight. With a single, swift intrusion it seized us, and set all the jangling bells of association in agitated motion. Out of a side-lane came a small procession of women bearing trays of flowers and sweets, and, walking between them, in the centre of the vivid group, a child-bridegroom and child-bride. The little boy, about eight years old, so valiantly accoutred with his miniature sword at his waist, and a turban precariously balanced on his round head, led his bride of seven or so. Though for the occasion she had assumed a maidenly modesty far beyond her years, she was curious-child enough to peep out from behind her veil at us. They looked like characters from a street play, thoroughly delighted with their central roles in a charming charade. And they posed for their photograph with disarming poise, like players at curtain-call. The procession was returning from the temple, after which the little bride would go back to her home. Eight years or so later, the young groom will come again to her village to fetch his bride and to perform the elaborate ceremonies of which this was a dress-rehearsal, a token and a pledge.

This encounter called to mind a conversation I had had with a bright-eyed ragamuffin, while sitting on a kerb-stone outside the village of Sanganer, near Jaipur, famous for its handmade paper and handblock printing. The youngster announced with much pride

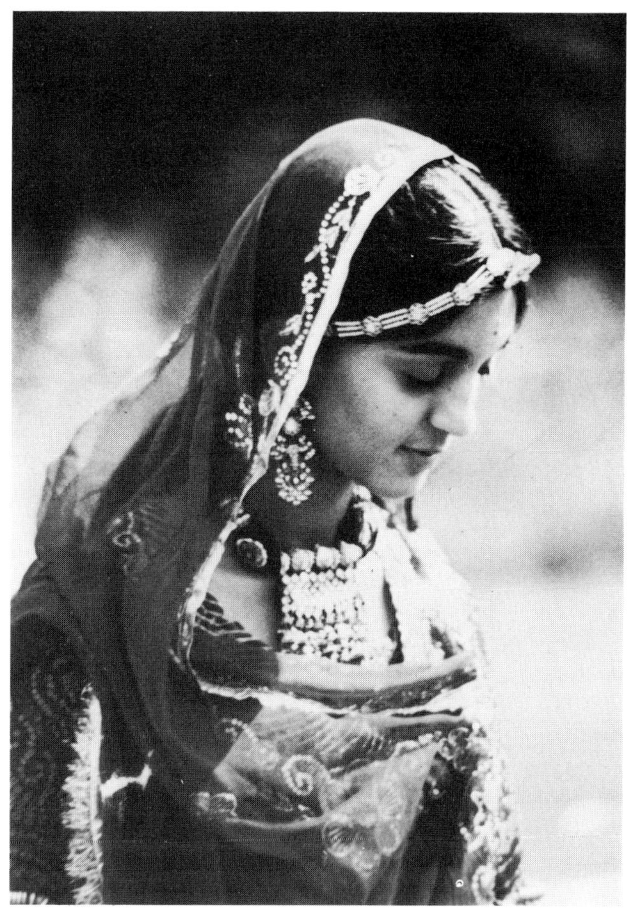

A Rajput princess

that he was married, and, pointing to a podgy brat of about six, so was his brother. But, he added in a tone of condescending commiseration, his friend, though older, had no wife. I had listened to his childish boast with astonished, if somewhat wry, amusement, wondering how the status quo would ever change when children were flung into the game of adult life at such an early age.

Child-marriage was one of the practices Mahatma Gandhi had persistently attacked. I recall reading an article in an issue of *Young India*, in which he wrote with distress about reports of a highly respected elderly gentleman of sixty having celebrated his marriage to a girl of eleven. Today, some forty years later, this deplorable aspect of child-marriage is no longer socially acceptable. The Lolita cult notwithstanding, no ageing roué in these days would dare risk his 'highly respected' reputation by such a misalliance.

The other aspect was the bleak future of the child-widow. Before 1947, the average life-expectancy of Indians was about 26 years. The mortality rate of children before the age of ten was as high as sixty per cent! The number of young women brushed aside into a forgotten netherworld between the living and the dead must have been appalling, since no Hindu girl of the higher castes could remarry, even if she had been widowed in childhood. Now the expected life-span is about 50 years, and more children survive into adulthood. So one can hope that the little people we met in Balotra will grow up to marry and live happily ever after.

Such marriages between children are a persistent rural custom because they are economical. Objectively viewed, they are possibly less reprehensible than the current mechanised urban practice of seeking life partners through newspaper advertisements. Although these pertain to alliances between young persons legally of age, the families thus brought together are total strangers to each other. The settlement of the dowry becomes a brazen attempt to extract the maximum advantage, with no palpable social pressure to exert a moderating influence. The recent spate of suicides by young urban wives because of the vicious demands made by the in-laws point to a dangerous trend when social institutions are no longer controlled by close-knit social units. In villages of the desert, the community is still a viable force. Families are known to each other, and in the case of child-marriage the dowry in the higher castes, or the bride-price among the lower, is paid in instalments.

Marriage remains the great focal event in Indian family life. At whatever social level, from the sophisticated, even Westernised groups, to the poorest, of whatever religion or caste, both for the individual and the family, marriage is the most significant and auspicious event of one's lifetime. The birth of a son is no doubt the desired and most

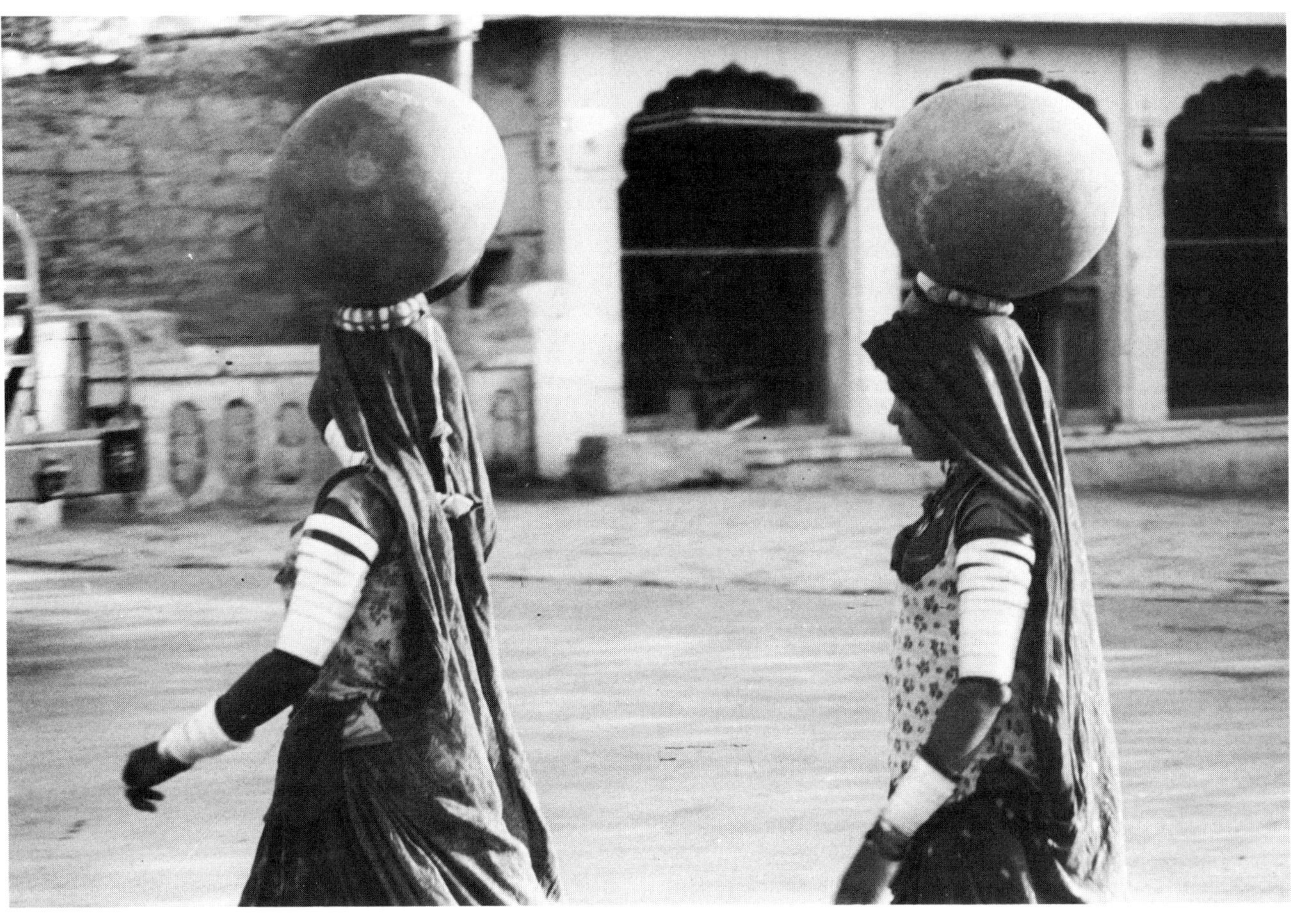

On the way to the well

welcome result, but birth, in comparison, is a private affair. A wedding is a social event and establishes the status of the family within the social milieu.

Given this context, it is completely acceptable that a brother should return all the way from England, at great cost, to attend his elder brother's wedding. And the surest means of getting a visa to visit Pakistan, otherwise extremely difficult to obtain by Indians, is to state as the purpose of the visit 'to attend the marriage of a close relation'.

*With hidden glances he looks back,
the bridegroom, clad in saffron.
Is my mother's brother coming?
He will care for the travelling companions.*

*With hidden glances he looks back,
the bridegroom clad in saffron.
Is my older brother in the marriage party?
He is its splendour and beauty.*

*With hidden glances he looks back,
the bridegroom clad in saffron.
Is my father's brother in the marriage party?
He is its splendour and beauty.*

In this Rajasthani folk song, the bridegroom is referred to as *Kesaria*, the 'saffron-clad one', saffron being the colour of joy and life-affirmation.

Folk songs relate to every trifling custom and ceremony that occurs during a wedding. There is an expressive term *nachor*, which means 'wring', but also suggests in its essence, 'distil', which accurately portrays the function of folk songs. They contain the distillation of experience at various levels of consciousness. For instance, the bride's hands and feet are dyed with intricate patterns made in a paste of dried henna leaves. Many songs refer to the henna-stained hands of the bride. The designs are floral and trellis patterns, or emblems of good fortune and fertility. Underlying these obvious symbols is the significance of hands dyed in henna, which are perhaps as potent a sexual stimulus for the Indian sensibility as lace lingerie is to the Western.

As part of her bridal finery, or *shringar* – a word that gathers in itself the whole ambience of erotic love – red lacquer bangles are slipped onto the bride's arms. How many women give a thought to the origin of the bangle which was the mark of slavery? The *churra*, as the red bangles are called, have acquired the proud status of an emblem of *suhag*, the auspicious state of wedded bliss. The nose-ring at the time of marriage replaces the clove or stud usually worn by unmarried girls. It is amusing to reflect that the dictates of whimsical fashion have restored this sign of abject slavery, the nose-ring, to use among fashionable urban beauties, whose otherwise 'lib' ideas would receive a jolt, were they to recall its original association with women slaves being literally 'led by the nose'!

The auspicious date of the wedding is fixed by the *lagan*, or saffron-stained letter from the bride's family, being received by the groom's. This is usually sent a fortnight before the event. Every day after that the bride and groom go through the *pithe*, or anointing ceremony, in their respective homes. It was intriguing to discover that in the case of Rajputs the *pithe* is only performed three days in advance. Once a girl has been anointed, the marriage must follow on the appointed day. Since the warlike Rajputs lived in unsettled conditions, and a warrior could be summoned to a sudden raid or border war, a common occurrence in the desert, the life of a Rajput was so uncertain that a fortnight was considered too long a period to risk. To ensure the presence of the bridegroom, the minimum period of three days became customary.

But not even this fine margin could prevent tragic misfortune overtaking the bride at the vedic fire-altar. Pabuji Rathor, the famous pastoral hero, was summoned by the message of Deval Charani while the ceremony was actually being performed. He had completed three of the seven required circumambulations round the sacred fire with his bride. His exacting benefactress taunted him with the remark that he sat under a bower of flowers, holding the hand of his Sodha princess, while the Charani's herd of cows was being stolen by his brother-in-law. Had he, a Rajput, forgotten his solemn vow? This made Pabuji leave immediately without completing the ceremony. When they brought his body back from the battle, the only comfort his unfortunate bride of but a few hours found was becoming *sati* on his pyre, in the hope of ensuring uninterrupted, eternal bliss in the hereafter – where hopefully there are no cow-stealers – in the company of her elusive lord.

For more than a century no Rajput has been hastily whisked off to answer a summary call to battle, so the need for such precaution no longer exists, but the practice lingers till today, a reminder of an exciting if hazardous past.

In the song, *kesaria*, the groom looks over his shoulder perhaps to ensure the presence of his relations as a bodyguard to protect him from sudden attack by marauders on the prowl for booty. An obvious target would be a *barat*, marriage party, and even today it attracts train or highway robbers, as we know from frequent newspaper reports.

As he takes leave of the women of his family, before the *barat* sets off, they sing to him *bana*, the songs of the bridegroom:

> *For you, O bridegroom,*
> *a step-well will be dug*
> *to bathe in,*
> *as you go to meet*
> *the fair flower, your bride,*
> *saffron hued.*

> *For you, O bridegroom,*
> *the neem will be planted*
> *to clean your teeth,*
> *as you go to meet*
> *the fair flower, your bride,*
> *saffron hued.*

> *For you, O bridegroom,*
> *a garden will be laid*
> *to rest in,*
> *as you go to meet*
> *the fair flower, your bride,*
> *saffron hued.*

> *For you, O bridegroom,*
> *wine will be served*
> *to drink,*
> *as you go to meet*
> *the fair flower, your bride,*
> *saffron hued.*

> *For you, O bridegroom,*
> *a feast will be prepared*
> *to eat,*
> *as you go to meet*
> *the fair flower, your bride,*
> *saffron hued.*

> *For you, O bridegroom,*
> *a coverlet will be spread*
> *to sleep on,*
> *as you go to meet*
> *the fair flower, your bride,*
> *saffron hued.*

When he arrives at the bride's home, the bridegroom is greeted by her friends who both flatter and tease him with verses that often are improvised to keep pace with the times:

> *The aeroplane flies in the skies,*
> *the car speeds along the road,*
> *instal a radio in your car,*
> *   young bridegroom.*
> *When the handsome bridegroom*
> * stands before them,*
> *the bridesmaids are bewitched.*
> *When the handsome bridegroom comes*
> * from the wedding ceremony,*
> *the maids sing songs of praise,*
> *   young bridegroom.*
> *When the handsome bridegroom*
> * comes to untie the bride's bracelet,*
> *he does so with his own hands,*
> *   young bridegroom.*

By touching with his sword the ornamental *toran* that hangs above the doorway to the bride's home, the Rajasthani groom evokes the ancient custom of marriage by capture, and calls to mind the famous abduction of Princess Sanyukta of Kanauj by Prithviraj

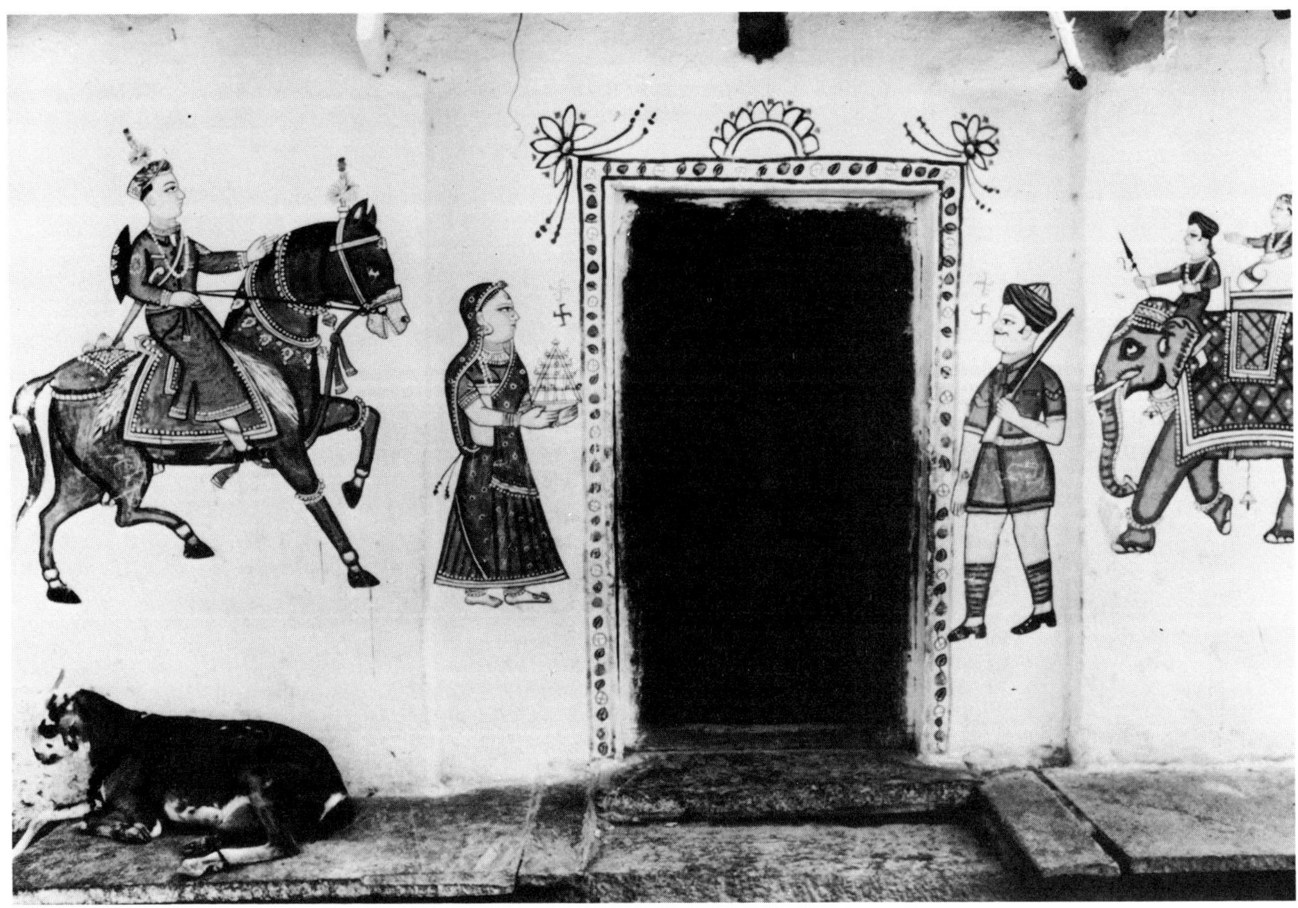

Typical wall-painting around the doorway to a home at the time
of a wedding

Chauhan of Delhi.

The piercing sweetness of the songs of the *doli*,
palanquin, at the time of the bride's departure from
her father's house with her husband, are a poignant
interlude at the end of the actual wedding, and signal
the hiatus between the ending of one phase of life and
another about to begin. The clinging, plaintive notes
of the *doli* ache in the memory of every Indian woman.

*The parrot to the garden came,
came the alien parrot;
he chose,
and took her away.
'Leaving us,
where do you go,
Little bride?'
The parrot of the in-laws came,
chose the cuckoo bird.
'Where do you fly,
cuckoo bird?'*

*'I ask you, my little bride,
leaving your loving father
where do you go, bride?
Leaving your loving mother
where do you fly,
cuckoo bird?'*

*'I ask you, my little bride,
leaving your loving brother
where do you go, bride?*

*Leaving your loving sister-in-law
where do you fly,
cuckoo bird?'*

*The parrot to the garden came,
came the alien parrot;
he chose,
and took her away.
'Leaving us
where do you go,
little bride?'
The parrot of the in-laws came,
chose the cuckoo bird.
'Leaving us,
where do you fly,
cuckoo bird?'*

Is it this idea of an end to the age of innocence and the
commencement of mature responsibility that
underlines the curious custom in Rajasthan of women
singing *moria*, peacock, outside the bridal chamber
on the first night spent in the bridegroom's home?

Moria relates the story of a bride who goes down to
the village pond to bathe. But she finds a beautiful
peacock which stands on the bank with splendid tail
unfurled, barring her path. She pleads with him to fold
his feathers and to allow her to reach the water, but he
refuses to do so. Instead he asks her to come away
with him:

*In the light of the moon
the sisters-in-law
went to draw water
from an enormous lake.*

*They set down their pitchers at the water's
 edge,
hung up their headrests from a jasmine branch,
then turned about
to take in the vision of the garden.*

*Plucking a tender plantain twig
they scrubbed their feet and washed them,
shining and cleaning laughing teeth,
they scrubbed their hands to wash them;
their smile shone full and bright.*

*A peacock sat at the water's edge
covering the lake with his wing.*

*'O bird of the rain god, move a little,
let me rinse and fill my pitcher.'*

*'From your face, set aside that veil,
beautiful woman, then rinse and fill your
 pitcher.'*

*'The veil, O peacock, is not lifted here;
it is only lifted
in the room of privacy,
in the room of leisure.'*

Unable to resist his beauty, the bride runs off with the bird. Her young sister-in-law, having witnessed the incident, informs her brother – the bride has eloped!

*'Look at the peacock, my sister-in-law,
his beauty twice outshines your brother's.'*

*'Go then with this peacock,
I'll wed my brother to a beautiful lady.'*

*'Take, sister, my necklace
inlaid with precious stones,
but do not tell your brother.'*

*'I'll burn and char
your precious necklace.
I will certainly tell my brother.'*

*In front went the splendid peacock,
with him she went, following.
On the straight road the peacock went,
and the lady walked in uneven gait.*

*'Sit around, brother, in idle pleasure.
Your bride meanwhile has crossed the bounds,
following the peacock over the banks.'*

*'Don't lie, sister, you lie!
My bride is in the pleasure room,
my bride is in the resting room.'*

*'Go, brother, to the resting room,
go to the place of rest,
crows and kites are flying there.'*

*The brother went inside, everywhere
crows and kites were flying there.*

A hunt for the couple follows. They are soon overtaken and captured:

*On horseback went a hundred and fifty men,
on foot another hundred and fifty.
On the straight road with the peacock
came with halting step the lovely woman.
They went inside the garden,
on a bended branch sat the peacock,
she rested against a tree trunk.*

*Sharp was the aim of the arrow,
he slew and covered the peacock—
the husband in his sovereignty.*

The bride is carried home and the proud peacock is slaughtered, his flesh is cooked and the poor girl is forced to eat of the dish as punishment. She submits but when her husband taunts her for her submissive acceptance of the death of her love, she suddenly revolts in a dramatic manner:

*'Cook that, my beauty, clean it well,
then you and I, we'll eat together.'*

*Served on silver vessels,
he and she ate together.
'You ran away, my queen, with him,
now you so lustily eat his flesh.'*

*In angry rage the lady rose,
she flung her bowl aside.
'Go, maid, to the bazaar straight ahead,
on my veil have embroidered a splendid
peacock,
Go, maid, to the goldsmiths' street,
On my bangle have engraved a shining
peacock.
Go, O maid, to the tattooer, and
on my eyes have marked my beautiful peacock.'*

What can be the reason for the singing of *moria* on the bride's first night in her new home? Is it a warning to the young woman about the sacred vow of marital fidelity she has undertaken, and the dark consequences of succumbing to illicit rapture? Or do its implications lie deeper, in the primeval notions of death and regeneration?

The macabre motif of a loved one killed, cooked and fed to the ignorant or knowing victim, is found in varying contexts in the myths of many cultures. The women who sing *moria* do so because 'it is the custom'. They are so used to the words, that possibly their bitter meaning or implication is lost on them. One can only hope the same holds true of the newly-wedded couple as they hear the haunting melody of *moria* outside their bridal-chamber.

On Being Born Female

Indications of attitudes towards girls and women reveal themselves in many ways, some more subtle than others. The birth of a son is announced by beating on a bronze *thaali*, plate. But at the birth of a daughter reluctant hands slap a dull sound on a winnowing fan. The brazen clang of the gong clamours for attention, while, in contrast, the sibilant effect of the *sarkanda* cane seems like an apologetic whisper. The contrast is apt.

The proud young mother of a son sends a message through the Sarus crane, a symbol of conjugal faithfulness and fertility:

> *Fly, fly my Sarus queen.*
> *Perch on my father-in-law's house.*
> *When he asks, 'Has a son been born?'*
> *reply, 'A prince has arrived;*
> *he will look after your home;*
> *Through him your family will live on.'*

While the father of daughters can only mutter:

> *To trudge a mile is no blessing,*
> *to have a daughter is no blessing,*
> *to be in debt to one's father is no blessing.*
> *The Lord rescue us from such misfortune.*

After World War II, in the 1950s, India had its first contact with an entirely new type of visitor from the West. These were young people, informal, open to unusual experiences and without prejudice. They were the forerunners of the 'flower children' who were to overwhelm us later, in the 60s and 70s. The earlier travellers took to the road in the wake of Kerouac's Dharma bums, with Ginsberg's poems of disenchantment ringing in their heads, but they were not yet the disillusioned drop-outs, the hippies seeking gurus in the East, in an escape from the satiating affluence of the later decades.

Among these young people was a French girl in her early twenties, a designer and photographer of talent who became a good friend. In 1958-59 she travelled extensively through India alone, by bus and third class railway, which was almost unknown for a single, white girl in those days. She stayed in out of the way villages with peasants and fisherfolk.

One of her ventures was a visit to the then almost legendary desert fortress-city of Jaisalmer. This was before the Indian army had built the present excellent highways that link Jodhpur and Bikaner to Jaisalmer, turning legend into reality.

When she left for Rajasthan, Annie had been armed with several letters of introduction to important officials, given to her by anxious Indian friends who found her casual naivete rather worrying. She however neatly circumvented such VIP chaperonage, and having met in Jodhpur an army captain who was going home on short leave to his desert village beyond Jaisalmer, she decided to accept a ride in his jeep.

They bumped their way over the ancient camel tracks to Jaisalmer, where Annie, enchanted by this wonder in the boundless Thaar, photographed the fort, made sketches and notes on its unique architectural features, and then went on to explore the possibilities of the captain's border home. No foreigner, leave alone a charming French girl, had ever visited this particular village before. Annie in her jeans and T-shirt, with her close crop of curls and boyish figure, was a seven-day wonder to the members of the captain's Bhati Rajput family.

The women, especially, were intrigued by this curious creature, who looked like a boy, was unmarried, travelled alone armed with only a camera, sat and talked with the men, smoked with them, and even joined in the formal ceremony of welcome on entering the house, by accepting a sip of opium from the palm of her host, Thakur Sahib, the captain's uncle. Annie in turn was no less intrigued by the strange world she had entered. There was only one source of water in the village, a large tank where the women filled their pots, washed clothes, bathed the children and watered the livestock. They lived segregated in the *zenana*, women's apartments, yet when they went about their daily tasks, they drew their colourful veils over their faces, left their backs and mid-riff bare, wore exotic embroidered bodices over skirts that swung provocatively at every step, and were literally covered from head to foot in exquisite silver jewellery.

The women of Thakur Shahib's immediate family did not join in these mundane chores. They observed strict purdah, never stepping beyond the boundaries of their fairly large compound. Annie also noted that these ladies wore gold ornaments, and the stuffs of their *ghagras* and veils were of fine material.

The men who surrounded her were no less exotic in appearance. With their vivid turbans of turmeric yellow, chilli red, chutney green and Indian pink, their eyes heavily kohl'd, their ferocious beards, they seemed to her like characters from some medieval, oriental extravaganza.

One thing puzzled her more than any other. A proud Rajput father repeatedly brought his baby girl to her to be petted. She finally asked the captain what was so remarkable about the child. He replied that she was the only *Rajput* girl in the entire village. The father was seeking approval of their distinguished foreign guest in order to justify to his family his unorthodox and courageous act in keeping his infant daughter alive.

To Annie, who had vaguely heard of female infanticide, this was a revelation. The situation having been explained to her, she made haste to cuddle the baby and to praise in extravagant mime the brave stand taken by the young father. She hoped she had struck through her gesture a blow against a horrifying custom, and helped to encourage other men to emulate this humane stand.

Female infanticide seems to have been an ancient Scythian practice, according to the early Mughal historian, Ferishta, who mentions the Ghakkars, a polyandrous Saka (Scythian) tribe inhabiting the banks of the Indus in early centuries A.D.:

> It was the custom among them as soon as a female child was born to carry her to the market-place and there proclaim aloud, holding the child in one hand and a knife in the other that any person who wanted a wife might now take her; otherwise she was immediately put to death.

This barbarous practice had remained firmly entrenched among certain Rajput clans during their centuries of supremacy and persisted up to recent times in remote areas. The reasons were mainly economic: the expense of providing dowries for daughters far exceeded the capacity of the increasingly impoverished families. Added to this was the custom of presenting as largesse absurdly inflated gifts of cash, land, clothes and jewellery to the innumerable household retinue, the Brahmin priests who officiated at all religious ceremonies, Charan bards who maintained the precious family genealogy, and Bhaats who recited the heroic ballads and legends connected with clan heroes and kings.

Apart from this overriding economic reason, the Rajputs had a sense of pride quite out of proportion to their actual standing. Since the father of a bride is compelled by custom to bow and touch the feet of the bridegroom and his father, the Rajputs attempted to save themselves this humiliation by the simple expedient of finishing off their daughters at birth, with a dose of opium.

In his *Annals and Antiquities of Rajasthan*, Tod makes a frank and pertinent comparison between the customs of medieval societies, East and West, on the matter of unwanted daughters:

> The same motive which studded Europe with convents, in which youth and beauty were immured until liberated by death, first prompted the Rajput to infanticide: and, however revolting the policy, it is perhaps kindness compared to incarceration. There can be no doubt that monastic seclusion, practised by the Franciscans in France, the Langobardi in Italy and the Visigoths in Spain was brought from Central Asia, the cradle of the Goths. It is, in fact, a modification of the same feeling which characterizes the Rajput: he gives the opiate to the infant, whom, if he cannot portion and marry to her equal, he dare not see degraded. (Vol II, p.741)

In England up to the nineteenth century, it was the common fate of younger girls in large Victorian families to remain unmarried, so that they could be available as unpaid housekeepers and nurses to look after the parents in their old age. After the death of the parents these poor spinsters spent their own declining years looking after the growing families of nephews and nieces or distant cousins, going from home to home, trying to make themselves useful to their more fortunate relations. This practice must have been in vogue during Tod's own lifetime, and it is significant that he does not consider it worth comment, while discussing the disadvantages of being born female. The customs one accepts as normal in one's own time and society do not strike one as wrong, but usually as inevitable, even if unfortunate.

The Census of India (1961) published a survey report on Bujawar, a Bhati Rajput village, which makes interesting reading on this subject:

> The infanticide of girls at birth has created a dearth of females among the Rajputs, and consquently nowadays it has become difficult for them to obtain a bride in the normal course. Only members of families who are well-to-do economically get girls in marriage without any difficulty. Persons whose position is not economically sound are required to pay a high bride-price. Many Rajputs have therefore to remain unmarried all their life.

No doubt Annie would be glad to learn that girls are now an asset.

Although it will still be a long time before they can be treated as individuals in their own right socially, women have a keen awareness of their pivotal role within the family. The household revolves around them and the influence of the senior wife and mother over the men in her fold is almost awesome in its propensity. She realises that she embodies in her person the power symbolised in the form of the mother goddess and occasionally she can view the chauvinistic antics of the male with humour:

> *Spin, spin, spin, O spinning wheel!*
> *With your aid*
> *I clothe myself,*
> *through your help*
> *I run my household.*
> *Spin, spin, spin, O spinning wheel.*
>
> *With my savings, O spinning wheel,*
> *with joyous ceremony*
> *I married off my sister-in-law,*
> *and through your help*
> *I adorned myself*
> *with a gold necklace.*
> *Spin, spin, spin, O spinning wheel!*
>
> *My luckless husband*
> *after twelve long years*
> *returned with the princely treasure*
> *of a single rupee.*
> *and that too a counterfeit coin.*
> *Spin, spin, spin, O spinning wheel!*
>
> *Of fragrant sandalwood*
> *is the precious spinning wheel*

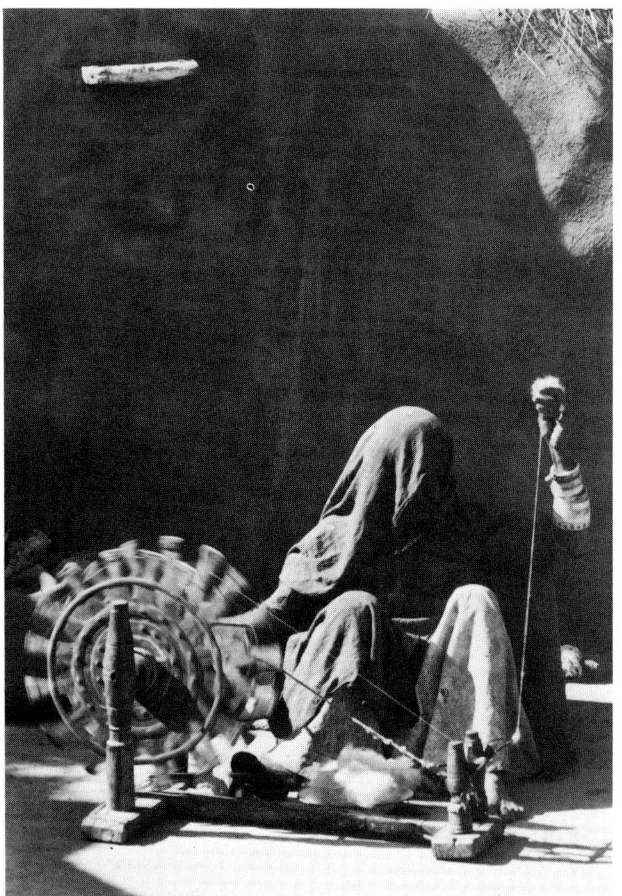
Woman spinning

In the love-song, *Hitchki*, hiccups, the young woman is confident of her charms even as she laments the absence of her lover:

*Days have gone by
since last I saw you;
months have passed
since we were together.
and still, my love,
you are so far away.*

*Oh these hiccups!
I think my darling
is longing for me.*

*The grains of my youth and beauty
are being pecked away
by the bird of time.
I warned you not to leave me.*

*Oh these hiccups!
I think my darling
is longing for me.*

In urban centres, even in the desert cities of Rajasthan, girls are now going to school and college in increasing numbers. In Jodhpur and Bikaner one sees them full of confidence cycling down the road to work in educational institutes and offices. But in the widely dispersed villages of the desert their position in the social system is still unenviable.

Mallinath Cattle Fair, Tilwara

The salt river Luni rises from the lake Ana Sagar in Ajmer and flows in a south-westerly course towards Balotra. Here it makes a wide loop, touching Tilwara, after which it turns directly south and flows down to lose itself in the sandy marshes of the Great Rann of Kutch.

Tilwara, near the old market-town of Khera, stands on the west bank of the curve taken by the river. The Luni is a seasonal stream, moody and erratic. It flows in a strong current during the monsoon months, and is known to overflow its shallow banks during the periods of heavy rain. These floods cause considerable damage during their brief duration, but once they subside, the river dwindles gradually to a thin trickle in the winter. In the spring season it no longer flows, its waters having been absorbed by the thirsty sands. All through the hot summer months its wide bed is a burning plain, parched and waterless, awaiting the rains.

In spring, the bend of the dry Luni becomes a vast beach and on this improbable site for a fortnight during the month of Chaitra (February/March) is held Rajasthan's largest traditional cattle-fair, dedicated to Sri Mallinath. A simple white temple, the shrine of this 14th century warrior-saint, stands on the high bank on the edge of the river at Tilwara.

The Mallinath Fair is not as well-known to outsiders as the one held at the sacred lake of Pushkar, which is celebrated on *Kartik Purnima*, the night of the full moon of November. Pushkar is an ancient place of pilgrimage and is the site of the only remaining temple in India consecrated to Brahma, the earliest deity in the Hindu trinity, whose worship gradually gave way to the other two manifestations of godhead, the austere Shiva, and the compassionate Vishnu. Pushkar is primarily a place of pilgrimage, and devotees come to bathe in the 'Lake of the Heavenly Lotus', to perform *puja* at the temple, and at night to float their offerings of lighted oil-lamps in leaf-boats on the holy waters of the lake. It is a solemn occasion and the fact that it developed into a large cattle-fair was secondary to its religious purpose.

Since Pushkar Lake is at the important centre of Ajmer and easily accessible, the influx of sophisticated urban visitors, foreign and Indian, is gradually changing the character of this fair from a religious rural occasion to that of a colourful, exotic event.

The fair at Tilwara is in the far-off region of Mallani. A metre-gauge railway line extends to the village, and the road from Balotra is partly dirt-track and partly

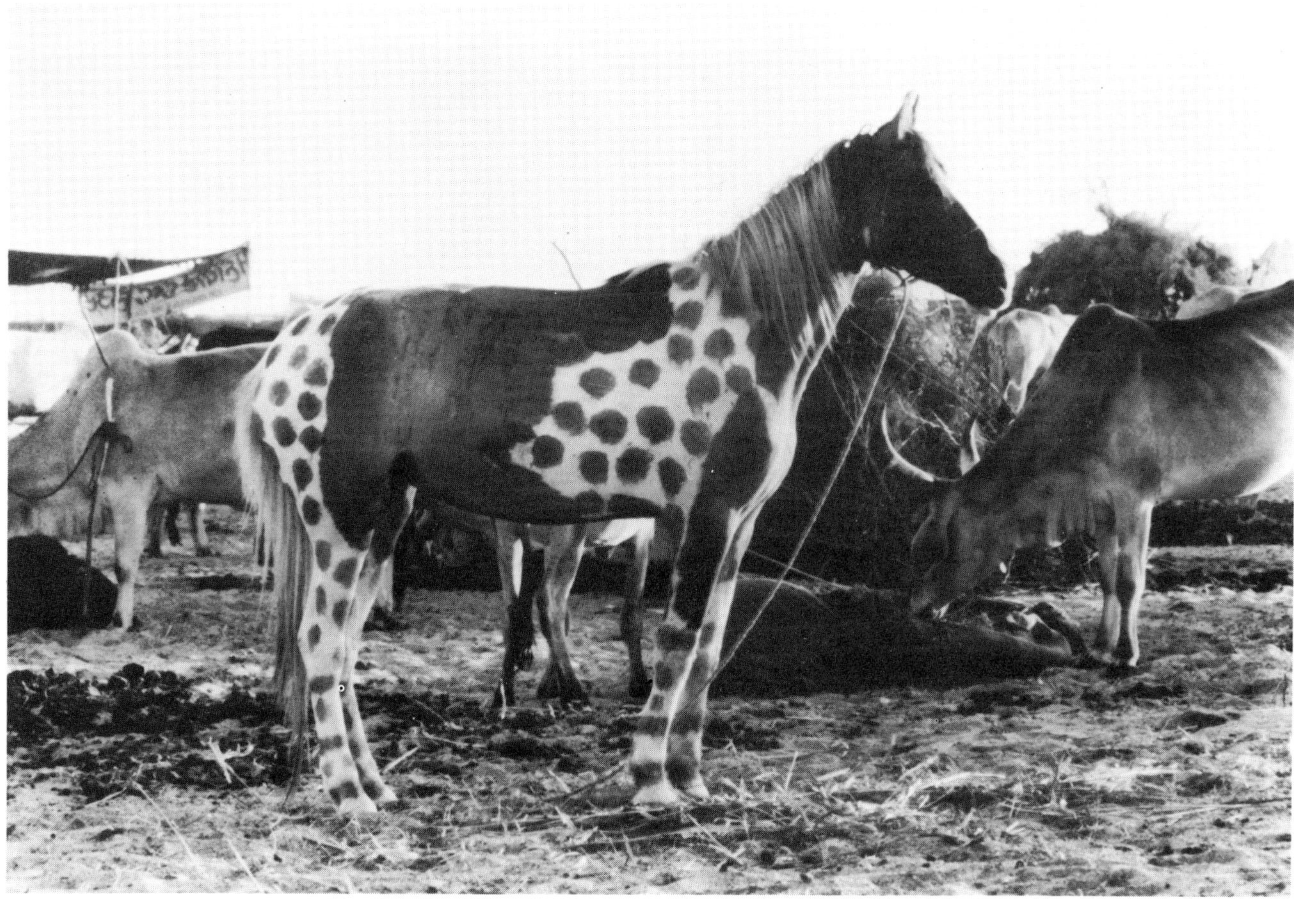

A piebald horse painted with daubs of henna

cross-country over the river bed. The event has a serious commercial purpose; it is a trade fair, and it has been held annually at this site for over six hundred years.

The Census of India Report (1961) on the *Fairs and Festivals of Rajasthan* carries an introduction in which a clear idea is given of the significant role that fairs played, and still continue to play, in the organisation of the social and economic life of the people:

> '. . . .they show what an extensive network of seasonal and perennial markets village fairs still provide to native craftsmanship and industry; they help to connect economic streams with social and religious movements; they suggest how a succession of small fairs in a time-series culminates in a very big fair, almost always in the heart of a particular area, and how this big event gradually subsides through another time-series of small fairs, so that an endless cycle of trade, social and religious intercourse is kept in motion; they can very greatly help in reconstructing ancient and not-so-ancient trade-routes in the country and the nature of the conveyance of goods by land and water and the means by which this may be facilitated, especially by making or repairing roads.

About five kilometres from where the village of Tilwara now stands lie the scattered ruins of the ancient settlement of Kher, which was an important crossroads of trade-routes from Sindh, Pali, Jaisalmer, Jalor and Mandor. Because of this it was a valuable possession for contending clans. Paramara, Chauhan and Rathor Rajputs held it at different periods from the 8th century onwards, while later the Bhatis, Jats and Muslims made constant efforts to seize it. Such disturbed conditions made Kher too hazardous a stop for the caravans, and so its importance as a trading centre slowly declined.

During these convulsive times, Mallinath, son of the Rajput, Rao Sulkhaji, ruler of Mallani, inherited the *gadi* of Mehwa in 1374. He successfully resisted the onslaughts of the Muslims, and his victories form the themes of many folk songs of Marwar. Mallinath is said to have had supernatural powers, and Tilwara became a place of pilgrimage during his lifetime.

The pilgrims who gathered together began to trade, at first in a small way by buying and selling the animals they had with them. After the death of Mallinath in 1399, a temple was built to him at Tilwara on the banks of the Luni, where he was worshipped as a local hero-deity. The first regular fair was organised by 'Mota Raja' Udai Singh of Jodhpur in 1599.

We were in the town by sunset on the eve of the fair and were fortunate to find accommodation at the Rest House in one of the large tents that had been pitched at the edge of the compound. As this was on a high bank above the bed of the river facing east, it gave us a vantage point from where we overlooked the entire expanse of the fair, and watched the sunrise next day. From the darkling river bed came the creak and rattle of bullock carts, mute cries of men as they set up their stalls, shreds of song, neighs, moans and grunts of animals, unyoked and unharnessed, settling down for the night. Like glow-worms, flocks of lanterns began to toss across the restless plain, clustering here and there to form pools of light. As we descended to the fair-ground, picking our way in the dark, like swimmers on a sloping beach, we slowly entered into a deepening ocean of sounds and smells. The odour of horse sweat and dung and the shuffle of hooves betrayed their encampment even before we discerned the animals in the dim glow of hurricane lamps, sleek, with shining coats and dainty fetlocks, some elaborately painted with daubs of henna. Nimble and graceful, they resembled the mounts of the soldiers we had seen on the walls at Parasrampura.

We met some Manganiyar musicians astride superb, high-spirited horses, and although we had by this time learnt never to be surprised by the hidden talents of these versatile friends, we were astonished to find that they were not only expert riders and connoisseurs of horse-flesh, but the main horse-traders at the fair!

The prize exhibits at the encampment, however, were the camels. It is difficult to associate tenderness and personal attachment on the part of the men for these towering animals, so apparently contemptuous, ill-tempered and unfeeling. But as they were obviously the most precious and useful of the desert creatures, their owners lavished much affectionate care on them and with evident regard for individual temperament and personality. Harnesses of multi-coloured straps, pretty pink and green ribbons and tassels, exquisitely chased metal saddles, more elegant and streamlined than any machine-made product; saddle bells and ankle bells and bells for the throat, with their distinctive musical jingles, muzzles woven in complex patterns; ornamented saddle bags and embroidered cloth trappings: no woman's boutique could have boasted apparel of greater appeal and charm, and appropriately enough, many of these items are made by the women in the families during their leisure hours:

Precious gorbandh!
How bright,
how intricate in pattern,
lovely to behold;
how gracefully you adorn
my camel's neck.

Grazing the cows
as they browsed in the fields,
I knitted the gorbandh.
Watching over the buffaloes
as they wandered in the meadow,
I strung the garland of shells

and made a pattern of network,
precious gorbandh!

My sisters-in-law
together wove the gorbandh.
And my husband's youngest sister
strung a gorbandh *of cowrie-shells,*
and the other ornaments
from the splendid city of Jodhpur.

How bright,
how intricate in pattern,
lovely to behold;
how gracefully you adorn
my camel's neck,
precious gorbandh!

Though the humblest and least spectacular of animals at the fair, the bullocks with their patience and meekness hold a very special place in the affection of rural folk. They are usually matched in pairs in terms of size and disposition for the cart-yoke and the plough. Sturdy, adaptable and uncomplaining, they are useful for a wide range of domestic and farm chores, and submit with resignation to an enormous amount of punishment. They serve as the farmer's scapegoat: all his bitterness, frustration and anger are vented on them, and they do not retaliate. There was a wide range of breeds at Tilwara, the most striking and bovinely majestic being the tall, wide-horned ones from Thaar Parkar.

I was surprised to learn that no cows are sold at the fair. A cow may be gifted to a daughter when she marries, or donated to the temple, or let loose to fend for herself, but only under the direst circumstances will an owner sell a cow, an act which expresses the farthest extremity of abnegation and despair. Even during the disastrous years of drought, 1968-69, herdsmen would anoint their cows with a *tilak*, a sacred mark, and abandon them in the desert, rather than sell them, as they feared they might end up at the butchers'. One can appreciate the sentiment behind such an act, but the fate of forsaken animals wandering in the desert till they collapsed to die of thirst is cruelty difficult to match.

Long trenches were being set up to serve as water-troughs for animals and small wells scooped out in the bed of the river. At a depth of half a metre the sand was damp, at one metre water appeared, and at about one-and-a-half metres it was astonishingly clear, sweet and potable. The miracle of sweet water in the mini-wells of this salt river bed lasts for about a fortnight, the period of the fair. This is, of course, regarded as the miraculous gift of the saint Mallinath to his faithful devotees.

Along 'main street' which ran from north to south of the open space, food stalls and restaurants had sprung up with surprising speed. Primitive though the arrangements appeared, they provided a wide range of eatables; freshly cooked vegetables, sizzling savouries, light snacks, sweet dishes, cold drinks, tea

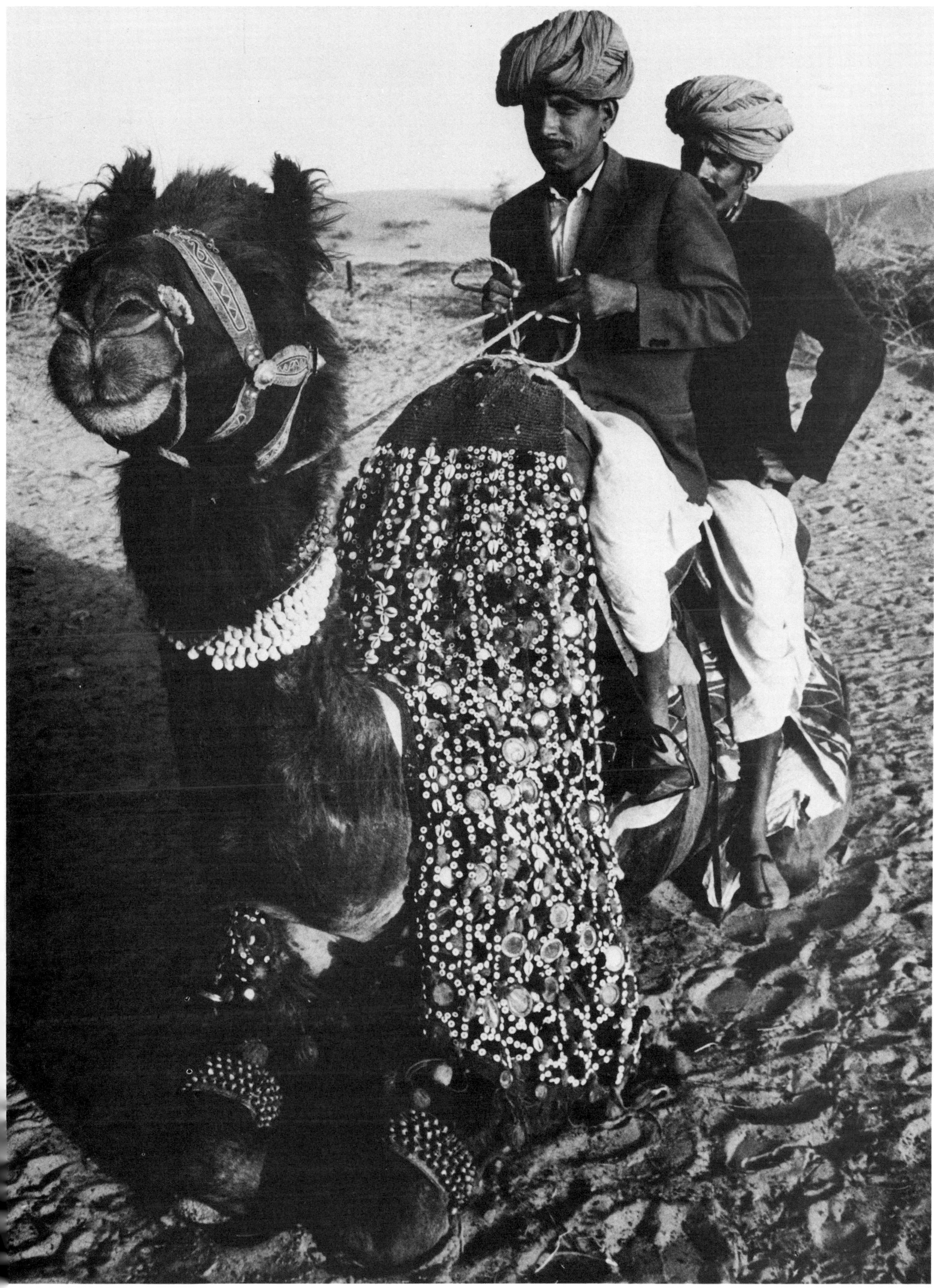

Caparisoned camel

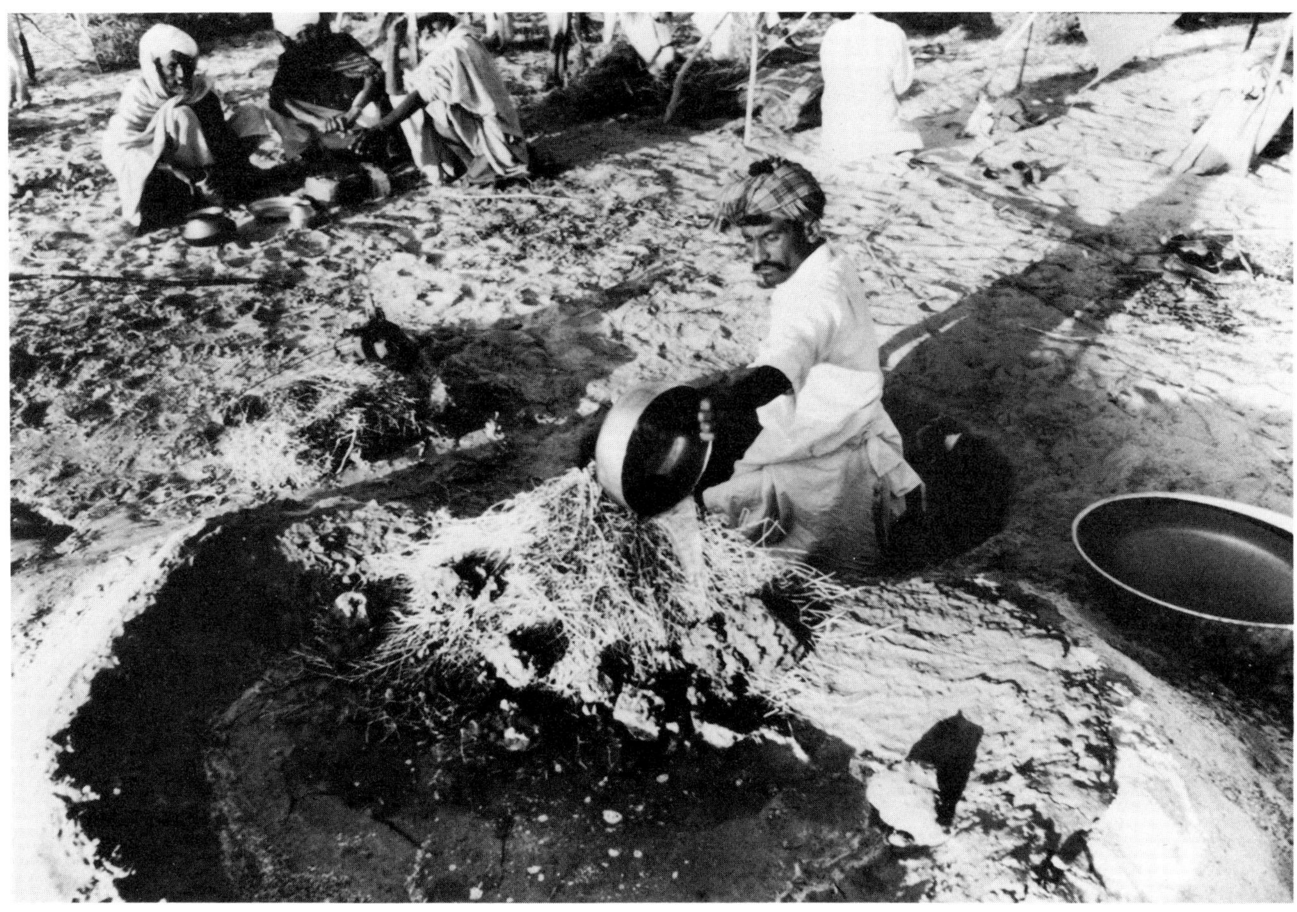

Fresh water is found at the depth of a metre in the banks of the
river Luni during the Mallinath fair

and coffee. And the service was almost round the
clock. At one of these we met Bansilal Chuiwala, a
popular actor, and manager of his own folk theatre
troupe. He invited us to the *khyal* performance which
had been scheduled for that evening. It was about
Raja Bharthari, a legendary hero, and this role the
handsome Bansilal would himself be playing.

Further along this thoroughfare were the usual stores
for knick-knacks. But in the serried lanes behind
these lay the scores of stalls that formed the heart of
the bazaar. We were amazed by the enormous
quantities and variety of goods for sale. There were
entire streets selling bamboo staves, from walking
sticks to stout poles, long enough to support a tented
pavilion; cots and cradles; turned wooden legs; wall
brackets and shelves; all types and sizes of baskets;
ropes of coir, hemp and plastic.

Another group of shops was stacked with huge metal
bins for cattle-feed; tin trunks in floral patterns and
shrieking colours; storage bins, cylindrical, square
and rectangular, from the size of waste paper
receptacles to chests six feet long; water cisterns;
sewing machine covers; funnels; jerry cans; oil cans;
kitchen shelves, larders, dangerous-looking
threshing machines.

Camel carts stood in rows in an area a furlong wide;
camel saddles, such as those we saw being fashioned
at Kanoi, were piled in precarious pyramids. Items of
saddlery, functional and decorative, were strewn in

wild profusion.

And then more humbly, but startlingly, in the midst of
all this, on his one metre square ground-sheet, was the
vendor of readymade spectacles, and ready-to-wear
sets of false teeth. These were certainly puzzling
items of merchandise, but the fact that there were at
least half a dozen such pavement opticians and
dentists in business indicated a fairly extensive
clientele, for the desert dweller is no spendthrift and
is cautious as to how he lays out his hard-earned
money.

Unlike the fairs we had seen at Mukam, Pushkar and
Kanana, Tilwara is almost exclusively a male event.
Very few women were to be seen, and the few we did
notice belonged to the nomad families camped on the
river bank, selling bamboo whistles, toys, beads and
laces.

In the first week, traders and herdsmen set up stalls,
or register their animals with the fair authorities. They
pay a small fee for this to the local government which
organises the fair and auctions the stall sites. For each
animal there is a charge of a few rupees, but
considering the fact that the number of these runs into
tens of thousands, the revenue raised must be
considerable.

It is in the second week that the fair comes truly into its
own. Buyers by then have come from all over
Rajasthan, and also from more distant places in
Gujarat, Madhya Pradesh and Uttar Pradesh. They

will have carefully examined the animals several times over before bargaining for those of their choice – all of which is conducted with much gregariousness and banter and dramatic action. We watched the horses, camels and bullocks being exercised morning and evening and put through their paces on the sandy stretch of the river bed for the benefit of customers.

Earlier, while walking along the dry course of the stream to the Manganiyar camp as darkness fell, Kothari had suddenly stopped at a particular spot, and stared fixedly in the direction of the white temple of Mallinath in the distance, as if recollecting something. On being persuaded, he told us of a curious experience he had had at about this place in the river some years before.

Late at night, after his companions had gone to sleep, Kothari had walked alone over the dry river sand towards the temple. On either side he could discern the forms of dozing cattle and camels huddled in groups. It was very calm and still, almost unnaturally so. Suddenly he heard a distant rumbling sound which seemed to be rising from the ground on which the temple stood. The reverberations grew louder and drew swiftly nearer. He noticed that animals somewhat far removed grew alert, then rose and stood stock still. Those closer by then lifted their heads, pricked up their ears and shifted restlessly, as though disturbed by the passing noise. Then he himself was transfixed with terror as the rumble rose to a roar, the earth quivered beneath his feet, and he felt waves of sound pulsate under and away behind him, to lose their fury in dying palpitations that ended in a far-away tremor at the southern end of the river bed.

All this, he explained, could not have lasted more than a few seconds in time. At first he thought it was an earthquake, but when he spoke of the experience to people at the fair, they said he had been the fortunate witness to a rare but renowned 'miracle'. The sound, they told him, was the thunder of horses' hooves as the saint Sri Mallinath, galloped past on a ghostly nocturnal visit to the shrine of the Bhatiani *Sati Rani* of Jasol, south of Tilwara, a sacred spot to which the saint periodically resorted to pay his respects.

It was quite dark by the time we reached the camp of the Manganiyars. Their horses were being fed and rubbed down. Their whinnying and stamping, clanking and snorting, formed an unorchestrated background to the ecstatic singing of the desert musicians. As the cow-dung cakes spluttered and flamed over the evening meal, we were roused by the call of the distant *naggara* which summoned the audience spread all over the vast expanse to the performance of the *khyal* of Raja Bharthari.

Khyal: Thoughts and Musings

For anyone engaged in research in the theatrical arts, the desert provides an inexhaustible living experience of every stage in the development of drama. In the fire-lit rites of exorcism taking place at a wayside shrine, or in the awesome *tantric* practices of the Meghwal *siddhnaths* of Nokhamandi, the earliest roots of theatre, as potent tribal magic, still exist. In the processions of women carrying trays of flowers and offerings, singing hymns of praise as they walk through narrow lanes to worship Sitalmata, or in the annual enactment of the story of Krishna by the *Ras mandalis* attached to temples, the close tie between religion and drama is obvious. The balladeer, singing and dancing as he recites the folk history of bygone rulers in intricate verbal rhythms, the humble puppeteer, travelling with his loaded donkey from village to village, the acrobats and freaks at every village fair, the inimitable art of the Manganiyar musicians, and the melodic beauty and irrepressible humour in the folksongs of the Langas, all contribute to the varied richness of a living experience of theatre. *Khyal* combines elements from many of these performing arts in which the desert is so prolific.

Khyal, which means thought or imagination, probably began as a game or contest between rival groups at village fairs. Two parties would sit opposite each other and improvise couplets in *sawal-jawab*, question-answer form. Lively exchanges and bawdy humour would be punctuated by individual displays of dance, song or acrobatic skills that posed a challenge to the rival group to equal or excel. Gradually some of these participants formed permanent performing troupes.

Khyal is the most popular of the several forms of theatre in Rajasthan. The plays are based on episodes from myths and familiar legends, and the basic plot is interspersed with interludes of witty repartee, broad slapstick and caustic satire. Characters from everyday life are lampooned: the avaricious money-lender, the hypocritical priest, the corrupt government official, the turn-coat politician, the befuddled husband of two wives. The *Khyal* players also do amusing take-offs of other itinerant desert performers, the Pabuji balladeers and the *kathputli* puppeteers. The more accomplished *Khyal* troupes are in much demand, and Rajasthani communities settled in such distant cities as Calcutta and Madras will often invite a *Khyal Mandali* for a month at a time to perform a cycle of their favourite plays.

The troupes are all-male, women's roles being enacted by female impersonators, some of whom are young boys of exceptional talent. Two of the female impersonators we saw that evening in rollicking sequences with ribald exchanges and scintillating dances would be acknowledged as theatrical artists of the finest cablibre anywhere in the world. The major roles are played by actors who are trained singers of the first order, and the range and volume of their voices leave one dumbfounded.

Indigenous theatre forms are a type of 'total theatre'. They invariably include music, dance, mime, the spoken word, stylised facial make-up, masks, jewellery, headgear and eleborate costumes. *Khyal* emphasises the musical aspect, and the main elements of the play are carried forward through the songs which are linked together with improvised dialogue. Dance is used for dramatic effect, in making entrances or exits, or to exteriorise an emotional state, such as joy, love, anger, fear or sorrow. Fights, wars and processions are portrayed through choreographic movement.

The dance is based on a rudimentary form of Kathak, which is the classical dance form of north India. Originating as a temple ritual around the myths and legends of Radha Krishna, Kathak later developed into a secular art and achieved its present precise and exquisite form in the 19th century courts of the Nawabs of Avadh.

The *Khyal* dancer combines the swift pirouettes characteristic of Kathak with the free, robust movements and expressions of Rajasthani folk forms. The vigorous dance patterns combined with the full-throated rendering of song make strenuous demands on the stamina and versatility of the young players whose audience at any one time may well number over ten thousand spectators.

Khyal's most illustrious female impersonator is the middle-aged, sinewy Ugam Raj. His supple body captures the essence of womanly grace, without the slightest element of caricature or vulgarity, and the expressions that play upon his face with the mercurial changes of the feminine temperament reflect the fine shades of each transient mood and emotion. His voice is a light tenor, gentle and caressing, which he retains at its natural pitch, but plies with such subtle delicacy and artifice that it evokes rather than imitates the feminine. He manages his own troupe and has received the highest national awards for his artistic accomplishment and his service to the cause of traditional theatre.

Bansilal, our host, is himself an actor-singer in the romantic tradition. He has a fruity baritone which he uses to stunning effect in passages of stirring histrionics or high-toned melodrama.

Performances often last throughout the night. The atmosphere is relaxed, even casual. People come and go; sip tea or munch peanuts, sleep through a sequence and are jerked into wakeful attention by the sudden eruption of the *naggara*, drums, into a rhythmic *tala* that heralds a climactic scene.

We had arrived at the theatre early. The stage, composed of wooden platforms, had been set up at one end, and on three sides of this, rugs were spread on the sand, for the seated spectators, beyond which the greater part of the audience would stand. The whole area was covered by canvas, like a circus marquee. A few folding chairs stood on either side of the stage and these could be picked up and used by anyone who did not wish to sit on the ground.

We were taken backstage by Bansilal to the improvised green-room, lit with bright petromax lamps, where the actors were busy with their make-up. Each actor sat on the ground with a small mirror propped up in front of him, quiet and concentrated, as with each touch of the pencil and each dab of the grease-paint he immersed himself deeper and deeper into his character. Unpretentious and humble as the scene was, it had a professional seriousness about it which was reflected in the hushed and reverential atmosphere.

The play *Raja Bharthari* is about a king who ruled a minor principality during the golden age of the Emperor Vikramaditya. Bharthari was an ideal monarch, but he had a fatal weakness: his all-consuming passion for his wife, Pingali. He placed his trust so completely in his consort that he confided in her the secrets of state and gave her the custody of the ring with the royal seal. Pingali betrayed that trust. She gave the ring to her lover, who passed it on to a favoured prostitute. From this unsavoury source it was recovered and returned to the king. Shattered by the treachery of his beloved and shaken by the knowledge of his own vulnerablity, Bharthari abdicated the throne, since he had proved himself incapable of protecting his people. He did penance in the forest and meditated at the hermitage of a saint. Finally he found peace, and was accepted as preceptor of the *ashram* when his *guru* passed away. In the meantime, Pingali, who had realised too late the folly of her rash action, tried in vain to hold back her husband from renouncing the world. He was adamant. Resigned to her fate, she entered the retreat, serving at the forest *ashram* where Bharthari was acknowledged as a saint.

Studying the reactions of the audience was as absorbing for me as watching the action on stage. Intent and concentrated during the scenes of the main plot, the spectators responded to a lyrical passage with an appreciative 'wah!' 'wah!' When the 'girls' came on in the interludes, they relaxed visibly, answering a particularly provocative gesture with a shower of small coins, which the performer gathered up while executing a swift acrobatic pirouette. At the climatic moment, when Bharthari learns of Pingali's betrayal, as Bansilal's magnificent voice broke and dropped to a shivering whisper, a half-uttered moan swept through the crowd with the sound of wind-whipped sand. They knew Bharthari's pain as their own and accepted, as he did, the verdict. It was not in the circumstances – the discovery of treachery, nor in the actions of others – the frailty of woman, that the fault lay, but in Bharthari's own fatal attachment to the object of desire.

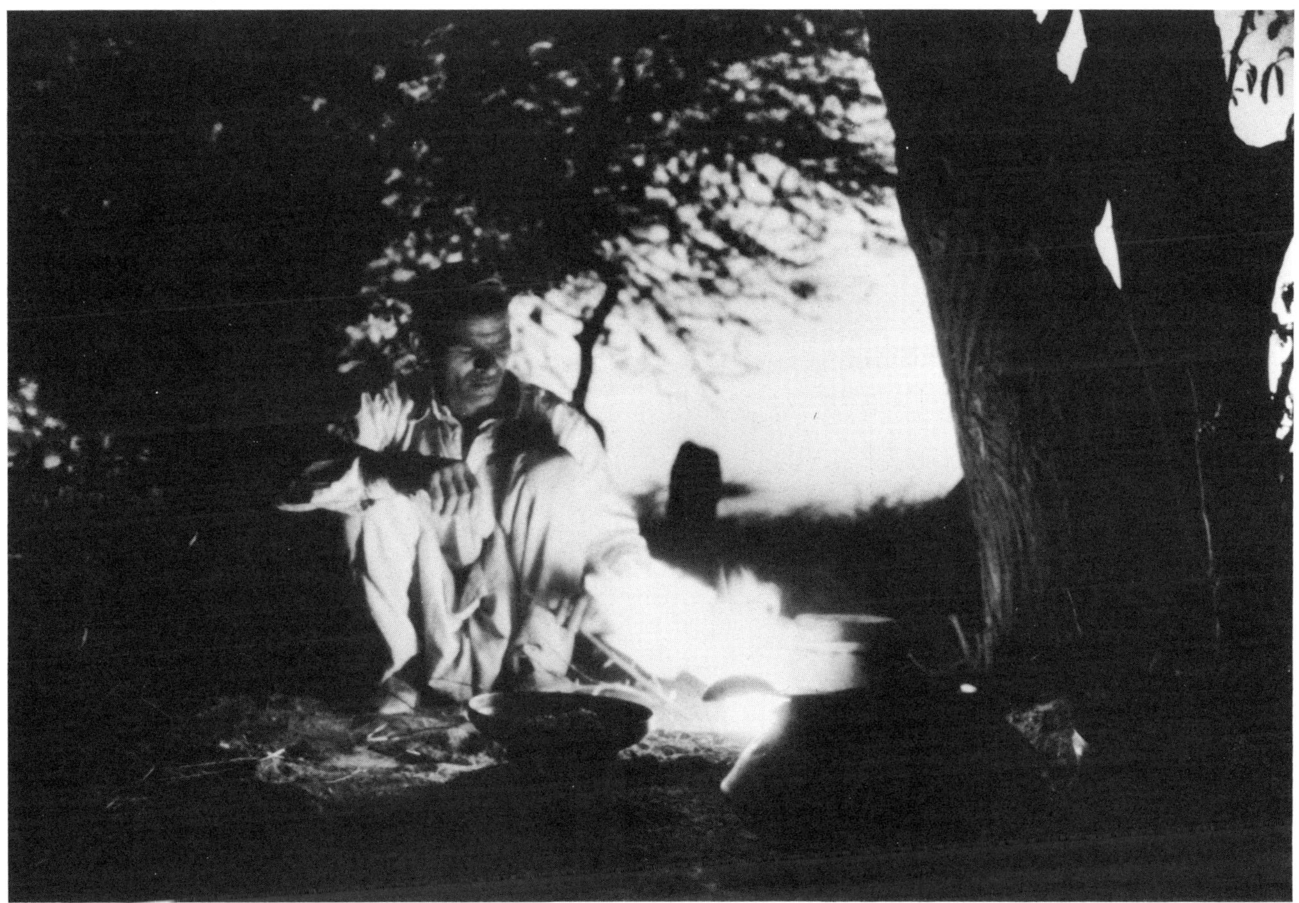

Preparing the evening meal at Tilwara

In a flash the *maya*, illusion, had dissolved like a mirage in the desert, taking with it the love, wealth, fame, power that the king, falsely, had held to be real. They could appreciate his decision, which to them seemed completely logical. They did not see renunciation as the result of a negative despair, but rather, as a positive response to a challenge that provoked a profound reaction: penance that led to self-discipline and meditation which resulted in perfect wisdom. A king's passionate love had been transmuted by the saint into compassion for all mankind.

Such are the eternal verities that hold the rude desert-dwellers enthralled. These ideas, unconsciously imbibed, are part of their philosophy of stoic acceptance that prepares them to face, 'one year in three, drought; one year in eight, famine,' and to welcome a cloudburst with a song, 'even so it is good that the rain must fall!'

How long will such ideas continue to be the mainspring of their lives? Do they recognise the challenge of the future, whose tentacles are everywhere reaching out to claw the fine mesh of their life-style? Do they realise that an alien goddess now entices them, with her inscrutable robot visage, a siren of the soft life? She is a *devi* who brings with her the irresistible temptations of material benefits, and who demands in return, as her blood price, their granite courage, their ancient faith, their thirst for the freedom inherent in the wide, arid spaces of Surya's domain, the desert Thaar.

A sharp rattle of beats on the *naggara* put an end to my musings. It was past midnight. We took advantage of the drum interlude to slip away.

We strolled back through the sleeping township of the fair. The last fires had been put out; the animals were at rest. A lambent moon floated in the serene, night-blue heavens. It was cold, with the dry, brittle chill of a desert night.

We paused in the middle of the river bed before ascending the bank to the Rest House. In the distance we could see the indistinct form of the white temple and hear, on the quiescent air, the faint pulse of the *naggara*. We stood and waited. Would the saint, Sri Mallinath, honour us with his blessings as he thundered by on his nocturnal mission to the shrine of the *Sati Rani*? But miracles do not occur every night, and the saint can divine the sceptic mind. He is not mocked.

Notes

Rajputs (literally 'sons of kings').

Originally not a caste but a class of fighting men of mixed origin. Certain clans came to power during the period following the break-up of the Gupta Empire, and several important dynasties were established (7th – 10th century) in the western region. Foremost were Gujara-Pratihara, Paramara, Solanki and Chauhan. They were followed (11th – 15th century) by the Sisodia, Rathor, Kachchwaha, Hada-Chauhan and Bhati clans. Altogether 36 families of Rajputs were recognised, and later claimed descent from the ancient Aryan martial caste of Kshatriyas: *Suryavansh*, solar clan of Rama, Prince of Ayodhya, and hero of the epic Ramayana; *Chandravansh*, the lunar clan of Krishna, Yadav King of Dwarika, and spiritual protagonist of the epic Mahabharata; *Agnivansh*, or fire-born clan, probably indicating a Vedic purification ritual whereby they were accepted into the Hindu fold as Kshatriyas. Genealogical 'purity' was zealously fostered and guarded.

The mystique around which the code of Rajput chivalry revolved and which lay at the core of Rajput culture, was based on the principle that they had the divine right to rule because they were divinely born. Rajput culture expressed its vitality not only in the martial arts but also in architecture, miniature painting, bardic poetry, music, dance, theatre and the crafts.

The Rajputs endeavoured to emulate the mythical heroes of the epic age, and to maintain and defend the faith and practice of Hindu ritual and worship. Faced by the increasing menace of Islamic invasions from the 11th century onwards, the Rajputs fought to preserve their independence. Although bitter inter-clan rivalries prevented combined efforts to repulse the invaders, several Rajput kingdoms successfully maintained their identity, despite set-backs, and through marriage alliances and treaties learnt to survive as rulers, even when subordinate to the Muslim overlords at Delhi.

Code of Chivalry

The Rajput was brought up to fight. War was his profession and vendetta a family obligation. Boys were considered adult at twelve and sent into battle clad in saffron, the colour of joy and life-affirmation. From their earliest years they were taught to use the bow and arrow, the sword and lance. Games of skill, wrestling, riding in reckless steeple-chase across dunes and jungle, big-game hunting and pig-sticking were their pastimes. The horse was their constant companion and they were deeply attached to favourite mounts. The chargers of certain princes were as famous as their legendary riders: Pabuji and his black mare Kali Kesar (Black Saffron), Rana Pratap and his blue horse, Chetak. The Rajputs kept pet cheetahs trained to hunt and flaunted falcons on their wrist. One of their riskiest sports was to ride at speed at a low-hanging branch and to swing up on it as the horse galloped under. A prince of Bundi broke his spine at this dangerous game, but the other participants continued undeterred.

Initiation into manhood was through the act of beheading a buffalo with a single stroke, an accomplishment to which they graduated by degrees, practising on sheep and goats. A favourite public spectacle was the mammoth animal fights, staged for royal guests between elephants, tigers and other wild beasts. It was not unknown for young princes to challenge one another to enter the animal arena. The fierce sport of Chaugan was gradually refined into the skilful and elegant game of polo.

Physical activity was balanced by a varied interest in other fields. Rajput princes were poets, connoisseurs of painting and music, astronomers and great builders. Their courts attracted celebrated musicians, dancers, painters and scholars. As with all desert dwellers, hospitality and loyalty were part of their creed.

They were deeply religious, and the early Rajput rule of the Pratiharas, Paramaras and Chauhans (8th – 12th century) is distinguished as a remarkable period of temple architecture of the Indo-Aryan type. Most of these temples were subsequently dismantled by Muslim conquerors, the pillars being used in Islamic mosques and other structures such as are seen in the Qutb complex in Delhi and the Arhai-din-ka-jhonpra in Ajmer. During the prolonged struggle with the Afghans and Mughals that followed after the 12th century, the later Rajput rulers concentrated on building their famous citadels in which the forts and palaces combine Hindu and Islamic architectural features in a pleasing fusion, characterised as the Rajasthani style.

Before the Islamic invasions Rajput women enjoyed considerable freedom. Accomplished in domestic crafts, they were also trained in the fine arts of painting, poetry and music, and were adept at riding and shooting. They joined in hunting expeditions and in competitions of target-shooting. As related in epics and legends, they seem to have enjoyed the right of *swayamvara*, maiden's own choice, which they exercised by garlanding the prince they had decided to marry, at a special function. They extended their own independent patronage, sponsored the building of temples and donated beautiful step-wells for the use of citizens. In the early period they appeared freely in public, participated in functions and took part in religious discussions. But later their freedom was curtailed, largely on account of the invasions and the practice of the intruders of taking women captives as part of the war booty, and the Muslim custom of purdah. The increasingly competitive spirit among Rajput rulers was manifested in the extravagant dowries they provided. Gamblers and profligate spenders, they developed an exaggerated sense of pride which was usually out of all proportion to their means. This was not only the weakness of princes but of anyone boasting Rajput blood. Daughters became an embarrassing financial burden and the position of women deteriorated.

Yet women continued to wield influence within the domestic circle, and although restricted by purdah still kept up their proficiency in the fine and martial arts. Incidents of queens and young brides who fought alongside their sons and husbands in defence of their citadels live on in many legends and bardic tales. Once married, a woman's life was entirely dependent on her husband's, for by the custom of *sati* she died on his funeral pyre.

The Rajput fought as an individual rather than as a member of a disciplined army. His was a bid for valour. When all hope was lost of being able to defend his fort, the Rajput ordered the rite of *johar*. By this terrible observance, all the women and children, led by the senior queen dressed in bridal finery, and the princesses of the royal blood, down to the humblest maid, entered huge subterranean vaults where fires had been lit, and perished in the flames. The men then opened the gates of the fort and, opium-maddened, fought to the death. By this suicidal code, the finest soldiers were sacrificed. Their famous strategic manoeuvre was known as the 'ghol'. They formed into a tight circle of mounted warriors and attacked at speed, breaking through the opposing forces. The effect was of a fast-moving human flailing machine. Once through, they reformed and charged again. This outmoded method was seen in use as late as in battles against the British. Their courage was never in doubt. Skinner's 'Yellow Boys' were named in tribute to the saffron-clad Rajput soldiery.

Charans

This caste was closely connected with the royal families. Charans performed a semi-religious function, conducting certain ceremonies, but since they bore arms and were non-vegetarian they could not claim the status of Brahmins or priests. They maintained the genealogies of the ruling families and were astute politicians. They negotiated treaties and arranged marriage alliances between opposing clans. They were emissaries of their rulers, and jealously guarded the honour of their princes, going to the extent of practising self-mutilation to vindicate any slight to the royal house. This rite was known as *tyagi* or *chandni* and could take the form of cutting off of limbs or ritual suicide, or even the sacrifice of their children in order to bring moral pressure on the offender. Their curse was greatly dreaded. They wielded considerable influence over the rulers who often bestowed on them extravagant gifts of land and jewels. Their women were held in awe as having mystic powers. Some became saints during their lifetime.

Bhaats

The balladeers of the desert are known as Bhaats. They could be called folk historians since their ballads recounted the deeds of the heroes, but these romantic and colourful accounts were certainly not factual or accurate. They were the 'media men' of the past, boosting morale, spreading news (and confusion), and using their extraordinary skills of song, mime and connected folk arts to help in the audio-visual impact of their art. They encouraged their Rajput rulers in extravagant spending at ceremonies, as they performed on such occasions and were gifted lavish presents. On the other hand, they preserved the arts and folklore from extinction.

Raikas

They are a caste of camel-drovers who lead a semi-nomadic life with their herds, leaving their women and children to cultivate the small land-holdings in their village. Their wanderings are seasonal, in search of pasture for their animals. They can recognise and track individual animals by their hoof-prints and are skilled rural vets. They are said to mix jackal blood with camel fodder to increase the stamina and strength of their animals. They are a handsome people and claim mixed descent from the union of Rajputs with Charan women. They worship Pabuji Rathor as their hero-deity and are said to have fought alongside that legendary pastoral figure in his battles. Because of his wanderings, the Raika is often referred to as the messenger of love in folk songs of the desert, carrying news of the absent lover to the beloved. In the past the Raikas were also employed as spies by warring clans.

Meghwals

Also known as Meghwal Bhambi, they are leather workers, tanners and skinners by profession. They are descended from *dasu*, slave, castes of antiquity, and till recently were regarded as 'untouchables', condemned to live beyond the boundaries of settled communities. The Meghwals themselves claim to be followers of Meghnath, a Brahmin, and describe themselves as 'outcaste Brahmins'. The legend: A family of four Brahmin brothers found a dead cow in their compound. There was no one to remove the carcass. Finally the youngest brother was prevailed upon to undertake this unpleasant task. On returning from the jungle where he had disposed of the dead animal, the young man was horrified to find the gates of the home barred to him. He was from then on an outcast. This is a variation of a familiar tale about castes that have been relegated to a low status.

Although they still follow the profession of leather-work, the Meghwals are gradually giving up skinning and tanning in order to improve their social position. They have eschewed eating carrion which they were compelled formerly to resort to, as they were forbidden to cultivate the land. They are now a 'Scheduled' or protected caste. A resilient and vigorous people, they have made great efforts to improve their lot. The Meghwals bury their dead, but this apart, their attempt is to adopt Hindu customs and ceremonies in order to gain respectability. Their deities are early gods and goddesses who are now identified with forms of Shiva and Kali.

Kalbelias (literally, 'conquerors of death')

Also known as *Jogis*, mendicants, they are a nomadic caste. Formerly they serviced the domestic looms, making and selling the spindles in villages of the hinterland. Expert hunters and trappers, they breed a special type of hunting dog, like a native whippet. The pedigrees of these hounds are carefully maintained. The bitch is not permitted to whelp for twelve seasons, and any breach of this rule imposes a heavy fine on the owner of the male dog. Girls bring pups as part of their dowry. Any outsider who wishes to marry a girl of the caste has to join the community, serving her father for several years and observing customary laws. He is then admitted to the caste and becomes a Kalbelia. The all-male *panchayat* decides disputes. The members sit in a circle, having deposited all weapons in a common pile, and must remain in session till a decision acceptable to both parties is reached. The expenses for food and drink during such sessions are borne jointly by members of the *panchayat,* who are later reimbursed by the person who loses the case. Fines are the usual punishment; banishment from the community is seldom invoked. Women enjoy a greater degree of independence than most other women of the region. They own their jewellery, and gifts in their dowry cannot be claimed by the husband's family.

Kalbelias travel in large groups, carrying their belongings on donkeys and in donkey-carts. They keep poultry and occasionally sell eggs and chickens. They are expert snake-catchers and charmers and worship the Nagdeva. Their most important festival is Nag-Panchami, dedicated to the serpent deity. They claim to cure snake-bite by using the extracted venom and also dispense herbal remedies and cosmetics to villagers. They are independent and jealously preserve their nomadic life-style despite the hardship involved. They are excellent singers and wayside performers, combining song and dance routines with snake and mongoose shows and sleight-of-hand tricks in their performances. Kalbelias bury their dead; they do not cremate.

Gadhia Lohars (literally, 'Blacksmiths of the Carts')

A caste of blacksmiths and tinkers, they travel throughout middle and north India in bullock-carts elaborately decorated with embossed and engraved metal, which are the hall-mark of their caste and trade. They claim to be descendants of the royal armourers and smiths attached to the Sisodia Rajputs of Chitor-Udaipur, the foremost ruling house of Rajasthan. After the third and last sack of the fortress-city of Chitor by the Mughal Emperor, Akbar (1567), the Lohars took a vow never to live in a settled home, or to eat after dusk, or to light a lamp, or to enter Chitor till the fort was restored to freedom. In 1956 Jawaharlal Nehru in an imaginative symbolic ceremony led the heads of several of these nomad groups into Chitor Fort, since they were now citizens of an independent nation. This attempt to settle the Lohars proved abortive despite several incentives, such as special free schools for their children and grants of land. Four hundred years of gipsy-living held more allure, and the Gadia Lohars still follow their nomadic existence.

Flora

Aonla (Phyllanthus embelica):   Tree with astringent, plum-like fruit.

Ak or *Akra (Calotropis procera):*   This is the main flowering shrub of the desert. It is in bloom for many months of the year. Its wood is used for making roofs or as fuel. The juice of its green shoots is used as medicine.

Ber (Zizyphus jujuba):   Principal fruit of the desert, the only desert produce that is offered as a gift. Its leaves called *pala (Zizyphus rotundiabia)* serve as rich fodder for camels, sheep and milch cattle.

Babul or *Keekar (Acacia arabica):*   The leaves and pods of the Babul are used as fodder, the bark for tanning hides. The wood is of an inferior quality, and is used for roofing, making cots and agricultural implements. The tree exudes valuable gum.

Bajra – Spike Millet: Forms the staple diet of the people. Crop is extensively sown after the first fall of rain. It is seldom watered or manured.

Jal or *Pilu (Salvadora Persica):*   Provides shade, its ripe fruit is eaten locally and its wood is used for roofing, cattle enclosures etc.

Jawar (Andropogan sorghum):   Indian millet.

Kair (Capparis aphylla):   A thorny shrub that sometimes grows into a dwarf tree. It has no leaves, but its twigs are evergreen and are used for feeding camels and goats. Its reddish flowers and tiny fruits are pickled or used as vegetables.

Khejra (Prosopis spicigera):   This is the most important tree of the desert. Once it takes root, it gets firmly fixed in the soil. It withstands shifting sands, rough winds, and acute scarcity of water. Every part of the tree is put to use. Its leaves and shoots are fed to animals. Its pods (called *sangri*) are used for human consumption. Its bark is stripped, dried and ground with grain to stretch limited food supplies in times of famine. Its wood is used as timber and as fuel. So valuable and essential is the *Khejra* to the desert people that in some areas it is worshipped during the Dussehra festival.

Phog (Calligonum polygonoides):   A common desert shrub of great utility. It grows in sandy soil and provides sustenance for camels for the greater part of the year. The twigs are used as fodder, the fruit as fuel.

Pipal (Ficus religiosa):   Not a desert tree. But is sometimes found growing near river-beds.

Rohira (Tecoma undulata):   A scarce but very important timber tree. Its wood is used for doors and windows, carts and agricultural implements. Bears handsome lily-like flowers.

Sewan (Panicum frumentaceum):   Tall, fine grass, excellent for sheep.

Musical Instruments

Dholak: Common drum. Left side of parchment is pasted from inside, giving a lower tonal quality. (Length: 41 cm, head diameter: 19 cm)

Duff: Iron rim frame. Parchment held by hoop, laced by leather braces on the back to small iron ring. Played by hand and stick. (Diameter: 52 cm)

Kamaicha: Bowed string lute. Hollowed out of single block of wood with integrated peg box, finger board and belly. Belly has large circular wooden resonator with parchment pasted over. Notched bridge. 4 main strings: 2 gut, 2 steel. 4 sympathetic strings on pegs on the right side of the body. 6 steel rings tied in peg box. A nut used only for a group of 9 steel strings which are bowed along with main strings. Bow long and curved, of wood and hair. (Length: 75 cm)

Khartal or *Kartal:* Pair of wooden clappers with jingles of brass inserted into wooden body. Played by one hand, held between thumb and four fingers. Occasionally the thin sides have thin metallic surface. (Length: 27½ cm)

Morchang: An iron frame with vibrating tongue. Held in the left hand, the frame is placed between the lips. The tongue is plucked with jerking movement by fingers of the right hand. The movement of the tongue is reinforced by intermittent blowing. (Length: 16 cm)

Narh or *Nad:* Flute made of kangor wood – a desert bamboo-like plant. Both ends open, 4 finger holes at lower end. Blown from upper end, held transversely. The blowing includes an element of throated throw of 'voice' which gives the flute its drone note. (Length: 54 cm)

Pungi: Two parallel bamboo pipes of equal length, each with a single beating straw reed which is inserted into the lower side of a gourd (fixed by wax) forming the chamber. The blow pipe is an extended portion of the gourd. Reeds tuned to a common pitch, one having a variable number of finger holes (5 to 8). One acts as drone, the other is stopped on finger holes. A third pipe is sometimes attached to exercise greater tone control.

Ravanhatha: Open string bowed chordophone. Belly of coconut shell, long bamboo body of 72 cm. Parchment stretched and laced on shell. Body does not serve the purpose of finger board. Two strings passed across notched wooden bridge, one (main) of hair, the other or more than two steel wires twisted into one. Between 3 to 16 sympathetic steel strings tied to protruding tuning pegs. Curved bow of wood or iron rod with jingle bells. (Length: 84 cm)

Satara: Whistle-blown double vertical flute made of two cylindrical wooden flutes of equal length. 6 ginger holes on the drone and 9 (3 redundant) on the main flute. Held jointly and blown simultaneously. Hole on drone flute can be stopped by wax to alter scale. (Length: 58 cm)

Shehnai: Single piece wooden tube with integrated wide bell opening, cylindrical bore, seven finger holes, and one thumb hole in rear. (Length: 32 cm)

Gujaratan Sarangi: Bowed string instrument. Main string of steel. Of the 4 strings, 2 are of gut and 2 of steel. 9 sympathetic strings on tuning pegs on the right side. (Length: 58 cm)

Sindhi Sarangi: 4 strings, 2 of gut, 2 of steel. Main string is of steel. 25 sympathetic strings tied to 16 tuning pegs on the right, 1 on the left and 8 in the peg box. One sound hole close to the body. (Length: 63 cm) Both the Gujaratan and the Sindhi sarangi are played by the Langa community.

Shree Mandal: Wood base with 17 to 27 steel strings, played with a plectrum.

(Catalogue of Folk Musical Instruments. Sangeet Natak Akademi, New Delhi.)

Bibliography

Abu'l Fazl, *Ain-i-Akbari,* trans. from the Persian, H. Blochmann, 2 Vols., New Delhi, Oriental Books Reprint, 1977.

Abu'l Fazl, *Akbar Nama,* trans. from the Persian, H. Beveridge, 3 Vols., Rane Books, Delhi, 1973

Asopa, J.N. *Origin of the Rajputs,* Bharatiya, Delhi, 1957

Al-Badaoni, *Muntakhabat-ut-Tawarikh,* Idarah-i-Adabiyat, Delhi, 1973

Bidwell, Shelford, *Swords for Hire,* John Murray, London, 1971

Brough, J. *Poems from the Sanskrit,* Penguin Classics, London, 1968

Burgess, J.ed. *The Indian Antiquary,* Vols. III and IV, Indological Book House, Varanasi, 1971

Elphinstone, Mountstuart, *An Account of the Kingdom of Caubul,* Oxford, 1970. Reprint.

Ferishta, Kassim, *History of the Rise of Mohamedan Power in India,* trans. from the Persian, John Briggs Calcutta, 1966

Goetz, Hermann, *The Art and Architecture of Bikaner State,* Bruno Cassirer, Oxford, 1950

Goudie & Hegde, *The Prehistory & Paleography of the Great Indian Desert,* Academic, London, New York, 1978

Heber, Rev. Reginald, *Narrative of a Journey Through the Upper Provinces of India,* John Murray, London, 1828

Jouhar, *Tezkereh-al-Vakiat, Memoirs of Humayun,* trans. Charles Stewart, Pustak Kendra, Lucknow, 1971

Jain, K.C. *Ancient Cities and Towns of Rajasthan,* Motilal Benarsidas, Delhi, 1972

Kosambi, D.D. *The Culture and Civilisation of Ancient India,* Vikas, New Delhi, 1970

Kosambi, D.D. *Myth and Reality,* Popular Prakashan, Bombay

Low, Sydney, *A Vision of India,* 1906

MacFarlane, Charles, *Our Indian Empire,* G. Routledge, London, 1848

Mundy, G.C. *Journal of a Tour in India,* John Murray, London, 1852

Pal, M.K. *Crafts and Craftsmen in Traditional India,* Kanak, Delhi, 1978

Parks, Fanny, *Wanderings of a Pilgrim in Search of the Picturesque,* Pelham Richardson, London, 1850

Roberts, Emma, *Scenes and Characteristics of Hindostan,* W.H. Allen, London, 1837

Roger, Alexander and Beveridge H. trans. *Tuzuk-i-Jehangiri,* Munshiram Manoharlal, Delhi, 1968. Reprint

Rawlinson, H.G. India, *A Short Cultural History,* Cresset, London, 1937

Roy, Pratap Chandra, trans. *Mahabharata of Vyasa,* Calcutta, Oriental

Sankalia, H.D. *The Prehistory of India,* Popular Prakashan, Bombay

Srivastava, A.L. *Medieval Indian Culture,* Shivlal Agarwal, Agra, 1963

Talbot, E.G. trans. *Memoirs of Babar,* Delhi, ESS Publications, 1924

Thapar, Romilla, *A History of India,* Vol. I, Pelican, London, 1966

Toy, Sidney, *The Strongholds of India,* Heinemann, London, 1957

Wilson, H.H. trans. *Rig Veda* (Sanskrit), Bangalore Printing and Publishing, Bangalore, 1946

Imperial Gazetteer of India

Oriental Annual

Sangeet Natak, Journal of the Sangeet Natak Akademi, New Delhi

Bulletin of the National Institute of Sciences, New Delhi, September 1952

Census Reports a. Village Surveys
       b. Fairs and Festivals of Rajasthan
       c. Glimpses of Rural Rajasthan

Lok Sanskriti (Hindi) Borunda   Tribe, Udaipur

India Magazine, New Delhi, September 1980

Guide to Rajasthan, Indian Tourist Development Corporation, New Delhi 1975

Index